Information Age Transformation Series

Effects Based Operations

Applying Network Centric Warfare in Peace, Crisis, and War

Edward A. Smith

CCRP
Publication
Series

This is a continuation in the series of publications produced by the Center for Advanced Concepts and Technology (ACT), which was created as a "skunk works" with funding provided by the CCRP under the auspices of the Assistant Secretary of Defense (C3I). This program has demonstrated the importance of having a research program focused on the national security implications of the Information Age. It develops the theoretical foundations to provide DoD with information superiority and highlights the importance of active outreach and dissemination initiatives designed to acquaint senior military personnel and civilians with these emerging issues. The CCRP Publication Series is a key element of this effort.

Check our Web site for the latest CCRP activities and publications.

www.dodccrp.org

DoD Command and Control Research Program

ASSISTANT SECRETARY OF DEFENSE (NII)
&
CHIEF INFORMATION OFFICER
Dr. Linton Wells, II (Acting)

PRINCIPAL DEPUTY ASSISTANT SECRETARY OF DEFENSE (NII)
Dr. Linton Wells, II

SPECIAL ASSISTANT TO THE ASD(NII)
&
DIRECTOR OF RESEARCH
Dr. David S. Alberts

Opinions, conclusions, and recommendations expressed or implied within are solely those of the authors. They do not necessarily represent the views of the Department of Defense, or any other U.S. Government agency. Cleared for public release; distribution unlimited.

Portions of this publication may be quoted or reprinted without further permission, with credit to the DoD Command and Control Research Program, Washington, D.C. Courtesy copies of reviews would be appreciated.

Library of Congress Cataloging-in-Publication Data

Smith, Edward Allen, 1946-
  Effects Based Operations: Applying Network Centric Warfare in Peace, Crisis, and War / Edward A. Smith, Jr.
      p. cm.
  ISBN 1-893723-08-9 (pbk.) -- ISBN 1-893723-08-9 (pbk.)
  1. United States--Military policy. 2. United States--Armed Forces.
  3. Military art and science. 4. World politics--21st century. I. Title.
  UA23 .S5238 2002
  355'.033573--dc21

                                                    2002012910

1st Printing 2002
2nd Printing 2003
3rd Printing 2005

Table of Contents

List of Figures

iv

v

Acknowledgments

In writing this book, I was privileged to be able to draw upon the work of the Information Superiority Working Group (ISWG) sponsored by the Office of the Secretary of Defense, upon the "Sensemaking Workshop" sponsored by the ISWG and the American Institute for Aeronautics and Astronautics, and the "Effects-Based Operations Workshop" of January 2002, in all of which I participated. The ideas presented also draw upon my own lessons learned from directing an extended series of Revolution in Military Affairs (RMA) Wargames conducted under the auspices of the Chief of Naval Operations and the Office of Net Assessment between 1995 and 1998. Similarly, these ideas draw upon lessons learned from participating in the effects-based operations play in the Navy's Global Wargames of 1999, 2000, and 2001.

I wish to express my special gratitude to Dr. David Alberts of the Office of the Secretary Defense (C3I) who suggested the book and then provided continued encouragement during its writing, and to Vice Admiral (ret) Arthur Cebrowski, U.S. Navy, who both instigated my initial effects-based studies during his tenure as President of the U.S. Naval War College and then encouraged me to proceed with the book when he assumed duties as Director of Force Transformation. I am and will always be grateful to Mr. John Garstka, Director of Concepts in the Office of Force Transformation, to Dr. David Signori of Rand Corporation, to Dr. Mark Mandeles,

President of the de Bloch Group, and Mr. John Robusto, Director of Network Centric Warfare at the Naval Air Warfare Command who volunteered to read this work and who provided valuable insights and suggestions.

Similarly, thanks are due to Dr. Richard Hayes, editor Joseph Lewis, graphic artist Bernard Pineau, and researchers Eric Cochrane and Brian Davis of Evidence Based Research, who lent discipline to my meanderings and put the work in a readable form. Special thanks are also due to Dr. Gordon Smith and my colleagues at Boeing's Washington Studies and Analysis office, who not only encouraged me to proceed with the writing but also assumed part of my workload to enable me to do so. Finally, I owe a particular thanks to my wife, Marie-France, who endured my "middle-of-the-night-inspirations-that-simply-have-to-be-written-down-right-now" and a home office that was for many months littered with books and papers.

However, all views expressed herein are the author's own and do not reflect either upon these sources or upon the Boeing Company.

Preface

It is fitting that this, the third book in our Information Age Transformation Series, be about effects-based operations (EBO). The first book in the series, *Information Age Transformation*, takes the view that DoD transformation is, in essence, about becoming an Information Age organization. The second book in the series deals with experimentation and argues that we need to modify, if not replace our somewhat linear requirements, doctrine development, and test and evaluation processes. This third book speaks directly to what we are trying to accomplish on the "fields of battle" and argues for changes in the way we decide what effects we want to achieve and what means we will use to achieve them.

Adaptation to the Information Age will require changes in the following four dimensions: mission space (what the military will be called upon to do), environment (the conditions, constraints, and values that govern military operations), concepts (the military business model or the way we do what we do), and the business side of the DoD (the way the organization supports value creation). EBO is about the first two of these four dimensions while Network Centric Warfare (NCW) addresses the last two. Hence, EBO and NCW form a synergistic treatment of military transformation. They deal with the why, what, how, and support of military operations.

Both EBO and NCW are, at their core, very simple ideas. Yet EBO, like NCW, often seems to be mischaracterized and misunderstood, much to the chagrin of its proponents. One theory that seeks to explain this notes that in the Cold War era, views of national security and the role of the military became narrowly focused. A military was to deter aggression and, if necessary, fight and win our nation's wars. Wars were implicitly defined as conflicts among coalitions of professional militaries. In many ways, Industrial Age warfare was very symmetric: air to air, tank to tank, submarine to submarine. Warfare and anti-warfare. Loss exchange ratios and FEBA movement made sense in this context. In other words, measures of attrition and territory, both directly related to military actions, made sense. Put another way, the means had merged with the effects.

Fast forward to now. The mission space and the environment in which we operate have changed significantly. No longer are the missions we are called upon to participate in purely or even predominantly military. The effects sought in many missions require a balance of military and non-military means to achieve. Thus, the tight coupling that once existed between means and effects exists no longer. But despite this reality, the former tight coupling between means and effects continues to permeate mindsets, processes, and measures. EBO serves to remind us that means and effects need to be explicitly linked, that traditional means may not be appropriate, and that we need to once again broaden our view of military operations.

EBO enables us to apply the power of NCW not just to traditional combat, as many are inclined to do, but to go beyond kinetic means to consider means in the information and cognitive domains to create effects in the cognitive domain across the full mission spectrum in peacetime and crisis response operations as well as in combat. EBO shifts our focus from targets and damage to behavior and the stimuli that alter behavior. As Dr. Smith argues, this broad multilevel interaction will form the basis of a new strategic deterrence.

Dr. Smith's blend of theory and practice explains and illustrates the why and how of EBO and its natural links to NCW. Upon completing the first three books in our Information Age Transformation Series, readers will have a comprehensive overview of what DoD transformation is all about and an idea about how to go about the business of transformation. Future books in this series will take a look at specific aspects of an Information Age transformation, including a look at a reconceptualization of C2.

David S. Alberts

Director, Research OASD(C3I)

Executive Summary

The terrorist attacks of September 11, 2001 fundamentally changed our security environment. The system of strategic deterrence in place since the beginning of the Cold War visibly collapsed. In place of mutually assured retaliation came the threat of terrorists armed with weapons of mass effect whom we may not be able to identify and who have no homeland at risk. The existing "balance of terror" became, with September 11th, unbalanced. Now we are trying to fashion a new strategic deterrence that relies not so much on retaliation as on prevention, either stopping the terrorists outright, deterring the sponsors, or convincing them that terror cannot succeed. Where strategic nuclear deterrence was the sine qua non of the Cold War, this new prevention-based deterrence demands a balanced application of both civil and military power to shape behavior. This shaping of behavior is the essence of effects-based operations.

To help us deal with the pressing problems of the post-September 11th world, we have three ongoing technological revolutions in sensors, information technology, and weapons. We can use the technologies simply to achieve incremental improvements in force effectiveness. But to do only this would miss their real potential. These

xiii

technologies can enable us to think differently about how we organize and fight. Indeed, this is what network-centric operations are about. But this is not enough. Network-centric operations are a means to an end. Their true impact derives from how they are applied. Narrowly applied, they would produce more efficient attrition, yet they clearly can do much more. The concept of effects-based operations is the key to this broader role. It enables us to apply the power of the network-centric operations to the human dimension of war and to military operations across the spectrum of conflict from peace, to crisis, to war, which a new strategic deterrence demands.

Defining Effects-Based Operations

The broad utility of effects-based operations grows ͡ ͡ the fact that they are focused on actions and links to behavior, on stimulus and response, er than on targets and damage infliction. They applicable not only to traditional warfare, but ͡o to military operations short of combat. Effects-ͤsed operations are not new. Good generals and ͤatesmen have always focused on outcomes and ͺn the human dimension of war (e.g. will and shock). Indeed, we can trace how the principles of effects-based operations have functioned in hundreds of crises and conflicts to distill a straightforward definition:

Effects-based operations are coordinated sets of actions directed at shaping the behavior of friends, foes, and neutrals in peace, crisis, and war.[1]

The concept of effects-based operations focuses "coordinated sets of actions" on objectives defined in terms of human behavior in multiple dimensions and on multiple levels, and measures their success in terms of the behavior produced. The "actions" include all facets of military and other national power that might shape the decisions of "friends, foes, and neutrals." Military actions, for example, might include air strikes, but also include a host of other military actions such as the role of maneuver, a major aspect of almost all crisis operations. Actions encompass operations "in peace, crisis, and war," not just combat.

If we look closely at real world crisis and combat operations, some rules of thumb for effects-based operations quickly emerge. Actions create effects not just on the foe but also on anyone who can observe them. Effects can occur simultaneously on the tactical, operational, military-strategic, and geo-strategic levels of military operations, in domestic and international political arenas, and in the economic arena as well. Effects cannot be isolated. All effects, at each level and in each arena, are interrelated and are cumulative over time. And lastly, effects are both physical and psychological in nature.

Operations in the Cognitive Domain

Effects-based operations can be described as operations in the cognitive domain because that is where human beings react to stimuli, come to an understanding of a situation, and decide on a response. To create an effect, an action first must be seen by an observer who will then interpret it and understand it against the backdrop of his or her prior experience, mental models, culture, and institutional ties, and translate this perception into a "sense" of the situation. Finally, this sense will be balanced against the options perceived to be available to produce a set of decisions and the reactions that constitute a response or "behavior." This cycle of actions and reactions will be repeated many times at multiple levels during the course of a crisis, a war, or even a peacetime interaction.

The cognitive cycle suggests three levels of complexity in effects-based operations.

First, we must somehow orchestrate our actions to present a particular picture to the observer. However, the observer will see not only *what* we do but also *how* we do it (e.g. the scale of our action, its geographic and operational scope, its timing, speed, duration and synchronicity). But, he will see only those facets of the action that his data and information collection capabilities permit.

Second, we must be able to identify a link between a particular action or set of actions and the effect we seek to create. But cognitive processes contain so many variables that we cannot reliably trace a cause and effect chain from a specific action to a specific reaction. Therefore, we need to think in terms of the kinds of potential physical and psychological effects (e.g. destruction, physical attrition, chaos, foreclosure, shock, and psychological attrition). These categories are not mutually exclusive but are elements in an overall effect that will vary from one situation to the next, from one level to the next, from one observer to the next, and over time.

Third, since effects are interrelated, the direct effects we create will tend to cascade into successions of indirect physical and psychological effects in ways that are different and not entirely predictable. Physical effects will tend to cascade in the manner of falling dominoes while psychological effects will tend to cascade almost explosively, limited only by the speed and scope of communications. Our operations may exploit these cascades to amplify the impact of our actions, or we may have to control them so as to prevent unwanted collateral effects.

To plan and execute effects-based operations, we need not know exactly how an observer will think or predict exact outcomes. Our object is to identify a series of the most likely outcomes that are sufficient for planning. For this, we need to know the nature of the stimulus we are creating and the decisionmaking problem it will present to observers, friend and foe alike. And, we need to know something of the observers' decisionmaking processes in order to understand the influences upon their decisions, such as institutional biases and prevailing mental models. Given this knowledge, we can estimate how the various aspects of our actions might be perceived and what options might be considered in response.

We must also be able to adapt agilely to changing situations. For this, we will require feedback as to whether our actions had the direct effect intended, and as to any change in behavior created. But how do we get this feedback? Clearly, there are many parts of the cognitive process we will not be able to observe. Nonetheless, there are observables we can exploit. If an action involves destruction, damage assessment is an index of whether the direct effect sought was achieved. Similarly, a system's physical performance can provide an index of direct effect. Likewise, assessment of an organization's performance can provide an index of its reaction to the stimulus. Finally, we might take a cue from indications and warning intelligence and aggregate large numbers of small indicators, any one of which might be meaningless by itself, but which can provide feedback on behavior when combined in the proper algorithm.

Network-Centric Operations: Options, Agility, Coordination, Knowledge Mobilization

Despite its complexity, the above is not an impossible task. We have been dealing with these challenges on an ad hoc basis throughout history. The good news is that we now can tap the technologies and thinking of network-centric operations to provide the four key ingredients of successful effects-based operations: options, agility, coordination, and knowledge mobilization.

Options

The ability to link diverse and geographically separated capabilities offers decisionmakers a wide range of options to tailor our actions precisely to a situation and set of observers so as to increase their impact. In a sense, networking permits the attrition-based metric of probability of kill (Pk) to be replaced by an effects-based metric "Po," in which the "o" is the probability of a given capability producing a useful option to deal with a given situation.

Agility

The responsiveness of networked forces with shared awareness and speed of command provides the agility to adapt to an intelligent adversary's actions by enabling us to shape and reshape our options and actions amid the give-and-take of battle and crisis operations.

Coordination

Shared situational awareness and understanding of command intent, coupled with the capacity for synchronization and self-synchronization, enable us to coordinate complex actions and effects that will produce a unity of effect across levels and arenas in which diverse actions build on each other synergistically.

Knowledge Mobilization

Finally and most importantly, success in effects-based operations will hinge on how well we mobilize knowledge and expertise to bear so as to provide timely, relevant support to decisionmakers at all levels. Flexible, responsive networking can bring this breadth of knowledge to bear.

In brief, network-centric operations are indeed a means to an end, and effects-based operations are that end.

---

[1]Effects-based operations are not defined in terms of a process because we logically cannot describe a procedure for planning and executing effects-based operations until we have first defined what those operations are.

Introduction

Come the Revolution...

As Chief of Naval Operations, the late Admiral Mike Boorda was pressed time and again to support a seemingly endless succession of new systems and platforms, each usually promoted by advocates attempting to portray their system in terms of some fashionable but only half-understood conceptual buzzword. Boorda's frustrated response to these "opportunities" was the pointed observation that "it sure would be nice if we had some clear idea what it was we were trying to do first."

Over the past several years, we have seen a succession of new civilian and military technologies and a series of new concepts. We have been offered the prospects of "force transformation" and a Revolution in Military Affairs (RMA) in various and sometimes competing forms. We have been confronted with the technologies of the information revolution and their application to something called Network Centric Warfare or network-centric operations. We have been asked to understand some apparently new concepts variously termed effects-based warfare, effects-based targeting, and effects-based operations. Quite understandably, this onslaught can leave us puzzling over how these pieces might fit together. Like Admiral Boorda, we are left trying to separate the worthwhile and necessary elements of the proffered transformation from those that would serve little purpose.

The key to dealing with this dilemma, as Boorda observed, is having some clear idea of what it is we are trying to do. Given the sweep and profound nature of the changes we face both in technology and in our security environment, especially after September 11, 2001, if we are to obtain that "clear idea," then we must proceed from the widest possible perspective and work our way down to the specifics. This approach is needed because the big picture encompassed by this wide perspective provides the context within which we can begin to understand and evaluate the changes being proposed. It provides a way of identifying where the pieces of the puzzle might fit, including those otherwise apparently irrelevant pieces that may prove critical to new ways of doing things. Also, it can give us a way of figuring out what pieces are missing and thus, what we need to invent and build if we are to succeed. In short, it can give us some sense of the direction and a set of priorities for getting where we want to go, which is the first step in any meaningful transformation of our military capabilities.

The purpose of this book is to begin to define one aspect of this big picture: how network centric-operations and effects-based operations fit together, and how they complement one another in meeting the needs of the new security environment. The starting point for this definition is the hypothesis that Network Centric Warfare and network-centric operations are not ends in themselves, but means to an end. They are tools to be applied to military operations. Their value derives as much from how we use them as it does from what they are. The concept of effects-based operations, of using military operations to shape the behavior of friends, foes, and neutrals in peace, crisis, and war, provides such an application.

Unlike network-centric operations, which have emerged from the technologies and thinking of the Information Age, effects-based operations are not new. Their roots can be traced back for centuries and are what good generals and statesmen have always attempted to do. When combined with network-centric thinking and technologies, however, such an operational approach offers a way of applying the power of the network to the human dimension of war and to military operations in peace and crisis, as well as combat. In essence, effects-based operations represent an opportunity to use networked forces to achieve nonlinear impacts and to expand the scope of action across the entire spectrum of conflict.

The focus in this book will be on defining the effects-based side of this equation. This focus reflects how the emerging literature on Network Centric Warfare has already done much to define the network-centric equation, but that there is no equal grasp of what effects-based operations are or how the two might be related. This book attempts to explain effects-based operations by constructing what might be termed an *extended working hypothesis*. It is not a definitive answer. We are too early in the process of defining network-centric operations, effects-based operations, and the requirements for a 21st-century military to generate one. Instead, the working hypothesis offers one logical way of assembling the pieces. Because any hypothesis is by nature imperfect and tentative, it must be broad enough to evolve as the technologies and the concepts of both network-centric and effects-based operations evolve. Indeed, a hypothesis with a broad reach in thought is likely to serve as a sound guide for what we are trying to do.

To support this working hypothesis, this book will rely heavily on common sense examples drawn from military history. These are calculated to convey a fundamental understanding of the enduring military principles and ideas behind both network-centric and effects-based operations.[1] They are intended as a jumping-off point for the more detailed operations research that must still be done, and not as definitive studies in themselves. However, the use of historical examples has another important use. It highlights the point that many of the ideas and principles inherent in both network-centric and effects-based operations are not new, but represent fresh applications and refinements of accepted, tried and true military thinking.

Transformation

There has been much discussion about the need for a transformation of American military forces to take advantage of the new technologies of the Information Age and to better enable those forces to handle the challenges of the post-September 11th epoch. But what is transformation? In his book *Information Age Transformation: Getting to a 21st Century Military*, Dr. David Alberts describes transformation as "a process of renewal, an adaptation to environment"[2] and points to both the changes in technology and the post-September 11th security environment as the driving forces behind transformation. He then goes on to lay out how Network Centric Warfare is the key to the transformation of a still largely Cold War military into an effective force for the 21st century. Where do effects-based operations fit in this transformation?

In creating a working hypothesis for effects-based operations, we will start with a form of transformation which has received much attention, the Revolution in Military Affairs. We will postulate that transformation constitutes a sharp break with the accepted way of waging war that enables one force to conclusively defeat another.[3] Such a framework is useful not because Network Centric Warfare and effects-based operations purport to be a true RMA (it is still too early to tell and, in any event, the transformation of a large military force is anything but rapid). Rather, the two concepts may be "revolutionary" because they propose a new form of warfare that might enable us to "conclusively defeat" an enemy. The lessons and caveats attached to the RMA therefore become factors to be considered in determining how we approach and implement network-centric and effects-based operations. They likewise provide an index of just how "transformational" the concepts of both Network Centric Warfare and effects-based operations really are (or aren't).

The most widely used example of a Revolution in Military Affairs is the 1940 blitzkrieg in which the German Army defeated the French and British Armies in northern France. The new "military" technologies[4] embodied in the radios, tanks, and close air support of the blitzkrieg were available to both sides in the struggle (actually, the British and French had more and better equipment than the Germans). But the Germans combined these new military technologies with a new, highly mobile concept of warfare, trained and organized their forces accordingly, and then devastated their opponents on the battlefield.

The example of the French and British debacle in 1940 provides two warnings that apply to any would-be revolution or transformation and to network-centric and effects-based operations:

- First, new military technologies, no matter how sophisticated, are not by themselves sufficient either to create an RMA or to deal with one. Unless the technologies can be translated into a revolution in warfare concepts, doctrine, and organization they will fall short of (or even fall prey to) a genuine RMA poised against it. Moreover, to the extent that new technologies give us an unfounded confidence that the old "tried and true" doctrine and concepts of warfare still work, they may conspire against us.

- Second, any successful RMA must function at more than the tactical level. At a purely tactical level, France's Maginot Line worked quite well. German forces did not come through its defenses. The fortifications remained intact and manned until France itself surrendered. The German blitzkrieg, on the other hand, worked because it generated sufficient shock to cause a collapse of resistance within the French political and military leadership, who then surrendered even though the means for conducting a continued resistance from North Africa were at hand.[5] Similarly, American forces in Vietnam were able to inflict defeat after defeat upon the Viet Cong and North Vietnamese military forces, but were unable to translate those defeats into a victory over North Vietnam. As long as it remains possible to win all the battles and still lose the war, an RMA must clearly have a strategic and operational dimension as well as a tactical application if it is to succeed.

However, there is also a third warning to be drawn from both the French Revolution and Vietnam: the Revolution that overturns the existing way of war may not involve "new" technologies at all. The lévée en masse that yielded the victories of the French revolutionary armies and Napoleon was not based on new technologies, but upon the application of standard 18th-century military technologies on a previously inconceivable scale. The need to sustain, move, and control such a large mass of forces necessitated changes in concepts of operations, doctrine, and certainly in the organization and command of the forces. Those changes and Napoleon's reorganization of the French state to support such an extensive military effort were the core of the Napoleonic RMA, and did not rely upon any new technologies possessed by the French.

Similarly, a military revolution might also center on a return to an older form of warfare, where that older form takes advantage of an opponent's relative inability to undertake a particular form of combat. General Giap's adaptation and application of Maoist principles of guerrilla warfare to defeating the United States in Vietnam might be classed in this category. Such guerrilla warfare required little application of new technology and deliberately avoided engaging U.S. Industrial Age forces in massed battles. Instead, North Vietnam's strategy centered on using a protracted, low level war to wear down American resistance at home.[6] Notice that in both the Napoleonic and North Vietnamese examples, the focus was not a different application of technologies as in the blitzkrieg, but something even more basic, an asymmetric *concept* of warfare. The approach to warfare used was revolutionary because it was able to meet and negate the impact of the strongest and most sophisticated armed forces of the day. It was not the nature of the means that was revolutionary; it was the result.

These warnings are clearly applicable both to network-centric, effects-based operations, and to the situation in which we have found ourselves as a nation since September 11, 2001. They tell us that the new thinking involved in the concepts is as important or more important than new technologies, and that a tactical-level revolution, however good it may appear, is not enough to win wars or to keep the peace. Similarly, any transformation that does not extend beyond new technology and systems to tactics, doctrine, organization, and concepts seems likely to fall short of revolutionary change. Moreover, if either or both the technology and the thinking fail to address the real uses to which the forces are to be put in a strategic environment, they are doomed to ultimate failure.

However, there is another dimension to the distinction between technologies and concepts that is essential to understanding both the nature of transformation and the nature of Network Centric Warfare and effects-based operations. In the 1940 blitzkrieg debacle, we can distinguish between two different revolutions.

On the one hand is what might be termed a Military Technical Revolution (MTR), that is, *the impact of new technologies and systems on existing concepts of warfare.*[7] On the other hand is a Revolution in Military Affairs, that is, *the application of those technologies to new tactics, doctrine, and organization and to a new concept of warfare.* This distinction between new technology and new thinking is particularly pertinent to our own situation in exploring the potential of Network Centric Warfare and effects-based operations. Consider that the new technologies of the Information Age are not an American or Western monopoly, just as the radio, the tank, and aircraft were not a German monopoly in 1940. In actuality, the technologies that support Network Centric Warfare and, indeed, the entire transformation we seek to create either are available on an open worldwide arms market or, even more importantly, are military adaptations of widely available civilian technologies. Indeed, in a macabre sense, this is what the airliner hijackings of September 11th represent.

As this suggests, we have no monopoly on change. The strategic environment that we face is one marked by a single internationally available Military-Technical Revolution that nations and even non-state actors will try to adapt to their particular needs with new concepts, doctrine, and organization. Each will try to create their own unique form of a RMA, often with us as the focus.

Furthermore, given the declining prices of the technologies of the information revolution, the threshold for access to this international MTR is no longer the possession of a world-class research and production capability. It is simply the availability of enough money to purchase the makings of a local capability and the ingenuity to operate the pieces as a system. As the terrorist attacks of September 11, 2001 indicate, that amount of money may be so minimal (the price of pilot lessons, airline tickets, and box-cutter knives) as to put the operation within the reach of even small groups and can be especially deadly whenever the will of those groups is great enough to generate people willing to commit suicide to further its ends. Even more ominously, if the terrorists have access to weapons of mass effect either independently or through state-sponsors, the threat may assume strategic proportions.

The keys to understanding and anticipating these would-be revolutions are likely to be assessing which technologies are likely to be chosen from this international grab bag and how they might be put together. In this context, the crucial determinant of the success or the failure of a future would-be network-centric or effects-based revolution is likely to lie in understanding the limits of both the concepts and technologies in meeting different strategic needs.

A Reality Check

These factors point to six common sense caveats that we will need to bear in mind as we attempt to understand the implications of Network Centric Warfare and to trace a theory and concept of effects-based operations.

1. Network-centric and effects-based operations may change the character of warfare; they cannot change the nature of war.

Coercion and manipulation will still be fundamental aspects of warfare and of military operations short of combat. Likewise, new concepts and technologies will not change the strategic imperatives that drive nations and non-state players in war and peace. Thus, the military solutions postulated in network-centric and effects-based operations will only be successful to the degree that they enable us to deal with these imperatives in peace and in war.

2. Network-centric and effects-based operations are not a substitute for military force.

Network-centric warfare and effects-based operations are about enhancing the impact and effectiveness of military force in a given tactical, operational, or strategic context. Success will be judged on the basis of results achieved rather than the novelty of the means used. A display of long-range precision bombing skills may be technologically impressive, but it will be of little use in coercion unless the targets that are struck hold a sufficient importance for the enemy either individually or in their aggregate to create the desired coercive effect. Similarly, however quickly we may move, and however successfully we remain inside an adversary's decision loop, the advantage of speed of command will avail nothing unless it enables us to do something to the enemy as a result.

3. Others will react.

Our network-centric and effects-based operations concepts and technologies will not and cannot be developed in splendid isolation and then sprung on an unsuspecting enemy. The technologies involved are too widely available and the discussions of their potential uses are too widespread for this to be a realistic possibility. The real question is not *whether* would-be challengers will react to our efforts to pursue network-centric and effects-based operations, but *when*, *where*, and *how*.

No prospective challenger can be expected to remain static and unchanging in the face of the efforts we are making. Therefore, if we use the new concepts to "fight the last war," if we study them in the context of past victories rather than past defeats, or if we measure them against an opponent who thinks and fights as we do (or even worse, as we would have him fight), we will yield any advantage to would-be foes who will not hesitate to exploit any vulnerabilities we have demonstrated. Indeed, others are already looking intently at the technologies that we are examining and adapting them to their own needs.

This implies that the development of network-centric and effects-based operations in the United States and the West will come as part of a protracted interactive process in which both we and our potential challengers are players. In this give and take, each side may be expected to adapt its technologies and thinking to evolving developments on the other side.[8]

4. Network-centric and effects-based operations are not a universal answer.

Network-centric and effects-based operations will not simply replace all other older forces and forms of warfare. They will open some new warfare niches even as they close others. And, the very nature of military competition should make it clear that would-be foes will attempt to exploit any warfare niche in which they believe the United States and its allies cannot successfully engage. Logically, these would-be foes will see exploitable niches wherever network-centric and effects-based operations are least applicable. Urban and guerrilla warfare, counter-terrorism operations, peacekeeping efforts, and hostage rescues are just a few examples. Even if aided by new technologies, such operations will remain manpower intensive and casualty prone and thus, attractive niches to be exploited by would-be foes.

To deal with these ever-changing challenges, we will still require a balance of military capabilities even as some of those capabilities become markedly better. The challenge will be to figure out how our concepts of Network Centric Warfare and effects-based operations apply to these challenges and enhance our ability to deal with them. The more applicable network-centric and effects-based operations are across the spectrum of conflict, the greater will be their impact.

5. Numbers still count.

New technologies, Network Centric Warfare, and effects-based operations do not remove "mass" from the military equation, but may reduce the mass of the military power needed to produce a given result. The desired outcome is still a decisive result, and some finite quantity of actions will be needed to achieve it. Sensor and information technologies, for example, can multiply the effect of each weapon fired by ensuring that each hits the right target at the right time, but some number of targets must still be struck to have the desired effect.[9] Similarly, an effects-based approach to warfare may enable us to achieve a nonlinear impact on the enemy, but some number of actions will still have to be undertaken to achieve that impact.

6. What if network-centric and effects-based operations don't work as planned?

Too many discussions of new technologies and concepts seem to assume that some form of a close-ended, one-time, limited objective strike or series of strikes will be decisive, and that a sustained campaign and/or the occupation of enemy territory will not be necessary (clearly not true in the U.S. operations in Afghanistan). Yet in our quest for some new blitzkrieg, we must always ask, what if the conflict turns out to be more like 1914 than like 1940?

The lessons of 1914 pose a very different set of *"what ifs"*:

- What if we must deal with an enemy so vast that even the most effective targeting effort must necessarily assume a very considerable scale?[10]

- What if intelligence is so poor that it cannot identify which targets might be decisive?

- What if there are no such targets?

- What if the enemy is so determined that he continues to fight in spite of the damage inflicted?

Even with all the new technologies of a military technical revolution, and even with a mature concept of a new kind of swift, precise war, we may still become embroiled in a long, large-scale conflict, or conversely in a protracted low-intensity conflict.[11] How would network-centric and effects-based operations function under these conditions and how would they contribute?

Since September 11, 2001, there is a new urgency in all of this. Transformation is no longer an academic exercise or another buzzword in defense acquisition. Rather, it is something toward which we are impelled by a basic change in our security environment that is every bit as profound and far-reaching as that of the beginning of the Cold War in 1947-1949. That change pitted the West against an international communist adversary armed with nuclear weapons in a balance of terror that endured for 40 years. Now, we face a security environment in which there is no such balance upon which to build. Terrorist opponents armed with weapons of mass effect can place our largest cities at risk, but there is little that we can place at risk in response. This time we must somehow fight a very asymmetric conflict whose focus from beginning to end will be in the mind of man.

It is already clear that the tools of the Cold War will not suffice to wage this war. We must, therefore, transform. But we must equally take care as to how we transform. As in the case of France in 1940, there is no second chance. Even the promise of network-centric operations will avail us little if they are applied to sharpening the tools of past wars or tools to pursue the wrong objectives.

This is where the concept of effects-based operations comes in. Effects-based operations focus on the mind of man. They are not a replacement for network-centric operations; rather they are the gateway to applying the tools of network-centric operations to the threat we now face, an asymmetric conflict that must be won in the mind of man.

The note of urgency behind the transformation should tell us something else as well. The transformation embodied in network-centric and effects-based operations cannot await the arrival of some new technology 20 years hence. Instead, network-centric and effects-based operations must be an application of both those technologies that we now possess and those new technologies we can create. In this sense, for all of the urgency, this process will remain more of an evolution in military affairs than a sudden revolution.

Getting There

It is worth noting that the Revolution in Military Affairs embodied in the blitzkrieg did not simply occur on its own. It was created. It required careful thought, considerable debate, and extensive effort to transform the German military of 1918 into that of 1940. Because of the internal soul-searching involved in such an effort, it is far easier to win support for radical change when the external pressures leave little room for anything else. This was certainly the case for Weimar Germany. However, such radical thinking and action are especially hard for a dominant power to undertake.[12] The very successes that produced its rise work against it. Admonitions such as "don't mess with success," and "if it ain't broke, don't fix it" become the rule of the day. This is far more than simply a conservative reaction. It is a recognition of the magnitude of the gamble that is involved in changing from a military structure and strategy that has worked and yielded the current dominance, to an approach that is new, untested, and may not work.

Here again is a reason for examining Network Centric Warfare and effects-based operations from a larger perspective. If we are to make an intelligent gamble on the future, we must understand not only how these concepts apply at the tactical level, but also how they enhance the nation's military power as a whole and enable it to better meet its strategic needs. However, here we have an advantage. If effects-based operations are not new but a restatement of hallowed military principles used by successful commanders and statesmen from time immemorial, then there is a large historical database that we can examine for clues as to how to proceed. This database also makes it plain that these commanders succeeded because they were able to apply the tools they had available to the problem of shaping a foe's behavior, much as we will be doing in the immediate future. One objective of this book will be to better define a broad unified concept and theory of effects-based operations so that we can better understand where and how the current tools of network-centric operations can be applied to doing just this.

Organization of This Book

This book starts by considering the asymmetric challenges posed by the new security environment of the post-September 11th world and the limitations of traditional attrition-based approaches to warfare in meeting them. It lays out a rough paradigm for looking at how Information Age technologies, the concept of Network Centric Warfare, and effects-based operations relate to one another. It then proposes a basic theory for behavior-based effects-based operations and derives a rule set from historical real world operations. The examples are then used to explore the three levels of complexity inherent in effects-based operations and the requirements for effects-based feedback to commanders. The concept is then extended to the peacetime missions of forward deterrence and reassurance. All of the pieces of the effects-based puzzle are in turn put together to look at an extended operational-level example. Finally, this book reviews the implications that effects-based operations hold for the further development of Network Centric Warfare and how the resulting network-centric and effects-based operations might contribute to the creation of a more effective homeland defense in the emerging security environment.

---

[1]Many (but by no means all) of these examples are drawn from naval history. This should not be surprising given the author's extensive background in the United States Navy and the tendency of all authors to focus on what they know best. However, the examples used are chosen to demonstrate a set of problems and solutions that extend far beyond the Navy or the Naval Service and that reflect the problems the United States military forces in general face in planning and executing effects-based operations

[2]Alberts, David S. *Information Age Transformation: Getting to a 21st Century Military.* Washington, DC; CCRP. 2002.

[3]As originally defined by Andrew Krepinevich, a Revolution in Military Affairs is a sharply discontinuous change in the efficacy of certain forms of military power stemming from the introduction of new technologies, concepts, doctrine and modes of organization.
Krepinevich, Andrew F. "Cavalry to Computers: The Patterns of Military Revolutions." *The National Interest.* Fall 1994. P.30ff.

[4]The evolution of two of these 1940 technologies (the radio and the airplane) depended about as much on innovations wrought by civilian industry as they did on improvements undertaken by government.

[5]The alternative advocated by de Gaulle and others was to move the entire French Government and as much of the French armed forces as possible to North Africa. This was staunchly opposed by the Vice Premier Marshal Pétain and a corps of defeatists in the National Assembly who voted to stay in France and later voted Pétain into power.

[6]It might be argued that guerrilla warfare was the RMA of the latter half of the 20th century as it brought down first the great colonial empires, then fought the United States to a standstill, and finally laid the seeds for Soviet collapse.

[7]If we consider terrorism as a form of warfare, then the use of airliners as large guided missiles would fall into this

MTR category.

[8]How long might the advantages that accrue from network-centric and effects based operations last before a reaction nullified much of its impact? In general, the bigger the challenge the RMA poses, the greater will be the efforts to counteract it, and the shorter the time it will retain a dominant advantage on the battlefield. Conversely, the more radical and overwhelming the RMA and the more difficult any attendant MTR is to replicate, the greater will be the impact and the longer the advantage is likely to last. While the impact of the blitzkrieg and the levee en masse lasted for two decades or less, the Western projection of military power by sea and the follow-on creation of Industrial Age military capabilities so overwhelmed the non-European world that the advantage endured for several centuries. The long-term success accrued less from the military technologies than from the fact that they evolved from a European societal and economic structure that was difficult to replicate. Hence, they and the colonial and mercantile empires they supported lasted until Japan, a nation that had successfully adapted the essential elements of European culture that gave them rise, finally challenged them.

[9]The contribution of information and knowledge superiority is that the more open to question the targeting is, the more it will become necessary to increase the number of strikes to have a reasonable chance of damaging those targets that will yield such a decisive impact. Conversely, if the quantity of weapons used fell to zero, the impact of that superiority, however fast or omniscient it may be, will still fall to nothing. However, there is still more to the equation.

The impact of numbers is not restricted to tactical exchanges. The more our RMA depends on a very limited number of precisely targeted weapons or actions, the more tempting it will be for an enemy either to calculate the damage he might incur and dismiss it, or to deal with the precision by presenting an overwhelming number of targets. Even more disturbingly, the fewer weapons we have available, the greater will be the pressure for us to gamble on targeting a very limited number of elusive and, perhaps, illusionary "golden" nodes (single points of failure calculated to bring enemy resistance to a halt) simply because there are not enough weapons for anything else. The danger of course is that, if we have guessed incorrectly, there are no further options.

A highly focused attack may work whenever the enemy is weak or his will is not great, and the destruction necessary to be decisive is relatively small. But the reality is that the bigger and more dangerous the opponent, the riskier it will become to

xl

base our strategy on assumptions about the fragility of enemy will. Such assumptions are themselves notoriously fragile and, if faulty, are more likely to lead to defeat than victory.

[10]The German invasion of Russia in June 1941 is a case in point. The force of the blitzkrieg that overwhelmed Poland in 1939 and France in 1940 was simply absorbed in the vastness of Russia, the same problem which had confronted Napoleon's RMA in 1812. The defeat of those enemy forces that could be engaged and the destruction of the infrastructure that could be reached in both cases was not decisive. The Russians refused to succumb, were able to generate more forces, and retained sufficient additional infrastructure beyond the reach of the invaders to continue to sustain armies in the field. A similar problem might confront the United States in the case of a war with China.

[11]Desert Storm succeeded as a new style conflict only because it ended when it did. Had allied forces been required to move from the open spaces of the desert into the heavily populated areas of Iraq, or had they been compelled to conduct house-to-house fighting in Kuwait City, much less in Basra or Baghdad, the resulting warfare would not have been swift and decisive, even if the final outcome remained the same. The cases of Vietnam or of World War II Russia are only marginally different in this regard.

[12]This is very much evident in the countervailing case presented by Great Britain in the interwar years. Although Britain entered the 1920s with superiority in all of the technologies that combined to sustain the blitzkrieg, and although Britain had initiated many of the concepts involved, it ultimately failed to transform its military in any revolutionary way.

CHAPTER 1

Why Effects-Based Operations? Military Operations in a New Security Environment

Network Centric Warfare and network-centric operations[1] are not ends in themselves. They are the means to an end. For them to have value, they must be applied to military operations, and they must improve the capacity of those operations to accomplish some strategic, operational, or tactical objective. Our working hypothesis is that effects-based operations (military operations directed at shaping the behavior of foes, friends, and neutrals in peace, crisis, and war) constitute the conceptual framework for this two-step process of turning our network-centric capability into a national advantage.[2] In essence, effects-based operations provide the "end" for our network-centric "means."

Effects-based operations are not new. Good generals, admirals, and statesmen have focused on

1

using military forces to shape the behavior of friends and foes for centuries. What is new is the potential application of network-centric thinking and capabilities to such operations. As suggested above, we must address two aspects of this marriage of network-centric and effects-based operations: what are the strategic, operational, and tactical objectives to be attained; and how might network-centric and effects-based military operations help us to realize those objectives? It is appropriate, therefore, to begin to answer the question "why effects-based operations?" by looking at our emerging security environment and the requirements that network-centric and effects-based operations must meet before beginning to discuss the nature of those operations in the following chapters.

The New Security Environment: September 11 and Beyond

The terrorist attacks of September 11, 2001 fundamentally changed our security environment. The system of strategic deterrence[3] that had fended off any serious attack on our homeland since the onset of the Cold War, and that had provided stability in a changing world, visibly collapsed. The Cold War face-off between powerful nation-states was replaced by a threat from non-state terrorists, potentially armed with weapons of mass effect, and dedicated to overturning what they perceive as an unacceptable status quo. The "balance of terror" tipped in favor of the terrorists. We now face the challenge of fashioning a new balance that relies less on the threat of retaliation and depends more on some form of prevention: stopping the terrorists outright; deterring their state-sponsors; and convincing all who would exploit terror that it cannot succeed.

These tasks demand changes in how we create and apply military power. The paradigms of the Cold War military order are no longer adequate. Whereas strategic nuclear deterrence had been the sine qua non of Cold War strategic deterrence, the new security environment calls for a more nuanced approach depending heavily on a forward, prevention-based, conventional deterrence and the balanced application of civil and military power. Where Cold War military effectiveness tended to be measured in terms of the destruction of forces and infrastructure, Information Age effectiveness is likely to focus on force agility and the ability to provide a wide range of options in peace, crisis, and war.

The Threat

The most pressing threats of the new security environment are violent reactions to the world's movement toward a single international system marked by the free movement of people, investment, goods, and ideas. The attacks of September 11th and the overt hostility toward what is perceived to be a heavily American globalization make it plain that this evolution will be neither easy nor without significant peril. Yet, this movement is not so much a function of American efforts to promote any ideology as it is due to the attraction that many aspects of the Western economic model hold. Notwithstanding recessions and inequities, the complex adaptive economic system that we call free enterprise has proven to be a much more efficient producer of goods and services than command economies or more traditional economies, an efficiency that manifests itself in the increased quantity of goods and services available. It is the promise not of mass consumption but of consumption by the masses, the idea that everyone can aspire to material goods and a better life, that is attracting support for change. In addition, the introduction of new information technologies stands to further enhance this productivity and attraction. America may aspire to influence the direction and timing of this change, but it cannot control it.

Democratic government, the complex adaptive political system, is the necessary complement to this complex adaptive economic system. Again, the reason is practical rather than ideological. Responsive government is needed to cope with the accelerating pace of political and social change that accompanies the free market and information-driven globalization, both to curb the potential abuses of the free market system and to enforce the competition that drives increased efficiency. In essence, it is the "feedback loop" that focuses the economic effort and ensures that efficient free enterprise does not sink into inefficient monopolies or corrupt oligarchies.

The movement toward a new international system has also been marked by an expanding information revolution and the spread of the free, mass culture of the West, abetted by a pervasive global media whose reach has been further expanded by the revolution in information technology (embodied in the Internet). This media revolution has not only heightened demand for the goods that a more efficient free market economy can bring, but also increased demand for more open and flexible government. Again, the information revolution is not the result of any American effort to create democratic bastions, support the free press, or promote information technology. Rather, it results from the spread of the information itself and the resulting increased awareness around the world of how life might be different and how governments might be better. This awareness lends force to the entire movement for change, political and economic, as well as social.

The course of this internationalization has not and will not be smooth. Expectations raised by the expanding media will exceed the ability of governments and economies to deliver.[4] There will be violent reactions and often destabilizing changes in established cultures and institutions. And, those who oppose change will see conflict as a way to disrupt the movement toward globalization. The anti-Western violence of al-Qaida is only one manifestation of a problem that is likely to continue as long as the process of globalization continues.[5] Herein lies the threat to American security. The United States can control neither the movement toward a new international system nor the violent reactions to it, yet the United States, its citizens, and its interests will clearly be a principal target. To make matters worse, the free trade and travel that are part of globalization make the United States and the West vulnerable in ways that they have never been before. Ocean barriers are no longer protection against terrorism in an era of mass air travel and still more massive trade.

Amidst this turmoil, a strategy of "forward defense" takes on a new meaning, and the traditional military missions of deterrence, presence, and crisis response take on a new significance. Over the past 50 years, the United States' forward defense strategy has rested on three pillars: the economy, politics and culture, and the military. Since September 11, 2001, this strategy has taken on a new urgency. The pace of the transition in which we are engaged is likely to be at least in part a function of the internal and regional stability surrounding it. The greater the instability and conflict, the slower the pace is likely to be and the more prolonged the threat to the United States. By aiding the transition to a successful and speedy conclusion, we therefore lessen the danger to ourselves at home and abroad. The forward strategy thus rests on a paradox. It must seek both stability and highly-disruptive change. How then do military forces contribute?

The Military Role

The lasting solutions to the unrest wrought by globalization are political, social, and economic in nature, not military. This is because the root causes of the instability are themselves political, social, and economic in nature.[6] Thus, the United States and the West can influence global evolution only to the degree that their businessmen, teachers, diplomats, and journalists are free to play a role. But, these varied roles, like the change as a whole, demand a basic local stability in order to succeed. While our forward military forces certainly may have a role in influencing local militaries, their crucial role is not as an agent of change. Their real role is to create and/or reinforce the stability that political, social, and economic change requires. The role of military forces is not to solve all of the social, political, and economic dilemmas; it is to buy time.

Military forces buy time in a very immediate sense by dealing with the symptoms of unrest: meeting threats to American and Western nationals; containing crises; supporting local efforts to handle unrest; and countering opportunistic threats from other local states. However, perhaps the most significant military contribution is not dealing with the symptoms of instability, but acting as the forward deterrent that underpins long-term stability, a force whose presence and capabilities support an enduring peace within which change can occur.

We can conceive of the economic, socio-political, and military roles in forward defense as a series of overlapping circles, depicted in Figure 1. Each element has a distinctively different function in the strategy. Each overlaps and supports the other elements. These overlaps are instructive. For example, by opening new markets, businessmen also engage in people-to-people contacts that help to expand the cultural and political frontiers. Yet, despite the overlap, the role of the businessman clearly remains economic. Similarly, a diplomat might aid business in opening new markets or expanding investments while continuing to execute U.S. policy. This overlap of functions is also apparent in the military domain. One role of military forces in

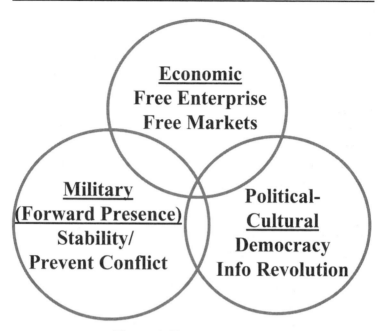

Figure 1. Forward Defense

forward defense, for example, may be to keep the seas safe for commerce. Another may be to engage people-to-people contacts, e.g. exercises with local militaries. However, while each of the latter roles may be important, they describe only those areas in which the military role overlaps and directly supports the economic and political elements. In this sense, they are missions that are peripheral to the actual and most critical military role of creating and maintaining the basic local stability. It is this role of deterrence and crisis response that is the true contribution of the military pillar.

In describing this role and the context of effects-based operations, our problem is complicated by the fact that we tend to look at military efforts in terms of reactive operations such as the evacuation of American nationals threatened by local terrorism, or crisis responses to block local aggression. Such operations deal with the symptoms of the instability and the incipient failures of local deterrence.[7] As such, they are but one part of the real contribution of constructing and acting as the guarantor of local stability.

Strategic Deterrence and the New Security Environment

Post-September 11th strategic deterrence has two dimensions: homeland defense and forward defense, deterrence and containment. During the Cold War, strategic deterrence tended to be defined predominantly in terms of strategic _nuclear_ deterrence. This is certainly understandable given the stakes involved in a nuclear conflagration, however this strategic nuclear deterrence was paralleled by a broader dimension that might be termed conventional or non-strategic nuclear deterrence.[8] Both remain a fundamental part of our security, but the latter dimension in particular lies at the heart of our post-September 11th problem and the need for effects-based operations.

Strategic Nuclear Deterrence

The nuclear deterrence of the Cold War rested on the threat of retaliation. It worked because each nuclear-armed power could threaten opponents with a set of consequences so catastrophic that neither side stood to gain. This "balance of terror" was the basis for mutual deterrence. As secure, second-strike capabilities emerged, and with them the perceived ability to retaliate even if the other side managed to deliver the first blow, this threat of assured retaliation became the "security" of a mutually assured destruction (MAD) which Cold War arms control agreements even codified into tightly written rules, replete with inspections to avoid technological surprises that might upset the deterrence system. Despite a number of tense Cold War military confrontations, the consequences of a nuclear exchange combined with the acknowledged difficulty of controlling the escalation of even a tactical nuclear exchange made nuclear conflict unlikely.

However, the very scale of the consequences involved in MAD set a credibility threshold. A nuclear war that would result in the annihilation of large portions of the population on both sides could only be credibly threatened to the degree that the issue at hand threatened the nuclear power's existence as a nation.[9] In essence, decisionmakers applied a "rational man" approach to MAD and concluded that no rational decisionmaker would accept the risk of such destruction for any but a life-or-death, vital national interest. Hence, if the threatened national interest was less important, the threat of nuclear war would become less credible. Beneath this sliding and somewhat uncertain threshold, there remained considerable room for conflicts in which vital interests were not engaged and, thus, in which strategic nuclear capabilities were largely inapplicable.[10] The strategic nuclear deterrents tended to cancel each other out beneath the credibility threshold and, within this sub-threshold region, each side was relatively free to pursue conventional conflicts with peripheral powers in Vietnam and Afghanistan, the Czech and Hungarian Revolutions, and the Grenada operation.

What then has changed? The stability of Cold War strategic nuclear deterrence rested in part on two facts: that an attacker could be immediately identified; and that the attacker had roughly equivalent forces or population at risk.[11] These facts assured the nuclear response and gave the regime of strategic deterrence much of its stability. Since the end of the Cold War, the problem has shifted to that of deterring a non-state adversary armed with weapons of mass effect and acting either alone or as the surrogate for some hidden state sponsor. Such an adversary has little at risk in such an attack. Indeed, the attack may be difficult to trace to a specific actor, state or non-state. Thus, the stability of assured retaliation has become a precarious balance between one side's ability to inflict an attack using a weapon of mass effect and the other side's ability to prevent it.

Conventional Deterrence[12]

This new strategic deterrence quandary poses a challenge to how we think about military power because it suggests that we must somehow deter a strategic attack with conventional military forces. In essence, it reverses the Cold War primacy of military forces in which strategic nuclear forces were the sine qua non of homeland security and both conventional deterrence and the forces to support it were considered a "lesser included case." In the face of the new threat to homeland security, it is nuclear deterrence that becomes almost a "lesser included case" of conventional deterrence. Forward deterrence, the maintenance of regional stability, and the containment of local crises that spawn both terrorists and their state support have become the key to assuring homeland defense to a degree never before seen.

However, we must be careful. Conventional deterrence is not simply a miniature version of its nuclear cousin with conventional weapons destroying pre-planned lists of targets. Rather, it differs significantly from nuclear deterrence in its complexity, its logic, and its execution.[13] At the heart of all deterrence is the question of *who* and *what* are to be deterred. In the case of Cold War strategic nuclear deterrence, this *who* and *what* tended to be relatively straightforward. By contrast, conventional deterrence encompasses a seemingly infinite and constantly changing variety of *whos* and *whats*, but few theories as to *how* to deter. Where the primary challenge in Cold War strategic nuclear deterrence was a symmetric opponent in the context of a major conflict, the *what* of conventional deterrence can be either asymmetric or symmetric, and thus can range from a terrorist cell to a large-scale conventional war, such as Desert Storm. Similarly, the *who* can range from a peer nation to urban terrorists and other ideological, ethnic, or religious non-state actors.

The logic of conventional deterrence revolves about two factors: the threat of unacceptable retaliation; and the ability to prevent a would-be foe's success.[14]

Retaliation

Like its strategic nuclear counterpart, conventional deterrence can rely on the threats of retaliation. We may threaten something a would-be enemy holds dear, using the same logic as strategic nuclear deterrence. However, where nuclear arms hold whole societies at risk, conventional weapons are limited to more finite targets or actions that only in some vast aggregate might purport to hold a whole society at risk. The key question in any threat of retaliation with conventional weapons is therefore: what precisely does the opponent hold dear? In some cases, that question may be answered with lists of targets. But, in the case of non-state actors or even states that simply do not have vulnerable forces, populations, or infrastructure, the problem again devolves to a question of understanding what factors play in the cognitive process of the leadership (e.g., the survival of the organization), and then threatening those vulnerabilities in some way.

Retaliation may also take the form of escalation, threatening to expand the conflict beyond the confines of a foe's desired battlespace. However, where the threat of nuclear escalation involves the crossing of a catastrophic threshold, in conventional deterrence this is more likely to be a process of probing and testing the limits of response. As this implies, the more flexible the capabilities of the deterrent force are, the more likely it is that the challenger's probe will be unsuccessful, and his threat will become less credible.

Over the years, the potential for conventional deterrence has been multiplied by a succession of developments. The development of precision weapons made it possible to destroy very specific targets reliably without a large-scale effort. Then, nodal targeting of the weapons bolstered the impact of precision weapons by enabling warfighters to focus destruction where it would create the greatest impact. Finally, the introduction of cruise missiles meant that these precision strikes could be accomplished without risking personnel, which made the political credibility of a threat far greater. Each of these elements has made retaliation with precision weapons appear to be increasingly attractive as a staple of conventional deterrence. However, a closer examination is warranted.

In fact, retaliation-based conventional deterrence runs into some of the same problems encountered in nuclear deterrence. It has a credibility threshold. The less direct the challenge is to the interests of the state threatening to retaliate,[15] the less credible any threat of a large-scale retaliation is likely to be, just as in the case of the doctrine of massive response.[16] But, there is a Catch-22 aspect to this. As the magnitude of the damage that can be credibly threatened decreases, the consequences and risks attached to the enemy action also decrease. And, the lower the risks, the more likely the deterrence is to be tested, as long as the adversary perceives the risks to be manageable. This suggests that as long as the challenger can control the level of conflict to avoid a large-scale reprisal, he would have considerable freedom of action. By contrast, if a challenger's probes were to be met with a tailored, graduated response including the possibility of vertical or lateral escalation, his risks would rise substantially.

To make retaliation still more difficult, all these risks-versus-gains calculations are likely to be heavily colored by what the adversary decisionmaker wants to see and by a consequent tendency to rationalize away the possibility of retaliation entirely or to minimize its impact. The more intellectually isolated the adversary decisionmakers are, the more likely such rationalization is likely to occur.[17] By extension, the greater the degree of rationalization is, the more likely a challenge will be to occur.

As the above strongly suggests, threats of retaliation at the conventional level are likely to be either difficult or ineffective as deterrents, especially in confrontations with asymmetric opponents.

Prevention

The more successful approaches to conventional deterrence appear to revolve around prevention: the foreclosure of any reasonable prospect of a quick or sure success.[18] Prevention therefore involves closing any military, political, temporal, or geographic niches[19] an adversary might seek to exploit. Logically, if would-be foes perceive that they cannot succeed in a course of action, then they will probably consider it pointless to proceed. Such foreclosure applies both to their dealings with other local powers and to dealings with a global power able to intervene in their area.

At the heart of foreclosure are the questions of what conduct we are trying to deter, and how an adversary might use the capabilities at his disposal to create and/or exploit a military, political, temporal, or geographic niche. That is, successful prevention hinges on our ability to identify the nature and dimensions of potential niches and demonstrating the capabilities to prevent the niche competitor from succeeding. Moreover, this construct is as applicable to confrontations with non-state terrorist organizations as it is to states.[20] Notice that this construct is open-ended on several levels. It does not necessarily imply a military-on-military confrontation or a formal campaign of any sort, although both may be part of an effort to foreclose. It does not necessarily imply a violent use of military force, though the actions of military forces are very likely to be part of any response. It will likely involve some mixture of political, military, and perhaps economic action to deal with a prospective niche that may itself contain such elements. And finally, the closure of the niche may depend either on an active foreclosure in which specific moves are countered by specific counter-moves, or on a passive foreclosure in which the continuing local security calculus itself discourages challenges.

The above discussion outlines a general framework for the complex and multi-faceted strategic deterrence we will need to pursue in the post-

September 11th security environment. It is a statement of the problem to which network-centric concepts and effects-based operations will be applied. In this sense, it is one part of the "end" toward which our network-centric "means" will be directed to produce a result. We still have to determine how the "means" will be applied to the tasks involved. This leaves us once again with the question: why effects-based operations? In essence, what would an effects-based application of network-centric concepts and capabilities contribute to solving the problems of the new security environment that our current approaches to warfare lack? To answer these questions, we need to understand what our current approach to warfare is, and just as importantly, how it has shaped our thinking about military power.

Attrition-Based Warfare, Asymmetric Conflict...and the New Security Environment

For better or for worse, our current approach to warfare, and thus to implementing a forward defense strategy and creating a post-September 11th strategic deterrence, remains largely focused on the destruction of an opponent's physical capacity to wage war.[21] That is, it remains attrition-based. Such attrition is neither wrong nor necessarily inappropriate. However, it is essential to our comprehension of the potential synergies of network-centric and effects-based operations that we understand why we have come to rely on attrition. Such understanding is inhibited by the fact that the term "attrition warfare" has a distinctly pejorative ring to it. Attrition warfare or attrition-based warfare is usually presented as the technological and conceptual antithesis of "revolutionary" military thinking or, indeed, as the form of warfare that network-centric and effects-based operations seek to replace. Or, it is still more narrowly used to describe a particularly bloody style of warfare epitomized by the World War I battles around Verdun.[22] Such easy dismissal yields little real understanding of what attrition warfare is, why it was adopted, or how effects-based operations might provide an alternative. Was attrition warfare simply a horrifically bad strategic choice? Or, was it dictated by some strategic imperative that made it a last resort? And, if the latter, how might network-centric and/or effects-based operations provide us with better choices?[23]

The first step in the process of understanding attrition is to recognize that attrition warfare, even in its bloodiest form, is neither a product of the Industrial Age nor of the modern nation-state. It has been found throughout history. Indeed, the Third Punic War between Rome and Carthage (198 B.C.) can be said to be the archetype of a total war, attrition warfare carried to its logical but extreme end. In that war, Rome defeated the Carthaginian army, destroyed the city of Carthage, and slaughtered its citizenry or sold them into slavery. By so doing, the Romans removed all of the physical means by which Carthage might wage war: men, arms, and agricultural infrastructure. No matter how much the surviving Carthaginians may have wanted to continue their struggle with Rome, they were rendered physically incapable of doing so. The driving force behind the totality of this destruction was a mutual hatred between Rome and Carthage that was pursued so implacably by the citizen soldiers of both states through a succession of wars that, as the Roman Senator Cato kept insisting, there was no alternative but that Carthage be destroyed.[24]

The evolution of the modern model of attrition warfare that has so shaped our thinking followed a similar logical trajectory. Although the modern concept of the citizen soldier arguably dates from the English Civil War and the early colonial and French and Indian Wars in North America,[25] it finds its clearest expression in the French Revolution's lévée en masse. The impact of mass conscription upon European warfare was profound. Whereas most 18th-century wars had been fought with relatively small, highly trained, professional "precision" armies, the lévée produced very large citizen armies driven by patriotism. Napoleon harnessed the military power of the lévée both by altering French military organization and doctrine to permit mass maneuver warfare and by reorganizing the French state and economy so as to be able to sustain enormous armies in the field.[26] The nationalistic underpinning of the lévée posed a problem for Napoleon's opponents because, to defeat Napoleon, they had to defeat not just Napoleon or his army, but the French nation as a whole, much as Rome found it necessary to destroy Carthage to defeat it.[27]

This same dilemma was at the root of the U.S. Civil War, and of the two World Wars. To the mass conscription and nationalism of Napoleonic mass warfare, these three wars added the resources of Industrial Age economies. The greater wealth, technology, and manufacturing capacity provided a way of regenerating and re-equipping defeated armies even as the growth of mass democracies reinforced the nationalism supporting large-scale conscription. However, the combination of nationalism and mass democracy also had another consequence. With large numbers of citizen soldiers dying in battle and entire populations involved in the war effort, it became increasingly difficult to accept 18th-century style negotiated settlements, such as the Congress of Vienna that ended the Napoleonic wars. Instead, wars were propelled to the infinitely more difficult goal of unconditional surrender. In essence, if government is truly to be "of the people, by the people, for the people,"[28] then it is no longer sufficient to defeat the opposing army in the field, for "the people" will simply generate a new army, as both France and Carthage had repeatedly done. Rather, to defeat a government of the people, you must wear down the people's resistance, or destroy their ability to put new forces in the field.[29] [30] During the Civil War, General Grant dealt with this unpalatable strategic necessity by trying to wear down the South's physical capacity to make war by killing or capturing its soldiers and destroying their support and re-supply infrastructure.[31] By placing unrelenting military pressure on the Confederate capital, he forced the South to commit its meager manpower to a grinding battle in which they could be destroyed. By using Sherman to cut the South in two and Sheridan to cut off supplies from the

Shenandoah Valley, and by using Union naval power to blockade or hold Southern ports, he eliminated the Confederates' ability to sustain any but a limited guerrilla war. Grant's was not an arbitrary choice, but a response to a harsh imperative. No negotiated settlement was possible because the one thing that the South and its electorate wanted, independence, was the one thing that the North could not grant without invalidating the entire cause for which it was fighting. There simply was no other way to defeat the South, nor, as the South itself discovered during the first half of the war, was there any other way to defeat the North.[32]

The World War I trenches bear an eerie resemblance to those of Richmond and Petersburg. Just as in the American Civil War, none of the warring powers in World War I deliberately set out to fight a war of attrition. In August 1914, both sides hoped to break their opponent's will in a swift campaign. Yet by October 1914, they found themselves entrenched on a static battlefield that stretched from the North Sea to Switzerland and from the Baltic to Romania, with their strategy reduced to grinding down their foes' military forces.[33] They too had no choice. The scale of the forces and resources committed was so vast and the foes so determined that no single battle or campaign could break their opponent's ability to continue the fight. Like the North and the South during the Civil War, both sides were able to sustain horrendous losses through 4 years of war, specifically because they all had some semblance of popular government and nationalistic fervor.[34] However, unlike the Civil War, neither side in the

Great War was able to destroy their opponent's economic and industrial capacity to sustain the armies in the field. Thus, in the absence of some signal success in either the Allied blockade or the German U-boat war, both sides were limited to one major course of action: grinding down the opposing army on the battlefield.

In the years after World War I, air power appeared to offer a logical way out of this dilemma. Bombers could strike directly into the enemy heartland and destroy the means of sustaining a conflict without the need for ground forces to break through enemy lines. Giulio Douhet, the Italian air power prophet, even hoped that such bombing would overcome nationalistic fervor and break the will of the civilian populace.[35] Yet, in the end, the strategic bombing of Germany and Japan during World War II was more reminiscent of the Civil War campaigns of Sherman and Sheridan. It destroyed centers of war production and cut the lines of communications by which production reached forces in the field,[36] but air strikes alone did not bring victory.[37] Similarly, the coordinated armor and air tactics of the World War II blitzkrieg appeared to replace trench warfare with a swift maneuver war. But, in the final analysis, despite the military successes against Poland, France, and initially against the Soviet Union, Germany was unable to translate military success into a strategic victory over all of the Allies. Nor were the Allies later able to translate their own blitzkrieg imitation into a collapse of German will. Rather, on closer inspection, the ultimate strategic and operational impact of the maneuver warfare in which both sides engaged was to gradually destroy enemy forces in much the same fashion that Grant had done in the campaign leading to the siege of Richmond and Petersburg during the Civil War. Like the South, German and Japanese will to resist endured until both countries were all but overrun or occupied.[38] As a result of this will to resist, despite its tactical and operational innovations, World War II remained fundamentally a war of attrition.[39]

Means and Will

What can we deduce from these examples? And what implications do they hold for Network Centric Warfare and the application of the network-centric revolution to effects-based operations? Four things are evident in the above history:

- First, attrition warfare was not an arbitrary choice. It was a last resort. No participant in any of the wars cited set out to fight a war of attrition.[40] On the contrary, all tried to fight a swift, decisive maneuver war, but found themselves confronted by a foe too big or too resilient for that to succeed. They were driven to attrition warfare when confronted by a hostile peer who would not yield as they had hoped. This strategic imperative was twofold. The resources available to a large industrialized state provided the physical means to engage in conflicts of a scale, scope, and duration that previously would have been unthinkable and enabled these states to redress battlefield defeats that, by Napoleonic standards, would have been decisive.[41] Equally important, the nationalism at the root of the nation-state's existence provided a cohesive popular will. That not only permitted them to endure battlefield defeats and terrible loss of life, but also compelled them to demand "unconditional surrender" of their foes rather than settling for a negotiated compromise in the manner of 18th-century diplomacy.

• Second, one cannot assume that an opponent will fight the kind of war planned. Opponents adapt to challenges in unexpected ways. The form these wars took was dictated by the interactions between the two competitors, not by any pre-war plans. The longer the conflict lasted, the more opportunity there was for adaptation. By extension, any new approach to warfare (network-centric operations and effects-based operations included) must be flexible and dynamic enough to deal with intelligent opponents.

• Third, the three great attrition conflicts examined, the American Civil War and the two World Wars, could be considered wars of attrition because the overall strategy of the participants depended on the cumulative destruction of their opponents' physical capacity to wage war in order to achieve victory. It was not because the combat operations needed to realize this strategy were limited to attrition for attrition's sake. In actuality, each side used maneuver, surprise, shock, attrition, and any other form of warfare that offered some prospect of success in meeting their attrition-based strategic objective.

• Finally and somewhat paradoxically, in all of these wars, the ultimate determinant of victory was not physical destruction, but the participants' will to continue the struggle. In each case, the underlying rationale for the attrition strategy was not to inflict the Punic War-style destruction of a total war (an extreme and almost impossible task in the case of a very large nation-state). It was to induce a collapse of the enemy's will. In each case, the warring parties resorted to attrition of forces and capabilities because they came to see such attrition as the only option available to them to provoke such a collapse of will. All parties to these conflicts almost doggedly sought to fight a swift decisive war of maneuver, often despite widely available evidence to the contrary.[42] Similarly, the participants almost invariably[43] sought their foes' surrender rather than a total Carthage-like destruction, even if only to avoid the horrible cost they themselves would incur in inflicting such a level of destruction, despite repeated insistence on "unconditional surrender."

This duality of these physical and psychological dimensions in the midst of attrition warfare points to the degree of complexity that is involved in understanding how we really wage war and why we succeed or fail. To win in each of the three conflicts examined, the victor had to overcome both some portion of the opponents' physical means of continuing the conflict and the opponent's psychological will to do so. Thus, with few exceptions (notably Verdun), what each side sought to accomplish by attrition was not simply destruction, but rather the reduction of the opponents' physical capabilities to some ill-defined or, perhaps, indefinable level at which that opponents' will to resist would collapse and they would surrender. This is significant because the reliance upon such a complex interaction of means and will suggests that success, even in attrition warfare, cannot be ascribed to some predictable function of force size and kill rate. Instead, it is the product of a complex, nonlinear relationship between physical destruction of some kind and degree, and a series of psychological processes taking place in the minds of human actors at each level of conflict over some period of time. This complex interrelationship of means and will appears greatest at the geo-strategic and military-strategic levels of conflict, but is certainly evident at the tactical and operational levels as well.

A Clash of Complex Adaptive Systems

The nonlinearity of the relationship between means and will also points to the utility of considering all conflict as clashes between complex adaptive systems. As described in complexity theory, such complex adaptive systems are entities that evolve and adapt to their environments.[44] As a result of this ability to learn and adapt, the behavior of complex adaptive systems can never entirely be predicted. This phenomenon is certainly evident in the history of warfare and specifically in the difficulty in predicting exactly when, why, and how a warring party's will might collapse under the stress of mounting losses. In the conflicts examined, the level at which the will of each losing country (and each military unit) broke varied greatly.

Three distinct examples of this variation are obvious in the conflicts surveyed. First, in the blitzkrieg of 1940, the French will to fight was weak at all levels from the onset and organized French military resistance ended early and abruptly, even though a substantial physical capacity to continue the struggle remained.[45][46][47] Second, during World War I, the will of the Central Powers was sufficient to withstand 4 years of heavy wartime losses, but by the summer of 1918, it was so worn down, especially in Austria-Hungary and Turkey, that resistance ended before the respective German, Austrian, or Turkish homelands were invaded, even though each had substantial organized military forces still in the field. But third, in the South in 1865 and in Germany and Japan in 1945, the will to resist was so great that, even after more than 4 years of war, and even after the destruction of most of each state's physical capacity to wage war, the will to resist remained strong.[48]

These examples are discrete cases on a continuum that, over the three wars, runs from Denmark's acceptance of German occupation without resistance in 1940 to the suicidal resistance of the Japanese on Okinawa in 1945. Moreover, a deeper probe of the French example indicates that the relationship between the blitzkrieg and the French collapse is by no means clear-cut. In fact, the blitzkrieg succeeded at least in part because it successfully exploited an underlying French psychological weakness that derived in part from deep fissures in French society and the leadership of the Third Republic.[49] Even then, as the subsequent activities of the Free French and Résistance underlined, the French popular will was not entirely broken so long as there remained a hope of overturning the German victory. By contrast, at the other end of the continuum, although the Allies anticipated analogous lingering resistance movements in Germany and Japan after their respective surrenders, none occurred, perhaps because there was no corresponding hope of ultimately overturning the Allied victory. The above examples point to a complex relationship between the attrition of physical means of waging war and the hoped-for collapse of will.

If we take this model of complex behavior combining physical and psychological dimensions and apply it, not just to the great wars, but also to the numerous smaller conflicts that have marked the past 50 years and the emerging post-September 11th world, another facet of the problem emerges: the impact of symmetry on the nature of the interactions.

Symmetric Versus Asymmetric Conflict

For all of the post-September 11th discussion of asymmetric conflict, it is curious both that there has been little agreement as to what constitutes an asymmetric conflict and that there has been little or no discussion as to an obvious first question: what is symmetric conflict? This question of symmetry draws together the threads of the issues of means and will, the roots of attrition warfare, and the nature of effects-based operations. The preceding discussion underlines the need to understand just how a conflict might be expected to evolve and therefore, how we might be called upon to adapt. In part, the direction of a conflict's evolution will be driven by culture and hence, will vary widely from one opponent to the next. However, it will also reflect what might be termed *the mechanics* of wars or crises in general. The relative symmetry or asymmetry of the will and capabilities of the opponents in a conflict or crisis is one significant factor in such mechanics.

Symmetric Conflict

The Civil War and the two World Wars were symmetric contests in the classic sense. Nation-states fought other nation-states or coalitions of nation-states.[50] War was formally declared or sanctioned in some manner and, atrocities notwithstanding, the warring parties observed a basic law of war, with violators prosecuted by the victors after the war. Navies fought navies. Armies fought armies. Because of these symmetries, the results of individual engagements and of protracted campaigns could be measured in classic Lanchestrian terms of forces and capabilities destroyed. Yet, there was an additional and much more significant symmetry to these wars. Both sides in each of these conflicts had both great means and great will (see Figure 2). In fact, it was the combination of the great means and the great will that could be brought to bear by competing nation-

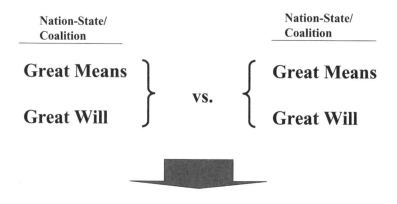

Attrition-Based Warfare

Figure 2. Symmetry of Means and Will = Symmetric Warfare

states that gave these struggles their character as protracted wars of attrition.

Consider the plight of General Robert E. Lee, the Confederacy's leading commander during the U.S. Civil War. Lee managed to defeat the Union Army of the Potomac about once every 4 to 6 months for most of the war.[51] Most of these defeats probably would have been considered decisive by the standards of the previous Napoleonic wars. However, in the Civil War, about 4 to 6 months after each of these "decisive" battles, Lee found himself confronting a larger, better-equipped Army of the Potomac. The North had the means needed to generate and equip new forces after each defeat, and it had the will to do so time and again. It is that symmetry of great means and great will on both sides that gave the war the character of a protracted attrition war. The same is true of the First and Second World Wars, and may be extended to the

Cold War as well. After 150 years of such symmetric, attrition-based warfare, this model of symmetric conflict has shaped our nation's conscious and unconscious perception of what war is or ought to be.

In these symmetric attrition conflicts, it may be argued, the bigger and more determined the two contestants were, the less likely it was that one of them would break quickly and the more likely the conflict would be both protracted and attrition-based. However, what if the opponents were not symmetric, but asymmetric?

Asymmetric Conflict

There has been much discussion of asymmetric conflict, but little agreement as to what constitutes an asymmetry. In some interpretations, asymmetries are considered to be any difference in military forces, equipment, training, or organization that might be exploited. While this is consistent with the maxim that warfare is about finding and exploiting asymmetries, it is equally applicable to the symmetric conflicts just discussed, each of which featured such asymmetries (U-boat warfare versus antisubmarine warfare for example), and does little to define the nature of the asymmetric conflict challenge we now face. In another vein, it is increasingly accepted that defining asymmetry in an asymmetric conflict involves a reversal of some or all of the symmetries we could observe in the three great "wars of attrition." Thus, nation-states may not fight other nation-states, but may be pitted against guerrillas, ethnic liberation movements, or even terrorists. Navies may not fight other navies, but instead be required to enforce embargoes or project power ashore against a variety of decidedly non-naval targets. Armies may not fight other armies, but have to contend with urban terrorists, guerrilla warfare, peacemaking, or peacekeeping operations, or, especially after September 11th, homeland defense against a terrorist threat.[52] However, if we follow the line of reasoning generated by examining the role of means and will in symmetric conflicts, another possibility emerges. The truly critical asymmetry may lie in the differences of will and means between the opponents because these differences shape the very mechanics of the conflict. This suggests that the real definition of an asymmetric conflict is one in which there is no symmetry of will and means.

What might an asymmetry of means and will look like? If a symmetric contest may be said to pit one adversary with great means and great will against another that also has both great means and great will, then an asymmetric contest might be expected to involve different combinations. The possibilities can be outlined in terms of a simple quadratic diagram (see Figure 3). The terms "great" and "limited," of course, are relative and simply denote the direction of the disparity of means or will between the two opponents. Still, they do serve to define some key elements in the asymmetry.

In a contest between an entity that has both great means and great will and an entity that lacks one or both, the side with both great will and means is bound to prevail. The outcome is likely to be swift

Great Means Great Will	Great Means Limited Will
Limited Means Great Will	Limited Means Limited Will

Figure 3. Asymmetry of Means and Will

where the challenger's will is weak and his means lacking. It may be less swift, but it will be just as sure, where the means are available but the will lacking, or where the will is strong but the means lacking.

A similar result is likely to emerge when one side has either great means or great will and the other has neither.

However, when the contest is between one power that has great means and limited will and another that has limited means but great will, the result is likely to be far from being either certain or swift. In fact, such a war is likely to involve protracted operations that are reminiscent of symmetric wars of attrition, even if the operations themselves may be very different in character. This would indicate a different paradigm for asymmetric conflict and a different set of mechanics at work.

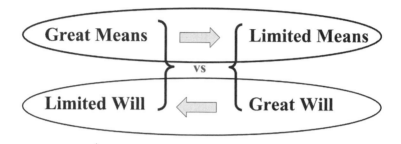

Figure 4. Asymmetric Conflict

In such a conflict, each side has an advantage over its opponent, but the advantages are very different in nature. Both the opponents and the strategies that they use may be fundamentally asymmetric. If we return to the basic warfighting maxim that success lies in attacking your opponent's weaknesses and not his strengths and by extension, that warfare revolves about the creation and exploitation of asymmetries, then we would expect each side to exploit its greatest strength and attack the other's greatest weakness. However, as illustrated in Figure 4, in this lopsided contest, there are really two different asymmetries that might be exploited. One side has an advantage in means. Logically, we would expect that side to exploit its advantage by attacking and destroying the other's more limited physical means, e.g. by pressing an essentially attrition-based approach.

The other side has an advantage in will. Therefore, we would expect that side to exploit its advantage by attacking its opponent's will to continue the struggle, e.g. an essentially effects-based approach focused on shaping the opponent's behavior. If we think about this type of asymmetric contest between a power of great means but limited will and another entity with great will but limited means, it is immediately obvious that numerous Cold War and post-Cold War conflicts fit the description. This is especially true if we accept that the entity with limited means may not be a state at all but a guerrilla group, an ethnic or religious liberation movement, or an international terrorist organization such as al-Qaida.

However, we must add a caveat here. Even in the heart of a massive war of attrition such as World War II, resistance movements in occupied Europe and the Philippines continued even after the conventional armies were defeated. These movements signal an important fact: An adversary need not be both powerful and determined in order to win. He need only be determined enough to overcome any disparity of resources between himself and his opponent. Stated differently, the more determined (or fanatical or desperate) the adversary is, the less reliant upon "means" he will likely be.

Moreover, as the last line suggests, such an asymmetric conflict need not be limited to war. The model applies equally or better to operations other than war across a spectrum from peacekeeping operations to crisis responses to terrorism. Indeed, it is the asymmetric rather than the symmetric model of conflict that appears prevalent since the end of

World War II.[53] Vietnam and the Soviet experience in Afghanistan offer good examples of asymmetries of will and means in war. Both were regional conflicts in which a small state or non-state liberation movement confronted a great power. Neither challenger possessed a size or resource base sufficient to support an extensive, highly mechanized war effort. Neither had the physical means to confront, much less to wear down, the physical war-making capacity of the United States or the Soviet Union in a symmetric attrition war. To have any hope of success, the challengers in both cases had to shift the focus from a contest of means in which the asymmetry worked against them, to one of will in which they held (or at least believed themselves to hold) an asymmetric advantage. In so doing, they accepted a continuing asymmetry of means that they could not in any event alter and concentrated their efforts on the parallel but opposite asymmetry of will. Their strategy, like that of a traditional symmetrical war of attrition, was cumulative. They understood that continued support by their opponent's public was the core requirement for a lengthy war. They concluded that the cumulative effect of protracted guerrilla operations could be to erode that support, even though the more powerful opponent retained military superiority in the field and continued to win battles and destroy elements of their own forces and capabilities.[54]

By zeroing in on the attrition of their opponent's political will as their strategic objective, they also defined a much more manageable military task. In this effects-based context, it was no longer necessary to launch large concerted attacks to destroy their foe's military capability and attain victory. Rather, the foe's will might be attacked by sustaining a rate and scope of relatively small attacks that was sufficient to inflict a level of casualties and damage that might be considered intolerable at home, regardless of whether they were militarily significant in the field. At the tactical and operational levels, this asymmetric use of limited military power left the American and Soviet militaries, designed for symmetric warfare with each other, with little in the way of military capabilities or support infrastructure that their large mechanized forces could attack. Enemy formations were kept too small, lines of communications too rudimentary, and the infrastructure too sparse for classic attrition-based warfare to work well. What is more, the dispersal had a second, derivative effect because it enormously increased the amount of effort required for the larger powers and their local allies to achieve military objectives based on attrition of physical means. The scale of their efforts often became so disproportionate to those of the guerrillas that it was questionable who was wearing whom down.

This asymmetric approach to warfare has been remarkably successful. Not only did it thwart superpower efforts in Vietnam and Afghanistan, but it also helped bring about the collapse of the Western colonial empires in the years after World War II.[55] This same asymmetric approach also has been manifest in a score of lesser encounters, crises, and Operations Other Than War from Somalia to Kosovo. It is also apparent in the reasoning of terrorist organizations from the Irish Republican Army to a long train of Middle Eastern terrorists. In each case, the challengers (states, non-states, gangs, terrorists, or warlords) believed that they simply had to be able to inflict sufficient pain over a long enough period of time to wear down a larger power's will and thus wring from it the concessions they sought.

In approaching such asymmetric conflict, it is easy to focus on the perceived lack of will on the part of a great power operating forward to protect what are often extended or unclear national interests. However, we need to carry this analysis an important additional step and focus on the will of the challenger. Is this will infinite? And if not, at what point might it break? We observed earlier that in the case of the World War II resistance movements, it was not necessary to be both big and determined to stand up to a big and determined foe. It was only necessary to be so determined as to overcome any disparity in resources. That is, the will required to succeed is relative. This suggests a relationship between means and will that is something along the following lines (See Figure 5).

The impact of means upon the outcome tends to vary arithmetically, while that of will varies geometrically. The more determined the foe, the less means he will require in order to succeed in the contest. The more constrained the task is, the greater the probability is of success with the means available. However, obviously if the means fall to zero, no amount of determination will suffice to make up the difference. This was the core reason for the Roman resort to a total war solution to the conflict with Carthage.[56]

$$\text{Probability of Success} = \text{Means} \times \text{Will}^2$$

Figure 5. Probability Equation

In the case of the World War II Résistants, the determination that balanced their lack of means derived from their firm belief that the Allies still fighting would eventually return with sufficient means to redress an imbalance.[57] In the case of the guerrilla movements, their determination did not necessarily stem from any realistic hope of outside intervention to redress the imbalance, but from a conviction rooted in a historical, national, or religious destiny. There was and is a sense of ultimate inevitability that fortifies the will sufficiently to sustain the long-term nature of a struggle and to endure the sacrifice of lives entailed. When this will is put into the context of a strategy that seeks to inflict damage and wear down public support rather than to gain a military victory, it can be sufficient to win.

If we apply the same logic to a different form of guerrilla operation represented by international terrorism, something similar emerges. There too, the will of the terrorists need only be great enough to balance the greater means available to their opponents. The terrorists may not be able to hope to match the means of a great, industrialized state, but assuredly believe that they have superior will. The roots of that will may be in nationalism or ethnic identity, as in the case of most of the guerrilla operations cited. But, those roots may also lie in the fact that the terrorists see themselves as part of an inevitable historical process or as divine agents whose deaths lead to martyrdom, as in the case of al-Qaida terrorists. Such a religious context can also yield the patience and endurance that comes from operating on a divine rather than human time line.

If we follow this logic to its conclusion, given sufficient will on the part of the terrorists, the means required for initiating and sustaining a long-term conflict may be very minor indeed. The World Trade Center bombing in 1993, for example, was the amalgamation of religious fanaticism and commercially available materials. The attacks of 2001 used commercial airliners as gigantic missiles. In each case, the willingness of the terrorists to accept their own deaths and of the terrorist leadership to trust to God and to ignore the follow-on consequences multiplied the impact of the minimal physical means available to them.

The New Security Environment: Asymmetric and Symmetric Conflicts

Does this mean that asymmetric forms of conflict have replaced the old attrition-based warfare driven by a symmetry of means and will? In fact, the definition of symmetric warfare in terms of will and means argues otherwise. If symmetric attrition warfare arose when circumstances pitted states and coalitions with great means and great will against one another, then it stands to reason that similar contests will tend to move in the same direction. This is borne out by recent history. Since World War II, classic, symmetric attrition wars have continued around the world. Desert Storm, for all of the apparent disparity of means involved, falls into this category, as do multiple wars between Third World states[58] including the Iran-Iraq War and a succession of Arab-Israeli Wars. This persistence of symmetric attrition warfare indicates that the conditions that gave rise to symmetric, attrition-based wars continue to exist. Asymmetric conflict has not replaced symmetric conflict; it has come in addition to it. In this same vein, we might expect that any eventual conflict with a proverbial "peer competitor" would, because of the symmetry that the word "peer" implies, resemble the symmetric attrition-based wars of the past more than any asymmetric conflict along the lines of those just discussed.[59]

The model for fashioning military power or for evaluating the applicability of network-centric and effects-based operations suggested here is not a tidy "either/or" of either a symmetric, attrition-based conflict, or an asymmetric, effects-based conflict. Rather, it is more along the lines of a continuum with a total focus on means at one extreme and a total focus on will at the other. This continuum would extend from pure attrition-based approaches to warfare (the total destruction of the Third Punic War) at one end to a pure effects-based approach (peacekeeping operations) at the other. Along this continuum, the mode of warfare toward which opponents will be drawn is a function of the degree of difference in their respective sizes, military capabilities, and determination.[60] The more symmetric the means and will of the adversaries are, the more likely they are to be drawn into a fundamentally attrition-based conflict that continues until one or the other contestant's means and/or will are exhausted. The more asymmetric the means and will of the opponents are, the more likely they are to take a more effects-based approach (for example, centered on a damage infliction strategy in a protracted low-intensity conflict) of which terrorism must be considered a form.[61]

The above continuum becomes a bit clearer if we compare the attrition-based and the behavior/effects-based approaches to conflict and begin to see where they differ and where they overlap (See Figure 6). In this comparison, the focus on means that is typical of a symmetric conflict produces what is essentially an attrition-based approach to warfare centered on attacking physical targets, usually to meet military objectives and usually to produce quantifiable results. This does not mean that the result is a pure attrition approach in which the only thing that matters is the destruction of forces and capabilities. Such attacks certainly may have psychological impacts in the manner of effects-based operations. The distinction is that in attrition-based operations, these impacts are usually a by-product of the attack, rather than its purpose. However, there is another important consideration. Because attrition-based approaches to dealing with conflict do involve physical damage to an opponent,

Focus: Will/ Behavior

— *Effects-Based*
  • Focus on "Actions" prolonged, low intensity conflict
  • Political Objectives
  • Nonlinear Results

— **Direct attack on will**
— **Peace, Crisis, War**
— **Deterrence:**
  • Unacceptable Damage

Focus: Means

— *Attrition-Based*
  • Focus on "Targets"/ "swift decisive" wars
  • Military Objectives
  • Quantifiable Results

— **Indirect attack on will**
— **War/Combat only**
— **Deterrence:**
  • Retaliation
  • Pre-emption

Figure 6. Comparing the Two Approaches

such operations are restricted to wartime or to combat operations short of war. In other words, some form of a state of hostilities is a prerequisite to their application. If opponents can deny us grounds for such a state of hostilities, they can invalidate any military strategy based on attrition.[62]

This same restriction applies in a different way to attrition-based deterrence. If one's only recourse is to destroy targets, then the deterrent value of military forces hinges on either their ability to retaliate by destroying forces and capabilities, or the ability to pre-empt an opponent's action with similar destruction. Both actions are credible only in extreme situations, at or near the onset of hostilities. Both have substantial political costs and risks including the possibility of reciprocal annihilation. Obviously, such threats are very unlikely to deter an opponent who sees the conflict in political terms in which such destruction might create opportunities in the world media, or who treats the destruction both as martyrdom and a confirmation of the attackers' intrinsic evil.

The above stands in sharp contrast to the elements of a warfare approach dictated by a focus on will and behavior. The military capabilities needed to attack the physical means of an opponent may be absolutely necessary to fight a symmetric war of attrition, but they may also be quite insufficient to deal with an asymmetric foe whose focus is necessarily on our political will or decisionmaking behavior. For such a foe, the focus is not on targets but on actions that are directed toward political objectives and that revolve about the opponent's will and decisionmaking structure, both political and military. In short, the approach to warfare is very fundamentally effects-based, directed at shaping behavior.

Unlike the attrition-based approach, the effects-based strategy is conceived and executed as a direct assault on an opponent's will and not a by-product of destroying his capability to wage war. For this reason, the role of the media and information is no longer that of an ancillary support for morale as in attrition-based campaigns, but as a central part of the effort to assault the public will. Because the target is human behavior, the results are not incremental, but nonlinear in the manner of the proverbial "straw that broke the camel's back." Pain is inflicted until the victim can stand no more. Further, because the actions undertaken and the pain inflicted need not involve destruction, they need not be confined to combat operations, but can span the spectrum from peace to crisis to war.[63] Finally, they can deter not simply on the basis of what can be destroyed either in retaliation or pre-emptive action, but rather by threatening a cumulative psychological attrition inflicted relentlessly over time.

While this latter model is drawn from observation of asymmetric conflicts, its use need not be restricted to those who would challenge a great power. Indeed, the cardinal advantage of the great power may prove to be that it has the option of following either an attrition-based or an effects-based approach, or some combination of the two that best meets its needs at any particular time.

The New Security Environment and Effects-Based Operations

What becomes clear in the foregoing discussion is that attrition-based operations, no matter how efficient we may make them, do not work very well against an asymmetric adversary who has minimized his dependence on conventional physical means of waging war. Still more importantly, the concept of attrition, because it does rely on destruction and thus on the existence of some recognized state of hostilities, does not apply where there is no state of hostilities, or if such hostilities are precisely what the military force is attempting to thwart. Because these operations short of combat comprise both the core of our national efforts to deal with the post-September 11th security environment and the vast majority of all military operations, we clearly need something other than an attrition-based metric for military operations and for our acquisition of effective military power. In brief, new information technologies and network-centric thinking must be put into a context within which they can address the complex interaction between nations, would-be nations, and other challengers in which the attrition of an opponent's physical means of waging war is not a central factor of strategy. The effects-based approach to military operations provides the gateway into doing just this.

But that is not all. Even in symmetric combat operations against a peer adversary in which attrition is a key factor, the focus on will and behavior promises to give our military forces the nonlinear impact they will need to succeed. Such capabilities could achieve our military objectives without the protracted conflict and massive casualties that have marked the great attrition wars of the past 150 years. In essence, although the warfare decisions that emerge from an effects-based thought process may still be denominated in terms of targets or forces and capabilities to be destroyed, the core of the approach is not the destruction of targets, but an action-reaction cycle in which success is defined by the behavior produced.

Finally, effects-based operations are not simply a mode of warfare. They encompass the full range of actions that a nation may undertake in order to induce a particular reaction on the part of an opponent, ally, or neutral. They represent a unified approach to national strategy that is as much at the root of peacetime operations as it is of wartime operations. Thus, the concept of effects-based operations becomes the key to applying network-centric capabilities and concepts on multiple levels to deal with a security environment that combines both old and new threats and that will require both combat operations and a broad range of operations short of combat, including those directed at establishing a stable deterrence regime on a global scale.

All of the above begs the real question: just what are effects-based operations? To proceed any further, much less to make the tantalizing marriage between network-centric and effects-based ideas a reality, we must first flesh out our definition and theory of effects-based operations, then describe its application to military operations, and finally assess how the efficiencies of network-centric thinking and capabilities might best be applied. This is the task of the following chapters.

---

[1]Network Centric Warfare can be concisely defined as the concept of linking all aspects of warfighting into a shared situation awareness and understanding of command intent so as to achieve a unity and synchronicity of effects that multiplies the combat power of military forces. Network-centric operations are then military operations across the spectrum of conflict from peace, to crisis, to war to which the concepts and capabilities of Network Centric Warfare have been applied.

[2]Logically, it is not enough to figure out how network-centric capabilities might apply to a given generic military operation. If that generic military operation serves little purpose in meeting our strategic, operational, and tactical objectives, then no matter how well we accomplish it, the capabilities will have little value.

[3]As a working definition, we can consider "strategic deterrence" to be the neutralization or foreclosure of direct threats to the peace, prosperity, and continued survival of the nation.

[4]Majid Khadduri, for example, traces the polarization of Arab society that resulted from expanding contacts with the West as the Arab leadership attempted to adapt an established system to new ideas without surrendering its Islamic identity. Khadduri, Majid. *Political Trends in the Arab World*. Baltimore; Johns Hopkins. 1972. pp. 2-7.

[5]Albert Hourani describes the economic, religious, and cultural reactions of the Arab world to spreading contacts with an intruding Western culture. He notes that one such reaction was the Islamist movement surrounding the Muslim Brotherhood and points to the work of Sayyid Qutb who, as early as 1964, was calling for a jihad "not for defense only, but to destroy all worship of false gods and remove all obstacles preventing men from accepting Islam." Hourani, Albert. *A History of the Arab Peoples*. Cambridge; Belknap/Harvard Press. 1991. pp. 445-6.

[6]The idea of a broader integrated involvement in change is not new and was noted very pointedly in the Iklé-Wohlstetter report in 1988.

Iklé, Fred C and Albert Wohlstetter, Chairmen. *Discriminate Deterrence, The Report of the Commission in Integrated Long-Term Strategy.* Washington. 1988. p. 15.

[7]A frequent criticism of military crisis responses is that ultimately they produce no discernible change in the local situation. However, if we consider the military role not as one of solving the problem but of buying time for an economic-socio-political solution, then the response takes on a new perspective. It may not at all be that the military intervention that failed, but that the political and economic tools available were not able to fashion a lasting solution in the period of time the military intervention bought.

[8]See Edward Rhodes, "Conventional Deterrence: Review of the Empirical Literature," Second Navy RMA Round Table, SAIC, Tysons Corner, Virginia, 4 June 1997.

[9]This was the essence of the French argument for an independent "force de frappe" which was deemed a credible response to any threat to France, whereas a U.S. response that endangered American cities might not be believable or believed.

[10]Iklé and Wohlstetter, p. 35. In actuality, through the course of the Cold War, each nuclear power recognized the dangers of an uncontrolled escalation that might grow from any military incident between them and was careful to avoid such armed confrontation.

[11]As part of the stabilizing mental model, each of the Cold War nuclear adversaries had a fairly detailed idea of what strategic weapons the other side had available and how they would be used. Thus, retaliation tended to be seen as a largely mechanical, "sensor-to-shooter" endeavor initiated by a national decision to respond.

[12]For purposes of this book, the term "conventional deterrence" is used to encompass everything but strategic deterrence, i.e. weapons of mass destruction or of mass effects.

[13]See the work of Prof. Edward Rhodes of Rutgers Center for Global Security and Democracy, "Conventional Deterrence: Review of Empirical Literature," Second Navy RMA Round Table, June 1998. "Conventional Deterrence," Comparative Strategy, Fall 2000. "Review Of Empirical Studies of Conventional Deterence," Working Paper, Columbia International Affairs Online (CIAO), Columbia University. July 1999.

[14]The latter is of course present in strategic nuclear deterrence in facets such as the secure second strike capability that denies an opponent the possibility of an incapacitating first strike.

[15]Under the United Nations Charter, states are given the right to self-defense but not to retaliation, thus many nations have tended to treat operations that would otherwise be considered to be retaliatory in nature as acts of self-defense in the context of this limited or conventional deterrence.
Waters, Maurice. *The United Nations.* New York; MacMillan Company. 1967. pp. 553-579.

[16]In the case of conventional deterrence, the unacceptable result most probably will not be the annihilation of society, but rather a political fall-out that could be counterproductive and that would, hence, negate the effect that the power had sought. Obviously, this sets up a sliding scale. The more important the interest to be defended is, the more acceptable any negative fall-out will be. The less important the interest is, the more likely it is that possible negative repercussions will outweigh any gains to be made from successful deterrence.

[17]Although it can be postulated that such a rational process of calculation would have little to do with the reaction of an irrational decisionmaker, it is probably closer to the truth to say that any senior level decisionmaker is, by virtue of having attained that position, rational. This does not mean that the rationality would match Western notions of a rational decisionmaker, but simply that some form of rational calculation will almost inevitably be involved in perceiving and reacting to the threat of retaliation. It is upon that calculation, in whatever form it takes, that deterrence relies.

[18]Rhodes, "Conventional Deterrence," p. 243.

[19]In fact, conventional deterrence centers on the "niche competitor," a foe that is constantly probing for niches within which he believes can compete successfully. Such niches may be defined in political terms as a challenge that the deterring power is unable to meet for political reasons or at acceptable cost, or with the temporal terms, such as the ability to engineer a military or a political fait accompli in such a short time as to preclude an effective response. The niche may be geographic, such as confining operations to an area to which the adversary cannot obtain ready access or in which his full capabilities cannot be brought to bear. Or it may be a warfare niche, a military challenge for which the deterring power has only a limited local or deployable capability. In general, the smaller the disparity in capabilities between the niche competitor and his opponent the larger the number and variety of the niches that are likely to be available to exploit, and the more frequent the challenges probably will be. Obviously, for the challenger, the key to success in such an endeavor is the ability to contain the conflict within the chosen niche. This imposes two constraints on his niche

strategy. First, he must be able to do something to achieve the desired effect within his chosen niche. It does no good to define a niche within which any action he undertakes will not produce a worthwhile result. And second, he must be able to discourage either vertical or lateral escalation that might move the confrontation out of the niche to arenas in which he cannot compete successfully. For example, the victim of the niche challenger might increase the level of the military confrontation by unexpectedly heavy reinforcement of forces in the confrontation, or might attempt to move the confrontation to other areas of competition geographic or otherwise.

The success of a conventional deterrent under these conditions hinges the ability either to counter any action the challenger might take within any given political, temporal, geographic, or warfare niche and/or to escalate a conflict beyond the confines of that niche.

[20]We can look at the threat from al-Qaida in this vein. The competitor seeks to avoid American retaliation by remaining anonymous or by so decentralizing his action that the military power of the United States cannot be brought to bear. Similarly, the terrorist cells seek to operate in a boundary niche between states, between external and internal security, and between peace and war

[21]The introduction of more efficient ways of applying military power to this end, whether by increasing the number of sorties and targets each day, or by nodal targeting to reduce the number of targets we need to destroy to incapacitate an opponent, do not change the fact that the fundamental objective remains the attrition of enemy capability to wage war.

[22]In 1916, the Chief of the German General Staff, General von Falkenhayn set out to exploit the German advantage in manpower by creating a situation in which would produce such a large number of French casualties as to gradually grind down the physical ability of the French Army to resist. Keegan, John. *The First World War*. New York. 2000, p 278.

[23]The dangers associated with a shift from attrition warfare to the unknown of Network Centric Warfare or a still evolving concept of effects-based operations are particularly significant for the United States, a country that was particularly well suited to fight and win such wars of attrition. From the epoch of the Civil War onwards, the American "nation in arms" had an economy and demography sufficient to support massive armies and an industrial production that enabled it to overwhelm its enemies war production. It also had the ability to mobilize national opinion and, hence, the political

capacity to outlast its opponents. Finally, because of its nearly insular geography, the United States (like Britain) could use the sea and its naval power to create a homeland sanctuary even as it projected its own massive military overseas to fight in the enemy's backyard.

[24]It might be argued that the Second Punic War, which decisively defeated Carthage, was the result of a successful attrition strategy and that the Third Punic War was a different "total war," though it remained a clear logical descendent of Cato's "Carthage must be destroyed" injunction. Goldsworthy, Adrian. *The Punic Wars*. New York. 1998. pp. 198ff.

[25]For a frontier settlement in North America, defense was not something to be provided by a distant army, however well trained. It was something to which every man and woman contributed because the penalty for failure was death. The result was the same militia system that so bedeviled the conventional British armies during the American Revolution. Burgoyne's defeats at Bennington and Saratoga, for example, were largely at the hands of a militia army that had not existed 2 weeks before the battles and did not exist 2 weeks later. The idea of the citizen soldier appears to have crossed the Atlantic with Lafayette who formed French citizen soldiers into what is now the Garde Républicaine. This idea was later adapted by Carnot into the lévée en masse. Galvin, John R. *The Minute Men*. Washington; Brassey's. 1989.

[26]Revolutionary France, like the late 20th-century United States, had the advantage of numbers. In 1800, France was by far the most populous country in Western Europe. It had a large and robust economy and an extensive civil infrastructure, particularly of roads. As a result, even as late as the 100 days in 1815, France was able to generate large armies on short notice. It was this size and capacity that sustained Napoleon through a quarter century of almost incessant wars. Durant, Will and Ariel. *The Age of Napoleon*. New York; Simon and Schuster. 1975. pp. 3-6 and 179ff.

[27]The Napoleonic wars introduced many elements of modern attrition warfare: massive forces, the nation in arms, and the destruction of the military means of a nation to resist. However, as a rule, these conflicts only indirectly touched on the civil means of creating military power, chiefly in the Continental System and the British Orders in Council. Thus, while Napoleon inflicted a draconian peace on Prussia after Jena, for example, he only sought to destroy the Prussian Army and not the means for Prussia to create military power.

[28]The Gettysburg Address. President Abraham Lincoln. 1863.
[29]Lincoln probably would have been horrified to see his words extrapolated in this way. But Lincoln appears to have understood their implications and the need for attrition warfare in defeating the South, supporting Grant's plan to wage such a war while at the same time repeatedly saying that he did not want to know what those plans were.
Sandburg, Carl. *Lincoln, The Prairie Years and the War Years*. Easton; Norwalk. 1984. pp. 464-5.
[30]Grant, U.S. *The Personal Memoirs of U.S. Grant*. Easton; Norwalk. 1989. p. 469.
[31]Grant writes that, although he had started the campaign in the West insisting that property rights be respected, he came to conclude that such an approach prolonged the war and that it was ultimately more "humane" to destroy all means by which the rebellion could be sustained.
Grant. *Memoirs*. pp. 191-2.
[32]This plan was outlined in April 1864 just after Grant took command of the Union armies and was elaborated successively over the course of the next 4 months.
Foote, Shelby. *The Civil War: A Narrative.* Time-Life, Vol. 10. Alexandria, Virginia. 2000. pp. 26ff.
[33]Hayes, Carlton J. *A Brief History of the Great War*. New York: MacMillan Company. 1925. pp. 41-55.
[34]Although sometimes ignored amid a lingering residue of World War I propaganda, 1914 Russia, Germany, and Austria-Hungary were all constitutional monarchies with functioning, democratically elected parliaments that voted to go to war and thereafter sustained the war effort by approving a succession of war budgets. It was not until the October Revolution of 1917 in Russia that this ceased to be the case. Similarly, it is noteworthy that Austria-Hungary's collapse and disintegration in October 1918 occurred in the context of its parliamentary system and without any effort by the monarchy or military to reverse that decision by force.
Keegan, pp. 415-416.
[35]Douhet, Giulio. *The Command of the Air*. Washington DC; Office of Air Force History. 1983.
[36]In the case of Japan's island empire, this interdiction was in great part the fruit of a submarine campaign that sank most of the irreplaceable Japanese merchant marine.
[37]Williamson Murray writes, "We now know that these massive assaults on Germany's cities did in fact impair German morale substantially. What British air theorists failed to take into account, however, was the reality that modern states (democratic as well as totalitarian) possess enormous powers

of compulsion. As a result, there was no outlet for the drastic effects that the bombing had on German morale – the concentration camp and the Gestapo were more than enough to keep the population in line."

Murray, Williamson et al. *An Historical Perspective on Effects-based Operations.* Institute for Defense Analyses, Joint Advanced Warfighting Project; Alexandra, Virginia. October 2001. p. 29.

[38]In the case of Japan, only outlying islands, e.g. Okinawa and Iwo Jima, were taken by storm and the government appears to have yielded in the face of the total destruction intimated by the atomic bombing of Hiroshima and Nagasaki. However, even in the face of these bombs and the Emperor's intervention, hardline military resistance to surrender continued. It is instructive that the Allies feared continued resistance by diehard elements of the civilian population and recalcitrant military even after a formal surrender.

[39]This look at attrition warfare can be taken a step further. The Soviet defeat in the Cold War may be laid to the Soviet Union's being overwhelmed by America's superior ability to maintain a large and rapidly modernizing military force while at the same time increasing its economic base. The Soviets were astute enough to recognize that their own inability to do both meant there would be an ever widening gap in capabilities and no Soviet hope of ever catching up. In effect, the United States and its allies won the Cold War by forcing the Soviet economic system into bankruptcy, that is, by destroying the Soviet means of continuing the competition without having to defeat Soviet forces in battle.

[40]The duel between Generals Pétain and von Falkenhayn at Verdun excepted. (Keegan, pp 278ff.) One can also make a case that Stalin realized from the start that he would have to fight a war of attrition against the Germans when they invaded and, indeed, such attrition warfare had historic antecedents in Kutuzov's winter campaign against Napoleon. Nevertheless, in the early stages of the German invasion in 1941, the Red Army defended forward and adopted a scorched earth policy only when the front collapsed.

[41]Grant, for example, says, "Up to the Battle of Shiloh, I ... believed that the rebellion against the Government would collapse suddenly and soon if a decisive victory could be gained over any of its armies."

Grant. pp. 191ff.

[42]This is most evident in the lead up to World War I when European military planners, with the model of the U.S. Civil War before them, nonetheless based their assumptions on the models of the 1866 Austro-Prussian War and the 1870-1

Franco-Prussian War. Those wars were swift and decisive and seemed to point to a military revolution based on mass mobilization and railroads, factors that caught the great powers up in the "Gun of August" entanglement of alliances and inflexible time lines.

Keegan, pp. 212-3.

[43]Notable exceptions were in World War II when the Nazis and Japanese sought to enslave the conquered peoples of Eastern Europe and China respectively, or the parallel but soon abandoned Morgenthau Plan by which the Allies were to have reduced post-war Germany to an agricultural state.

[44]Murray Gell-Mann, "The Simple and the Complex," in David S. Alberts and Thomas J, Czerwinski. *Complexity, Global Politics, and National Security.* Washington, DC. 1997, pp. 10-11.

[45]At the time the French government capitulated, plans were being implemented to shift the center of French resistance, together with the French Navy and as much of the Army as could be transported, to North Africa which itself contained a sizeable French army.

Churchill. *Their Finest Hour.* p. 201.

[46]William Shirer traces the divisions between right and left in French society back to the beginning of the Third Republic in 1872.

Shirer, William L. *The Collapse of the Third Republic, An Inquiry into the Fall of France in 1940.* New York: Simon and Schuster. 1969.

[47]These differences came to a head during the socialist government of Léon Blum in the 1930s.

[48]Ready, J. Lee. *World War Two: Nation by Nation.* London; Arms and Armour. 1995. p180ff, p. 116ff.

Colton, Joel. *Léon Blum, Humanist in Politics.* New York; Knopf. 1966.

[49]As a result, in the aftermath of June 1940, French at all levels and of both right and left tended to see the 1940 defeat as the inevitable result of the policies and weaknesses of the Third Republic itself.

Smith, Allen. *The Road to Vichy, The Writings and Journals of Constant Caulry, 1938-1945.* Unpublished thesis, College of William and Mary; Williamsburg, Va. 2002. pp.3-7.

[50]The Confederacy is included as a nation-state.

[51]Johnson, Robert and Clarence Clough Buel eds. *North to Antietam: Battles and Leaders of the Civil War.* New York: Castle Books. 1956. pp. 449-695.

[52]Gray, Colin. "Thinking Asymmetrically in Times of Terror."

Parameters. Spring 2002, p. 5ff.

[53]It is certainly tempting to imagine that a confrontation with another large industrial power on the order of Germany or the Soviet Union is unlikely for well into the present century. It is also tempting to imagine that any future confrontation with a lesser adversary will proceed in the manner of a Desert Storm. However, the World War I example carries a warning. The great power strategists and planners before that war had the clear example of the American Civil War before them. Yet, they chose to study different examples, those of the Austro-Prussian War of 1866 and the Franco-Prussian War of 1870-1, wars that seemed to confirm the validity of their preferred approach to war and left them unprepared for the conflict of 1914-1918.

[54]There is an assumption here that the challenger can be sure that his own public support will outlast that of the larger power. This is not a foregone conclusion. For one, the robustness of the larger power's public support is likely to be a function of how directly the challenger threatens what that public perceives to be its vital national interests, such as the safety of its citizens. Too much of a challenge, thus, can provoke the larger power's public and create an equality of will between the two sides yielding the victory to the bigger side. Similarly, the challenger must pay attention to his own support, much as Mao enjoined guerrillas always to be able to swim in the sea of the local peasantry.

[55]Consider that, in the 20 years after the end of World War II, the great colonial empires of the British, French, and Dutch collapsed in disarray even though parts of those empires had been held securely with minimal military forces for two to three centuries beforehand. The colonial powers fought to maintain or restore a local hegemony, but this goal was not strongly shared by electorates at home with the result that the tolerance for physical attrition of any kind was extremely low, a distinct contrast with the situation in World Wars I and II. The indigenous rebels, on the other hand, fought to oust a foreign power and establish a national entity. In so doing, indigenous leaders often built on an extensive knowledge of their imperial enemy. Many had been educated in the "mother country" and perceived that there was no stomach for the commitment of blood and treasure that would be required to hold the empires by force. While not all of the colonies were the scene of guerrilla warfare, the British experience in Malaya and Kenya, the French in Indo-China, Madagascar, and later Algeria, and the Dutch in the East Indies, all pointed to the difficulty of attempting to halt opposing guerrillas if independence were not granted.

[56]Goldsworthy, pp. 353-6.

[57]One might also speculate that the failure to generate an equivalent resistance movement in Germany in 1945 stemmed from the basic lack of any such hope.

[58]"Third World" is used here in Nehru's original context, that is, states that were not formally members of either the NATO or Warsaw Pact.

[59]However, we must add an additional important caveat here. In the final analysis of each of these wars and conflicts, symmetric and asymmetric, the choice of what kind of war to fight was not for one side's planners and strategists to make. Their enemies chose. They chose by not "breaking" as the strategists had planned. They chose by how they decided to fight, by their stalwart reactions to defeats and losses of men and materiel, by the resources they committed, and by the will to resist that they were able to generate and maintain.

[60]If we take this observation a step further, the more successful we are in implementing an American military revolution, the more asymmetric our opponents must become if they are to have any chance of challenging us successfully.

[61]Strausz-Hupé, Robert. "The New Protracted Conflict." Orbis. April 2002.

[62]One might argue here, for example, that treating a large scale terrorist action as a criminal matter rather than as an act of war also has the effect of ruling out the attrition-based responses for which American and Western militaries in general are best equipped.

[63]In fact, the almost Manichean dichotomy of military operations into war versus "operations other than war" reflects a holdover from Cold War thinking in an age whose military challenges are more properly described by a continuum that runs from peace through crises of every sort, to wars that are equally varied in size and scope.

CHAPTER 2

Network-Centric Operations: The Starting Point[1]

Given the radical change in the existing world order that we have experienced since the end of the Cold War and particularly since September 11th, it is hardly surprising that we should begin to think not only of "transforming" our military forces, but also in terms of some form of "revolution" in military affairs (RMA). While transformation[2] offers the prospect of multiplying the power of our own military forces, perhaps the more compelling argument in its favor is the specter of a successful RMA in the hands of an opponent producing a devastating defeat. Indeed from a semantic standpoint, the real military revolution in our modern world would be one that overthrew the existing world order and not one that somehow sustained it.

In this regard, perhaps the most poignant message carried by the story of the French collapse in the 1940 blitzkrieg is not so much the desirability of finding an American RMA as it is the absolute necessity to avoid being surprised and defeated by someone else's RMA. In the final analysis, our

59

interest in Network Centric Warfare may not be so much a question of figuring out how to be the Germans of 1940. More than anything else, it may be determining how to avoid being the French. This unstated fear of being on the losing end of an RMA is the underlying motivation of much of the RMA debate. That same fear is also at the root of much of the growing interest in effects-based operations.

The blitzkrieg example underlines something else as well. In many respects, a military development may be revolutionary not because of the speed with which it takes place, or because of the novelty of the means used, but because of the result it achieves. A revolution in military affairs is revolutionary because it constitutes a sharp break with the accepted way of doing things, a change that enables the RMA military force to defeat an opponent conclusively.[3] The problem is that peacetime tests of such a prospective military revolution can never fully replicate either combat conditions or the uncertainties of war. However closely an opponent's activities have been monitored, and however frequently the elements of a would-be RMA have been practiced, the outcome and success of the prospective revolution will never be known until it's too late[4] and the battle is won or lost.

It is in this context that both Network Centric Warfare and effects-based operations must be considered. Either separately or together, both Network Centric Warfare and effects-based operations may be said to constitute an embryonic, would-be military revolution. Neither is entirely new in the sense that both can be traced to fundamental military principles long antedating the Cold War. However, both take on a significant new dimension in the Information Age. Both are also evolving significantly in response to the changing missions and threats of the post-September 11th world. Both display a renewed focus on more traditional military operations rather than a Cold War-style strategic nuclear standoff. Both reflect attempts to think differently and to harness new technologies. Finally, like other would-be military revolutions of the past, both may ultimately be confronted with a challenge that their advocates had not anticipated and they may fail. Herein lies the core challenge. How do we best adapt the new technologies and the new thinking to the missions our military forces are likely to face in our new security environment while recognizing that others in that world will be attempting to create their own revolutions with us as the target?

Network Centric Warfare, Technological Revolutions and Combat Efficiency

It seems appropriate that any discussion of transformation should start with Network Centric Warfare, the concept of linking all aspects of warfighting into a shared situation awareness and shared understanding of command intent so as to achieve a unity and synchronicity of effects that multiplies the power of military forces. The Department of Defense Report to Congress on Network Centric Warfare of July 2001 notes that Network Centric Warfare involves networking in three domains of warfare (the physical, information, and cognitive domains) so as to "generate increased combat power by: better synchronizing effects in the battlespace; achieving greater speed of command; (and) increasing lethality, survivability, and responsiveness."[5] In their seminal book, *Network Centric Warfare, Developing and Leveraging Information Superiority,* Alberts, Garstka, and Stein describe "Network Centric Warfare" in this manner:

> NCW is about human and organizational behavior. NCW is based on a new way of thinking, network-centric thinking, and applying it to military operations. NCW focuses on the combat power that can be generated from the effective linking or networking of the warfighting enterprise. It is characterized by the ability of geographically dispersed forces to create a high level of shared battle space awareness that can be exploited via self-synchronization and other network-centric operations to achieve commander's intent. NCW supports speed of command, the conversion of a superior information position to action. NCW is transparent to mission, force size, and geography. Furthermore, NCW has the potential to contribute to the coalescence of the tactical, operational, and strategic levels of war. In brief, NCW is not narrowly about technology, but broadly about an emerging military response to the Information Age.[6]

Network-centric operations, then, are the application of the concepts and principles of Network Centric

Warfare to military operations across the spectrum of conflict from peace, to crisis, to war.

As this description suggests, Network Centric Warfare and network-centric operations are closely aligned with the emerging new technologies of the so-called Information Age. But, the description does more than that. It implies that the new technologies by themselves are not enough and that the real potential of network-centric operations stems from some innovative thinking as to how to use these technologies. Thus, in the manner of Dr. Krepinevich's definition of a revolution in military affairs, the new technologies must be accompanied by changes in organization, doctrine, and tactics, just as the inter-war years' new technologies, radios, aircraft, and armor needed to be used as a different combined arms force to create a blitzkrieg RMA. There is still another dimension to this combination of new technologies and new thinking. Network Centric Warfare may also provide the means for executing an old concept, effects-based operations, in a new way that is both precise and dynamic. It is this prospect that will be explored in this book.

The common thread that runs through the definition of Network Centric Warfare, the introduction of new technologies, and the exploration of a concept of effects-based warfare is the search for greater combat efficiency. That is, the purpose of each technology and concept is a reduction in the relative amount of military or other power needed to undertake a given mission, to fulfill a given task, or to create a specific outcome. The attraction of

Network Centric Warfare and effects-based warfare is the prospect that they can yield improved combat efficiency. The challenge is to understand how they might do this and what combination of technologies used in support of which concepts would yield the greatest combat efficiency.

We need to be careful in how we proceed. The Alberts et al. description of Network Centric Warfare implies a distinction between a military technical revolution (MTR) and a RMA similar to that drawn in the Introduction to this book. Whereas the MTR applies new technology to existing ways of war, the RMA combines new technology with new tactics, doctrine, and/or organization, e.g. the blitzkrieg, or combines new or existing technologies in a new concept of warfare, e.g. the levée en masse and the Napoleonic revolution.

If we apply this construct to Network Centric Warfare and effects-based operations, three distinct levels of potential improvement in combat efficiency begin to emerge. The first level of improvement would derive from the application of new technologies to existing forces, doctrine, tactics, and organization and the existing concepts of warfare. The second level of improvement would derive from the adaptation of doctrine, tactics, and organization to optimize the impact of the new technologies. Finally, the third level of improvement in combat efficiency would then derive from the application of the new technology and thinking to a different style of warfare, an avenue we will explore in effects-based operations.

The idea of combat efficiency and the three levels of potential improvement in efficiency, each tied to different aspects of the RMA debate, offer a framework for more detailed consideration of how both Network Centric Warfare and effects-based operations fit into the larger picture of the new security environment, what military forces do in it, and how they are organized.

First Level Improvement in Combat Efficiency: New Technologies

The most straightforward and understandable potential improvement in combat efficiency is to be derived from applying the emerging military and dual-use technologies for forces, doctrine, organization, and tactics to existing concepts of warfare. The use of new technology to multiply the impact of military forces seems almost axiomatic and, indeed, is the staple of the current acquisition process. The only challenge would appear to lie in determining which technologies in which combinations hold the most potential. Still, this is not as simple as it sounds.

Three Technological Revolutions

The driving force behind the discussion of Network Centric Warfare has been a revolution in information technology that has been building over the last decade and more. Still, this information is only part of the picture. In reality, we must think in terms of an interlocking set of three different technological revolutions: one in sensors, one in information technology, and one in weapons technology.[7]

- *Sensor Technology*. The revolution in sensor technology is twofold: one element is the move toward sensors that are able to achieve a comprehensive, near-real-time surveillance over vast areas, and the other is a move toward smaller, cheaper, more numerous sensors that can be netted to detect, locate, identify, and track targets.[8] The latter is of particular significance. Not only will the sensors produced by the revolution be smaller, cheaper, and therefore, much more numerous, but they will also be of an almost bewildering variety. Each will test some specific set or range of phenomena, e.g. acoustic, seismic, and infrared, with each stream of information integrated both with that of different sensors and over time. Together, these trends can provide the quantity and quality of data to create a "situational awareness" that is "global in scope and precise in detail."[9] Already, this trend is being reflected in the expanding efforts of the U.S. Army and U.S. Marine Corps to exploit fields of unattended ground sensors, including some insect-like mobile sensors. It is also reflected in the U.S. Navy's exploration of a concept of an "Expeditionary Sensor Grid" of thousands, if not tens of thousands, of sensors that might be deployed by an operational commander in tiers of overhead, unmanned aerial and surface sensors spread across a forward battlespace on and under the sea, ashore and in the air.

• *Information Technology.* The true utility of the new sensors described above can only be appreciated if we think of them in the context of sensor fields or entire surveillance systems. The military success of the sensor revolution is contingent upon an equal and parallel success in networking them into a system of systems. New information technology provides this network backbone. It lends the sensor revolution a real military significance. The reason is twofold. First, the networking allows us to expand the capability of the sensors both by better integrating the data collected, and by allowing the sensors to interactively build on one another's efforts. This latter networking can in turn permit a dumbing down of the sensors involved so as to make them still cheaper and potentially more numerous. Second, the scope and scale of the data provided by the sensor revolution is likely to be of such a quantity that it would be unmanageable save for an information revolution that will bring the geometric increase in computing power necessary to process, collate, and analyze the resulting quantity of sensor data. In short, without networking, the sensors could achieve only a very limited part of their impact and their numbers and diverse data streams might even become counterproductive.

What is more, the revolution will also provide the means of distributing information to any designee or "shooter" anywhere in the world at near-real-time speeds. Unless the "command and control"[10] of the forces receiving the sensor information were equal to the task, the influx of information would likely overwhelm commanders and become dysfunctional. Thus, the information revolution must also contribute the means of ensuring both that the right information reaches the right decisionmaker at the right time in the right form, and that the decisionmaker can make the best use possible of it in executing command intent, however it may be expressed. If we take this latter thought a step further, we can also look for information technology to provide better information and displays to help decisionmakers appreciate the rapid successions of complicated tactical and operational data that make up a modern engagement. Still more importantly, we might use the new technology to address the still more complex, subjective, and usually ambiguous information inherent in exploiting the human dimension of war.

• *Weapons Technology.* If the network-centric revolution was limited to the first two technologies alone, a battlefield commander might find himself inundated with a quantity of targets that would completely outstrip his supply of weapons. The third component of the triple revolution provides the means of exploiting these sensor and information revolutions. The focus of this weapons revolution is not toward increasingly precise weapons but toward smaller, cheaper, and more numerous weapons that are precise enough to exploit the data provided by sensors and information systems. Like the information and sensor revolutions, the revolution in weapons is twofold. Better streams of targeting data can permit a "dumbing down" of expensive guidance packages and thus reduce costs. And, new designs, better electronics, "lean manufacturing," and mass production of much larger numbers of weapons can decrease the cost for a given level of accuracy and capability.[11] Indeed, the sensor and information revolutions enable us to think not only in terms of cheaper missiles, but also in terms of unmanned combat air vehicles that can be far cheaper than manned platforms as the delivery means for this new generation of cheap precise weapons.

...and Combat Efficiency

If we accept that the first level of improvement in combat efficiency stems from applying these new technologies to the existing ways of war, then the major challenge in attaining the first level of improvement in combat efficiency is figuring out which technologies in which combinations might best enable us to meet our strategic objectives and provide the best return on our investment. The question of which combinations work best is particularly important. As our outline of the three revolutions indicates, the real impact of the technologies upon warfare derives from the synergies of combining different technologies drawn from different revolutions.[12] Improved sensors can help us to find more targets more quickly and accurately and to detect enemy actions and reactions sooner. But, the amount of data these sensors can provide would overwhelm us without better information systems to process and handle the data stream. Better information technologies similarly might enable us to move data and information faster and to disseminate both combat information and directives more rapidly and with less error. But, the combinations of sensors and information systems we create could simply leave us with massive amounts of targeting information if we did not have the larger numbers of weapons needed to exploit that information, and so on.

The idea of combining a variety of different technologies to achieve new synergies seems axiomatic. The difficulty is in determining which synergies are likely to result and how these will evolve over time. In this vein, the triple technological revolution poses five challenges with which we must deal:

- First, the three technological revolutions are largely independent of each other and, thus, will almost inevitably be out of synch. This is especially true since the sensor and information revolutions are largely being developed by civilian industry and follow a timetable that bears little relationship either to developments in the other revolutions or to military need.

- Second, there will be a continual interaction among the new technologies. Innovations in one area may be expected to have a direct impact on the utility of technologies in other areas. For example, the new information technologies that permit sensors to be more autonomous might enable an expansion in the size and scope of the sensor fields that can be managed within an existing surveillance system. Furthermore, developments in one area may spark changes in others. Improved guidance on weapons or the introduction of improved unmanned combat air vehicles, for example, could change the nature and function of sensor fields.

- Third, the synergies that emerge from the interaction of the new technological developments can be both positive and negative.[13] Although we are accustomed to thinking of one technology building on another, in fact, some of the synergies may actually be negative. A slower pace of development in one technology revolution could inhibit progress in another, such as bandwidth restrictions limiting the size of sensor fields that can be monitored. Additionally, a new technology in the hands of a would-be opponent could potentially defeat the purpose of an entire development effort. A series of developments in information technology that permit us to centralize command and control, for example, may create a vulnerability that a precise weapon can exploit. Still more likely, if new information technology were used to drive a centralization of command instead of a de-centralization, it could reduce our agility just when it is most needed to deal with adversaries who have used new sensors and information technologies to de-centralize their operations.

• Fourth, as the last point suggests, because much of the triple revolution either is in civilian, "dual use" technologies or is readily available on the international market, there is no American or Western monopoly on the systems emerging or how they are adapted to military use. To the contrary, other states and non-state actors may pick and choose from a global technological "grab bag" to create their own would-be revolution, a revolution that may well be focused on defeating the United States and the West. As the cost of the new technologies declines over time, furthermore, the number of actors who could potentially afford the technologies needed to pose an asymmetric threat will expand, multiplying the number and variety of potential applications of the technologies we must confront. Moreover, because smaller actors and non-state actors must rely on commercial-off-the-shelf technology, they can largely avoid cumbersome acquisition procedures that afflict the asymmetric foes. This can give them an advantage in speed and surprise. In essence, as soon as they can identify a technology synergy and buy it, they can exploit it.

• Fifth, none of the three revolutions is close to being finished. Each of the technological revolutions is likely to continue to expand and accelerate in the decades to come. Each new development can spawn new potential synergies like a succession of ripples spreading out over a lake. Thus, our problem is not simply that of finding a one-time revolutionary synergy for our own use, but rather that of managing a stream of potential synergies, many of which might be used against us.

In brief, the three technological revolutions present a nearly infinite and constantly changing plethora of potential military synergies that will change even as we attempt to apply them to existing concepts, doctrine, tactics, and organization. Given the fluidity and complexity of the three technological revolutions, how do we identify those technologies and those combinations that offer the most potential, both for ourselves and for our would-be opponents?

To some degree, by applying the principles of "system of systems" engineering, we can identify some of the potential synergies, test them, and incorporate them into our deliberate planning process. Better sensors and information clearly could create better situational awareness and thus reduce fratricide and enable us to detect enemy moves as they occur. Better targeting data would mean that fewer weapons would be required for a given mission, and so on. Although this multiplying web of potential synergies may sound complex, the impact of the new technologies can be readily quantified. By comparing the results of a given mission or tactic using older systems and forces with the results of the same mission or tactic using new systems or forces, we can obtain very exact results.

However, this ability to quantify is seductive. Because comparisons of limited changes in existing systems can yield very exact results, we can find ourselves in the position of the man looking for his lost keys by the light post because that is where he can see best. Similarly, if we focus only on that which we can quantify, we stand a good chance of making only incremental changes in current capabilities since that is what we can best quantify, a fault for which the current acquisition system has been frequently chastised. The result would be to end up improving our capacity to fight the last war, like France in the face of the blitzkrieg.[14]

It is worth noting in this regard that, during the inter-war period, the most impressive military technological advances and investments were made by France, not by Germany. These technologies, embodied in the Maginot Line, were tested and evaluated, and "proven" to be an order of magnitude more effective than the fortifications of World War I.[15] Nor were the French unaware of the emerging technologies of their epoch. In 1940, French tanks were often better than their German counterparts and their aircraft were more numerous.[16] However, what shaped the blitzkrieg was how the Germans used the technologies they had available and their organization, strategy, and tactics.[17]

The key question raised by the technological revolutions outlined above is the same one that distinguishes a MTR from a RMA. That question is not: how do we use the new technologies to execute our current tactics and doctrine better? It is instead: how might the new technologies enable us to do things differently? This, indeed, is the essence of transformation. The challenge posed by this question is to create doctrine, organizations, and tactics that optimize emerging technologies or that incorporate them into new concepts of warfare that better adapt our capabilities to the changing security environment. In the final analysis, without the new thinking, the new technologies are likely to increase efficiency in a way that is largely arithmetic and incremental in nature. They enable us to execute today's tactics and operations in a quantifiably better way, but they still leave us with traditional, tightly controlled, and synchronized operations that are hierarchically planned and executed.[18]

We can palpably sense that there is something missing in this technology-focused, first level of improvement in combat efficiency. Not only does the application of new technologies to existing concepts, organization, doctrine, and tactics beg the question of what those same technologies might have done in a different context, but it largely ignores an even greater issue. The post-September 11th missions our military forces now face are not and will not be the same as those for which our Cold War platforms, organization, and tactics were designed. The evolving synergies of the triple technological revolution draw us to look at a second level of combat efficiency in which changes in technologies are coupled with change in how we think about war. This next level of combat efficiency has come to be embodied in the idea of Network Centric Warfare.

Second Level Improvement in Combat Efficiency: Network Centric Warfare

Fittingly, the concept of Network Centric Warfare builds on some key warfare changes that can grow from the three technological revolutions. One such change is the use of sensors and networking to improve situational awareness, precision, and self-synchronization to carry out more operations during a given period of time and to focus those actions on the right target at the right time to optimize impact. The speed and precision brought by networking can likewise provide the potential to exploit very specific battlefield opportunities and to operate at a pace calculated to overwhelm an enemy's capacity to respond. Also, network-centric capabilities portend a highly agile force able to change from one rapid, precise operation to another at will, and able to compress complex targeting processes to fit the nearly real-time dimensions of the battlefield. Finally, networking also has the potential to increase the amount and quality of the information and knowledge available to commanders at every level both on and off the battlefield. For our understanding of Network Centric Warfare and its role in improving combat efficiency, the critical point is not that these capabilities may exist, but rather how the capabilities come together in Network Centric Warfare and how the resulting network-centric operations are more efficient.

The concept of Network Centric Warfare now evolving applies the new technologies to two ends: to explore new ways to do existing missions better;[19] and to find ways to undertake missions that we might never before have attempted. The latter is a critical part of dealing with a fast changing security environment and especially the threats of asymmetric threats. The Navy Warfare Development Command's draft "Capstone Concept for Naval Operations in the Information Age" begins to define a working concept for the application of these Network Centric Warfare concepts to military operations. The Capstone Concept refers to network-centric operations "as the art of deriving maximum force power through the rapid and robust networking of diverse, well-informed, and geographically separated warfighters" so as to "enable a precise, agile style of maneuver warfare."[20] What does that mean, and how does it increase combat efficiency?

Proponents of network-centric operations explain the impact on combat efficiency in this manner. In traditional military operations, a mission is assigned and planned, forces are generated, and operations are executed to concentrate power on an objective. This is a highly coordinated, "stepped" cycle (see Figure 7): periods of relative inaction, during which forces are generated and actions coordinated (the flat part of the step) alternate with periods of action, when combat power is applied (the vertical part). However, if forces were networked to create a near-real-time situational awareness, then we could act continuously along a relatively smooth "combat power curve." We would no longer need to pause before deciding on further action; the information and coordination needed would already be there.

The shared situation awareness promised by network-centric operations would also permit a flattened decentralized command structure in which decisions could and would be made at the lowest practicable level of command. Combined with self-synchronization, it would permit us to reclaim the "lost combat power" between the

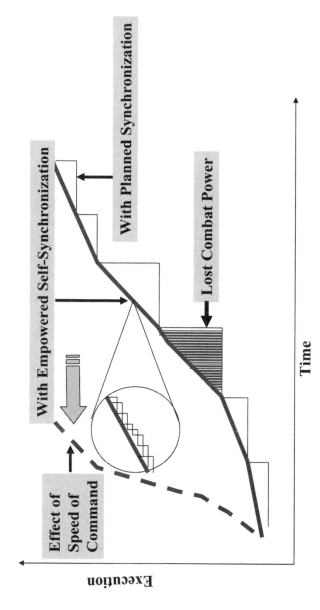

Figure 7. Self-Synchronization and Speed of Command

optimal combat power curve and the steps of the planned synchronization as illustrated in the diagram. Finally, as we train and organize to work with these capabilities and perfect our decisionmaking, the pace of these semi-independent operations might accelerate further to permit a steeper combat power curve and with it a new, more rapid speed of command.

Speed of Command

Although equating accelerated self-synchronized operations to increase combat efficiency makes intuitive sense, it needs further explanation. One way of doing this is to look at the diagram's "steps" in the context of the Observe, Orient, Decide, and Act (OODA) loop concept proposed by Colonel John R. Boyd, USAF. However, instead of treating the OODA loops[21] as circles, we can look at them as a succession of linear cycles overlaid on the steps described. Col. Boyd's Observe, Orient and Decide phases then would equate to the flat part of the step while the Act phase would be the vertical or action part of the step (see Figure 8). Plotted on axes of time (x) versus cumulative application of military force (y), the "steps" then become OODA cycles with each Act adding to the total of the military force applied.

If we were somehow able to compress the length of time required to complete an observation of the opponent's actions sufficient to make a decision, and/or if we were similarly able to shorten the time needed to re-orient our activities and then to decide

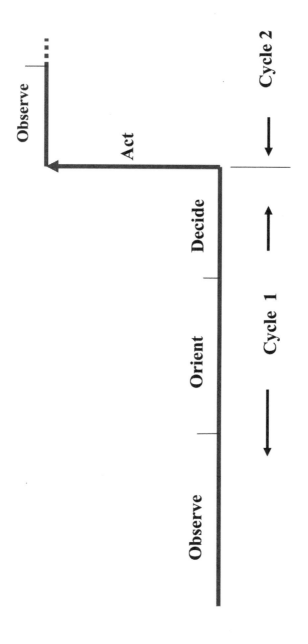

Figure 8. The OODA Cycle

on a course of action, then the impact on the combat power curve would be to greatly increase its slope (see Figure 9).

The result would be the increase in the speed of command theorized in Figure 7, our original diagram.

While this may be sufficient to explain the diagram in Figure 9, it falls into a trap. We seem to equate the length of the OODA loop or decision cycle with the pace of operations. Yet, we know that much more is involved in conducting military operations.[22] We know that to act, we must do a great deal more than simply observe, orient, and decide. Actions are physical in nature and require physical preparations as well as decisionmaking. Accordingly, we must look beyond the OODA decision cycles to a larger dimension that might be termed a "combat power generation cycle." That cycle encompasses not only the act of observing, orienting, and deciding, but also the whole range of parallel physical acts necessary to actually generate combat power, or act.

Self-Synchronization

This broader conception of the combat power generation cycle introduces new dimensions to each phase of Boyd's OODA loop. For example, the "observe" process includes both the decision to observe certain activities and the physical actions needed to acquire the intelligence, surveillance, and targeting data and to transmit it to the right people or systems. New sensor and information technologies can compress this process significantly, but there is a limit to how much.

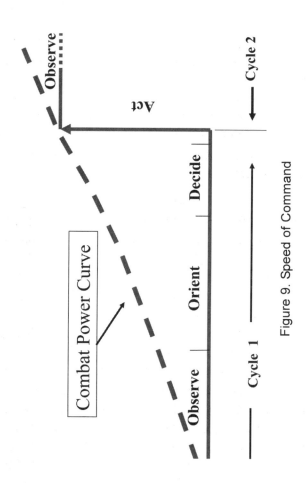

Figure 9. Speed of Command

Moreover, to optimize the impact of precision, we need more than sensor-based awareness; we need to identify specific vulnerabilities. To do that, we need to know the enemy better. Although this "knowing" draws on sensor information and as a result, will be subject to some time compression, the knowledge also depends on regional expertise and on intelligence databases developed long before the battle begins. Thus, the new sensors and information technology can only shorten the cycle to the degree that the physical actions needed for long-term collection and analysis have already been completed and that knowledge is already available on the network.

A similar limit emerges in the "orient/decide" phase.[23] Better awareness helps us avoid mistakes and use assets more efficiently, but we must still complete a set of physical actions to generate military power. We may have to move the carrier within range of the objective, plan and brief the mission, fuel and arm the aircraft, and launch them.[24] We may also have to deliver follow-on air strikes to achieve an objective. The pace of these actions is determined by the physical capabilities of systems and people. An aircraft carrier can move only so fast and its flight deck operations can be hurried along only so much. Efficiency is as much a function of how we organize, train, and equip our forces as it is of how the information flows. The same is true of the "act" phase. Once in the air, aircraft must proceed to the target and then, at a time dependent on a series of physical constraints (the speed of the aircraft, range of its weapons, and the distance to be traveled), launch their ordinance.

To increase the impact of network-centric-derived speed of command and thus combat efficiency, we must accelerate both parts of the combat cycle, the OODA cycle and the process of generating combat power. A strike sortie generation demonstration conducted by the U.S.S. Nimitz (CVN 68) in 1997[25] provides a good example of how these two elements come together. The Nimitz demonstration used a rudimentary network to aid targeting and decisionmaking, but then focused on optimizing the battle group, the carrier, and the airwing to make better use of the increased information that the network made available. Among other things, it added pilots to its embarked airwing,[26] introduced new high-speed cyclical operations,[27] and relied on accompanying missile ships for air defense of the battle group. The result was a fourfold increase in sorties over a 4-day period. Arming each aircraft with multiple precision weapons, each of which could reliably destroy an aimpoint, further multiplied the effect. The battle group thus established a faster, more efficient power generation cycle, one that (when combined with network's ability to identify the "targets that count" in commensurate numbers) produced an order of magnitude increase in the group's combat efficiency.[28]

This achievement is significant for several reasons. First, the Nimitz operation shows that using better equipment, organization, training, and information can shorten the combat power generation cycle, and thus take advantage of network-centric speed and awareness. However, it also indicates something else; the time required for combat power generation will vary with equipment, training, and organization, just as it did on the Nimitz before and after new measures were implemented. That suggests that dissimilar military forces have power generation cycles of radically different lengths. For example, the length of the Nimitz's cycle would differ from that of a squad of SEALs (U.S. Navy special operations forces) inserted from a submarine, or of a cruiser firing Tomahawk land attack missiles, or of a squad of Marines in a firefight, or of bombers operating from bases in the continental United States (see Figure 10).

The Nimitz demonstration also points to another differential in the impact of training and organization. Thus, not only are different kinds of units differently equipped and therefore subject to different physical limits in how fast they can react, but different units of the same type will have received different levels of training and display different proficiencies that will also have an impact on the speed of their performance.

In a traditional battle, the commander manages the complex interaction among these different combat cycles by coordinating subordinate units so that their respective "act" phases strike the enemy at the same time or in some prescribed sequence. Indeed, one can hardly imagine the D-Day landings in the absence of such coordination to mass the fires and effects of the massive Allied forces. And as the complexity of the Allied landings underlined, the more diverse the forces involved, the greater the coordination problem is likely to be. The difficulty is that by coordinating to this degree, the entire effort is held hostage to the speed of the

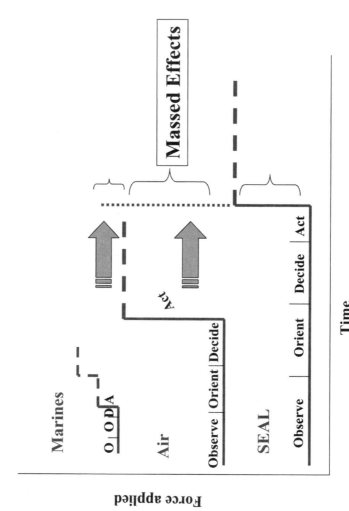

Figure 10. Synchronizing OODA Cycles to Mass Effects

slowest combat cycle, with all other units deliberately kept from achieving their optimum tempo of operations so as to mass the effects needed or to be mutually supportive. Therefore, the commander deliberately foregoes additional cycles of applied power that might have been generated by quicker paced forces, and so less power is applied overall (see Figure 11). In short, "by optimizing mass, we minimize efficiency."[29]

As if this were not enough of a challenge, most of our wartime operations do not involve uniquely U.S. forces. The norm is a coalition operation of some form. Thus, the problem is not only the differences between unit types and levels of proficiency on the U.S. side, but an even greater variance between U.S. units and the analogous Allied units. Each Allied unit almost inevitably will have different equipment and different training as well as in all likelihood different rules of engagement. These will in great degree govern the varying lengths of the coalition's combat power generation cycle (see Figure 12).

In fact, the pace of coalition operations are very much governed by these factors to the point that the overall combat power generation cycle of the coalition as a whole may bear little resemblance to those of the individual players. While these problems can in some respects be ameliorated by integrated alliance working arrangements such as in NATO, in general, the problem encountered by the commander in coordinating the "act" phases of multiple forces and multiple allies increases almost exponentially as the number of coalition partners increases.

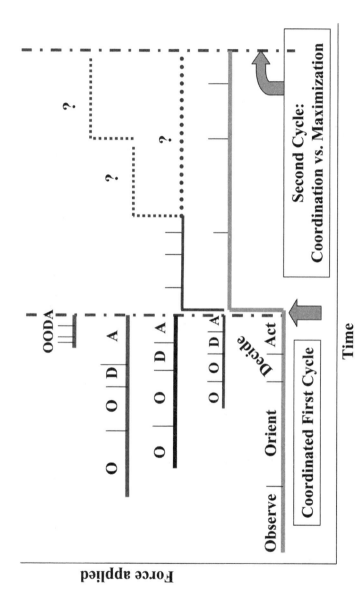

Figure 11. Coordinated Attack...Then What?

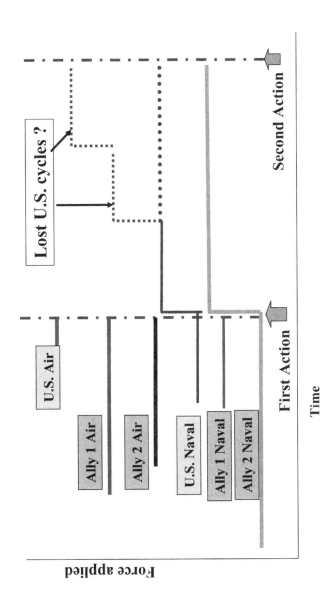

Different kinds of forces and different ROE to be coordinated

Figure 12. Coalition Operations: International Self-Synchronization

Shared Situation Awareness, Shared Understanding of Command Intent

How does Network Centric Warfare better enable the commander to deal with this complex challenge and optimize the pace of his operations?

Increases in an individual unit's speed of command, or decisionmaking, can certainly enable us to reduce OODA cycle lengths and thereby increase the pace of operations, to a point. Similarly, better equipment, organization, and training of that unit can also increase its pace of operations. But, the key question that emerges from the discussion above is not about individual units, but about how disparate units of all descriptions can be coordinated to increase the overall pace of operations and firepower of the force as a whole, whether it is entirely American or a coalition. The implied solution is to somehow permit each unit to operate at its optimal pace, thus reclaiming the "lost combat power." But, how do we do this without making the overall force dysfunctional and, perhaps, fratricidal?

Here is where the agility derived from Network Centric Warfare becomes important. This agility and the speed and precision it exploits all derive from the amalgam of information tools, sensors, and communications that constitutes the information back plane of network-centric operations. The network permits us to undertake more actions in a given time, to focus those actions better, to act and react faster, and to do so with more certainty. That is to say that networking permits our military forces to become more efficient.

The contribution of Network Centric Warfare centers on creating a shared situational awareness and a shared understanding of "command" intent.[30] The assumption here is that, if unit commands down to the tactical level have a general awareness of the overall situation and a specific awareness of their position in it, then they will be able to operate freely and coordinate among themselves so as to optimize the capabilities of each unit. The ability to use the shared situational awareness in this manner is clearly much more than linking sensors and commanders. Like the Nimitz demonstration, it derives from adopting different organization, training, and doctrine to build on the awareness. It also involves looking at the shared situation awareness beyond the tactical level. For the concept to work, operational level commands and above must be confident enough in the quality of the sharing to be able to decentralize decisionmaking for maximum effectiveness where feasible, and retain control where it is needed. This also implies different senior echelon training, organization, and doctrine, a change that needs to stretch all the way up to the national leadership. Finally, if we are ever to put to rest the oxymoron of rapid coalition operations, the shared awareness and the changes in organization, training, and doctrine must likewise extend to potential partners.

As the latter two prospects highlight, shared situation awareness by itself is insufficient. The commands sharing the awareness must likewise be linked by a shared understanding of the command intent without which their actions are likely to become dysfunctional. In fact, the decentralization of command that breeds the greater combat efficiency hinges on such shared understanding. Again, such shared understanding depends as much on organization, training, and doctrine as it does on the information links among the commands. Furthermore, even more than with shared situation awareness, such shared understanding of command intent requires looking beyond the tactical level of military operations.

This does not mean that a detailed understanding of the national leadership's objectives and policy intent need be inflicted on the harried tactical level commander. It does mean that the command intent at each level must reliably reflect the intent of the next higher echelon of command. That descending chain of command intents is likewise the fruit of training. However, it is something more. The understanding we seek is not so much the result of shared information as it is of shared knowledge, both of the situation and the objectives. It is this latter sharing that is at the heart of most of the coordination problems associated with coalition operations.

In the final analysis, the driving force behind both the shared situation awareness and the shared understanding of command intent is less a question of simply increasing combat efficiency than the need to avoid defeat. To deal with changes in the enemy threat or to take advantage of emerging battlefield opportunities, we must be able both to conduct rapid, semi-independent operations and to mass forces and effects as required. We must be able to change the mode, direction, and objectives of our actions just as much as we need to bring speed and precision to targeting.

Identifying Synergies of Thinking and Things

If we must choose the best technologies in the best combinations to optimize combat efficiency, and if we are to combine them with the right organization, training, and doctrine to exploit shared situational awareness and understanding of command intent, how are we to determine which are the best solutions? How do we measure the value of the alternatives? How much is the proverbial "pound of information" really worth?

The problem of assessing multiple different impacts encountered in dealing with myriad interacting new technologies is multiplied here by the need to monitor how each contributes or fails to contribute to the new tactics, doctrine, and organization we are exploring. The result is a complex problem with a seemingly infinite number of variables. Even though any precise quantification of the value of information may not be possible in the sense of assessing new technology alone, there clearly are new ways of assessing and measuring outcomes that are now emerging. These approaches focus upon measuring outcomes with and without key network-centric capabilities such as shared situation awareness and self-synchronization.

In fact, this is what the Navy's Fleet Battle Experiments (FBEs) and the Joint Forces Command's experimentation program in particular have been attempting to do, both with respect to the concepts themselves and with respect to the incorporation of new technologies into those concepts. Nor are those the only such experiments. The Department of Defense Report to Congress on Network Centric Warfare points to "a growing body of evidence that provides an existence proof" of the central ideas of Network Centric Warfare.[31] The report goes on to note:

> The most compelling evidence identified to date exists at the tactical level in a broad range of mission areas. This evidence has been assembled from a variety of service and combined experimentation and operational demonstrations, as well as high intensity, tactical conflict situations. Examples were identified that supported the relationship between:
>
> • Improved networking capabilities and increased information sharing
>
> • Increased information sharing and increased shared situational awareness
>
> • Increased shared situational awareness and improved collaboration and synchronization
>
> • Increased mission effectiveness as a result of the presence of one or more of these factors.

Although these results are certainly not quantifiable in the same sense that the acquisition process has come to expect of weapons and platforms, the experimentation to date[32] provides clear indication of the synergies between the new technologies now available and some new thinking as to how to best wage war. These synergies are the basis for the second, higher level of combat efficiency that is attainable with network-centric operations. Indeed, they are already sufficient to indicate that the second, network-centric level of improvement in combat efficiency is clearly well beyond that achievable with the new technology alone. Furthermore, the simple fact that we are still referring to "experimentation" has another important implication: that we have not yet fully explored just how great an increase in combat efficiency might ultimately come from combining the new technologies with network-centric thinking.

Third Level of Improvement in Combat Efficiency: Effects-Based Operations... Efficiency to do What?

Although the results of the experimentation with network-centric operations are certainly promising, they are not the end of the story. What we have described is the nature of the network-centric "means" we seek to create. What we have yet to address is how we might use that tool's enhanced operational efficiency. Now we must ask: efficiency to do what?

If we say nothing further at this point, that application will, by default, reflect the tried and true concepts of some form of attrition-based warfare. It is easy for us to look at the applications of speed of command and self-synchronization and the uses of shared situation awareness and shared understanding of command intent considered so far and to think only in terms of improvements to our ability to destroy enemy forces and infrastructure. That is, just as in the case of the first or MTR level of combat efficiency, network-centric operations by themselves and in combination with new first level technologies can amount to little more than "better, faster, more" attrition.

At first glance, this statement appears dissonant. Surely, the changes wrought by new technologies and Network Centric Warfare must enable us to something more than just improve the efficiency of our attrition? The discussions of Network Centric Warfare certainly give us a hint of something more. We are told that network-centric operations may enable us to "get inside the enemy's OODA loop," or that we can use the increased pace of our operations to overwhelm the enemy and lock him out of an effective response. Still, even these hints of something more almost inevitably seem to devolve into metrics that are still defined in terms of targets destroyed, in terms of attrition of enemy forces and capabilities: (1) because we were able to operate inside the enemy OODA loop, we were able to destroy the opposing force; (2) because the enemy was unable to respond effectively, we were able to destroy his infrastructure with relative impunity, and so on.

Yet, the real efficiency that we seek with our new technologies and network-centric thinking is something very different from such destruction. It is to foreshorten the combat itself by breaking our enemies' will to resist, even though they may retain the forces and capabilities to do so. How then do we make the leap to a level of efficiency that would permit us to break our enemies' wills rather than grind down their means of waging war? How will the new technologies and concepts of network-centric operations apply to the use of military power short of destroying the opposing forces and capabilities (the operations short of combat that make up the vast majority of what a military does)?

To answer these questions, we must first answer a different question: what are effects-based operations?

---

[1]Parts of this chapter were originally published as "Network Centric Warfare: What's the Point?" United States Naval War College Review. Winter 2001.

[2]The Department of Defense Report to Congress on Network Centric Warfare defines transformation as "the evolution and deployment of combat capabilities that provide revolutionary or asymmetric advantages to our forces." Report to Congress, p. 2-2.

[3]See also Norman Friedman, Thomas C. Hone, Mark D Mandeles. The Introduction of Carrier Aviation into the U.S. Navy and the Royal Navy: Military-Technical revolutions, Organizations, and the Problem of Decision. Office of Net Assessment, 1994.

[4]Andrew W. Marshall, "Opening Remarks," *Navy RMA Roundtable*, June 4, 1997, SAIC: 1997.

[5]Department of Defense. Network Centric Warfare, Department of Defense Report to Congress, 27 July 2001. Washington, D.C. 2001. p. 3-10.

[6]David Alberts, John Garstka, and Frederick Stein. *Network Centric Warfare, Developing and Leveraging Information Superiority*. Washington; CCRP. 2000, p. 88.

[7]Morrow, Walter. "Technology for a Naval Revolution in Military Affairs," Second Navy RMA Round Table, 4 June 1997.

[8]By extension, this revolution would then include all of the elements of the global locating capability, e.g. the Global Positioning System (GPS), that enable us to locate objects precisely either for surveillance or for targeting weapons.

[9]Morrow. "Technology."

[10]There is some question as to whether the term "command and control" might itself be archaic in an era of complex, high-speed interactions. Indeed, the prospect of some new arrangement for the direction of forces and actions seems to be a necessary ingredient for the implementation of both Network Centric Warfare and effects-based operations.

[11]This trend is already evident in the falling unit price of the Navy Tomahawk cruise missile from $1.2 million 10 years ago, to less than $700 thousand in 1998, to the prospect of $300 thousand or less before the next decade is out - a roughly 50% drop every 10 years. Murphy, RADM Daniel. "Surface warfare." Navy RMA Round Table. June 4, 1997. A similar case might be made for the JDAM munitions.

[12]In the U.S. operations in Afghanistan, for example, the Predator unmanned aerial surveillance vehicles were armed with Hellfire missiles, thus combining sensors and weapons systems into one package with the package supported by increasingly accurate and comprehensive information systems. The combination of technologies and at least the limited introduction of Network Centric Warfare lent new meaning to an old concept of "armed reconnaissance" and provided a new paradigm for technology synergy.

[13]The situation is analogous to the triple revolution in guns, armor, and propulsion that marked warship design in the 50 years between 1862 and 1912. That three-fold revolution introduced a period of trial and error experimentation and forced such rapid change in warship design that new units were obsolete within a few years of fleet entry. It also brought forth Mahan and a fundamental rethinking of what navies could do.

[14]In a period of very rapid, multi-faceted technological change, this tendency is aggravated by the fact that it is very likely that many, if not most, of the technological synergies we are encountering will only be fully understood over time. To make matters still more difficult, the interactions of diverse new technologies can only be fully understood as they are applied to defense problems in the field. To make matters worse, the nature of those defense problems themselves will be constantly evolving. This means that, for all of our efforts to test and plan, we will not be able to predict entirely or quantify in advance all the potential results of the technologies we introduce.

[15]Probably the most innovative military technologies of the 1920s and 1930s were those incorporated into the vast array of defensive works on France's frontier with Germany known as the Maginot Line. The French problem was not a lack of innovative military thinking as to other alternatives. Charles De Gaulle's *Fils d'épée* (1934) clearly laid out many of the principles adopted by German panzer commanders in the blitzkrieg. Similarly, the problem was not a lack of experimentation. The French Army Staff conducted numerous wargames throughout the period, most of which validated their thinking. Their problem was rather that they applied their military technical revolution to the wrong concept.

[16]May, Ernest R. *Strange Victory, Hitler's Conquest of France.* Hill and Wang. 2000. p. 209.

[17]What the French lacked was the organization, doctrine, and tactics of the blitzkrieg and, as Williamson Murray points out, the French staff was unable to deal with the pace of operations that these innovations generated.

Murray, p. 21.

[18]To some degree, this same quandary is also evident today in the debate over Network Centric Warfare. All too many attempts to describe Network Centric Warfare and its impact on military operations have centered on the network and on the new information technologies that can be used to create more efficient sensor-to-shooter sensors and communications architecture. In this "if you build it, they will come" approach, the architectures and information technologies (the technological revolutions) are seen to be the core of the problem, and that the RMA will be born directly out of its successes. While the link between new information systems and improved combat efficiency is certainly true, the "if you build it, they will come" approach runs into many of the same problems and limitations of the MTR. The performance of a sensor-to-shooter architecture, for example, may be very testable and quantifiable, but it could still leave us endlessly refining the "SCUD hunting" problem of the last war, rather than dealing with emerging asymmetric challenges. And, the farther the approach strays from existing paradigms, the more difficult it becomes to quantify. More importantly, the MTR approach largely fails to answer how and why the new architectures and technologies translate into new capabilities like "shared awareness" and "speed of command," or how these enable us to "get inside the enemy's OODA loop," much less to what avail.

[19]The Navy's old Ocean Surveillance Information System (OSIS) combined with the Joint On-line Tactical System

(JOTS) in the context of the Combined Warfare Commander (CWC) concept certainly represent at least an embryonic form of what we now know as network-centric operations, which dates back more than 15 years. However, the efforts of the ongoing series of Navy Fleet Battle Experiments clearly move toward a level of interaction these earlier systems could not foresee.

[20]Navy Warfare Development Command. Draft Network Centric Operations: A Capstone Concept for Naval Operations in the Information Age. p. i.

[21]The OODA cycle was originally used by Col. Boyd to characterize a fighter engagement but it has been come to be applied to the decisionmaking process in general. While certainly an oversimplification of a much more complex interaction, it does offer a shorthand version of the process and is used here in that sense.

Colonel John A. Boyd, USAF. "A Discourse on Winning and Losing." Air University Lecture. August 1987.

[22]At this point, in fact, we begin to see the limitations of the overly simple, tactical level OODA loop model.

[23]In Boyd's tactical engagement loop, "orient" and "decide" are separated into two phases, however, this separation becomes difficult to distinguish in more complex operations, especially at the operational and strategic levels of war. As used in this paper, the orient and decide phases are combined and used to define the period of time necessary to generate the right force to achieve the right effects.

[24]In the 2001-2 Afghan operations, we are already seeing an impact network-centric situational awareness on this process. Aircraft were often launched and targets provided en route or, especially in the case of long-range bombers, were changed several times en route. Yet, despite the increased efficiency wrought be the changes in command, control, communications and information, the aircraft in question still had to go through the same physical processes to launch or to be "turned around" between cycles.

[25]The results of this demonstration are detailed in a two-volume study by the Center for Naval Analyses. See Angela Jewell et al. "USS *Nimitz* and Carrier Airwing Nine Surge Demonstration." Alexandria, Virginia; Center for Naval Analyses, 1998.

[26]In the Nimitz case, the airwing composed of low maintenance, quick turnaround F/A-18s that could readily undertake five or more sorties per day.

[27]The carrier airwing started with intense "flex-deck" operations, but soon discovered that the flight deck became

unworkable. They therefore switched to an aggressive concept of cyclical operations that enabled them to launch more aircraft while maintaining better order on the flight deck. Interview with RADM John Nathman, USN. February 11, 1999.

[28]This was echoed in the 2002 report of Commander Carrier Group Eight on operations in Afghanistan. The report noted that naval air strike operations had moved from a paradigm of two aircraft per aimpoint to one of two aimpoints per aircraft, in essence a fourfold increase in striking power.

[29]Comment by Colonel John D. Sullivan, USAF ret., Boeing Washington Studies and Analysis.

[30]That is, the mission and objectives toward which the command's actions are to be directed and the manner in which that mission is to be accomplished. Depending on the organization and doctrine of the forces involved, this intent may be highly specific and directive in nature or, in the context of Network Centric Warfare, it may be general enough to permit individual units to adapt to the changing battle and to take initiative to exploit fleeting battlefield or other operational opportunities.

Alberts et al. *Understanding Information Age Warfare*. pp. 167ff.

[31]Network Centric Warfare, Department of Defense Report to Congress. 27 July 2001, Washington, DC. 2001. pp. 8-8ff.

[32]In *Understanding Information Age Warfare*, Alberts et al. cite examples of the Navy's Fleet Battle Experiment Delta and the Air Force's F-15 link 16 experiments. In the former, the addition of some rudimentary shared awareness and a greater degree of self-synchronization to a routine defensive problem resulted in a tenfold decrease in the number of "leakers" at the same time as it permitted a 10 percent decrease in the number of air sorties. In the latter, the introduction of link 16-derived situational awareness, even on only a limited proportion of the F-15s engaging, resulted in a twofold increase in the number of kills.

CHAPTER 3

What Are Effects-Based Operations?

What are effects-based operations? Are they simply another name for a more sophisticated version of nodal targeting, or perhaps, another twist on the connection between attrition and "will" that operations research analysts have been puzzling over for decades? Or are they something more, a broader and more integrated approach to military operations as a whole that, when combined with new technologies and network-centric thinking, might enable us to deal differently with the challenges we face and help us to exploit our military power operations short of combat?

In one guise or another, effects-based operations have always been with us. They are what good generals, admirals, and statesmen have always tried to do: to focus on shaping the adversary's thinking and behavior rather than on simply defeating his forces. They are at the heart of the writings of Sun Tzu and of Clausewitz on military operations. Moreover, as the allusion to both military and political leaders indicates, effects-based operations are neither simply a mode of tactical level warfare nor peculiarly military in nature. They also encompass the full range of political, economic, and military actions that a nation might undertake to shape the behavior of an enemy, of a would-be opponent, and even of allies and neutrals. These actions may include destruction of an enemy's forces and capabilities, that is, attrition-based operations. However, the objective of an effects-based strategy and of those actions that advance it is not simply to destroy physical capabilities, but to induce an opponent, neutral, or ally to pursue a course of action in keeping with our interests.

The concept of effects-based operations is a broad framework which includes ideas like "nodal targeting" and "attrition-based operations," but which offers the scope and flexibility to do much more: to look at military operations in peace, crisis, and war, and to do so in the context of a cohesive overall national political, economic and military effort.

This sweeping postulate poses a set of significant questions to be addressed in this book. How would we define a working concept of effects-based operations? How might such a concept change the way in which we operate our military forces and apply our military power? How might we actually operationalize that concept both in combat and in day-to-day military operations? And finally, how should it shape our understanding of Network Centric Warfare?

Toward a Concept of Effects-Based Operations

The preceding chapters' discussions of levels of improvement in combat efficiency, attrition, means and will, and symmetry in conflict indicate that effects-based operations increase combat efficiency (1) by concentrating efforts on enemy will so as to foreshorten combat, and (2) by applying network-centric operations not just to combat but across the spectrum of conflict. In fact, these two ideas also provide significant clues as to how effects-based operations work and as to the nature of the relationship between Network Centric Warfare and effects-based operations.

Will and Behavior

Contained in the discussion of attrition-based warfare is the idea that attrition, however efficient it might be made, e.g. by nodal targeting, remains at best an indirect assault on the true determinant of a conflict's outcome: the will of the enemy to continue the struggle. This question of will is fundamental to both the symmetric and asymmetric models of conflict, but in very different ways. In the symmetric, attrition-based contests, the destruction of the physical capacity to wage war gradually deprives a foe of the physical means for continuing a struggle that he is otherwise determined to pursue. In the asymmetric contests, the destruction is aimed at creating a psychological or cognitive effect.[1] That is, in the asymmetric, essentially effects-based contest, the objective is to break the will or otherwise shape the behavior of the foe so that he no longer wishes to continue the struggle, or to disorient him so that he can no longer fight or react coherently.

While physical destruction remains a factor in effects-based operations, it is the creation of such a psychological or cognitive effect that is the true focus of the effects-based approach. It is also the real context for assessing the combat efficiency of network-centric and effects-based operations. For example, the increased precision, speed, and agility promised by the networking of sensors, forces, and commanders certainly portends an ability to undertake very rapid and very precise actions on the battlefield. The potential availability of an increased knowledge and understanding of the foe through the network points to a new ability for commanders to configure their battlefield actions so as to achieve a highly specific "effect" defined in terms of enemy behavior. In essence, the combination of network-centric capabilities with an effects-based approach appears to present us with a new potential for attacking the elements of enemy will directly and thus, circumventing or, at a minimum, diminishing our reliance on sheer physical destruction.

Operations in Peace, Crisis, and War

The discussions of attrition-based warfare also point to an obvious fact. Although our efforts to improve the combat efficiency of our forces and to apply the concept of Network Centric Warfare are focused on combat operations, the vast majority of our military operations do not involve either combat or destruction. To be certain, a military force that cannot fight the nation's wars is worth little, but it is equally true that one capable only of warfighting will be of small help in preventing wars, containing conflict, or building a stable deterrence, which are the key missions in dealing with the post-September 11th security environment.

We must also take this logic an important step further. We need to recognize that the behavior we seek to shape is not simply that of our enemies. Our military actions are and must be equally directed at shaping the behavior of friends and neutrals.[2] No successful alliance or coalition operation has ever been conducted without taking into account the impact of its actions on each of the partners. Likewise, no crisis reaction or peacekeeping operation can remain focused solely upon an aggressor without considering how other regional states will react. The political reality is that although we may focus upon defeating an enemy, our military operations almost always must also seek to support our allies and to reassure neutrals, as well as simultaneously deterring other would-be adversaries who might potentially join the foe in opposing us.

This aspect of effects-based thinking lies at the center of coalition operations of all stripes and characters.[3] In fact, thinking in terms of effects-based operations can provide a basis for looking at how military operations might best be orchestrated to shape the behavior of friends and would-be foes alike so as to prevent war and preserve peace. The effects-based approach can also provide us with a framework for considering not just how to apply network-centric operations to battle, but also how they might be used in a variety of roles across the entire spectrum of conflict from peace to crisis, to war.

The above presents a possibility for applying the new technologies and thinking of Network Centric Warfare to something more than combat and more than the destruction of an opponent's physical means of waging war. By combining the concepts of effects-based operations and Network Centric Warfare, we can address the complex interaction between nations, would-be nations, and other challengers, particularly asymmetric opponents in which destruction is either not the central factor of strategy or is to be avoided.

Defining Effects-Based Operations

The shift in focus from "weapons on target" to "focused actions" to shape the behavior of enemies and allies suggests a broad definition of effects-based operations along the following lines:

> Effects-based operations are coordinated sets of actions directed at shaping the behavior of friends, neutrals, and foes in peace, crisis, and war.

Notice that this is a definition of effects-based *operations*. Effects-based *warfare* would be the subset of these operations pertaining to combat or wartime operations,[4] while effects-based targeting (at least of the kinetic variety[5]) would be in turn a subset of effects-based warfare. Notice, too, that we are defining the operations themselves and not a "process." Logically, unless we first define what effects-based operations are, we cannot begin to address a process for how we might plan and execute them. Accordingly, we will start by defining the key terms in our effects-based concept and a set of rules derived from observed uses before trying to identify a process for carrying the concept out.

The definition of effects-based operations above emphasizes a broad understanding of actions or sets of actions and their links to behavior. The term actions is deliberately broad so that it can subsume not only military actions, but also political, economic, or other actions by a government, as well as those of non-governmental and international agencies and non-state actors.

The term *behavior* is also left broad so as to encompass not only that of foes, but also that of friends and neutrals. The latter reflects not only the links and considerations that must remain a critical facet of successful coalition operations, but also leaves the term *foes* loose enough to encompass both an adversary in combat operations and an opponent in a confrontation that does not result in combat.

These distinctions reflect the reality of today's broad-spectrum military operations and, indeed, the highly varied use of military power throughout history. The actions military forces may be called upon to undertake certainly can and must include combat and specifically strike operations, but military forces clearly do a great deal more. Indeed, the most frequent and persistent military mission has been that of preventing war, usually by deterring conflict or containing any crises that might escalate into war. In these endeavors, military forces are routinely used in conjunction with political and diplomatic action to shape the behavior of observers (friends, foes, and neutrals) either by their actions or by their very presence in a particular area. And historically, national command authorities have used these actions very deliberately to create particular effects. In brief, past actions of military forces have clearly constituted effects-based operations even though they did not involve combat.

Defining "Effect"

If we are to pursue this definition of what might be termed "full spectrum effects-based operations" into a more detailed concept, we must first be clear as to what we mean by the word effect. The term *effect* has been routinely used in military writings to imply everything from outcomes or results, to operational objectives, to the blast radius of a weapon's warhead. To make matters worse, much of the discussion of effects-based operations to date has tended to focus on kinetic effects, that is, the impact of blowing something up (a use that, in many ways, is scarcely distinguishable from the attrition-based model examined in the previous chapter).

Most frequently, the term *effect* is used in a target-planning connotation to denote the impact of a particular target's destruction upon some larger operational or strategic dimension, notably in Colonel John Warden's concept of the concentric circles of vulnerabilities in an enemy system.[6] In this context, the effect is not only that of the direct impact, that is, the destruction of the target, but also that of the chain of successive events or indirect impacts that arise from that direct impact. The process of identifying the potential nodes in this chain or cascade of subsequent consequent indirect effects and then exploiting them is the basis for most of the current nodal targeting efforts. However, in each case the focus of such effects-based nodal analysis is on using some form of target destruction[7] as the agent for generating the subsequent cascade of effects.[8]

For the purposes of this work, we will take a different tack and explore the more general operational connotation that is suggested both by the broad requirements of our security environment and by Sun Tzu's injunction that "to subdue the enemy without fighting is the acme of skill."[9] We will postulate simply that:

An effect is a result or impact created by the application of military or other power.

Such power of course may be applied at the tactical, operational, military-strategic, and/or geo-strategic level of conflict.[10]

The breadth of this definition implies that effects may be either kinetic or non-kinetic, and may equally be either physical or psychological/cognitive in nature. Thus, one effect may still be the destruction of opposing forces and capabilities. However, this broad definition of effect, like that for effects-based operations, also leaves room for many more possibilities that can stretch well beyond our still fundamentally attrition-based framework. It includes, for example, the use of maneuver to create effects and the application of military power to the creation of conventional deterrence.

Notice, too, the use of the phrase "application of military or other power." The phrase is deliberately broad so as to encompass those effects that can derive from uses of military power that do not involve destruction, or that come from the use of other forms of power, or that arise from a conjunction of different forms of power. This reflects the reality of a world in which military power is not applied in isolation but is invariably part of an overall national package.

Notice as well that the words *other power* are not further defined. This implies that we may look not only at the effects that might be wrought by other elements of national power, but also that effects may derive from applications of power by actors that are not nations, including non-state actors such as terrorists, guerrillas, and ethnic or religious liberation movements.

With these broad definitions, we have the latitude to explore both how network-centric operations might more directly shape behavior whether in combat or in situations short of combat, and how military actions complement political and economic power in creating effects.

A Stimulus and Response Model of Effects-Based Operations

These definitions of effects-based operations and effects lead to another critical question: just how do the actions we take, military and otherwise, influence the behavior of adversaries and other observers?

A psychologist looking at our efforts to define effects and effects-based operations would swiftly conclude that what we were talking about was nothing more than a series of stimulus and response interactions. That is, the behavior we seek to shape is nothing more than a response to a stimulus or set of stimuli. By threatening or administering some form of punishment or by offering some inducement, the stimuli motivate the recipient toward a particular course of action or behavior. In fact, this idea of stimulus and response is a good shorthand description of what we are attempting to do with effects-based operations. The challenge we confront in planning an effects-based operation is figuring out what the right stimulus is to produce the response or effect that we seek.

One way of shaping an opponent's behavior in a particular direction is fairly obvious. Killing a foe certainly and definitively shapes his future behavior. Similarly, the physical destruction of a foe's forces, capabilities, and infrastructure will also shape that foe's future behavior. Simply put, the removal of particular capabilities forecloses to the enemy any courses of action that might have depended on their use and thus, options that the opponent might otherwise have pursued. In other words, by destroying the capabilities, we create a physical effect that in some way delimits the enemy's physical behavior.

To take a much considered example, the destruction of Iraqi SCUD missiles and their launchers during Desert Storm would have foreclosed their use as terror weapons, a kind of behavior that the Iraqi regime might otherwise have chosen to adopt. This train of logic is at the root of much of attrition-based warfare[11] and of most nodal targeting efforts. It is also the basis for much of the current concern with "time critical strike" and "time critical targeting."

However, the 50-year history of crisis response operations signals that there is much more to the concept of effects-based operations than this rather narrow and still largely attrition-based understanding. By looking at actions in terms of stimulus and response, we open a different door. Actions become stimuli. They are no longer restricted to moves that destroy physical capabilities, but include all moves that a military force makes that might influence a decisionmaking process.

This broader concept opens the way to address not only the links between physical actions and physical effects, but also those between physical effects and effects that are psychological in nature. And, it also permits us to consider the impact of the very same actions upon friends and neutrals. Thus, while the proximate physical effect sought in hunting Iraqi SCUDs during Desert Storm was to forestall Iraqi use of those weapons, the real underlying reason was the need to prevent the Iraqi regime from undertaking a series of physical actions (attacking Israel) that would have led to a potential Israeli retaliatory strike, which could have undermined the cohesion of the coalition. From the perspective of the United States, this larger political-military dimension of SCUD hunting was a critical factor that would determine whether the American-led coalition could be held together and thus, whether the desert war itself could be conducted. In short, the importance of the political-military and psychological effects of the SCUD hunting tended to far outweigh the significance of any immediate physical effects generated by the SCUD hunting or of any military objectives that might have been met by using the assigned air sorties against other military targets. How then do we address this larger dimension of the stimulus and response model?

The Navy Warfare Development Command's draft Capstone Document takes a step in this direction by proposing that we can combine a superior knowledge of the enemy and of a given situation with the increased speed, precision, and agility to attack enemy decisionmaking. The Document suggests that we might use the newfound network-centric attributes to induce chaos, to shock the enemy into submission, or to "lock out" any coherent response as an alternative to attrition-based modes of warfare.[12]

What is significant here is the Document's acceptance of the fact that the objective of network-centric operations may no longer be in the physical domain, that is, destroying enemy forces and capabilities. Instead, the Document treats destruction as but one means of attaining the objective of setting in motion a psychological process of perceptions and decisionmaking. As the Document makes clear, network-centric operations can involve the use of military power to affect the psychological or reason and belief domains of warfare.

If we follow the logic of the Document a bit further, network-centric, effects-based operations would be about focusing knowledge, precision, speed, and agility not on more efficient destruction, but upon the enemy decisionmakers and their ability to take coherent action. The knowledge, precision, speed, and agility created by network-centric operations become the tools of a realm of effects-based operations centered squarely in the human dimension of war. At a general level of abstraction, this prospect is enticing, but the proponents of Network Centric Warfare are less clear as to exactly how the increased speed, agility, and knowledge wrought by the network translate into the needed effect. Nonetheless, there are hints throughout the literature on Network Centric Warfare and in the experimentation conducted by each of the Services as to how this might be done. For example, "getting inside the enemy's OODA loop," "lock out," and creating an "overwhelming pace" of operations are effects-based applications of network-centric capabilities. These ideas provide a jumping-off point for exploring the concept of effects-based operations.

Stimulus and Response in Military Operations

Instinctively, we can appreciate that the ability to penetrate the "enemy's OODA loop," to anticipate enemy actions and to foreclose them before they even begin would be a powerful capability. However, just how does this process take place and what have network-centric capabilities to do with it?

To answer this question, we need to return to the OODA cycle diagram outlined in Chapter 1 (see Figure 13). However, this time we will look at the cycle from a different perspective. In the diagram above, the "act" phase or the application of combat power can be seen in two ways. From the perspective of straightforward physical attrition, the "act" attacks, destroys, or in some way degrades the enemy capability to wage or sustain a war. Indeed, this is our almost instinctive reaction to the diagram. Yet, from the cognitive perspective, the same "act" can be seen as a stimulus, that is, something that enemies "observe" and must factor into their decisionmaking processes and which may have an impact on their choice of action (see Figure 14).

Notice that the action involved may be the same in both cases: blowing something up. Only now we are considering what the impact of that target's destruction will have on enemy will and psychology and not just on his physical capabilities. Logically, the more significant the action, the greater impact the stimulus will have on the enemy decisions and ultimate behavior.

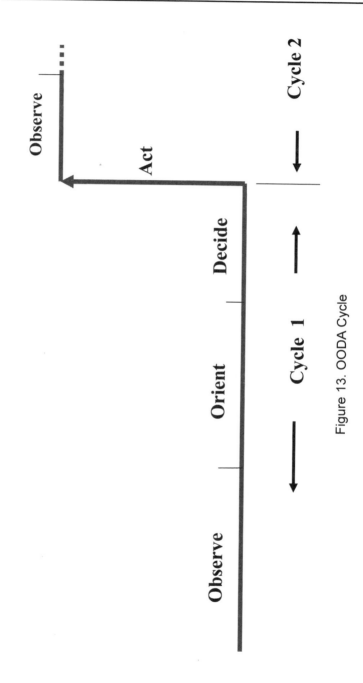

Figure 13. OODA Cycle

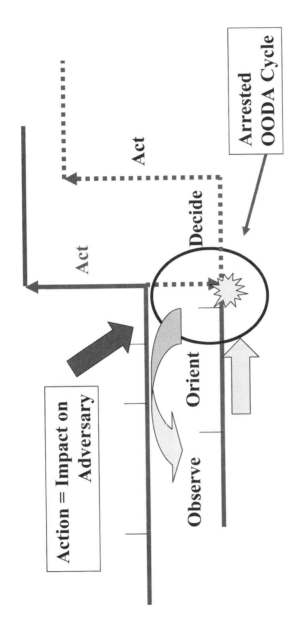

Figure 14. Interaction Between OODA Cycles

If the stimulus is significant enough, the effect may be to force enemies to reconsider their courses of action and, perhaps, to begin their OODA decisionmaking cycles all over again, re-observing, re-orienting, and re-deciding before acting. That is to say, we would not so much "get inside" their OODA loops as we would disrupt them.

We can also extend this logic. A succession of such significant stimuli might not only disrupt a foe's decisionmaking cycle but could even create an almost catatonic condition of "lock out" in which the enemy is continually re-observing, re-orienting, and re-deciding to the point that he either cannot react coherently or cannot act at all.

Midway

One historical example of a decisive stimulus and response interaction occurred during the Battle of Midway in June 1942 (see Figure 15). In that battle, intelligence derived from coded Japanese messages enabled the United States Navy to anticipate the Japanese attack, to detect enemy carriers before their own were found, and to launch an air attack first.

However, the real story here lies in the decisionmaking process in the Japanese command. When the Japanese commander, Vice Admiral Nagumo, received a reconnaissance report of an American carrier in the area (the first dotted line in Figure 15), he reconsidered the attack on Midway that was about to be launched, re-oriented his effort, and ordered his aircraft rearmed for fleet action.[13]

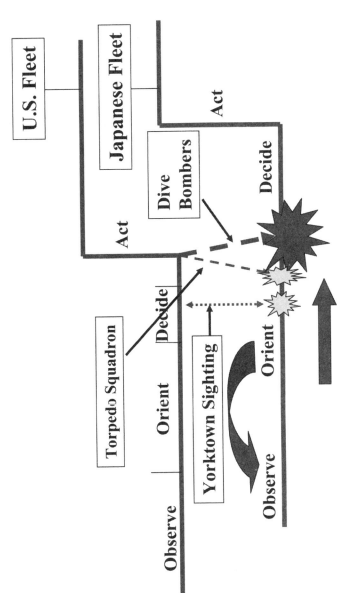

Figure 15. Battle of Midway (June 1942)

Then, as the planes were being rearmed, Nagumo's fleet was attacked by carrier-based American torpedo planes. Finally, as his protective combat air patrol was intercepting the American torpedo planes, the American bombers struck (in Figure 15, the second dotted arrow), catching the Japanese carriers with decks full of planes and bombs.

Consider what happened at Midway from the standpoint of our stimulus and response model. The Americans had planned a tightly synchronized air operation. The American dive-bombers and torpedo planes were to have attacked simultaneously so as to overwhelm and dilute the ability of the Japanese combat air patrol to defend their fleet, a standard and logical military course of action. When the different elements in the American attack became separated, this traditional, attrition-based American plan failed, but in the process of failing, it produced an entirely unplanned but fortuitous serendipity of effects-based interactions: two stimuli and then a devastating attack.

The first stimulus to impact upon Vice Admiral Nagumo's very professional military decisionmaking process was a sighting of an American carrier, the U.S.S. *Yorktown*, by a Japanese reconnaissance aircraft. The Japanese observation, which the Americans were naturally trying to avoid, presented Nagumo with the prospect of an American naval threat to his force and an opportunity for a decisive naval battle. In essence, it compelled a re-orientation of the Japanese effort. The fact that Nagumo's fleet was preparing to do something quite different (attack ground targets on Midway) meant that the aircraft for the Midway strike had to be rearmed for a fleet engagement. Nagumo, unaware of the presence of the two additional American carriers in the area, decided to risk an immediate rearming of his strike aircraft for a fleet engagement.

With the rearming underway, the second stimulus came, in the form of the attack on the Japanese fleet by unescorted American torpedo planes.[14] Despite heroic efforts by the American aviators, this costly act did not succeed in inflicting any physical damage on the Japanese fleet. However, it again intruded upon the Japanese decisionmaking cycle, this time at the level of Nagumo's subordinates, by necessitating two defensive tactical actions that proved to have serious consequences. First, the Japanese carriers were forced to maneuver radically to avoid the American torpedo attacks and in so doing had to curtail the rearming of strike aircraft and halt any aircraft launches. Second, the Japanese combat air patrol defending the fleet descended from their stations high over the fleet to chase the torpedo planes. Those decisions paved the way for a largely unopposed attack by the American dive-bombers that appeared over the Japanese fleet well after they had planned to do so, but at just the right tactical moment to take advantage of the Japanese confusion. Their attack dealt deathblows to four Japanese carriers in the ensuing 11 minutes, devastated the carrier air arm of the Imperial Japanese Navy, and proved to be the turning point in the Pacific War.

In this example, two stimuli, the sighting of the U.S.S. *Yorktown* and a tactically ineffective torpedo plane attack together had a decisive impact on the Japanese decisionmaking cycle. They occurred at just the right time to force the Japanese to re-orient their efforts and to re-decide their existing course of action, first at the operational level and then at the tactical level. The responses to the stimuli together proved fatal to Japanese ambitions in the Pacific.

Notice that in the Midway example, American success was not the result of ingenious planning or any application of a concept of effects-based operations. It grew from a series of serendipitous blunders. Yet the message is the same. A series of stimuli (that need not involve any physical destruction at all) can produce a response that will determine the outcome of a battle and perhaps a war. The stimuli unwittingly applied by the Americans had focused on the human dimension of the battle and secured a very nonlinear outcome. The challenge for network-centric and effects-based operations is to repeat such an effect reliably, predictably, and at will. How might the new technologies and network-centric thinking of our first two levels of combat efficiency help us to do this?

The question suggests a series of "what ifs." For example, if we compare the Japanese and American combat cycles at the time of the torpedo attack, it becomes evident that the cycles were out of phase (see Figure 16). Had they been in phase, both sides would have observed each other at the same time, oriented their efforts accordingly, and decided and acted similarly.[15] In that case, the

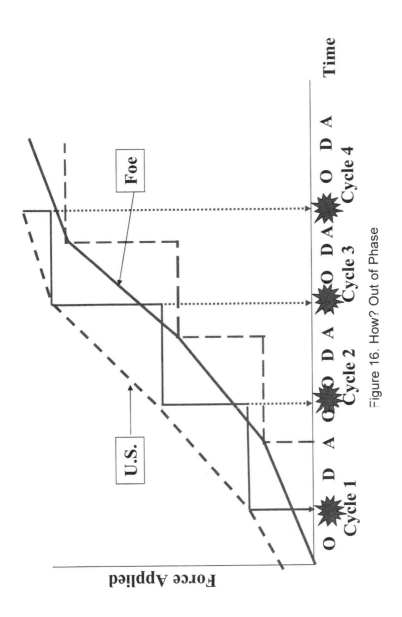

Figure 16. How? Out of Phase

American and Japanese strikes would have passed each other in the air and struck empty decks on both sides, without the disastrous consequences for the Japanese, but possibly with dire results for the smaller force of American carriers. But thanks to their intelligence coup, the American side completed their decisionmaking process in time for the torpedo bomber action to hit the Japanese when they were still re-orienting their efforts to attack the American fleet. The American success rested partially on careful preparation (the intelligence, reconnaissance, and early launch of aircraft) and in part on the good fortune of the *Yorktown* sighting and the disjointed arrival of the torpedo and dive-bomber strike elements over target.

To emulate the stimulus and response sequence of the Midway example, we would have both to time the enemy decisionmaking cycle precisely and correctly, and to coordinate our own stimuli/actions to occur at exactly the right time. This would require not only the situational awareness that in 1942 enabled the American fleet to launch its strikes first, but also the knowledge of the enemy needed to identify and exploit the critical junctures.[16] Also, we would have to be able to coordinate our actions so as to control them with an exactitude sufficient to exploit the timing of enemy decisionmaking. There is a fundamental problem here: intelligence simply will not yield such knowledge of the enemy reliably, consistently, or at all levels, nor will it be able to predict the impact of a random stimulus like the *Yorktown* sighting.[17]

How else then might the new technologies and network-centric operations enable us to create the same effect upon an enemy decisionmaking cycle as at Midway?

One solution is simply to multiply the number of opportunities to repeat the Midway incident. The more frequent the stimuli, the greater the chance that they will occur at the right time to obtain the desired effect on the enemy decisionmaking process. Shortening the length of our own overall combat power generation cycle would multiply the number of impacts on adversary decisionmaking over a given period and, thus, increase the likelihood of striking at the "right time" to disrupt the adversary's cycle (see Figure 17). But, as we have seen, the power generation side of the combat cycle can only be compressed so much. Using existing organization and doctrine, there are only so many large strike waves that can be launched in a given time and thus, only so many stimuli that can be applied.

Still another approach would be to organize and plan differently. We could, for example, build on the concepts of self-synchronization and shared situation awareness enabled by networking to launch smaller, more numerous operations, each of which might generate a stimulus sufficient to affect the adversary's decisionmaking cycles.[18] The length of the combat cycles of individual units might remain the same, but the actions of each might be staggered and overlapped so as to produce and sustain a rapid succession of stimuli being applied to enemy decisionmaking (see Figure 18).[19] This approach has an obvious limitation: the more we diminish the size of our actions, the more vulnerable

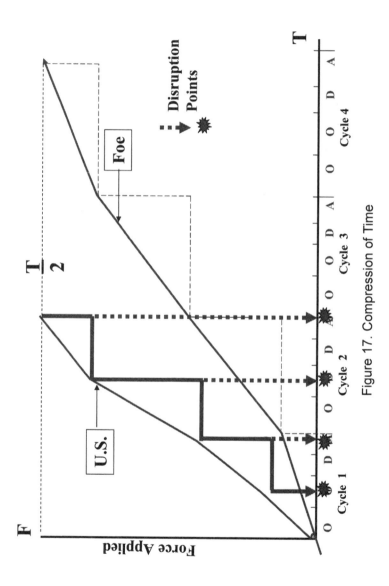

Figure 17. Compression of Time

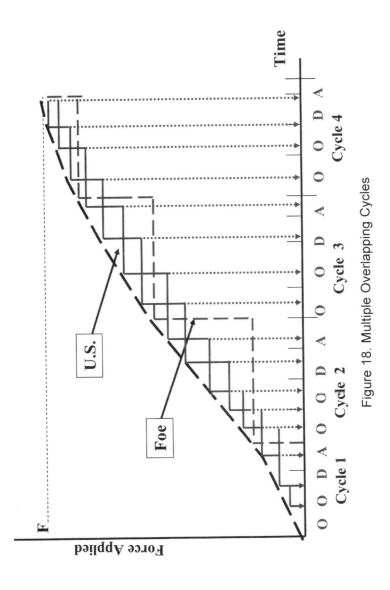

Figure 18. Multiple Overlapping Cycles

the individual units will be to being defeated in detail. However, if we were to exploit a synergy with new sensors and communications, the resulting improvements in situation awareness and commanders' knowledge of the enemy might enable us to anticipate enemy actions and optimize forces either for disruptive effect or for mutual support.

Finally, we could both multiply the number of cycles and compress the time needed to execute each cycle (see Figure 19). In essence, we would use our network-centric capability to liberate individual forces to operate at their optimum combat cycle and by so doing increase the number of combat power generation cycles we execute. Ideally, these stimuli could be made numerous and varied enough to overwhelm enemies with new developments, forcing them continually to revisit decisions, pause for further observations and perhaps, redirect efforts even to the point that they never actually take action. Indeed, this approach seems to come closest to combining the elements of self-synchronization and speed of command contained in the "Cebrowski curve" outlined in Chapter 2.

The latter two approaches in particular suggest a very different effects-based analogy from that of Midway (see Figure 20). Instead of a rapier thrust into the enemy decisionmaking process at precisely the critical time, we would unleash something akin to a swarm of bees. Even though no single unit in the attacking swarm would have a decisive impact, the overall effect would be to leave the victim swinging helplessly at attackers coming from all directions, and unable to mount any coherent defense save

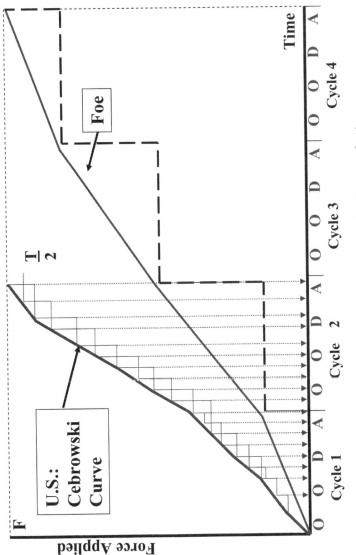

Figure 19. How? Time Compression + Multiplying Cycles

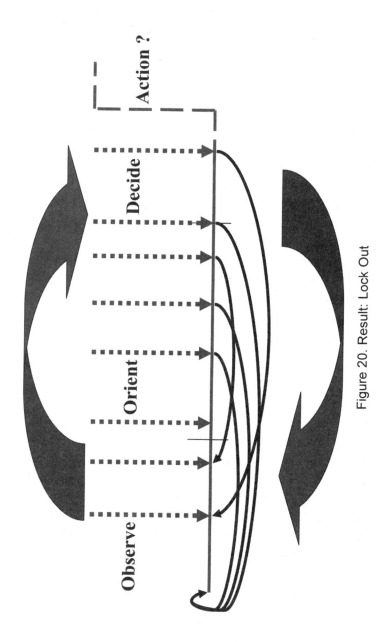

Figure 20. Result: Lock Out

retreat.[20] In essence, we provide so many stimuli that adversaries can no longer act coherently, but would be constantly forced to recycle their decisionmaking. Repeated often enough, the stimuli applied to the enemy decisionmakers could result in an almost catatonic inability to act: a lock out.

This swarm approach poses new challenges. How do we coordinate the swarm so as to achieve military objectives other than interfering in enemy decisionmaking? How do we know when to mass forces or effects so as to avoid being defeated in detail? How do we assess the effectiveness of our efforts and then feed the results of these assessments into the next round of orient, decide, and act phases? Will enemies know they have been defeated and cease to resist? Or, will they simply continue to swat at the attacks until they can no longer do so, and continue a blind attrition war?

To be effective, the swarm will need to work toward a unified set of military objectives under the same command intent. But to achieve the brief cycle times, the elements of the swarm must be self-contained and self-coordinated. In short, our forces would need to become self-synchronized and self-adaptive.[21] These are key capacities that we hope to draw from network-centric operations, but they find their nonlinear payoff in an effects-based operation directed at the human dimension of war, in this case enemy decisionmaking.

Shock and Chaos As a Response

The Midway example and the above "what ifs" point to a theoretical relationship between the technological and network-centric levels of improved combat efficiency and a third effects-based level of improvement on at least the tactical level. However, we need to take the reasoning another step to look at a more general application on the operational and strategic level.

The connection between the swarms of stimuli and lock out indicates the possibility of the stimuli creating at least one classic psychological effect encountered in military operations, the creation of chaos on the battlefield. The principle of chaos in warfare is not new.[22] Clausewitz talks in terms of exploiting the fog and friction of war to drive the enemy into a rout, that is, into a state of chaos.[23] By examining how technology-based and network-centric-based efficiency coupled with effects-based operations might stimulate and exploit battlefield chaos, we can establish at least one such general application of our stimulus and response model of effects-based operations to military operations as a whole.

Recent writings on chaos theory[24] have drawn a comparison between the concept of chaos in physical systems and its application to warfare. In exploring chaos in physical systems, the boundary region between chaos and order is particularly significant because small inputs or changes in system parameters there can have very large impacts, even causing the entire system to collapse.

If we extend this thinking to effects-based operations, this phenomenon would equate to creating a situation in which relatively small applications of military or national power at the right time might have disproportionate and potentially decisive impacts. This was certainly reflected in the Midway example, but bears a fuller explanation.

Defining the Edge of Chaos

How do we define this "edge of chaos" boundary region in terms of effects-based operations? A simple approach is to define the edge of chaos in terms of the intensity of the military operations, specifically the pace versus the scale/scope of operations. These can be plotted along the x and y axes of a graph (see Figure 21).

We can understand intuitively that the more we increase the pace of our operations (x), the more difficult they will be to manage. Similarly, the greater the scope and scale of our operations (y), the more difficult they will be to control. By extension, we can surmise that at some point along the x-axis, there are operations so rapid that we would not be able to coordinate them, and that somewhere along the y-axis are of such a size or scope that we would lose control of our forces. In brief, we can identify two transition points from order into chaos. Figuratively then, the edge of chaos would be a line drawn between these two points that touches all the combinations of scale/scope and pace of operations that define the limit of our control. Beyond the line lies the zone of chaos where operations are so large and/or so rapid that we cannot hope to execute them and remain a coherent viable force. Within the line lie all of the operations we can control, the zone of order.

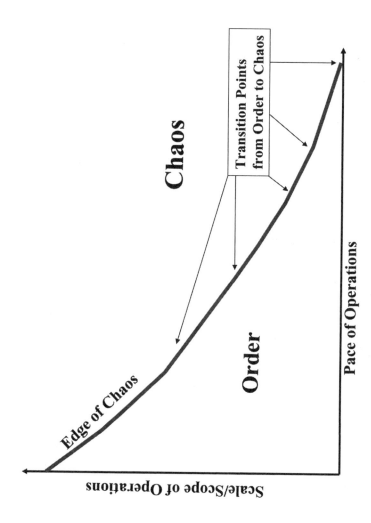

Figure 21. Defining the Edge of Chaos

In this context, chaos encompasses all those military operations that are uncontrollable, and are therefore unfocused, incoherent or chaotic, such as in an "every man for himself" battlefield rout.[25] The opposite of this battlefield chaos is order where military operations are of a scale, scope, and pace which can be controlled, coordinated, and focused on a given objective.

Exploiting the Edge of Chaos

How can we identify and exploit this operational boundary? The starting point is the realization that the edge of chaos is not fixed (see Figure 22). It changes constantly. As the U.S.S. *Nimitz* flight sortie in Chapter 2 demonstrated, the use of better organization, training, and equipment can enable a unit to operate safely at a much higher pace and scale of operations. That is significant because it implies that the edge of chaos for any unit is mutable. A highly trained and organized force using sophisticated equipment will be able to operate safely at a pace and scale of operations that would push a less well-trained and equipped force into chaos.[26] Better equipment, training, and organization enable us to drive our transition points further out along the x- and y-axes and define a new edge of chaos. This kind of improvement is what the new technologies and network centric thinking in the first two levels of combat efficiency are all about.

The mutability of the edge of chaos is significant in another respect. If we consider that the manning, training, organization, and equipment of no two units is ever likely to be identical, it implies that no

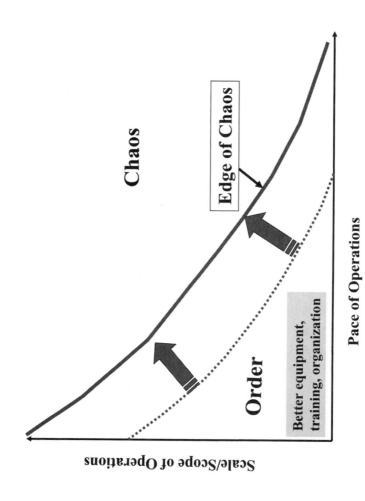

Figure 22. Defining the Edge of Chaos

two units will ever have exactly the same edge of chaos. By extension, the edge of chaos will also vary from one force to the next as each force comprises different units, differently equipped, manned, trained, and organized.

Opposing forces in any battle, therefore, are likely to have their own very different edges of chaos. This would suggest a situation more along the lines of Figure 23 in which the two very different edges of chaos of the opponents define three distinct zones.

Zone 1 is the zone of chaos. It encompasses all the combinations of scale/scope and pace of operations in which neither side will be able to control or direct its actions in any coherent way.

Zone 2 defines a complex, asymmetric region in which the better-equipped and trained force and/or the force with the better tactical, operational, and strategic concept of operations can coordinate its operations while the less-well-trained and equipped or the less-well-adapted side cannot.

Zone 3 is the zone of order. It encompasses all the combinations of scale/scope and pace of operations that both sides will be able to manage more or less comfortably.

By definition, neither side can operate successfully in Zone 1. Conversely, neither side would derive any particular advantage from operating in a way that permits its enemy an orderly and focused response in Zone 3.[27] By contrast, the boundary region, Zone 2, offers the possibility for the kinds of disproportionate impact foreseen in chaos theory. It

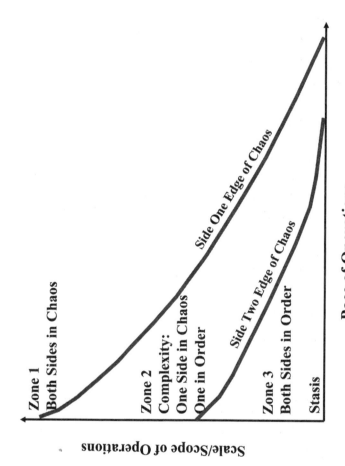

Figure 23. Operations on the Edge of Chaos

is a regime of inherent asymmetry in which the less capable side can be confronted with a dilemma. If it attempts to respond in kind, it risks losing control and lapsing into chaos, but if it fails to respond, it will likely be pummeled into submission by its opponent. At best, the asymmetry condemns the less capable actor to pre-planned, time-late responses.[28]

In essence, the diagram describes what we hope to obtain by adopting new technologies and integrating them into a network-centric concept of operations. The goal is to create an information and speed advantage sufficient to comfortably handle a scale, scope, and pace of operations that is manifestly beyond that of any prospective opponent, and then to exploit that superiority by operating in that advanced zone of complexity. What has this got to do with chaos, effects-based operations, and the exploitation of the human or psychological dimension of warfare?

Chaos and Behavior

If we look at this three-zone model from the perspective of effects-based operations, this logic can be carried another step. Our exploitation of the zone of complexity need not be limited to destruction and more efficient attrition. It can also serve to exploit the human dimension of warfare. For example, if we were consistently able to operate beyond the other's edge of chaos, we may be able to induce a state of despair in which further resistance either is, or appears to be, futile. Focusing efforts on precisely those psychological vulnerabilities most likely to drive the enemy into chaos can accelerate this process.

One good historical example is the 1805 Battle of Trafalgar in which Admiral Horatio Nelson destroyed the combined French and Spanish fleets. The crux of the action was Nelson's bold movement to break through the French-Spanish battle line in two places and then concentrate his forces on bite-sized portions of it (see Figure 24). Although the idea of defeating the enemy in detail is certainly understandable in the context of attrition-based warfare, the real key to Nelson's success was the effect that his bold maneuver had on the French and Spanish ability to control their forces and the chaos it created.

The basis for Nelson's confidence that his own forces could undertake such a risky operation and

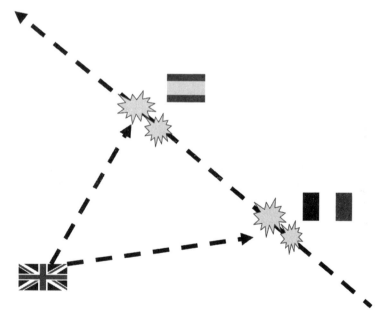

Figure 24. Battle of Trafalgar (1805)

be successful was what could be described as a "cerebral networking" among Nelson and his senior captains. That network had been formed by years of combat operations together. Nelson was confident that all of his subordinates would perceive the developing situation in the same way, that they would have a shared situational awareness.[29] He was equally sure that his commanders not only understood his intent, but that they would aggressively exploit any opening in the enemy line and carry out mutually supportive actions without further direction. For that reason, Nelson could limit his final directive before the battle to a single, inspiring, if not otherwise very helpful, "England expects every man to do his duty." Nothing more was needed. The commanders knew what to do.

This contrasts sharply with the situation of the opposing commander, Admiral Pierre de Villeneuve. His force was larger and in many ways technologically superior, but it lacked any semblance of the cerebral networking Nelson had forged. The French commanders had largely spent the war years blockaded in port. They distrusted Admiral Villeneuve even as Villeneuve distrusted his own judgment. Added to this was the problem of coordinating the French fleet's operations with those of a Spanish fleet, with which the French had never before operated.

Under these circumstances, the best Villeneuve could do was to form his combined fleet into a conventional 18th-century line of battle, in which two ordered, parallel battle lines would pound each other until one or the other struck their colors, blew up, or sank. When Nelson refused battle on these terms and instead broke through the French-Spanish line, the pace of operation that he forced on the French-Spanish immediately exceeded their ability to cope and invalidated their numerical superiority. Villeneuve largely lost control of his forces. In such conditions, his ships only became part of general chaos, and in fact, a substantial proportion never entered the battle.

If Trafalgar had been simply a classic symmetric, attrition-based contest, the outcome might have been determined by the fact that the French and Spanish had more ships, more guns, and a much heavier broadside throw weight.[30] Instead, it hinged on the ability of each side to respond not simply to the stimulus of an attacking fleet, but with the pace of those stimuli. When that pace proved to be more than the less well-trained and less confident French and Spanish fleets could handle, they lost.

If we compare this to the Japanese reactions in the Midway example, it becomes evident that we are dealing with two different kinds of psychological impacts.[31] In the Japanese case, the fleet was well-trained and equipped and had operated extensively together and was operating against a numerically inferior opponent. The stimuli presented by the Americans did not result in chaos but nevertheless forced the Japanese commanders into a series of bad decisions. In the case of Trafalgar where the French and Spanish force was well-equipped but not well-trained and had not operated extensively together, the stimuli presented by Nelson's attack so overwhelmed the force that once combat was joined, the French commander was unable to direct the battle in any coherent way. In both cases, the numerically inferior force won the day. In both cases, it was the impact on decisionmaking that appears to have been decisive.

Chaos, Stimulus and Response, and Asymmetric Warfare

In the Battle of Trafalgar, the range of combinations of scale/scope and pace of operations that the French and Spanish could handle, their edge of chaos, clearly lay entirely inside that of the British Fleet. This gave the British the decisive advantage in what was otherwise a symmetric contest. This leads us to another question. Both Trafalgar and Midway were essentially symmetric confrontations in which two very similar forces fought each other to a conclusion. Indeed, the edge of chaos diagram that we have used seems to assume a situation in which the two opponents have similar objectives and forces, but in which one or the other has superiority in information and speed of command. What if the opponents had been asymmetric?

In an asymmetric contest, there are likely to be two major differences from this state of affairs. The forces are not likely to be similar in character and the strategies and courses of actions followed by each side are likely to be very different. If we were to depict this in terms of two edges of chaos, it is unlikely that one side's edge would fall entirely inside that of the other (see Figure 25). Instead, there would be some kinds of operations in which one side could engage but in which the other could not or would not engage, e.g. terrorism. It is also likely that one side might be able to generate a pace and scope of operations that exceeded that of the other in a particular area. For example, a large conventional military might be able to mount and control a scale of operations that a guerrilla force could not, but the guerilla force in turn might be able to generate a pace of small-scale operations that the larger force could not. This suggests that in an asymmetric contest the two edges of chaos might well cross each other to produce not just a single zone in which one side was able to dominate, but a second asymmetric zone, in which the advantage was reversed.

This reversal underlines a factor evident in both the Trafalgar and Midway examples. The side that is bigger and better equipped does not necessarily win the battle. Faster, better, and technologically superior capabilities may still leave room for successful competition. One side in the conflict might choose to fight asymmetrically. For example, they might choose to trade centralized control for speed and scope of operations, that is, to define a niche within which they can compete.

In so doing, that side might voluntarily forego some of its ability to mass effects on a specific objective. If the desired effect derived from the pace and scope of the attacks rather than from the amount of destruction, or from cumulative impacts rather than from specific, then this trade-off may be very acceptable. In other words, the challenger could confront a technologically superior enemy by creating a new asymmetric zone in which small,

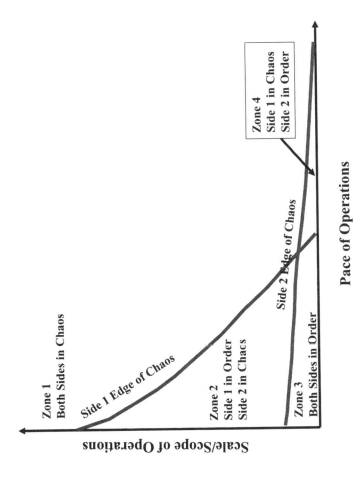

Figure 25. Intersecting Edges of Chaos

decentralized units could operate successfully, but in which an opponent using large formations under centralized control could not respond coherently.

The importance of this fourth asymmetric zone is even more evident if we plot the respective edges of chaos on a graph with three axes: one for pace, one for scale, and a separate orthogonal axis for scope (see Figure 26).

This depiction highlights two aspects of decentralization: forces can be broken into smaller self-synchronized units; and, they can be dispersed over a wide area to make a coordinated and timely response by the other side more difficult. This corresponds rather closely to Maoist theory of guerrilla warfare. Guerrillas use dispersed formations so small that they can no longer be targeted effectively by heavier government forces. These bands then conduct many small raids so rapidly that the raiders are gone before opposing forces can be brought to bear. Since the desired psychological effect, the attrition of an opponent's will, depends more on pace and scope than on damage to specific targets, control can remain highly decentralized and still succeed. This was the essential problem the United States confronted in Vietnam.

To this example, we must add another, for the model corresponds rather closely to what might be expected of terrorist operations below even the level of military operations represented by guerrilla warfare. In a terrorist operation, the emphasis is on an even more widely dispersed force with whatever control and support needed provided via a loose

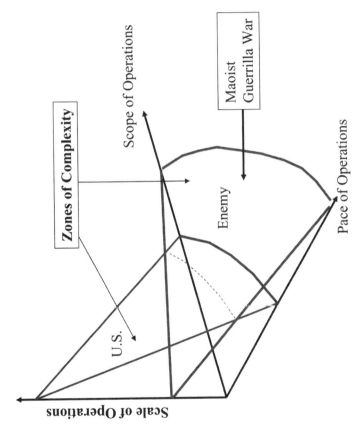

Figure 26. Edge of Chaos – Three Axes

nodal network in which each node functions in a manner that is largely separate from the others.

This latter decentralization can be expected to vary with the amount of support and direction needed. For example, to the extent that local materials and personnel can carry out assigned operations on their own, or to which the timing of the operations need not be very precise, the individual nodes can function at a minimum scale and with little direction. The more precise the timing required, the greater the scale, and greater the necessity for nonlocal materiel such as weapons of mass effect (WME), the less able the terrorist organization will be to decentralize and the more vulnerable it will be to our own coordinated operations.

These examples imply a new understanding of chaos as not necessarily a loss of control over one's forces. It could also mean a situation in which the size of the forces involved and the length of the delays associated with generating and using them consistently prevent one side from accomplishing its objectives.

...and Network-Centric Operations?

How do network-centric operations address this low-tech asymmetry? One answer is based on the knowledge and situation awareness brought to bear by the network. If the guerrillas' actions or the terrorists' actions can be anticipated or instantly detected and responded to, then much of what guerrillas and terrorists gain by dispersing and decentralizing can be negated. In effect, networking permits the high-tech side to move its edge of chaos further out along the x- and z-axes of the diagram until decentralization no longer confers any advantage on the guerrillas or terrorists. Also, where the guerrillas, urban fighters, or terrorists might opt for increasing the number and decreasing the size of their operations by decentralization, a network-centric force might do the same (for example, by resorting to a ground war of small units aided by superior situation awareness).

Alternatively, the network-centric force could increase its pace, using the network to manage high-speed complex operations. For example, given the relatively slow pace of operations that might be expected of a decentralized terrorist organization, the network-centric force could act and react faster. In each case, network-derived situation awareness combined with self-synchronization would enable the network-centric forces to operate as a self-adjusting, military version of the "complex adaptive system" while at the same time retaining the ability to mass superior effects at will.

Fleshing Out the Concept

What we have done in the preceding pages is to layout a rough framework for a working concept of effects-based operations and to show how that concept links the first two levels of improvement in combat efficiency to a third and larger effects-based efficiency. The historical examples of Midway and Trafalgar further demonstrate how the concept is in fact reflected in real-world operations. We can see in the responses of Admirals Nagumo and de Villenueve to the stimuli presented by the actions of Admirals Spruance and Nelson and their forces. Yet there is a great deal missing here. We do not know what went on in the minds of the four admirals, of their staffs, or of their subordinate commanders that may have influenced or decided the responses chosen. This is to say that we have not yet traced our working concept through the cognitive domain, the area in which the nonlinear psychological effects that we seek to create and exploit actually reside.

---

[1]As used here, the psychological effect denotes all of the non-physical impacts resulting in behavior, while the cognitive effect refers to the impact on a decisionmaking process.

[2]In this "shaping" of friends and neutrals, military actions fall into much the same role as diplomatic actions, not compelling or forcing a certain behavior, but of reassuring or supporting so as to induce it.

[3]This factor, sometimes dubbed the CNN factor after the role played by the media in Desert Storm, has been an increasingly critical part of military operations and is likely to grow as Information Age technology links a global public. This is a key element of the "globalization" process addressed in Chapter 1.

[4]Alberts et al. make a similar distinction between network-centric operations, the application of network-centric technologies and thinking to all military operations, and Network Centric Warfare, their applications to the subset of those operations involving combat.
Alberts et al. *Understanding Information Age Warfare.* p. 58.

[5]Targeting is used here in its most frequent context of attacking and inflicting damage on physical entities. However, it should be noted that the term may also be applied in the sense of information operations that cause no physical damage.

[6]Col. John A. Warden III, USAF. "The Enemy as a System." *Airpower Journal.* Spring, 1995. pp. 41ff.

[7]This includes the use of offensive information operations to

destroy or corrupt an adversary's computer or other electronic systems, even though no visible physical destruction may be entailed.

[8]The question of direct and indirect effects and the problems of planning cascades of effects in the context of an effect-based operation will be explored in some detail in Chapter 7.

[9]Samuel B. Griffith. *Sun Tzu, The Art of War.* Oxford, 1963. p. 77.

[10]The word conflict is used here in its international relations sense of a contravening interaction between opposing actors that may or may not involve military action and may or may not include inflicting damage.

[11]In the Third Punic War (199 B.C.), for example, the Romans foreclosed any further hostile behavior on the part of the Carthaginians by destroying the entire power base, tearing down the city, and selling the population into slavery.

[12]Ullman, Harlan and James Wade, Jr. *Shock & Awe: Acheiving Rapid Dominance.* Washington, DC: NDU. 1996.

[13]Nagumo's force had already been under attack from U.S. land-based aircraft, but considered the real threat and opportunity to be the American carriers.
Prange, Gordon W. et al. *Miracle at Midway.* New York, 1982. pp. 231ff.

[14]The torpedo planes attacked in three uncoordinated waves the effect of which was to keep the defending Japanese fighters at sea-level for a protracted period of time.
Prange, p. 257.

[15]This is to say, the technologies that might have permitted one or the other side to act faster or with more power (level one efficiency) or to comprehend the situation and decide faster (level two efficiency) would have been the decisive factors.

[16]In the Midway example, because the forces were very similar in character, the length of the U.S. and Japanese OODA cycles would have been roughly similar. In a conflict between two dissimilar forces, that would not be the case making the OODA cycle that much more difficult to predict.

[17]Despite the best surveillance picture or situational awareness we can generate, the ultimate determinate of the speed and direction of the enemy decisionmaking cycle will be the enemy himself. Such knowledge of the enemy is not the result of sensor data but of analysis based in large part on sporadic human intelligence reporting. We cannot, therefore, depend on having the intelligence when we need it or, indeed, on collecting the needed data at all.

[18]Note that in each case the total amount of force applied

remains constant and what varies is the way in which that force is used.

[19]Indeed, this begins to approximate the optimum combat power performance curve used by VADM Cebrowski in the graphic used to demonstrate the impact of self-synchronization that we saw in Chapter 2.

[20]In fact the desperate actions of the American escort carrier force attempting to block the advance of a powerful Japanese battleship force toward Leyte Gulf in October 1944 provide just such an example. In that engagement, the threatened escort carriers launched any aircraft that could fly, including those that were unarmed or armed with munitions that could have no possible physical effect on the heavily armored Japanese force. The American pilots attacked the armored bridges of the Japanese ships with ineffectual machine gun fire, and when their meager ammunition was spent, resorted to "buzzing" the Japanese ships without firing. The effect was to so confuse and bewilder the Japanese commander, VADM Kurita, that he ordered the withdrawal of the force, even as it was on the verge of victory.

Friedman, Kenneth I. *The Afternoon of the Rising Sun, The Battle of Leyte Gulf*. Novato, California. 2001. pp. 283ff.

[21]Both of these factors were key aspects to the success of the American air attacks during the Leyte Gulf Battle. Pilots, who very well appreciated the nature of the danger the Japanese force posed, were merely told to attack the enemy with whatever they had. The perpetual buzzing of the Japanese bridges was the result.

Friedman, p. 285.

[22]It should be noted that the idea of inducing chaos will hardly be a new concept to ground forces for whom the primordial challenge is to control very large numbers of actors in battle. In the ground context, "breaking the enemy will to resist" equates to causing the enemy to lose control and disintegrate into a chaotic "every man for himself" rout. While this understanding remains operative to be sure, the focus of the chaos sought here lies at the operational and even the strategic level even more than of the battlefield.

[23]Watts, Barry. *Clausewitzian Friction and Future War*. Washington, DC; National Defense University. 1996. pp.105ff.

[24]Maj. Glenn James, USAF, uses the example of a water faucet that will drip with an annoying regularity. As the flow of water is increased, the frequency of the drip increases but the regularity remains. However, when the flow is increased even minutely beyond some definable rate, the drops no longer have time to form and the drip changes abruptly to a sporadic (chaotic) flow. The very minor increase in flow has caused the

physical system to become chaotic.

James, Maj. Glenn, USAF. *Chaos Theory, The Essentials for Military Applications*. Newport Paper 10, Naval War College, Newport, R.I. 1997. p. 15-16.

[25]It is worth making a distinction here between a tactical level chaos that induces the enemy to take flight and a strategic level chaos that may induce irrational behavior by a power with nuclear weapons. Between these two extremes lies a zone in which inducing "shock and awe" is a tool that can be used to achieve specific effects calculated to support our political and military objectives. However, implicit in the idea of effects is a risks-versus-gains analysis that applies to chaos as to all other effects.

[26]In the Nimitz demonstration, the air wing set out to conduct "flex-deck" operations which were thought to offer the fastest turnaround and sortie generation. What they soon discovered was that this "clobbered" the deck making it difficult to move even as many aircraft as they routinely did. In effect, they had reached the edge of chaos for flex-deck operations. Then, they adapted to the new requirement, and instituted a new form of accelerated cyclic operations that not only avoided the previous bottlenecks but enabled them to operate comfortably at the new higher pace.

Nathman, Op. Cit.

[27]In a strategic nuclear confrontation such as those during the Cold War, it was necessary to operate in this zone of order so as to avoid the risk of an irrational act or uncontrolled escalation.

[28]One example of this is the October 1973 Arab-Israeli War. The Egyptian Army's "edge of chaos" could not hope to match that of the Israelis. Therefore, the Egyptians were forced to resort to a highly planned pre-emptive operation in which virtually all actions were pre-scripted. That gave them an initial success in crossing the Suez Canal, but left them largely incapable of responding to Israeli counter-action.

[29]The two fleets took more than three hours to close. This would have allowed ample time for the commanders to observe the enemy line and any potential gaps in that line that they might exploit. The cerebral networking provided a common understanding of how such gaps might be exploited and how each might provide mutual support and exploit any further opportunities that might be observed during the battle.

Marcus, G.J. *The Age of Nelson, The Royal Navy 1793-1815*. New York. 1971. pp. 276ff.

[30]The British advantage also stemmed from how they used the capabilities at hand. This was not only at the operational

level, e.g. the cerebral networking of commanders, but also at the tactical level in gun handling. Intense training enabled British ships to get off almost twice as many rounds per minute as their French and Spanish counterparts, essentially nullifying the French-Spanish armament advantage. This amounts to a 19th-century equivalent of the Nimitz strike sortie generation demonstration and reflects the degree to which training can change the edge of chaos of a given unit. Ibid.

[31]It is significant to note that, in our Midway example, the reactions of Japanese commanders remained very professional throughout the engagement. There was no panic. Japanese forces remained under control and withdrew in good order. Their defeat in the battle stemmed from a series of responses that were impelled by the timing of the American stimuli. Each decision/response was perfectly rational in its own right, but foreclosed options that, had they been pursued, might have changed the course of the battle. For example, Nagumo's decision to rearm the aircraft on deck foreclosed an immediate launch of the aircraft, which might have made the carriers less vulnerable. The combat air patrol commander's decision to descend to attack the incoming American torpedo planes decimated that threat, but it prevented an effective defense against the American dive-bombers.

Pranger, pp. 257ff.

CHAPTER 4

Shaping Behavior: Operations in the Cognitive Domain

The key to our working concept of effects-based operations as well as to the non-linear payoff that we hope to obtain from Network Centric Warfare is a process that takes place in the mind of man. Our definition of effects-based operations proposed that there are actions that shape "the behavior of friends, neutrals and foes." This cause and effect link was certainly apparent in the examples of Midway and Trafalgar, but to make the concept a useful tool, we must understand not simply that a response occurred, but also why it produced the effect that it did. Without this connection, we cannot replicate the actions required to change behavior successfully or make any reliable use of the concept. To address the "why" of the stimulus and response, we must understand something of the cognitive processes involved in observing and responding to a stimulus.

157

Beyond the OODA Loop

Colonel John Boyd's OODA loop reduces the cognitive process to a tactical short hand of Observe, Orient, Decide, and Act. In this OODA loop context, we can intuitively understand, for example, that operating faster than our opponent confers an advantage. Indeed, in the context of the one-versus-one, air-to-air engagement from which Colonel Boyd originally derived the OODA loop, the mental processes involved seem fairly clear and straightforward.[1] The fighter pilot first observes his opponent's presence or action, orients himself to deal with it, decides upon a course of action, and then acts to execute it. The opposing pilot similarly observes that action or reaction, orients himself to deal with it, decides on a course of action, and acts. Victory then goes to the pilot who can act and react faster. Similar tactical level OODA loops can be divined for everything from a submarine engagement to a firefight on the ground. However, the OODA loop construct also leaves some critical questions unanswered. For example, at what pace of operations might we expect to overwhelm that opponent and why would this be so? How might we shock that opponent, induce despair, or break his will? It should be apparent that there are very real limits to how far can we take this somewhat simplistic tactical level example.[2]

The general concept of an OODA loop or decisionmaking cycle certainly has value when applied to operational level interactions and higher, as in the Battle of Midway. Yet, it is also evident in both the Midway and Trafalgar examples that these operational level interactions are vastly more complex than the one-to-one, air-to-air engagement, and that the complexity increases still more at higher levels. Moreover, however decisive Midway and Trafalgar may have been at the operational level of war, neither ended the war. It took another 3 years after Midway to defeat Japan, and the Napoleonic wars dragged on for another 10 years after Trafalgar.[3] Both battles were but one factor in a complex series of factors that determined the nature of the decisionmaking at the military-strategic and geo-strategic levels.[4]

The military-strategic and geo-strategic dimensions of the two examples point to the need to consider actions in terms of a multi-level, multi-arena impact that spans friends and neutrals as well as enemies. After all, this larger framework is the context into which each of the battles ultimately had to fit, but this necessary contextualization also presents a very different set of problems from the tactical military action we are accustomed to considering. Not only do these different dimensions of upper level interaction operate on an entirely different timeline from that of tactical OODA loop engagements, but they force us to consider that the nature and timing of actions and reactions are at least as important as their speed. They also force us to think not just in terms of the personal behavior of the other pilot in a fighter engagement, but also in terms of institutional or organizational behavior of increasing complexity.[5] In fact, the farther we move away from the tactical level OODA loop, the more we are obliged to look to what might be termed "operations in the cognitive domain."

Operations in the Cognitive Domain

The cognitive process by which humans perceive and decide is clearly at the center of the human dimension of war. It is the ultimate locus of the non-linear effects we hope to obtain from both network-centric operations and effects-based operations. Our ability to understand this process is the basis both for any hope of foreshortening combat by convincing an adversary to yield and for determining how we might create effects without fighting. Finally and perhaps most significantly for our current strategic environment, it is the battleground for asymmetric conflict in peace, crisis, and war.

Three Domains of Conflict

The 1999-2000 work of the Information Superiority Working Group sponsored by the office of the Secretary of Defense (C3I) and the March 2001 workshop on "sensemaking" conducted by the Department of Defense's Command and Control Research Program (CCRP) and the Command, Control, Communications, and Intelligence Technical Sub-Committee of the American Institute for Aeronautics and Astronautics (AIAA)[6] took the OODA loop several steps further. They described the process of decisionmaking involved in the OODA loop in terms of three different domains: a physical domain, an information domain, and a cognitive domain (see Figure 27).

All military operations were considered to occur in the context of these three domains. Physical military actions took place (the physical domain), the actions

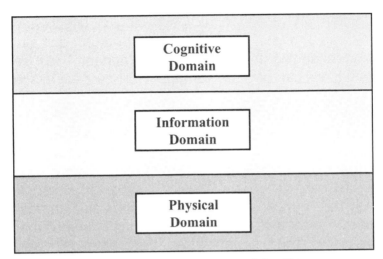

Figure 27. Three Domains of Conflict

were detected and reported to higher authority (the information domain), and decisions as to how to respond were made by commanders at various levels (the cognitive domain). However, there was also recognition in the working groups that the domains extended well beyond just military operations to all of the actions that a state, government, or a non-state actor such as a terrorist organization might take. By extension, the domains might be considered to subsume all of the processes involved in any effects-based operation and, by further extension, all of those processes that network-centric operations must serve if they are to have any value.

The three domains provide a general framework for tracing what actually goes on in the stimulus and response process inside human minds and human organizations, and how physical actions in one domain get translated into psychological effects and then into a set of decisions in another domain. Understanding this process is important because with it, we can begin to comprehend how people and organizations perceive a stimulus or action and why they respond or react in the way they do and thus, how we might shape behavior.

The Physical Domain

As the name suggests, the physical domain encompasses all the physical actions or stimuli that become the agents for the physical and psychological effects we seek to create[7] (see Figure 28).

These physical actions can include a military force that is simply in the right place at the right time to have an impact. Such a force becomes an object to

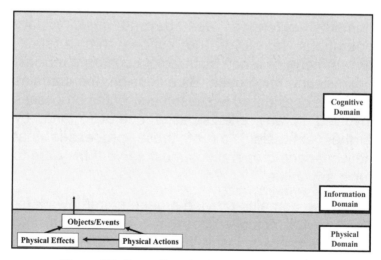

Figure 28. Operations in the Physical Domain

be observed and reported, as in the case of the Japanese reconnaissance reports of the American carrier *Yorktown* during the Battle of Midway. It may also take the form of a military operation, such as the follow-on American torpedo plane attack on the Japanese fleet, an event that is observed and affects subsequent decisions.

However, we must not restrict our consideration to military forces and military operations. If we look at the military-strategic and geo-strategic dimensions of the battles of Midway and Trafalgar, it becomes clear not only that these naval actions were only part of a much larger military effort, but also that the entire military effort was part of an overall national effort. Thus, the physical actions we must consider are not only those of military forces, but also those that occur in other arenas of national power and may be political and economic in nature, as well as military.

If we carry this into the context of the three domains, then the actions in the physical domain may be political, economic, and/or military in nature, and all must be equally considered to be objects or events in the manner of the diagram in Figure 28. All can certainly affect the opponent's decisionmaking process or, in the context of the workshop's deliberations, can change the way in which an opponent or other observer understands or makes sense of a developing situation.

At the other end of the action-reaction cycle, the physical domain also encompasses those physical effects created by our actions. These are of two types: the direct effect or actual physical impact of an action; and the indirect or derivative physical effects that flow from and are caused by the direct effect. All of these successive effects are physical in nature and lie in the physical domain.[8]

To understand how these objects, events, and physical effects shape decisions, however, we must move beyond the physical domain to the information and cognitive domains.

The Information Domain

The information domain includes all of the means by which we become aware of the objects and events or of a situation as a whole. In tactical terms, this domain encompasses the essential elements first of monitoring the battlespace and then of managing our actions so as to achieve our military objectives. The information domain includes all sensors that monitor physical actions and collect data. It also includes all the means of collating or contextualizing that data to create an information stream, and all the means of conveying, displaying, and disseminating that information. In essence, the information domain is the means by which a stimulus is recognized and conveyed to a human or to a human organization[9] (see Figure 29).

Although this process of collecting and reporting to create a shared situation awareness tends to be the focus of most of our attention in network-centric operations, it is just half of what transpires in the information domain. This domain also encompasses all of the means of conveying the

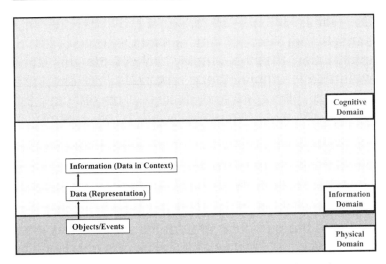

Figure 29. Operations in the Information Domain

decisions, plans, and orders that translate a cognitive response into physical actions. This domain is the focal point of efforts to apply new information technologies to tie the disparate elements of the information domain together and thereby permit faster, more flexible, and more precise network-centric military operations.[10]

A Surveillance System of Systems

There is a critical caveat to this process of collecting and conveying data and information and the "awareness" that it produces. In order to illustrate that we are all prisoners of our own senses, Plato uses the example of a man confined in a cave since birth who cannot see the "real" world but only the shadows that the "real" world makes on the wall of his cave.[11] Similarly, in observing the physical actions that will drive decisions, we are all prisoners of not only our senses, but also of the sensors and sources of information that we employ, and of the decisions we make to employ these resources. We can think of these resources and decisions as defining the nature of a surveillance system or system of systems of sensors.[12] Each sensor, like our own senses, sees only part of what may be transpiring at any given time. Any individual sensor may be limited to a specific geographic area or physical environment, just as a surveillance satellite can only see the particular area of the earth that is in its field of view, or only what is in line of sight. Equally, the sensor may monitor only a specific set of physical phenomena such as a particular part of the overall frequency spectrum.

The success or failure of the surveillance system does not hinge on any single all-encompassing sensor, but on how each sensor in a network interacts with the others to provide the information needed, much as vision, hearing, touch, taste, and smell conspire to present a picture to the human mind. Indeed, this balancing and networking of sensors is one of the core principles of network-centric operations, with each sensor contributing some part to an integrated whole. This is to say that the capability of the surveillance system as a whole is a function of the capabilities of the sensors we chose to include in that system of systems. Thus, the probability of detecting a particular object or event at any given time would depend on the decisions made regarding what the surveillance system needs to detect, which sensors are needed to assure such detection, where they are deployed, and how they report and to whom.

This is where we begin to straddle the line between the information domain (in which actions are observed and reported) and the cognitive domain (in which decisions are made).

The Nature of Awareness

At the center of the cognitive domain decisions regarding the nature and organization of the surveillance system are three questions: What are we trying to do? What kind and level of awareness do we need to do it? And, what information do we need in order to create that awareness? The answers to these questions determine how we balance the various sensors and sources in our surveillance system of systems so as to achieve an adequate level of awareness.

Our awareness requirements will probably revolve around acquiring a defined level of data and information on our security environment. In a tactical combat environment, this data and information would likely include the location, activities, and capabilities of our own forces and those of our allies and coalition partners (Blue), opponents or potential opponents (Red), and any other significant player (White) (see Figure 30). We would further seek to situate these observers in an environment that might extend to include factors such as terrain or sea-state, weather, lighting, and what we know of the intentions of each actor.[13]

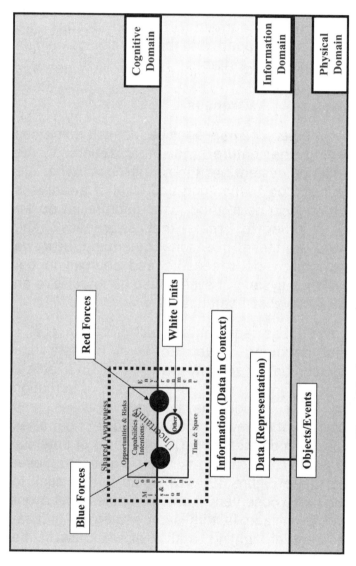

Figure 30. Operations in the Information Domain

Even for a country as wealthy as the United States, the resources to be applied to the task of observing will never be unlimited. Thus, the decisions we make regarding the situation awareness to be created will always involve balancing the data gathering and information resources available on the one hand with the degree of uncertainty (or perhaps ignorance) that we are willing to accept on the other.

The impact of such decisions is far-reaching. The missions we can undertake, the tactics and strategy we can support, and the threat environment within which we can operate will be constrained by the situational awareness we create. The fighter pilot in our OODA loop will be able to observe only to the degree that his sensors or some external input enable him to do so.[14] These sensor-based constraints will also be carried over into planning. A guerrilla band or a terrorist organization, to take an example, might not be able to plan on the availability of timely, comprehensive satellite data. But, they might deal with this constraint by redefining their strategy and mode of operations to take into account the degree of shared awareness possible with the data and information that they could obtain.

This shared situation awareness also has temporal and spatial dimensions. In creating a surveillance system of systems, we would also need to strike a balance between the extent of the physical and geographic space that requires monitoring and the timeliness of the reporting possible. With a finite number of sensors, as the geographic area to be searched increases, the more the sensors will have to be dispersed, the more frequent will be the holes in coverage, and the lower will be the probability of detection.

Notice that in each of the above cases, the awareness produced by the sensors is shaped by the way in which the risks and opportunities of a given strategy or operation are weighed. That is, the character of the information domain and the nature of what can or cannot be observed are irrevocably tied to the processes of decisionmaking in the cognitive domain.

Human Information

In the discussion of the information domain thus far, we have focused on the problems of sampling the physical phenomena of the battlespace environment using sensors that are mechanical and electronic in nature. However good these sensors are or may become, they have two major limitations:

- First, they focus in large part on an immediate and distinctly military battlespace consisting of the tactical picture needed for the operational level of war. But this means that the system only monitors and reports a relatively small proportion of the total data that might be available on objects, and then in only one sector of the physical domain.

- Second, they largely ignore what might be termed *human information*,[15] the panoply of data on objects and events derived from human sources.

This broader definition of human information extends to the full range of data and information from human sources in much the same way as a distinction is drawn between raw sensor data that is collated to create information and analyzed to create intelligence. However, it presents a new problem and challenge for the information and cognitive domains. Human-derived information is by nature uncertain and, to some degree, ambiguous. Not only are human senses and recollection more fallible than mechanical and electronic sensors, but the reporting may deliberately set out to deceive (disinformation) or it may be clouded by what the reporter wishes to see, or by the degree to which he understands what he observes (misinformation).

At the tactical level of operations, the human data input might take the form of a local resident telling a peacekeeping patrol about some past or potential guerrilla activity in an area. At the operational and military-strategic levels of conflict, this human information may take the form of more conventional human intelligence, intelligence exchanges, contacts with nongovernmental organizations, or open source information. At the geo-strategic level it would likely be part of a broad input of information not only from military or intelligence sources, but also from the data gathering and information sources of the government as a whole. For example, data would be drawn from other government agencies, international organizations, allies, neutrals, private individuals, and the media, all of which have acquired increased importance in the post-September 11th security environment.

As the above suggests, human-derived information is far more difficult to handle than sensor data. It does not lend itself well to automation[16] and offers no prospect of a sensor-to-shooter link that, after all, attains its high rate of speed by "getting the man out of the loop." On the contrary, the ability of human-derived data to translate into information and expand awareness depends on the ability to put the man back into the loop.[17] Just as the creation and organization of a system of systems of sensors requires considerable decisionmaking, so too does the handling and analysis of human-derived data and information. Creating human information that is useful to the commanders and warfighters involves a cognitive process on the part of some analyst. That analyst may be the stereotypical intelligence analyst, or an expert brought into the problem on an ad hoc basis. But, it also may be the soldier on patrol in a peacekeeping operation who is and must be the expert on the area he is patrolling. In this capacity, he must evaluate and deal with all sorts of human information on an immediate and continuing basis. This implies a different dimension of the cognitive domain than the essentially sensor-based tactical decisionmaking, one that turns on the assessment of what information to believe and what not to believe. In short, it hinges on human judgment. This cognitive context may potentially be as simple as a peacekeeper's day-to-day knowledge of the neighborhood he is patrolling or it may be as complex as trying in June 1942 to estimate all of the eventual repercussions of the victory at Midway.

The Cognitive Domain

The cognitive domain is the locus of the functions of perceiving, making sense of a situation, assessing alternatives, and deciding on a course of action. This process relies partially on conscious reasoning, the domain of reason, and partially upon sub-conscious mental models, the domain of belief. Both reason and belief are pre-conditioned by culture, education, and experience. From the standpoint of a stimulus and response model of effects-based operations, the cognitive domain is where the stimulus actually produces some response and shapes behavior. As such, it is the real focus of any effects-based operation.

We have just seen the amount of decisionmaking behind the creation and orchestration of data gathering in the information domain. Obviously, the human decisionmakers and the human organizations that directed the surveillance effort arrived at some way of balancing their assigned missions with the materiel and other constraints imposed, and of balancing time and space, and opportunities and risks. But this overview leaves a question: How did they arrive at a notion of what the correct balance was?

The same question confronts us when we look at the information domain from the perspective of how decisionmakers deal with the information that the surveillance system produces. One element of the answer revolves about the mantra of conveying "the right information to the right person at the right place in the right form." Too much information presented too quickly overwhelms decisionmakers, while too little leaves them making decisions in a vacuum. The wrong displays can confuse and disorient. The right ones can permit them to handle more information and make better decisions.

All of these considerations are important, but they are all fairly clear human engineering problems and are relatively easy to solve. The real challenge at the center of effects-based operations is how human decisionmakers perceive the actions in the physical domain as reported to them, and then how they make decisions. Yet all of these questions in both of these areas drive us back to the same fundamental questions: How do human beings perceive a developing situation, make sense of it, assess the choices available and come to a decision as to a course of action?

Knowledge and Understanding

The sensemaking conference and successive sessions of the Information Superiority Working Group observed that the decision processes in question and the ability to deal with information hinged on what the human decisionmakers themselves brought to the situation (see Figure 31). In part, this human dimension reflects the condition of the individual decisionmaker and factors such as emotions, physiology (especially fatigue), and beliefs. But it also reflects a deeper and more fundamental question of how human beings in general perceive and understand a given situation.

As a general rule, human beings approach problems with a particular frame of reference that

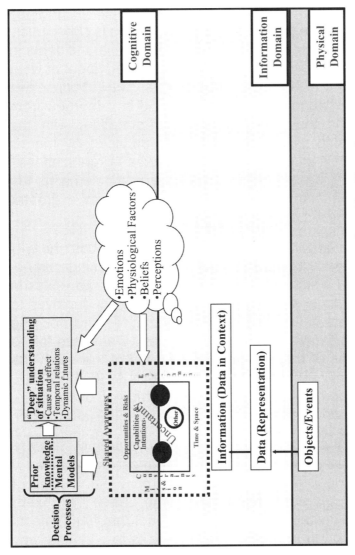

Figure 31. Operations in the Cognitive Domain

grows out of an individual's prior knowledge, education, and training, all within the context of a particular culture.[18] The decisionmakers and humans in general tend to reason largely by analogy. A given set of circumstances is consciously or unconsciously compared with similar incidents in the past or with a generalized mental model of what "ought to be." The deep and largely subconscious understanding of the situation then emerges from noting the nuances of the information, with the missing pieces of the puzzle provided by mental models or prior experience. Human organizations[19] might be expected to approach problems in the same manner, although potentially with a greater diversity of knowledge and experience.[20]

Prior knowledge and mental models, both heavily influenced by national and decisionmaking culture, have a significant impact on cognitive awareness in two dimensions: the sensors or sources deployed to collect data and process information; and how the information created is treated and translated into a sense of the situation. In the case of the latter, the result can clearly be dangerous if there are misperceptions of either the information or the entire situation, regardless of the quality of the information.

As the above suggests, the tendency toward crucial misperceptions will be most pronounced if the decisionmakers have little or no knowledge of the outside world, or who have a fixed, ideologically-based mental model that flatly rejects any other model or actively seeks to eliminate any other point of view.[21]

The issues of prior knowledge of culture, training, education, and mental models are crucial because they affect how a situation is perceived and thus, the rest of the cognitive process. They will determine how decisionmakers are likely to pursue the cause and effect logic, the way in which they view time, and the kinds of alternative futures they can foresee, which are all elements at the root of our concept of effects-based operations. For example, decisionmakers with an otherworldly mental model might pursue what they see as a divinely-inspired cause and effect logic with an eschatological understanding of time in which the events of this world simply work toward an infinite divine plan. Unless we can understand this context in some manner, we will be unable to comprehend the potential outcomes of a given situation, much less calculate what actions on our part might produce a given psychological effect and the behavior we are striving to shape.

Sensemaking and Decisionmaking

Together, the prior knowledge, mental models, and resulting understanding of a situation provide the basis for sensemaking. The process of sensemaking has been referred to as fitting together the pieces of the puzzle (information, constructs drawn from prior knowledge and mental models, ambitions, emotions) into a story that conveys an intuitive appreciation of the situation. This story embodies cultural values, and it contains some idea of a dynamic future, and it also may contain an intimation of alternative paths to different futures (see Figure 32).

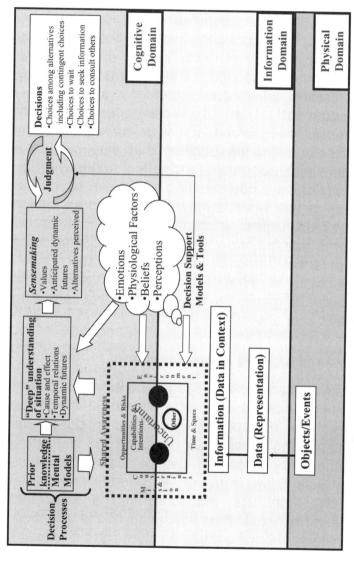

Figure 32. Sensemaking and Decisionmaking

This process of sensemaking provides the basis for defining the choices of courses of action available for a potential response. Such a choice, of course, might be to undertake no action at all, either because no action is deemed necessary or advisable, or because it is decided to await further developments. Inaction may result from a decision to seek further information, for example, by changing the data gathering focus of the surveillance system or by applying different models and tools to the collection and assessment. The decision might also be to avoid immediate reaction in favor of consultations.

The decision might equally be to take action. In this case, an additional decisionmaking process would determine which of several potential actions would best meet the contingency at hand. The decisionmakers would go through their own assessment of the physical and psychological effects to be sought and the pros and cons of the various physical actions that might lead to creating those effects. In any individual effects-based operation, each of these options (to act, to wait, or to probe further) then would be tested against the understanding developed during the sensemaking process.

Acting

Once a course of action is decided, that decision must somehow be translated into physical action. This process would again cut across the information domain to undertake something in the physical domain (see Figure 33).

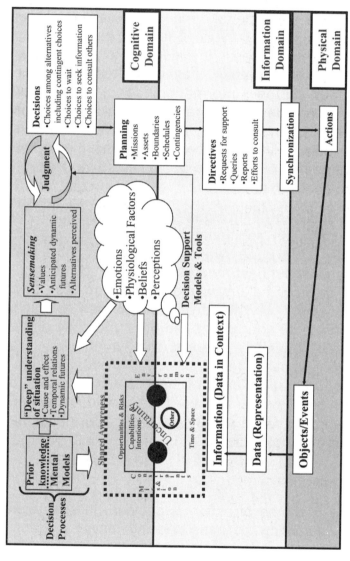

Figure 33. Reactions in the Physical Domain

The planning process, like situational awareness, straddles the divide between the cognitive and information domains. The process encompasses defining and deconflicting the actions and communicating a full understanding of the commander's intent to the units executing the directives. This is no small challenge. Planning must take into account a host of factors that stretch well beyond the immediate battlespace or other area of conflict. To make matters worse, this effort to orchestrate the entire task runs into the same Platonic problem we encountered in observing and reporting data. No action will ever be executed in exactly the way the commander intended. No matter how well the commander's intent may be communicated, the understanding of that intent will vary across multiple levels and multiple arenas, as well as across coalition members. Just as each individual's training, experience, mental models, and idiosyncrasies are different, so too will their understanding be different. If the backgrounds of the individuals in question differ greatly, the chances of a miscommunication will be high.

The more complex the action and the greater the number of arenas and levels of command that we attempt to coordinate, the greater will be the likelihood of distortion and misunderstanding. Improving command and control communications can help, but the real problem lies in the interface between the cognitive domain and the information domain. It is the problem of communicating understanding, both to planners who must understand what is possible with the assets at hand, and to warfighters and other actors as to the commander's true intent.

The more uniform the experience or prior knowledge base of planners and actors, the less the problem is likely to be. The more diverse the experience base is, the greater the likelihood of a misunderstanding.

Action-Reaction Cycle

Finally (and ideally), this process will produce a set of synchronized and coordinated physical actions aimed at creating some physical and/or psychological effect on the opponent and thus, affect that opponent's behavior in an acceptable direction. This is to say that the entire process described from the physical actions to the collection of data to the sensemaking, and the execution of a response is but one half of a cycle in which each side in succession observes and responds to the actions of the other. The physical action produced by the planning and execution process then becomes a stimulus that the opponent will observe, consider, and react to (see Figure 34).

This description of a complex process fraught with uncertainties, although necessary to an understanding of what we are attempting in effects-based operations, is by no means restricted to effects-based operations. On the contrary, we can see in it a description of military operations in general. It is an OODA loop written large and in some significant detail. It is not new. It is in many senses a timeless description of the challenges involved in any military operation. It can be traced through the 1805 Battle of Trafalgar and through the 1942 Battle of Midway.

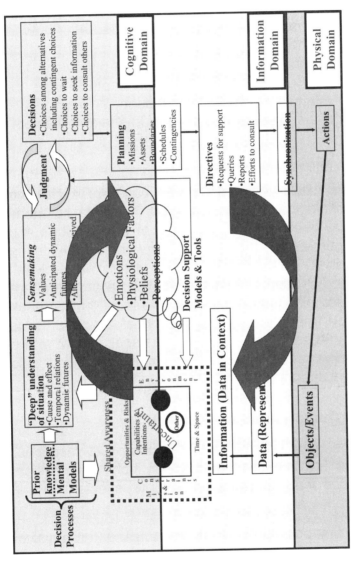

Figure 34. Action-Reaction Cycle

From Cognitive Cycles to Effects-Based Operations

What does this cognitive cycle tell us about how to choose the right actions to create the right physical and psychological effects to shape behavior? The cognitive cycle provides the conceptual base for understanding three essential aspects of actions or stimuli that we are trying to use to shape behavior.

The Nature of Actions

If we follow the logic of the cognitive cycle, the psychological effects we seek to create so as to shape behavior are the result of observations and the perceptions that these observations evoke in the observer. This implies that the effects we seek will be reliant upon those aspects of our actions that are observable. That means that we must look at each action from the standpoint of what an observer is likely to see. Seen from this perspective, what the observer sees is not merely *what* is done, but also *how* it is done.

The Cumulative Impact of Actions

In the entire cognitive cycle we have just described, there are only two points at which any physical actions we may take can create effects that will influence behavior.

The first point of entry is obviously that the physical actions either create the physical effects (e.g. destruction of forces and capabilities) that may foreclose certain behavior, or that they constitute the object or event that is being observed, reported, and perceived, and to which the observer ultimately reacts.

The second, less obvious point of entry is the history of previous physical actions that may have been seen by the same observers, such as the responses to earlier crises and other contingencies in the same area or in similar situations. These previous actions form a large part of the prior knowledge described in the cognitive cycle. They are the reference points against which the observers and decisionmakers measure the current physical action and thus, the basis for their perceptions.

Perhaps as important, these previous actions shape the observers' unconscious mental models of what course a given set of actions is likely to follow and therefore will be the basis for how the observer assesses a variety of dynamic futures. The history of previous actions provides a ready gauge of likely cause and effect relationships and time-delay expectations. In a still broader context, the history of previous political, economic, and military action in similar situations are an essential part of shaping the deep understanding that goes into the sense that the observer makes of a given situation. Phrased differently, the aggregate of our previous actions precondition observers as to what they should expect to see. The above underscores a cardinal principal of effects-based operations. The effects-based operation does not begin with the physical action we may decide to execute. It begins with all those actions we have taken in the same area well before the current action was ever considered at all. If the history of our previous actions supports the immediate physical action we are undertaking and the psychological effect we are trying to create, then we may build upon the observers' expectations. If that history would contradict that immediate action and the effect we seek to create, then we may have to overcome the earlier impressions to achieve the effect we desire.

The Nature of the Observer

The cognitive cycle underlines how different observers with different levels and kinds of experience, mental models, national or organizational cultures, and understandings of the situation will make sense of the same action in different ways and reach different decisions as to how to respond to the stimulus.

Although this variable has obvious implications for how information is perceived and handled within a given state, it has even more of an impact when we remember that any action we take will be seen by more than just one human observer. Indeed, our definition of effects-based operations specified that they shaped the behavior "of friends, foes, and neutrals," each of whom will see the same action from a different perspective and in a different light. Moreover, although the process outlined in the cognitive cycle may be understood in terms of a state or government reacting to a stimulus, the same process would apply to a non-state actor such as a terrorist organization. Their reactions would be a function of what they were able to see, how it was reported and understood, how it was correlated and contextualized, and how it was balanced against the options open.

...and Effects-Based Operations?

How applicable is this entire construct to effects-based operations? There are two potential criticisms that must be taken into account. First, it may be argued that underlying the entire construct is a presumption of rationality on the part of the observers and decisionmakers involved and that without such rationality the entire construct becomes questionable. Second, it may similarly be argued that there are so many variables at play in the cognitive process that it cannot be universally applied.

The first question was, in fact, addressed by the Office of Net Assessment of the U.S. Defense Department in a summer seminar.[22] The seminar's conclusion was that the decisionmakers in a confrontation would be rational. The working groups observed that attaining a leadership role, whether in a government or an organization, can be understood to demand a substantial degree of rational thinking and calculation, even though this rationality may not be the same rationality that a Western mind would pursue.

If we accept that the decisionmakers in a confrontation are likely to be rational, then we can postulate that the process described above will remain roughly the same, even though the filters (culture, education, and experience) may be vastly different and produce vastly different outcomes. Very simply, what we are describing is the process by which the human mind functions and despite cultural differences, the same general process remains valid across such boundaries.

However, perhaps the most pointed response to such a critique is simply to apply the construct to a series of real-world operations and to look at how these mechanics operate in the context of those operations. To the degree that the mechanics are constant across multiple operations, then we can begin to deduce the parameters of the operations in effects-based operations in the cognitive domain.

---

[1]Boyd, p. 42.

[2]In *Understanding Information Age Warfare,* Alberts et al. refer to the OODA loop as a "traditional view of command and control processes" but also make the argument that it oversimplifies even a "traditional" hierarchical joint command structure.
Alberts et al. *Understanding Information Age Warfare.* pp. 131-133.

[3]Muir, Rory. *Britain and the Defeat of Napoleon, 1807-1815.* New Haven; Yale University. 1996.

[4]A distinction needs to be drawn between the *military-strategic* level of decisionmaking by Theater Commanders and the Joint Staff focused on higher-level *military* decisionmaking, and the *geo-strategic* level of decisionmaking by the national leadership focused on the aspects of *national* power, including political and diplomatic risk assessment.

[5]We can think of these successively more complex systems in the context of James Grier Miller's "Living Systems" (p.755) theory of seven levels of complexity operating from the level of cells all the way through that of supranational or

international systems. In effects-based operations, we are dealing with at least four levels of the system: groups (individual military units), organizations (Joint Task Force), communities (the military), societies (nation-states), and possibly, supra-national groupings such as the international community. Each of these levels shares certain characteristics and certain mechanical processes with the others. Thus, the theory offers the prospect of some internal rational order amid the complexity of the maze of human organizations. That structure offers some hope that we can plan and execute effects-based operations focused on behavior and can provide a key to figuring out how to handle the complexity involved.

Miller, James Grier. *Living Systems*. Denver. 1995. pp. 9ff.

[6]"Report of the Workshop on Sensemaking, 6-8 March 2001." DODCCRP/Evidence Based Research; Tysons Corner. 2001. The comments included here also reflect the notes of the author, who was a participant in the workshop.

[7]The assumption here is that all actions must have some physical dimension to them in order to be either objects or events that can be observed and reported. The physical component of such an action may be as great as a large scale amphibious assault or as little as the keystrokes required to insert a computer virus into the internet.

[8]At the same time, all of the above objects, events, and chains of physical effects clearly can be seen to have an impact that lies beyond the physical domain, a second and distinctly different chain of derivative effects. Clearly, Vice Admiral Nagumo, the Japanese commander at Midway, made decisions based on a report of a sighting of a U.S. carrier, and his subordinate commanders made tactical decisions because of the American torpedo plane attack. Thus, an action in the physical domain resulted in a stimulus in the cognitive domain that in turn resulted in a series of command decisions at various levels that altered Japanese behavior during the battle. It is equally true that the chain of physical effects deriving from the destruction of a railroad bridge might be expected to set off a series of decisions at succeeding levels of command. These cascades of direct and indirect physical effects will be discussed in detail in Chapter 7.

[9]As noted in *Understanding Information Age Warfare*, a direct observation by human senses (the Mark 1 Mod 0 eyeball) does not pass through the information domain in the connotation of electronic sensors and information systems. Nevertheless, the processes and limitations of the human senses are very closely analogous to those of the electronic sensors and information systems. Because they perform an

analogous function, it is useful to consider them in the same information domain for purposes of effects-based planning and execution.

Alberts et al. *Understanding Information Age Warfare.* p. 12.

[10]Alberts et al. note that "information is the result of putting individual observations (sensor returns or data items) into some meaningful context. Data is a representation of individual facts, concepts, or instructions in a manner suitable for communication, interpretation, or processing by humans or by automatic means."

Alberts et al. *Understanding Information Age Warfare.* pp. 16-17.

[11]Jowett, J.B. trans. *Plato's Republic.* New York; Modern Library. 1982.

[12]We will follow here the distinction made by Alberts et al. that direct sensing is the application of human senses to surveillance in a way that unites the sensing and the cognitive function of perception in an individual. Indirect sensing denotes a situation in which mechanical or electronic sensors detect and forward data or information to a human observer who perceives a situation as a result and thus becomes the entry point into the cognitive domain.

[13]In an asymmetric conflict environment (guerrilla warfare, urban terrorism), this information requirement would extend across the full range of what might otherwise be considered police data or even financial data.

[14]In fact, one of the major attributes of network-centric operations is that it would enable such external inputs from a network to increase the scope of the area that the pilot could observe.

[15]This human information is distinguished from *human intelligence* (HUMINT) sources, a term that usually connotes data derived from the reporting of open and undercover agents of some sort and that has been assessed in some way for its reliability or credibility. The term *human information*, as applied here, encompasses all of the unevaluated information that derives from both traditional open sources and from incidental observations and reporting by human beings.

[16]There are rich possibilities for the use of new information technologies such as data mining in extracting relevant data from large amounts of text and the creation of analytical models to search for new ways to contextualize that data. However, like the creation of a system of surveillance sensors, even the data mining and the tools require extensive human judgments as to what should or should not be the focus of the data mining and what should or should not go into

the models used.

[17]The analysis process that transforms such human information into HUMINT deals with these problems by aggregating the reporting to look for consistencies over time or by comparing such information with other reporting on the subject area that has proven reliable.

[18]Alberts et al. point to four different ways in which knowledge can be loaded into the cognitive domain:

The education, training, and experience of an individual;

Direct experience with the physical domain;

Interaction with other human beings; and

Interactions with the information domain.

Alberts et al. *Understanding Information Age Warfare.* p.18.

[19]Because commanders act and react in the context of some organization and are influenced by the differing perceptions of multiple players in that organization, if we are to understand what goes on in the cognitive domain, we need to think in terms of *command intent* rather than *commander's intent,* even though the ultimate decision continues to rest with the commander.

[20]This will vary with the decisionmaking culture. A culture that discourages anyone but the chief or a limited number of decisionmakers to speak will be limited to their experience base alone. One that encourages the expression of divergent viewpoints will benefit from a wider base, but may be subject to an information overload. Practically, decisionmakers tend to gravitate to a limited number of counselors whose judgment is trusted and who put information into an experiential framework shared by the decisionmaker. Robert F. Kennedy's description of the American decisionmaking process during the 1962 Cuban Missile Crisis is a case in point.

Kennedy, Robert F. *Thirteen Days, A Memoir of the Cuban Missile Crisis.* New York; Norton, W. W. & Company, Inc. 1969.

[21]In this sense, Osama bin Laden and his admirers can be described as Islamist fascists.

[22]Office of the Secretary of Defense, Office of Net Assessment. 1995 Summer Study, Author's notes.

CHAPTER 5

The Rules of the Game: Putting Effects-Based Operations into a Real-World Context

In the cognitive cycle, as in the definitions of effects-based operations, effects, and the stimulus and response model, we can begin to see the outlines of a fundamental general theory of effects-based operations. We must now take this theoretical understanding another step and see how it applies to real-world operations. There are two ways in which this might be done. If we assume that both network-centric operations and effects-based operations are entirely new concepts for which there is no precedent, then we would be obliged to examine the theory in the context of controlled battle experiments in the hope that those experiments could be made to resemble the real world. However, if we accept that the basic principles of network-centric operations are not new, and that effects-based operations in one form or another have always been with us, then we can also test the theory directly by looking at how it is reflected in real-world conflicts.

In this chapter, we will approach the effects-based problem from this latter direction. With the theoretical underpinnings of the preceding chapters in mind, we will examine a series of real-world operations, both to test the theories and to deduce a set of effects-based operating principles, or "rules of the game." In choosing which set of military operations to examine, we will move our focus away from warfighting. Whereas the previous examples (Midway, Trafalgar, the great attrition wars, and Vietnam) were all wartime combat models, this time we will turn to examples of military operations short of combat. After all, if we are to assess the full range of military actions that might provoke responses and change behavior, we must look beyond combat operations. In each case, we will seek to understand why, how, and which actions produce effects: the set of operating principles or rules of the game. By looking at a variety of cases over time, we will try to assess the general applicability both of these operating principles and of our emerging theory of effects-based operations. Finally, by concentrating our attention on crises short of hostilities, we will also begin to address how effects-based operations apply to the peacetime and crisis response operations that have constituted the vast majority of our military operations for the past half-century and more.

To support such assessment, there is a substantial database of operations short of combat to draw upon. If we use the generally accepted method of counting U.S. crisis responses developed by Barry Blechman and Stephen Kaplan in the late 1970s, we can identify approximately 400 crisis response operations of varying sizes and descriptions that have been conducted by U.S. military forces since the end of the Second World War.[1][2][3][4][5] Very few of these 400 crisis responses by military forces, which included some of the largest scale military operations of the Cold War, actually involved combat. However, almost all did involve the use of some form of maneuver, as opposed to strike operations, to create effects and to change behavior.[6] And, almost all paid nearly as much attention to shaping the behavior of friends and neutrals as they did to shaping the behavior of prospective foes. Thus, the crisis response conflicts provide ample grounds for both testing the theory and ascertaining how it operates in the real world.

As a more manageable number of examples than the 400 or more responses cataloged, we will examine a set of three major crisis reactions by the Soviet Union and the United States that occurred in the Middle East between 1967 and 1973:

- The June 1967 Arab Israeli War;

- The September 1970 Jordanian Crisis; and

- The October 1973 "Yom Kippur" Arab-Israeli War.

From the standpoint of our ex post facto experimentation, this set of examples has a number of advantages. Each took place in the same basic geographic area and security environment: the Cold War Middle East (see Figure 35). The three crises also involved many of the same players and demonstrated a significant scale and scope of interaction over a period of time that is short enough to make changes in technology and weapons among the principles a negligible factor. And, the actions of the players are fairly well documented in accessible, unclassified sources. These factors indicate that we should be able both to pick out consistencies in behavior from which to draw our rules, and to trace a learning quotient from one crisis to the next.

There is also an additional significant point to be considered. In each of these crisis reactions, as in the earlier 1962 Cuban Missile Crisis, any resort to hostilities by either the Soviet Union or the United States against the other would have marked a dangerous and perhaps catastrophic failure of military power. This is to say that they represent the antithesis of an attrition-based approach to military operations. For the two superpowers in their interaction with each other, the destruction of forces and capabilities was not an option to be considered in order to create effects. Thus, the results or effects of their operations cannot be assessed in terms of attrition models. But, they are explicable in the context of a stimulus and response, effects-based operation model in which sets of military actions coupled with actions by other elements of national power produced the desired changes in behavior. That is to say, the crises are good mirrors of exactly the kind of issues raised in the preceding chapters.[7]

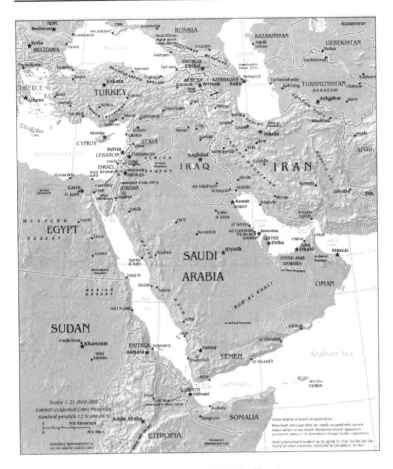

Figure 35. The Middle East

The Crises

The Arab-Israeli War, June 1967

The June 1967 crisis is significant for two reasons. It is the first incident in this series of Soviet-American confrontations in the Middle East, and therefore provides a baseline case for assessing how the two powers adapted and learned over the course of the three crises. Also, it is the only one of the three crises that involved an attempt to put together a coalition military operation.

The roots of the crisis lie in escalating terrorist operations into Israel that took place throughout 1966 and early 1967. On May 12, 1967, amid the threats and counter-threats surrounding these attacks and a new Egyptian-Syrian defense pact, Israel threatened to take unspecified retaliatory action in the event of continued terrorism across its border.[8] Syria immediately accused Israel of mobilizing its armed forces for an attack on Syria and invoked the defense pact. In response, Egypt mobilized its armed forces on May 14, ordered its forces into the previously demilitarized Sinai Peninsula area on May 18,[9] and finally declared a blockade of the Strait of Tiran on May 22.[10]

Britain and the United States initially reacted to the crisis by trying to create an international naval force to transit the strait and break the blockade and promptly started to mass naval forces in the Red Sea for such a demonstration of power.[11] On May 30, Israel gave the superpowers a deadline of 1 to 2 weeks for this effort to succeed.[12] But, the effort soon ran into problems. The principal superpower naval force east of Suez was a British carrier battle group in the Red Sea.[13] Not surprisingly, Britain immediately became subject to Arab threats to British oil supplies and financial stability. As a consequence, Britain announced that it would withdraw from the effort on May 31,[14] and with the British withdrawal, the attempt to use coalition military power to avoid the conflict failed.

On June 5, in the face of mounting war preparations by its Arab neighbors, Israel attacked first Egypt, then Syria and Jordan. The United States and the Soviet Union initially attempted to avoid any direct involvement in this developing conflict and kept their respective naval forces in the Mediterranean Sea at a distance from the war zone.[15] But, as the Arab-Israeli war intensified, both the Soviet and American military forces throughout the region were put on alert and moved closer to the conflagration. Soviet warships equipped with anti-ship missiles took up tattletale stations in close proximity to major American units, while armed U.S. carrier aircraft closely monitored the major Soviet units in the area. Both sides likewise began to reinforce their naval forces in the area. The tense naval standoff quickly came to involve 47 American ships and 25 Soviet ships.[16]

The face-off continued until June 10 when, in the face of an increasingly successful Israeli invasion of Syria, the Soviets threatened to intervene directly in the struggle to stop the Israeli advance toward the Syrian capital of Damascus. In response, the United States sent its Sixth Fleet, then stationed south of the central Mediterranean island of Crete, toward the conflict area at high speed.[17] At the same time, the White House communicated to the Soviets that any such direct Soviet intervention in the war would be unacceptable, that the United States wanted to control the situation and that, in any event, the Israelis were not going to force their offensive as far as Damascus. When the Israeli drive indeed halted short of Damascus, the confrontation ended, but left Israel in control of parts of Egypt, Syria, and Jordan including the Sinai Peninsula up to the Suez Canal, the West Bank territories of Jordan, and the Syrian Golan Heights.

The Jordanian War, September 1970

In the wake of the terrorist attacks of September 11, 2001 and the subsequent U.S. operations in Afghanistan, the Jordanian crisis of 1970 is particularly interesting. It involved both state-to-state conflict and interactions, and interactions with a number of non-state players, a group of Palestinian terrorist organizations loosely sponsored by Syria. The operations therefore involved not only the client states of the Soviet Union and the United States as in the 1967 war, but also included terrorist operations carried out by various Palestinian factions to threaten the United States and Israel, and to induce a collapse of the Jordanian government.

The Jordanian crisis grew out of a series of confrontations in the spring and early summer of 1970 between the Jordanian Army that remained loyal to King Hussein and groups of Palestinian guerrillas and terrorists supported by Syria and (indirectly) by the Soviet Union.[18] The tense situation was aggravated by additional Palestinian terrorist actions in Jordan, including an attempted assassination of King Hussein on June 9,[19] the assassination of the American Defense Attaché to Jordan on June 12, the seizure of 60 Western hostages at an Amman hotel, and by an ongoing series of hostile encounters between the Israelis and both Egypt and Syria.[20]

As the situation in Jordan worsened, the United States tried to use its political and economic influence both to broker a Jordanian-Palestinian settlement and to engineer a cease-fire in the ongoing fighting between Israel and its neighbors.[21] The diplomatic effort failed in all respects. By September, the situation in Jordan was deteriorating rapidly. On September 1, Palestinian terrorists attempted yet another assassination of King Hussein. Then on September 6, the Palestinians began a series of airliner hijackings, including American aircraft and United States citizens, dispatching the aircraft to airfields in Cairo and Jordan.

This action was accompanied by renewed demands on the Jordanian Government both by the terrorists and by other Palestinian factions.[22] These events in turn were followed by open conflict between Palestinian guerrillas and the Jordanian Army and by a Syrian invasion of Jordan in support of the Palestinians. To everyone's surprise, the Jordanian Army defeated the Syrian invasion and asserted control over the Palestinian terrorist camps.[23]

In response to the deteriorating situation in Jordan, the United States began to concentrate naval forces in the eastern Mediterranean and dispatched an additional carrier battle group from the Puerto Rico area, in case some form of intervention became necessary. Then, in the face of the Syrian invasion, the United States warned the Soviets and the Syrians that if the invasion continued, the U.S. would not stop any Israeli action and might indeed intervene directly itself, and began to put airborne forces on alert.[24] In the following days, as the Syrian (and Iraqi) invasion continued, American forces in the European Theater were put on alert and the U.S. Sixth Fleet was reinforced with an additional carrier battle group.[25] In response, the Soviets continued their own reinforcements to their Mediterranean fleet.

During the ensuing Soviet-American military confrontation, both sides maneuvered naval forces in the area but deliberately kept their most powerful units outside the eastern Mediterranean area of the conflict. Although the confrontation ended when the Jordanian Army defeated the Syrian and Iraqi invaders and surrounded the principal Palestinian terrorist bases, both the Soviet and American naval forces continued to reinforce and to maneuver warily in the Mediterranean for several additional weeks.

The Yom Kippur War, October 1973

The 1973 Arab-Israeli War was occasioned by the continued Israeli occupation of Egyptian, Syrian, and Jordanian territories that had been captured in the 1967 war and by the failure of the United States or any other actor to find a negotiated settlement to return these territories.[26] In some ways, the 1973 war resembled that of 1967. It too was principally a conventional military conflict between states, rather than a combination of state-sponsored terrorist actions and conventional operations. However, unlike the 1967 "Six Day War," the 1973 war was long and more closely fought with the local antagonists, rapidly exhausting their supplies of weapons and munitions.

The war started on October 6, 1973 (on the Jewish holy day of Yom Kippur and in the midst of the Muslim holy month Ramadan) and began with both a surprise Egyptian assault across the Suez Canal accompanied by a Syrian thrust into the Israeli-occupied Golan Heights.[27] The Egyptians quickly established a bridgehead on the Israeli-occupied side of the canal and expanded it over the next 8 days. The Syrians, after an initial success on the Golan Heights, bore the brunt of the Israeli response and by October 10, they were falling back. By October 14, the two sides were deadlocked, but over the following week, the tide began to turn heavily in Israel's favor. A cease-fire was attempted on October 22, but it failed. A second cease-fire went into effect on October 24. After a tense U.S.-Soviet confrontation, the cease-fire finally took hold on October 25, ending the war.[28]

Given the initial Arab successes in the war, the Soviet Union promised "full support."[29] However, when the Syrian situation began to deteriorate sharply on October 9-10, the Soviets began a large-scale airlift to Syria. The United States initially played down any resupply effort and sought Soviet cooperation in finding a diplomatic solution to the crisis. However, the U.S. began resupplying Israel on October 7 and then, as Israel began to run out of arms, began a large-scale resupply effort on October 13.[30]

The Soviet and American military approaches to the crisis mirrored this evolution. Initially, both sought to maintain a "low key, even handed approach toward the hostilities"[31] and kept their respective fleets operating in an area south of Crete. This changed on

October 9-10 as the Soviets placed units with anti-ship missiles as tattletales near the major U.S. units, and then began a rapid, large-scale reinforcement of their Mediterranean fleet.[32]

When the first cease-fire failed to end all hostilities on October 22, the Soviets threatened Israel with "grave consequences," alerted its airborne divisions, began to reconfigure its airlift so as to be able to send the airborne divisions into Damascus, and increased the pace of its naval reinforcements.[33] On October 24, in a brusque note to President Nixon, the Soviets threatened to send their military forces into the Middle East to enforce a peace, a potentially dangerous move considered unacceptable by the United States. This was followed by a threatening "anti-carrier" exercise by Soviet ships in the Mediterranean directed against U.S. forces in the area.[34]

In response to the Soviet actions, the Americans first sent to the crisis area an additional carrier that previously had been held in the western Mediterranean as a demonstration of the U.S. desire to keep the crisis low key. Finally, in response to the Soviet threats of October 22 and 24, the United States went to a general alert, increased the Defense Condition, alerted the 82nd Airborne Division, and reinforced the Sixth Fleet with an additional carrier group that had been held outside the Mediterranean. The resulting tense Soviet-American naval confrontation continued through the first week of November until it was apparent that the cease-fire was holding and both sides began to draw down the forces in the area.

Observations

While the above recounting of three very significant crises and the Soviet and American reactions is necessarily very cursory, there are several aspects of our broad definition of effects-based operations that are immediately evident in even this loose account of the military interactions of the three crises.

- First, although the numbers of Soviet and American forces involved were very large and the interactions between their naval forces in particular were often very intense, none of the operations involved actual combat. Indeed, one of the principal objectives of both the Soviets and the Americans in each case was to avoid such hostilities, the result of which could be a rapid and uncontrolled escalation into a nuclear conflict. Thus, despite the significance of the major naval and other military interactions involved, none of those critical interactions had much at all to do with any semblance of an attrition-based model of warfare.

- Second, in each case, it was actions, especially the maneuvers of the Soviet and American fleets, and not weapons that were carefully targeted by operational commanders and national leaders alike to shape the opponent's behavior[35] and that of local clients, allies and neutrals. The critical question was not what was destroyed, but how certain military actions would be perceived and by whom.[36]

• Third, all of the military operations in each of the crises, however large they may have been, were but one part of a still larger, longer, and more complex diplomatic, political, and economic effort involving all the regional actors. Neither the military actions of these actors nor the effects they created could be separated from their political-diplomatic context. Rather they had to be coordinated with other actions to achieve an overall effect.

• Finally, the interactions of both fleets during the operations were dynamic. The fleets' actions did not at all resemble the execution of a preplanned target list followed by bomb damage assessment and planning for a second strike. Instead, the maneuvering interactions of both the Soviet and American forces were as dynamic as those of a tactical OODA loop, but were as interrelated, complex, and multi-faceted as those suggested by the cognitive process outlined in Chapter 4. Moreover, the cognitive cycles observed at the tactical and operational levels were very much connected to equivalent cycles at the military-strategic and national levels of interaction. Indeed, the fleets and their actions became a primary way of one superpower signaling its intentions to the other,[37] and thus of shaping national behavior.

The above certainly indicates a dynamic in the use of military forces that is very different from attrition-based models and cannot be readily explained in such terms. What additional lessons can we draw from these three crisis response operations, and what do they tell us about the nature of effects-based operations and the prospective role of network-centric thinking in them?

Effects-Based Operations: Rules of the Game

If we look more closely at what was going on in each of the above three crisis response operations and at those aspects of each side's behavior that carried over from one crisis to the next, we can begin to discern some general operating principles or rules of the game for effects-based operations. At the root of these parameters is a very fundamental observation: that the military responses in each of the three crises consisted of a succession of what might be termed action-reaction cycles (see Figure 36). That is, they can be described in terms of a series of two-sided interactions in which each side tried to persuade its

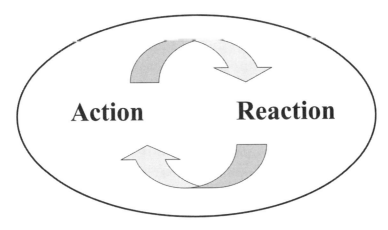

Figure 36. Basic Building Block: Action-Reaction Cycle

opponent to adopt a particular course of action while dissuading it from alternate, unacceptable courses of action.[38] These behavior-driven action-reaction cycles between intelligent adversaries were the basic building blocks of the crisis operations observed. They are equally the basic element in effects-based operations.

These action-reaction cycles could be observed repeatedly at multiple levels throughout each of the three crises:

- At the tactical level, the cycles were most evident in the maneuvers and counter-maneuvers of the Soviet and American warships in the Mediterranean. This was especially apparent in the repeated movements of the air or surface tattletales used to monitor and (if need be) to attack the opposing units, and the subsequent efforts of their targets to evade or guard against a sudden missile strike.

- The cycles were also evident at the operational level in the interaction between the Soviet Mediterranean Eskadra[39] as a whole and the U.S. Sixth Fleet, especially in what has been termed a strategy of "inter-position" in which each fleet sought to interpose itself between the opposing force and its clients.[40]

- The cycle was also seen at the military-strategic level in confrontations between U.S. and Soviet military power that stretched well beyond the Mediterranean battlespace. In all three cases, the superpowers' military efforts involved diverting forces from other theaters or from the homeland to reinforce the forces in the Mediterranean area. In the 1970 case, these efforts even included Soviet preparations to fly airborne divisions into Syria, and in the 1973 case, it included both a similar Soviet action and a U.S. general alert that included strategic nuclear forces.

- Finally, the cycle was perhaps extremely evident at the national level as the drama of the crisis was played out among the American and Soviet governments, their clients, their allies, and neutrals in a drama that spanned both politics and economics, and both the national and international arenas. In this latter contest, the U.S. sought to block any direct intervention by Soviet military forces and to discourage Soviet support to Arab clients, while the Soviets sought to do the same to the United States, and both sought to posture for a wider Arab audience.

In each of the three crises, the success of the overall national level effect sought depended at least in part upon the tactical and operational level signaling effects created by military forces on-scene.

If we can discern these building blocks at each level of interaction, what more can we deduce as to the nature of effects-based operations?

Rules of the Game

Actually, the three crisis response operations surveyed and, indeed, the entire history of Cold War crisis responses by the United States, point to six basic rules of the game that describe and define an effects-based operation. The first three of these rules are roughly analogous to those in a game of chess, while the last three step beyond the chess game to a far greater degree of complexity, specifically because they center on the human (cognitive and behavioral) dimension of the interaction.

1. Actions create effects.

In a game of chess, it is not necessary to take a piece to have an effect on the game. Many or even most of the moves we make during the chess game probably will not involve taking an opponent's pieces. We might simply put an opponent into check, for example. Or our moves might be directed at foreclosing a future move by the opponent, or at positioning a piece for a future move we might wish to make. Each contributes to the course of the game; each creates an effect.

Throughout all three of the Soviet-American naval confrontations in the Mediterranean between 1967 and 1973, the focus was similarly on moves or actions rather than on targets and destruction. The actions of the Soviet and American military forces did not need to include the destruction of opposing forces and capabilities in order to have an impact or to create a desired effect. Quite the contrary, the destruction of forces in the crisis area, whether those of the opposing superpower or those of its local client states, would have meant an unacceptable increase in the scale and scope of the local conflict, an eventuality that both the Soviets and Americans sought to avoid. Indeed, it was just such a possibility that brought the most intense moments of both entire confrontations. Both sides appreciated the dangers that any hostile military action between them, even an accidental one, could pose, including an uncontrolled escalation to nuclear conflict.[41]

Additionally, especially during the 1973 war, there was also a perception by the two superpowers that the clients might also be attempting to provoke just such an exchange, as a way of solidifying their protector's involvement in what was becoming an increasingly desperate situation for both clients.[42] In fact, however tense they became, most of the military operations stopped at a level of actions well short of the violent use of military force. Yet, this did not mean that either the actions or effects of the military forces involved were inconsequential, as the dispatch of the entire Battle Force of the U.S. Sixth Fleet toward the coast of Syria in the closing days of the 1967 War bears out. It meant rather that to produce the right effect, the military action used could not depend on destruction for its effect.

During the vast majority of these encounters, each side maneuvered for tactical advantage, often aggressively as in the case of the Soviet anti-carrier exercise in the closing days of the 1973 crisis, while at the same time deliberately and carefully avoiding combat. The focus of the actions undertaken was to use maneuver itself as the agent for creating the desired effects. Indeed, the coordination of both the Soviet and American ships, aircraft, and submarines participating in these cycles throughout the three operations bore all of the marks of maneuver warfare in their agility, flexibility, and responsiveness. The encounters were maneuver warfare without the warfare. They were engagements in which maneuver by itself created the desired effect.[43]

Moreover, this paradigm of "maneuver warfare without the warfare" is not peculiar to these three crisis reactions. It has been a recurring facet of almost all of the 400 or so crisis responses that have taken place over the last 50 years.[44] In many respects, the maneuvers of the fleets engaged in responding to the three Middle East wars resembled nothing so much as a modern version of 18th-century positional warfare. They were military operations in which the object was not to destroy the opposing army but to so out-maneuver it as to foreclose any possibility of success and thus, force its cession. These maneuver responses resemble many elements of what was termed "gunboat diplomacy" in the 19th century, a form of positional warfare at sea.[45] This idea of an effects-based maneuver warfare without the warfare not only appears to be the paradigm for the majority of the military reactions to crises over the past half century, but also that for the world of asymmetric challenges that we are likely to have to face in the 21st century.

Given these examples, we can hypothesize that in effects-based operations, it is not necessary to destroy an opponent's capabilities in order to have an impact or in order to create an effect. This is not to say that effects-based operations exclude the destruction of capabilities and targets. They do not. It says rather that there was much more to creating a desired overall effect than striking a target or destroying opposing forces, and that the destruction of forces and capabilities may be but one way to accomplish an effect, and not necessarily the best one.

2. Effects are cumulative.

A chess game is comprised of a series of moves that continue until a capitulation, a checkmate, or a draw. The moves in the game do not occur in isolation. In each move, pieces may be lost, formations dispersed, and intended moves foreclosed with the effect of that move cumulatively setting the parameters for succeeding moves. The effect of a move may be felt either directly and immediately because it forces an opponent to react in the next move, such as by putting a king into check. Alternatively, it may be felt indirectly or not until later in the game, such as in the impact of the loss of a powerful piece. As the latter implies, the ultimate effect of a given move may not be entirely known at the time and may well be represented in serendipitous or unintended consequences in subsequent moves.

In the Soviet and American responses to the three Middle East crises, the action-reaction cycles clearly followed a similar pattern. At the tactical level of these operations, there were long successions of air operations[46] and of tattletale and counter-tattletale operations on a given day, and from one phase of the crisis to the next as each side maneuvered for tactical advantage. In these successive cycles, the lessons learned from one interaction immediately affected the actions and reactions of the succeeding cycles.

At the operational level in particular, each side began to develop a knowledge base of what to expect of the other and of how to adapt to the situation in the Mediterranean. This experience and knowledge base changed how each side's military forces reacted as any individual crisis progressed, but also transferred from one crisis to the next. For example, in the 1967 crisis, the Soviet ability to reinforce its Mediterranean fleet promptly was constrained by the provisions of the Montreux Convention requiring 4 days advance notice for all warship transits of the Bosporus and Dardenelles, but by 1970, the Soviet Navy Staff had hit upon the idea of making "contingency declarations" of intent to transit. In normal operations, these declarations could be left unfilled, but in time of crisis, all the contingency declarations made could be met, thus enabling Soviet warships to exit the Black Sea in greater numbers. This permitted the Soviets to augment their forces in the Mediterranean Sea by larger numbers of ships in 1970 and 1973 than in 1967.

It can be surmised that military and other interactions in peace, crisis, and war will follow a similar general rule. In effects-based operations, therefore, actions and their effects are not and cannot be isolated. They are interrelated. The effect created by one interaction carries over into the next cycles to create a cumulative overall effect. One action or effect thus paves the way for the next in a succession of interactions. Forces lost and capabilities destroyed cannot be applied to the next action. Similarly, troops whose confidence has been crushed in one interaction cannot be expected to respond aggressively in the next confrontation.

The same is true of the cumulative effect from one crisis or conflict to the next. In this succession of actions and effects, the effect of an interaction may be direct and immediate, an impact that either independently or when added to what has gone before causes a change in current behavior. Or it may be long-term, a part of a continuing history of actions and effects that will ultimately shape perceptions or otherwise produce an aggregate impact.

3. Any action-reaction cycle will have both active and passive participants.

The idea of cumulative effect can be taken a step further. Consider that in a chess tournament, the impact of a move is not confined to a single interaction during a game. Instead, it will influence how the opponent plays in succeeding moves or even in succeeding games. Moreover, each move or series of moves, like those of a chess master, may be studied for the novel way in which they deal with a given situation on the board or for what they say about an individual player's thinking. These lessons can then be carried over into other encounters. Furthermore, this learning process is not confined to the two active protagonists. It applies to all those who can observe the game or who can study it in some fashion. In this manner, the impact of a move may extend not only to re-matches with the same players, but to all who can put the knowledge to use for their own ends, either against one of the players being observed or someone else.

In each of the three Middle East crises, we can observe a similar pattern. The interactions between the Soviet tattletales and their American prey in each crisis were essentially action-reaction cycles involving two active players in a tactical level engagement. But, surrounding these active players in each case were successive layers of interested parties. These passive players might not be directly involved in this tactical engagement, but would be immediately and directly affected by its outcome.

In the event that the interaction were to take a wrong turn (i.e., an American ship ramming a Soviet tattletale or a Soviet tattletale firing a missile), these passive actors would have quickly become active participants in any resulting conflict. The aircraft in combat air patrol stations might have been ordered to attack any Soviet unit that opened fire, and Soviet tattletales trailing other major American combatants might similarly have opened fire on their charges as the conflict spread.[47] In fact, this spread of action from the active players to a widening circle of observing players (potentially to a nuclear exchange) was exactly what the operational commanders, the national military staffs, and the national commanders on both sides feared in all three crises.

On another level, the client states of both superpowers were also passive players in each of the three superpower confrontations. They were not directly involved in the Soviet-American military interaction centered on the tattletales, but they were close observers who were very concerned with the outcome of any such engagement. Indeed, particularly in the 1967 and 1973 crises, they tended to see any engagement as a gauge of each superpower's commitment to its clients and thus, of the latitude they had in pursuing their own war aims.[48]

The set of passive actor-observers also included NATO and the Warsaw Pact Alliance partners of the Americans and Soviets respectively. These powers, apart from the abortive role of Britain in 1967, and Hungary permitting Soviet aircraft in their airspace in 1967 and 1973, took no part in the crisis, but likewise would have seen Soviet and American interactions as a gauge of their commitment as allies. Finally, there were all of the regional states that were not involved in the Arab-Israeli or Jordanian conflicts, but whose future behavior would at least in part be shaped by those outcomes. These states (e.g. Libya and Saudi Arabia) were also closely following the course of Soviet-American military confrontations.

In short, the actions of the superpower protagonists from the tactical level upward were being observed in one fashion or another by the whole world. At a minimum, these observations would have translated into revised military assessments as to the capabilities of each superpower to carry out a role in the region and into political assessments as to the reliability and worth of each of the protagonists as an ally. Thus, in each case, the effect of an action assumed many different dimensions that stretched well beyond the initial tactical battlespace and the original active players.

Whereas the above three rules have clear analogies to a chess game, they also hint at a more complex interaction that transcends the kind of competition reflected in a game of chess. And, the 1967, 1970, and 1973 crises used to illustrate the first three rules demonstrate some more complex interactions than any reflected in the chess game. This more complex dimension emerges in the remaining three rules, which focus on the human dimension of the interactions and the way in which each action-reaction cycle is seen and understood by observers.

4. Action-reaction cycles occur simultaneously in multiple dimensions.

In each of the three crises, the action-reaction cycles could be seen to occur on four different levels:

- At the tactical level, there were tattletale and counter-tattletale operations and close air surveillance operations.

- At the operational level, there were maneuvers to interpose the forces of one or the other fleet between the opponent and that opponent's local clients in the war.

- At the military-strategic level, there was a race to substantially reinforce the naval units in the crisis area and in the 1973 crisis, to resupply clients on both sides by air. Other forces were put on alert. Nuclear forces were held pending a close monitoring of the opponent's forces for any sign of change.

- Finally, at the geo-strategic level, there was a considerable political, diplomatic, and sometimes economic effort undertaken by both the Soviets and the Americans in each of the three crisis reactions.

In each of the three crises, interactions at each level and in each arena took place simultaneously. What happened or failed to happen on one level in one arena influenced what happened in all. In an example of inaction, the failure to counter Arab financial pressures on Britain in 1967 nullified the only military force in the region capable of averting a conflict, Britain's "East of Suez" carrier battle group.

Thus, in place of a single chess game, we have multiple complex interactions on four levels and in three or more arenas. This only stands to reason since the actors and behaviors we wish to influence in effects-based operations also reside on four different levels of the military arena and at multiple levels of the political and economic arenas.

5. All actions and effects at each level and in each arena are interrelated.

It is clear, especially at the geo-strategic level, that the military actions in the three Middle East crises took place in the context of complex diplomatic, political, and economic maneuvering. The crises also amply demonstrate that the actions and effects on all of these levels and in all these arenas were interrelated. This was certainly very evident in the concerns of both Soviet and American operational commanders that some unintended action might set off an uncontrollable succession of events. Although this was apparent in each crisis, it was most pronounced as in the 1970 crisis when the

U.S. Sixth Fleet commander ordered his flagship alongside that of the Soviet Fleet's flagship so that both ships would be subject to any attack that might grow out of an incident.[49] The commanders' concern was military in nature, but both commanders clearly appreciated that any such encounter would quickly spread outside the military arena to the political and economic.

In the crises, the diplomatic activity obviously included explanation of Soviet or American positions and actions to allies, neutrals, and/or potential adversaries. This was an essential element in defining the military actions required to support the creation of a unified national level effect. In the days before the 1967 War for example, much of the diplomatic activity centered on putting together an international naval force that could break the Egyptian blockade of the Gulf of Aqaba before the Israelis undertook any action.

In a different vein, the Arabs (and particularly Saudi Arabia) applied significant economic pressure on Great Britain to foreclose a potential British military action. Similarly, during the 1973 crisis, the Arab states led by Saudi Arabia attempted to foreclose American military support for Israel by cutting off American oil supplies with an oil embargo.

However, there was also another dimension of this interrelationship in view. As Rule Two indicated, the actions of the players were also cumulative over time. After its abortive involvement in the 1967 war, for example, Britain never again played a leading role in a Middle East crisis. In 1970, British forces kept well clear of the developing crisis, and by 1973, they had been entirely withdrawn from both the Mediterranean Sea and the area "East of Suez." Similarly, the U.S. and Soviet reactions to the crisis were mutually studied and figured in the actions that each took in subsequent crises.

If we accept, as outlined in Rule Two, that actions and effects cannot be isolated and that they produce cumulative effects, then as another general rule, it follows that all of the above interactions: at all levels and arenas must also be treated as interrelated and cumulative over time. Thus, it is not only what we do now that might create an effect on another level or in another arena, but also how that action appears in the context of what we have done in the past. The effect of any individual action, thus, stands to be enhanced or diminished by the cumulative context within which they were undertaken.

6. Effects are both physical and psychological.

The chain from physical actions to psychological effects can be observed in each of the three Middle East crisis responses. It is perhaps most evident in the dispatch of the U.S. Sixth Fleet toward the Syrian coast in 1967 in response to the Soviet threat to intervene on behalf of a hard-pressed Syria. However, it is more uniformly present in the large scale, visible reinforcement of naval forces in the Mediterranean that both sides undertook in all three of the Middle East confrontations. Although neither the abrupt dispatch of the Sixth Fleet nor the substantial reinforcement of forward forces resulted in any semblance of attrition-based damage to forces and capabilities, we can nonetheless see connections between the physical and psychological effects. In each case, a physical action (ship movements) had a direct physical effect. The event was observed and reported. That direct physical effect gave rise to a series of subsequent actions and decisions, which manifested as changed behavior. The reinforcement of forward forces typically set off similar movements of opposing forces to counter or monitor them, and in decisions by policy makers to further reinforce their own forces in the area. In the case of the Soviets in 1967 and again in 1973, the psychological effect was evident in the decision not to enter the struggle on behalf of Syria.

However, if we look more closely still at the crises, we can also discern that these reactions to a single tactical or operational level action evoke a chain of reactions that span all the levels of command and across multiple arenas.

It should be readily apparent in the discussion of each of the rules that effects have both physical and psychological dimensions. The relationship between physical actions and physical effects is already familiar. A bomb is dropped and physical destruction ensues. But the central thesis of effects-based operations is that physical actions, destructive or nondestructive, kinetic or nonkinetic, can produce physical *and* psychological effects.

The psychological effects in the decisionmaking processes of allies, neutrals, and enemies become manifest in their behavior. That is, we can detect the psychological effect of our actions upon observers by noting how they react or alter their behavior in response.

Actions and Effects

The rule set and examples outlined above supply a general framework for pursuing an effects-based operation that is consistent with the model of the cognitive cycle outlined in the preceding chapter (see Figure 37). Yet, they still leave us far from any sort of cause and effect chain.

What were the criteria for choosing a particular action at any given time during the crises? That question actually implies two different questions:

- First, what was it in the nature of a specific action that induced decisionmakers to believe that it would have the desired impact on the other side or upon other observers? How did they decide, for example, what (to use Admiral Zumwalt's words) was a low-key response? Such a decision presupposes that we can identify which aspects of any action observers might see as low-key and which they would not. If we are to operationalize effects-based operations, we must have an idea of what attributes of our actions will have desirable effects and then be able to control them so as to obtain those effects.

- Second, how do we choose what effects to create? It is clear in the examples that the effects sought existed at multiple different levels and in multiple arenas. The basic rule set

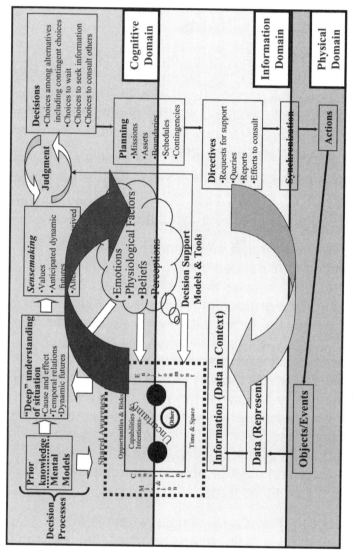

Figure 37. Action-Reaction Cycle

likewise tells us that all of these are interrelated with the effects in one arena or level determining the success or failure of those in another arena or level. Yet, the effects demonstrated in the examples were almost universally of a general nature and primarily at the geo-strategic or military-strategic levels. How then do we identify the effects we need to create and then link them to the actions needed to create them?

The above suggests the need for a more nuanced understanding of both the nature of actions and effects, especially as the terms apply in the context both of the rules sets and of the real-world examples above. This is the function of the next chapter.

---

[1]The vast majority of these responses were small-scale and largely utilized those military forces already on-scene or in the region of the crisis. According to the Blechman and Kaplan study, *Force without War*, this figure stood at 331 as of 1978. As later updated by Siegel and the Center for Naval Analyses using the same methodology, the figure amounted to more than 400 crisis responses by U.S. military forces by the end of 1996.
Blechman, Barry M. and Stephen S Kaplan. *Force without War*. Washington, DC; Brookings. 1978.
[2]Zelikow, Philip D. "Force without War, 1975-1982." *The Journal of Strategic Studies*. March 1984.
[3]Siegel, Adam. *The Use of Naval Forces in the Post War Era: U.S. Navy and U.S. Marine Corps Crisis Response Activity, 1946-1990*. Alexandria, Virginia; Center for Naval Analyses. 1991.
[4]U.S. Air Force, Air Staff. *The United States Air Force and U.S. National Security: A Historical Perspective*. Washington, DC; USAF Historical Office. 1991.
[5]U.S. Army Concepts Analysis Agency. "Crisis Response." unpublished paper. 1992.

[6]Obviously, if we follow the logic of the cognitive domain, one must maneuver something that observers can see and must take into their decisionmaking. Thus, the maneuver to which we shall refer is a maneuver of capabilities that achieves its effect in part from what those capabilities are and in part from where they are and when.
Barnett, Roger. *Naval War College Review.* Spring 2002.

[7]The author was assigned to the U.S. Sixth Fleet during the 1967 and 1970 crises and monitored the Soviet response to the 1973 crisis from the Navy Field Operational Intelligence Office, authoring a series of classified articles on the latter.

[8]Israel had launched an earlier anti-terrorist operation against the Jordanian town of Es Sammu in November 1966.

[9]The Sinai had been de-militarized in 1956 as the requisite for Israeli withdrawal from territories it occupied in the 1956 war.

[10]Abu-Lughod, Ibraham. *The Arab-Israeli Confrontation of June 1967: An Arab Perspective.* Evanston; Northwestern University. 1970. pp. 49-51.

[11]Johnson, Lyndon Baines. *The Vantage Point: Perspectives of the Presidency, 1963-1969.* New York. 1971. pp. 290-291.

[12]Johnson, p. 294.

[13]The sole subscribers to the force in addition to Britain were the United States, which had two over-aged destroyers in the Persian Gulf, Australia, which was to send two cruisers, and the Netherlands, which volunteered to send an officer to command the force.
Finney, John W. "Backing Reported for Plan to Test Aqaba Blockade." *New York Times.* June 1, 1967. Page 1, Col 8.

[14]Wilson, Harold. *A Personal Record.* Boston. 1971. p. 396.

[15]President Johnson first set the American limit at 200 miles from the conflict area, then later reduced it to 100 miles. The sole exception to this limit was the USS *Liberty*, an intelligence collection ship that was monitoring events from waters off the Gaza strip until the Israelis attacked it (ostensibly accidentally) on June 10. Neither side had air or ground forces in the area, although the threatened Soviet airlift into Syria would have involved both.
Johnson, pp. 298 ff.

[16]*New York Times.* June 11, 1967.

[17]President Johnson wanted to maneuver the U.S. Sixth Fleet so as to signal the Soviets that the United States would respond, but with a measured military action. Aware that Soviet intelligence collection ships were monitoring the fleet, he had it reverse course and head toward the Syrian coast, but to avoid alarming the Soviets, he apparently wanted the

ships to proceed at a "normal" cruising speed. However, he made the mistake of asking his Secretary of Defense Robert McNamara what a "normal" cruising speed for the fleet would be, and received a reply of 25 knots (about double the normal cruising speed).

Johnson, pp. 302-303.

[18]Nixon, Richard M. RN. *The Memoirs of Richard Nixon.* Norwalk. 1978. p. 485.

[19]Kissinger, Henry A. *White House Years.* Boston. 1979. p. 595.

[20]*New York Times.* June 12, 1967 and June 28, 1967.

[21]Nixon, pp. 483 ff.

[22]*New York Times.* September 13, 1967.

[23]Kissinger, p. 628.

[24]Kissinger, pp. 629.

[25]This build up continued on September 23 even as the Jordanians began to drive the Syrian forces back across the border so as to maintain pressure on both the Soviets and their Syrian clients.

Kissinger, p. 630.

[26]This situation was particularly troublesome to the Egyptians. The cease-fire line of 1967 ran along the course of the Suez Canal, which consequently could not be used. This deprived Egypt of a substantial source of revenue and foreign exchange and made them dependent on annual compensation payments from their Arab neighbors, a situation unacceptable to Sadat.

Sadat, Anwar As. *In Search of Identity, An Autobiography.* New York; Harper. 1978. pp. 188 and 215.

[27]Jordan, in no position to fight, studiously avoided any involvement in these assaults despite heavy pressure from other Arab states to do so.

Kissinger, Henry A. *Years of Upheaval.* Boston; Little Brown. 1980. pp. 490 and 494.

[28]Sobel, Lester A. *Israel and the Arabs: The October 1973 War.* New York: Facts on File, Inc. 1974. pp. 90-111.

[29]The Soviets had had some advance notice of the operation and on October 5, scrambled visiting ships from Egyptian ports and evacuated civilian personnel from the country.

Kissinger. *Upheaval.* p. 466.

[30]Nixon, p. 514.

[31]Zumwalt, Elmo. *On Watch.* Washington, DC; Zumwalt. 1980. p. 435.

[32]Zumwalt, p. 442ff.

[33]This included a helicopter carrier battle group and a series of additional submarines increasing the total to more than 80, a total that ultimately included some 96 units.
Zumwalt, p. 442.

[34]Israelyan, Victor. *Inside the Kremlin During the Yom Kippur War*. University Park; PSU Press. 1995. pp. 169-170.

[35]This was certainly underlined in the 1967 Arab-Israeli War by President Johnson's use of the movements of the Sixth Fleet to signal U.S. resolve to oppose any direct Soviet intervention in Syria. But, it was equally apparent in the White House order to send an aircraft from the Sixth Fleet into Israel to suggest combined Israeli-American planning during the 1970 crisis, and in the movements of the Sixth Fleet, the alert of the 82nd Airborne Division, and the increase in the overall Defense Condition (DEFCON) during the 1973 crisis.
Kissinger. *Upheaval*. pp. 469ff.

[36]Kissinger. *White House Years*. p. 614.

[37]Since the major units of each fleet in all cases were under close and continuous scrutiny by the other, any change in activity, size, or location were promptly reported to higher levels of command if not directly to the respective national command authorities.

[38]Edward Luttwak uses the term *suasion* to encompass the idea that a single action can be either persuasive or dissuasive, depending on who is observing the action.
Luttwak, Edward. *Strategic Power, Military Capabilities, and Political Utility*. Georgetown. 1976. p. 26.

[39]The designation *Eskadra* signified an operational organization that was theoretically more than a squadron and less than a fleet, but which might be expanded as much as necessary to cope with an evolving situation, in the manner of a U.S. task force.
http://www.fas.org/nuke/guide/russia/agency/mf-med.htm. John Pike. September 16, 2002.

[40]One variant of this strategy was the placement of the U.S. Sixth Fleet in an operations area south of the island of Crete in both the 1967 and 1973 crises. That position, although away from the immediate conflict area, was also astride the flight path of the Soviet aircraft resupplying Egypt and Syria.
Howe, Jonathan. *Multicrises: Sea Power and Global Politics in the Missile Age*. Cambridge. 1971. pp. 57ff.

[41]Then Vice Admiral Isaac Kidd, U.S. Navy, commented that he was so concerned with this possibility that, during the height of 1970 crisis, he put his flagship alongside the Soviet flagship. In this position, missiles or bombs aimed at one would be sure to strike both as a demonstration that he had

no intention of initiating hostilities.

Kidd, Isaac C. ADM. "View from the Bridge of the Sixth Fleet Flagship." Proceedings, February 1972. Interview with the author. November 10, 1972. p. 31.

[42]From the Egyptian and Syrian standpoint, the desperation stemmed from their apparent inability to halt the Israeli advance on their respective capitals. From the Israeli standpoint, it was desperation born of logistics and the inability to replace the arms and munitions expended without a massive American airlift. These factors became key ingredients in the superpowers' ability to force both sides to the negotiating table.

Sobel. *Israel*. p. 97.

[43]We have to be careful to add a caveat that the impact of the maneuver derived in part from the fact that the forces used could have opened fire and inflicted destruction.

[44]Blechman and Kaplan, p. 271.

[45]Cable, Sir James. *Gunboat Diplomacy, The Sea in Modern Strategy*. London. 1971. p. 76.

[46]These were primarily carrier air operations on the side of the Americans in all three crises, but included air resupply operations by the Soviets in 1967 and air resupply by both Americans and Soviets in 1973. These interactions were usually dissimilar in that the Soviet reaction to a carrier launch cycle was usually to report the launch and track the aircraft, and the American reaction to resupply flights was similarly to track and report them. Both actions, however, carried an implication of an ability to attack or otherwise halt the air action if need be.

[47]This was especially true since these tattletales were not judged to have a combat life of more than a few minutes after hostilities began. This tended to make the entire engagement a precipitous "battle of the first salvo."

Kidd, p. 32.

[48]Kissinger. *Upheaval*. pp. 579ff.

[49]Then VADM Isaac Kidd. Interview with the author. November 10, 1972.

CHAPTER 6

The Challenge of Complexity

Perhaps the most striking aspect of both the cognitive cycle and the foregoing rule sets is the sheer complexity of what we are trying to do in planning and executing effects-based operations. Indeed, we can delineate three distinct areas of complexity: orchestrating the right actions to create the behavioral effects we want to produce; determining which cascades of direct and indirect effects are likely to stem from our actions; and determining which effects we have actually created. The challenge, moreover, is not only to deal with these complexities, but also to exploit them to our advantage in the manner of the "edge of chaos" discussed in Chapter 3.

The historical examples of combat and crisis operations demonstrate that this challenge, however daunting it may appear, can be met. Great leaders have always been able to manage this feat to some degree. That is one reason why they are considered "great." Our challenge is to figure out how to apply new technology and the network-centric thinking of the Information Age to this task. To this end, we must dissect the complexities involved and study how leaders have dealt with those complexities in the past.

Complexity One: From Actions to Effects

At the heart of the concept of effects-based operations is the idea that our actions can affect the outcomes of an interaction. At least in a general sense, we can certainly see this to be the case in the three crises reviewed as well as in earlier examples from Trafalgar and Midway. Yet, implicit in the idea of planning and executing an effects-based operation is the notion that the link between the actions we execute and the effects they create is more than a general loose relationship, and that with specific, well-chosen actions we can drive specific effects to take place.

The problem with this supposition is the complexity of the task involved. The rule set in the previous chapter makes it clear that we are treating a process in which the actions and effects in question are interrelated across four levels (tactical, operational, military-strategic, and geo-strategic) and across at least three arenas (political-diplomatic, military, and economic) and are cumulative over time.

If we consider this process in the context of the Middle East crises, it also becomes apparent that the actions we use to create effects can be of nearly infinite variety.[1] Similarly, the review of the cognitive cycle indicates that the way in which these actions, past and present, will be perceived varies from one observer to the next. Finally, the rule set cautions that any action will be perceived by and have some effect on multiple and often competing observers. The task of translating actions into effects clearly is not impossible. After all, this is exactly what the participants in each of the three Middle East crises were doing.[2] How did they do it?

If we think about what went on in the crises, the decisionmakers routinely accepted a degree of uncertainty in their calculations. This is very different from the certitude we normally think of in a precision strike whose outcome is denominated solely in terms of bomb damage and levels of physical destruction. They accepted the complexities involved in inducing the desired behavior and, in a sense, heeded the Aristotelian injunction to be "satisfied with the degree of precision that the nature of the subject permits, and not to seek exactness when only approximation is possible."[3] In essence, they bounded the complexity by looking at and choosing certain kinds of actions that were likely to produce certain kinds of effects so as to find a workable answer.

It seems clear that the starting point for answering these most fundamental of effects-based questions is to understand better what we mean by the terms *actions* and *effects*, and how they apply in the real-world operational context that we have laid out in the principles of effects-based operations. The cognitive cycle gives us a hint of how to proceed: that the impact of actions and the nature of effects both are the result of how observers perceive, understand, make sense, judge, and decide. It is this human dimension of interactions, whether in peace of in war, that we must address if we are to understand either the nature of actions or the effects that we might create.

The Nature of Actions

In discussing the cognitive cycle, we noted that the impact of a physical action on an observer stemmed not only from *what* was done, but also from every observable aspect of *how* it was done. It seems clear then that our concept of the nature of actions must proceed from one basic question: what aspects of an action are observable?

As we saw in the crisis reactions, the number of permutations in actions that an observer might theoretically see could be nearly infinite. However, such an open-ended approach is of little value in defining a working concept. What we must do is to bound this infinity by thinking of an action in terms of a particular set of variables, the sum of which will be observed, interpreted, and understood by an observer in their cognitive processes.

To plan an action, we must consider all those variables that might describe that object or event and then determine what part of that description might reach one or another observer through the information domain of sensors and information systems that each has created (see Figure 38). Notice that we have not said that this multi-faceted description of an action equates to the observer's *perception*. The perception is the initial impact that a particular set of action variables will have on a specific individual with a specific background in a

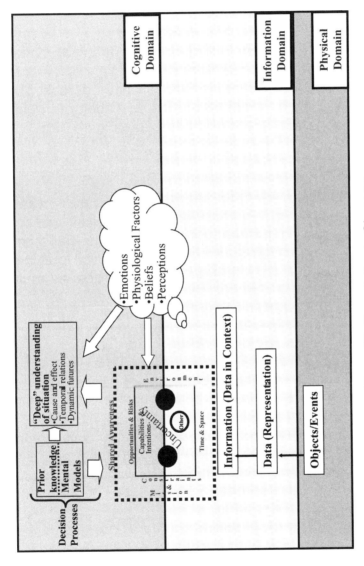

Figure 38. From Action to Observer

specific set of circumstances or situation. Our concern for the moment is more limited. It is to determine what the variables associated with the *what* and *how* of an action might be.

If we think about the physical actions that took place during the battles of Midway and Trafalgar and in the three Middle East crises, we can trace at least six different major observables that describe both what was done and how it was done (see Figure 39).

1. What

The starting point is obviously the question of "what is done," the nature of the physical action undertaken. In other words, what is the object or event to be observed? This physical action may be the destruction of forces and capabilities as in a

What is Done	How it is Done
What	Scale
With What	• Force Used
	• Impact
	Scope
	• Geographic
	• Operational
	Timing
	• Speed
	• Duration
	• Synchronicity
	Visibility

Figure 39. Observable Attributes of Physical Actions

traditional warfare model. It may equally be a terrorist bombing. However, as we have seen in the case of the Battle of Midway, the action need not involve destruction. It may be as simple as being at a particular place at the right time, as the aircraft carrier *Yorktown* was at Midway. Or it may be a movement toward a place as in the case of maneuver, a recurring feature of each of the Middle East crises. Or, it may be what is *not* done and where a unit is *not* present, as demonstrated by the deliberate efforts by the United States to keep forces out of the crisis area that characterized all three Middle East crises.

For the opponent observer/decisionmaker, this "what" is the aspect of the stimulus that might be expected to provoke one series of shaping questions: What did my adversary do? What action was taken or what capability was destroyed? How will it affect me or how might I have to alter my current course of action to deal with it? The "what" encompasses most of the reactions upon which nodal targeting or a carefully crafted target list might focus. But the "what" also extends to military maneuvers or simple presence that might induce observers to ask questions such as: Where did the force interpose itself? What action did it take and how might that action inhibit my current and future operations? Moreover, these kinds of observations are not restricted to the states and governments doing the observing, but would apply equally to non-state actors, such as terrorist organizations. This is especially true if the physical means of such groups are limited to the point of offering few targets subject to physical destruction.

Because the observers in question will not be limited to adversaries and would-be opponents, the actions will also be seen by and affect the decisions of friends and neutrals, both passive and active players, as well as our own public. These questions might take a somewhat different direction, but focus on a similar end: How does the action affect me and the course of action I am currently pursuing with regard to the United States, or the region, or my neighbors?

All of the above considerations were reflected in the responses to the Middle East crises, but there was something more as well. In the 1967 War, President Johnson was concerned not only with *what* the Sixth Fleet was doing (heading toward Syria), but also *how* it was doing it (its transit speed). This interest is understandable in the context of the crisis because of the signal that the Fleet's speed would carry to the Soviets. However, it would also have been important to the White House because the length of time it took for the transit determined the timing for the next diplomatic and political actions the United States might have to take.

This distinction between what an action is and how it is executed is the basis for the five remaining elements of an action.

2. How

The first and perhaps most visible element of this "how" is the nature of the power used to undertake the action. The choice of power will tell observers a great deal both about the action itself and the direction of any continuing chain of interactions, both essential parts of the sensemaking and decisionmaking processes. Obviously, it makes a great deal of difference whether an action or stimulus is solely or primarily political, economic, or military. And, it also matters what kind of military force is used or threatened.

The choice of military force, for example "boots on the ground," might presage a willingness to take risks or to undertake an extended commitment, while a relatively low cost threat, such as a missile strike, might signal a lack of commitment. The message sent by this choice can be either positive or negative depending upon the situation and opponent. "Boots on the ground" in one circumstance may indicate an issue so important as to be worth risking substantial casualties. In another situation, reliance on ground forces could signal an opportunity for the opponent to adopt a damage infliction strategy as part of an asymmetric attack on our will. Similarly, a resort to standoff precision missiles may signal a lack of willingness to take casualties, or by denying any exploitable vulnerability, it may indicate a ready ability to act again because the operation can be sustained without appreciable political fallout.

In the Middle East crises, the forces of choice were naval units, airborne divisions, and transport aircraft. The naval forces in particular were applicable to a local face-off. They offered credible, forcible options such as putting Marines ashore and air strikes, but they could also be maneuvered to support political-diplomatic efforts. In all three cases, one key to this use in crisis resolution was that each action taken would be immediately reported to the opposing side by the tattletales observing both sides. Similarly, the activity of the 82nd Airborne Division and its Soviet counterparts were closely monitored and reported, as was the overall alert status of military forces, and particularly strategic nuclear forces, on both sides.

We can equally turn this around and look at the question from the perspective of the types of operations or weapons (kinds of force) used by terrorists. The hijacking of airliners with the eventual release of the passengers and crew, as in the 1970 crisis, might be expected to create one reaction. The hijacking of similar airliners and their use with passengers and crew as gigantic missiles in the World Trade Towers attack conveys a different magnitude and character threat, while their use to deliver a weapon of mass effect against a large city would convey yet another level and character threat.

3. Scale

The scale of the action has two dimensions: the scale of the effort involved in the action and the scale of the impact. Together they set the quantitative size of the problem the enemy observer or decisionmaker must deal with.

Obviously, a single missile might destroy a single target and create an effect, but it seems evident that a different scale of effort, using 100 missiles on the target, will create a very different impression upon the observer, for good or bad. Similarly, using 100 missiles against a single target has a very different significance from their use against 100 different targets.

Moreover, the effect created by the same scale of effort will vary from one observer to the next and from one situation to the next. Was a 100-missile strike a disproportionate response? Was it sufficient to induce shock and to deter future actions or is a greater scale of effort and impact required? Would a strike by a single missile against a single target convey an impression of weakness or of confidence in an ability to detect and strike exactly the right target at exactly the right time?

From the standpoint of friendly or neutral observers, these same questions would contribute to defining the credibility of both a threat and a response. Their observations might reassure them as to the viability of U.S. commitments, or define the extent of the problem they would face in trying to challenge us. While these questions underline how separate the question of scale is from that of focus, they also point to the need to tailor the scale to a particular set of observers and a particular situation.

The impact of scale on the Middle East interactions was very evident. In all three of the crises, military forces, and the naval forces in particular, offered potential variations along at least three different continua: the scale or numbers of units added or subtracted; the distance from the crisis area; and the level and type of activity undertaken. All three variables figured prominently in each of the crises, but the choices as to which to emphasize hinged on a risk analysis. Moving a force closer to the crisis area or increasing the aggressiveness of its actions appear to have been considered riskier alternatives than increasing numbers, with the former used only where the very short time-span of interactions left no other military alternative. In fact, the naval confrontations in the 1970 and 1973 crises were some of the most massive uses of Soviet and American military power during the 40 years of the Cold War.

However, there was a second reflection of this concern regarding the scale over the span of the three crises. Not only was there concern with the reinforcement and counter-reinforcement of naval units during the crises, but also as planning carried over from one crisis to the next. Thus, the number of ships involved in the confrontations grew substantially from the 1967 crisis, to the 1970 crisis, to the 1973 crisis. Indeed, the scale and pace of such a build-up was deemed so critical by the Soviets that they set up a system of contingency declarations for transiting the Bosporus and Dardenelles, which endured for more than a decade after the crises.

4. Scope

Scope encompasses two dimensions, one geographic and the other operational.

- Geographic scope defines the physical battlespace within which the foe may be obliged to act or within which he may be vulnerable. The broader the area is, the greater his problem is likely to be. For example, a barrage of 100 missiles aimed at a single target will be observed to present a different challenge from a similar scale strike directed at

100 separate targets spread across the breadth of a country. The former would permit the foe to concentrate his defenses around one or more key targets. The latter would put him in the quandary of either having to dilute the defense so as to try to defend all potential targets, or concentrating it around the wrong target and leaving the others without any defense at all.

However, there is another aspect to geographic scope: where can forces be brought to bear? The impact of this aspect of geographic scope of operations was most apparent in the abortive Anglo-American attempt to break the Egyptian blockade of the Strait of Tiran in 1967. When the use of British naval forces was foreclosed by Arab economic pressure on Britain, the United States and its would-be coalition partners were unable to get sufficient forces to the scene in time to meet an Israeli deadline, and the effort failed. In essence, the Arabs managed to construct a challenge, the geographic scope of which exceeded the abilities of the American and Australian forces.

A variant of this challenge occurred in the air resupply efforts of both the Soviets and Americans during the 1973 crisis. In the Soviet case, warships armed with surface-to-air missiles stationed at the Hamamet anchorage off Tunisia could readily attack the American aircraft resupplying Israel as they passed through the air corridor in the Strait of Sicily, a route dictated by the refusal of America's European allies to grant overflight permission.

Similarly on the American side, the concentration of the Sixth Fleet carriers off Crete and Cyprus put them athwart the routes that Soviet transports needed to take to reach Egypt and Syria.

• Operational scope defines the nature of the battlespace or the warfare environments (air, sea, undersea, ground, space) where the foe might be challenged. However, it simultaneously defines those warfare areas where the foe is not likely to be challenged and that, therefore, might provide opportunities to counter or balance the threats that can be posed. For example, an inability to deal with land or sea mines might signal a way of slowing or stopping a "boots on the ground" challenge. In general, the greater the number of warfare environments subject to a credible challenge, the more stressing the threat is likely to be seen to be by the would-be adversary. A complex, multi-dimensional threat will simply tax an adversary's assets and command and control to a greater degree, and it is more likely to keep him guessing as to where the full weight of any attack or maneuver will be placed.

The influence of operational scope was demonstrated in the Soviet-American face-offs in all three crises. Both sides were largely limited to naval forces for the confrontation because neither had a frontier with the parties involved, nor air bases or troops in the area.[4] However, the operational scope of what the respective forces were able to do differed greatly. The American force with its carrier air power and amphibious capability had a far wider operational scope, one that encompassed a full range of air operations from surveillance to strike at sea and ashore. The Soviets had the advantage of anti-ship missiles mounted on its heavier combatants as well as missile-firing submarines. In the aggregate, these different advantages tended to cancel each other out, which is perhaps one reason that the contest became primarily one of numbers.

5. Timing

Timing encompasses three different dimensions: speed; duration; and what might be called "synchronicity."

- Speed is the ability to execute an action or reaction rapidly enough to create a desired effect. This may mean creating an operational tempo that is so overwhelmingly fast as to allow no coherent response or as to induce shock or chaos. Or it may mean being able to react quickly enough to changes in either the warfare environment or the political arena to foreclose courses of action that the foe might wish to take. Both these ideas are reflected in the concept of "speed of command." Thus, for the foe, speed defines one set of problems with timing actions for maximum effect and another in coping with the pace of operations. The former portends foreclosure of desired courses of action and the latter holds the potential for shock and chaos.

  The closing hours of both the 1967 and 1973 crises present a clear example of this requirement for speed in creating an effect. In each case, the effect created by an overall national action hinged on the ability of the Sixth Fleet to demonstrate American resolve by its maneuvers, and the ability of the Soviet intelligence collectors to immediately detect those maneuvers and report them directly to Moscow. A similar but less pressing example occurred in the 1970 crisis when U.S. airborne units in Germany were put on alert at least in part because such an alert would be speedily reported to Soviet Intelligence.[5]

- Duration, or the period of time over which an operation is or can be sustained, defines how long a foe might have to endure an action, and by extension, whether he or she can hope to outlast it. An action that can only be initiated once or that cannot be repeated very often invites the foe to "ride it out" before returning to previous behavior, whereas one that has no such limitation invites a conclusion that the pressure is not going to end without a change in behavior.

The build-up of Soviet and American naval forces in the Mediterranean in each of the Middle East crises was at least partially directed at convincing the opponent and its clients of a willingness to "stick it out." Despite any efforts to limit access, the ships could be maintained on station virtually indefinitely and if necessary, resupplied from home waters.[6] In a larger dimension, for at least the Sixth Fleet, there was also the history of continuous operations in the area since 1948. There was no expectation on the part of either the Soviets or their clients that the American force might be withdrawn, only a question as to where it would operate, in what numbers, and with what capability.

- Synchronicity, or the ability to cause actions to occur at exactly the right time or in exactly the right sequence to achieve a disproportionate impact, defines the level of difficulty of the military problem a would-be foe faces. The wider the diversity of closely timed operations the foe might face, the more difficult it will be for him to counter them and the more likely it is they will result in a cascade of problems for the observer that he will be unable to control.

The Soviet anti-carrier exercise that took place in the closing days of the 1973 crisis (a demonstration of the Soviet Fleet's capacity to launch a sudden and coordinated missile strike that could incapacitate or sink all the U.S. carriers in the Mediterranean) is certainly one demonstration of synchronicity, and one obviously calculated to have more than just tactical significance. However, such synchronicity is also apparent in the timing of Sixth Fleet actions to coincide with notes exchanged between Moscow and Washington, as well as in the alerts to airborne forces on both sides.

6. Visibility

As the diagram of the cognitive process suggests, any action that is observed, whether it is intended to be or not, and whether it is part of a particular effects-based plan or not, will create some effect. Conversely, any action that is not observed, no matter how carefully planned and orchestrated it may be, will create no psychological effect.

The visibility of actions, whether directly or through sensors and information systems including the media, is key. If the foe or local audience cannot see the scale, scope, and timing of our actions (including "virtual" actions) or cannot even get a report of the actions in a manner that is timely enough to enter his decisionmaking process, then they will have no impact beyond their attrition value, if any. For example, a virtual action that cannot be seen or evaluated by the observer is likely either not to enter into his calculations at all or, perhaps, to be dismissed as a hoax. But that is not all. If the dimensions of our actions are misreported and misperceived, the observer may react in a way that is very different from what was intended. Or he may overreact, a particularly dangerous prospect when confronting a foe armed with weapons of mass destruction. Knowing what the foe or other observers and, by extension their individual surveillance or other collection systems, are likely to see becomes a critical factor in effects-based planning.

While there is clearly a need to appreciate what observers are likely to see and react to, there is also an opportunity in considering the visibility of our actions because it provides one more variable that can be manipulated and controlled to create the desired effect. If our knowledge of the observer's sensor system and how it operates is sufficient, for example, we may be able to orchestrate our actions so as to control what is observed and when.

These factors were evident in the use of naval forces to signal intentions to the Soviets. Presidents Johnson and Nixon were very much aware not only that U.S. maneuvers were being closely monitored by the Soviets, but also of what would be reported and how fast it would reach the Soviet decisionmakers in Moscow. Thus, each president was able to use the maneuvers of the fleet with considerable finesse. However, the same visibility was conferred on the reinforcements entering the Mediterranean. Soviet movements through the Bosporus were to some degree signaled several days in advance by the contingency declarations for warship transits, but then were confirmed when the ships making the transit were directly observed. Similarly, U.S. forces held in the Atlantic became visible, and therefore became elements in the confrontation when they transited the Strait of Gibraltar into the Mediterranean, where they were equally monitored by the Soviet intelligence collectors.

We need to expand this focus further. Both the United States and the Soviets had large and sophisticated surveillance and intelligence collection systems to detect changes and relay information to decisionmakers. This was not the case for the local nations nor was it necessarily true for the allies of the two superpowers. Typically, the surveillance systems of the local states did not extend very far off their coasts and their intelligence collection was largely limited to human intelligence that was often late. Thus, news of movements or other actions could not be locally ascertained. While this might have permitted the concealment of military efforts almost at will, it had a down side. In each of the three crises, false reporting of U.S. military action in support of Israel, e.g. reports of U.S. carrier aircraft participating in the initial air strikes of the 1967 war, could not be confirmed or denied by trusted local sources and, thus, spread wildly.

Together, these six attributes constitute a list of the variables inherent in any military action. Stated differently, they constitute the aspects of our physical actions that may be orchestrated so as to create a desired physical or psychological effect and produce a particular behavior.[7] In essence, they provide a yardstick against which we can begin to measure the actions that we might want to execute in order to create a particular effect.

Effects: To Do What?

We earlier defined *effect* as "a result or impact created by the application of military or other power." Most discussions of effects-based operations seem to focus on very specific actions being orchestrated to create very specific effects. On the surface, pursuing this correlation would seem like a logical way to proceed. After all, effects-based operations revolve about the assumption of a causal link between a given action and a given outcome or, stated differently, between a stimulus and a response. Indeed, this same assumption is at the root of our expectations for a higher order, third effects-based level of combat efficiency. Nor is this all. The sheer complexity of the interactions described in the previous rule set highlight the impossible scale of the challenge we would face in trying to predict an exact link between actions and reactions at any but a purely tactical attrition-based level at any one level of conflict. And it seems nearly impossible to do so across the whole multi-level, multi-arena, multi-actor interaction described much less in a manner dynamic enough to be able to deal with a changing battlefield situation.

Unfortunately, this relationship between an action, however carefully crafted, and an effect can never be reduced to a simple cause and effect logic chain. As we could see in the cognitive cycle, there are too many variables involved in the process of moving from perception, to decision, to discernible behavior and the process is, thus, too complex to be rendered into such a neat chain.

At the root of all of this complexity lies a fundamental reality. Effects-based operations are about the human dimension of conflict. They revolve around the interactions between two or more of the most quintessential of complex adaptive systems: human decisionmakers and human organizations. The behavior of complex adaptive systems is, by definition, nonlinear. Indeed, it is exactly this human-based nonlinearity that we are trying to exploit in our effects-based operations. However, the nonlinearity implies that any link between an action and the subsequent behavior of human decisionmakers cannot be entirely predicted.[8] Thus, the cause and effect linkages between a particular stimulus and a particular response on any but an immediate tactical level are (and are likely to remain) neither clear nor quantifiable. At Midway, for example, despite the United States' ability to break Japanese codes, no one on the American side could have predicted either VADM Nagumo's exact reaction to the sighting of the U.S.S. *Yorktown* or the subsequent chain of events. This is true even though in retrospect we can discern a clear stimulus and response chain.

If we cannot expect to trace or predict a clear, one for one, cause and effect relationship between actions and human behavior, and if effects-based operations are by their very nature about exactly this human dimension of conflict, then how are we to plan and execute effects-based operations?

One way of dealing with this nonlinear challenge is what might be termed the *behavioralist approach*. The hope here is essentially that we might use the increasing computer power of the information revolution to profile the opposing decisionmakers so precisely as to be able to predict their reactions to the stimuli posed by any particular action.[9] But there is a drawback. A profile of sufficient depth to predict reactions would require such a depth of knowledge, not only about the decisionmakers themselves but also of all the factors impacting on their decisions, as to render it highly unlikely that the knowledge would be available when needed. Developing and maintaining such a database, or even simply obtaining the depth and quality of inputs needed would be a Herculean task, even with modern data mining technologies. Understanding how to put the data together in a model that took into account all of their implications in the context of an alien culture would be still more difficult. Moreover, the resulting profiles, whether computer assisted or not, would only be as good as the data and information programmed into them. Finally, if this task were multiplied across all the levels of potential decisionmakers in all the nations and non-state actors we might encounter, the scope simply of the collection effort required would rapidly reach an impossible scale.

A variant of this behavioral approach is the idea of using game playing theory.[10] That is, if we could replicate the conditions of the interactions themselves and, with computer assistance in the form of perhaps hundreds or thousands of virtual runs, and if we could reduce these interactions to some predictive model, we would be able to produce at least a set of probabilities for certain actions producing certain effects. This approach, of course, assumes that the game play from player to player is constant enough to model reliably.

Both of the above approaches certainly can contribute to an understanding of the observers and the processes involved in moving from action to effect to reaction. And, both offer real possibilities as analytical and decisionmaking tools. Yet, the real message seems to be that any approach that focuses on tracing an exact link between a given action and a very specific effect is doomed to failure. Herein lies a paradox. The nonlinearity of human reactions that makes the assessment of the cause and effect link so difficult is precisely what gives effects-based operations their disproportionate impact. How then are we to exploit the very nonlinearity that plagues us?

We can begin by accepting that the interactions we seek to trace are fundamentally nonlinear. The conflict we seek to portray is very much a clash between complex adaptive systems and there are real limits to what we can predict in such clashes. Professor Alan Beyerchen has noted that much of the enduring value in Clausewitz's writings stems from the fact that "he understands that seeking exact analytical solutions does not fit the nonlinear reality of the problems posed by war, and hence that our ability to predict the course and outcome of any given conflict is severely limited."[11] How do we apply these injunctions to looking at effects?

Let us return to the Midway example. We have said that we could not predict the exact nature and timing of Vice Admiral Nagumo's response to the sighting of the *Yorktown*. But, we can try to bound the problem. For example, the American operational commander, Vice Admiral Spruance, and his staff could understand very well both that the Japanese would be looking for his ships, and that Nagumo's most likely reaction to a sighting would be to launch aircraft for a naval battle. This is to say, he had a good general understanding of the most likely impact of an American stimulus and of the most likely Japanese response. He might also have surmised that the arrival of the torpedo planes would cause the Japanese carriers to maneuver so radically as to be unable to launch or recover aircraft. And, he might have predicted as well that, if that arrival occurred before that of the dive-bombers, the Japanese Combat Air Patrol (CAP) would probably descend to intercept the torpedo planes and leave their protective CAP stations uncovered.

Thus, even though the exact chain of events remained unknown and unknowable, Spruance could have used his understanding both of the operational situation and of the fundamental military choices his counterpart would face to deduce a series of most likely actions and reactions. That is, he could roughly predict at least a limited cause and effect chain. If he had also had adequate and timely information on the location and movements of Japanese forces, both air and sea, and of the timing and sequencing of Japanese air operations, he might have been able to exploit this general understanding to create intentionally the effects that the sighting and the disjointed American attack actually created by pure chance.

The Midway example suggests that we should not try to think of effects-based operations in terms of finding and exploiting very specific actions-to-effects linkages, but to look instead at a more general relationship between the potential actions described by the variables and various kinds of effects. That is, we should bound the problem of a potentially infinite number of effects in the same way as we did the potentially infinite number of actions. To do this, we might parse the infinite range of possibilities into a finite set of categories that can give us some idea of what kinds of effects that we might seek or that we might produce in a given set of circumstances. Then, from the categories, we might proceed to an understanding of how the different influences that each represents together add up to an overall effect able to alter or shape the behavior of foes, friends, and neutrals.

Kinds of Effects

In the Middle East crises, as in earlier historical examples, we have seen recognizable evidence of certain kinds of effects. The destruction of forces and capabilities at the center of attrition-based operations was certainly one such effect either in the form of destroying a specific force or target, or in that of the gradual wearing down of an opponent's forces and capabilities. Similarly, the chaos manifest in the French and Spanish fleets at Trafalgar would appear to be another kind of effect, and the shock that rippled through France in May 1940 yet another. Finally, the maneuvers of naval forces in the three Middle East crises from 1967 to 1973 illustrate what might be termed "foreclosure" as yet another kind of effect. We can begin to discern the outlines of six different categories (see Figure 40).

Although the effects in these categories are produced by some physical action, the effects themselves fall into two general areas: those effects that are predominantly physical in nature, and those that are primarily psychological. The physical effects alter behavior by dealing with the physical means of an observer to wage a war or to carry out a course of action. The psychological effects alter behavior by affecting the cognitive processes of the observers so as to shape will. The physical effects are focused on destruction and the incapacitation of forces and

Physical	Psychological (Reason/Belief)	
Destruction	Chaos / Entropy	
Physical Attrition	Foreclosure	
Chaos / Entropy	• Passive	
	• Active	
	Shock	
	Psychological Attrition	

Figure 40. Kinds of Effects

capabilities, including by rendering an observer incapable of mounting a coherent action (chaos). The psychological effects span the domain of reason, the rational decisionmaking process, and the domain of belief, the emotional impacts on decisionmaking. They lap over into the physical domain where they induce chaos, but focus on foreclosure, shock, and psychological attrition.

1. Destruction

Destroying an opponent's physical capability to do something is clearly an effect. In fact, the destruction of an opponent's forces and capabilities is the cardinal physical effect specifically because it may be successful regardless of whether it produces a psychological effect. If we kill the foe or destroy his physical means of resisting, his options for responding will be reduced to nearly nothing, no matter how great his will to resist. This, as we have seen, was the underlying desperate logic of symmetric attrition warfare.

While this logic has been challenged by the asymmetric warfare focused on will, destruction has a real and continuing validity. This is especially true at the tactical level where there is no time to consider whether an opponent's behavior has changed and every reason to suppose that a behavior that has changed once can just as rapidly change back again so long as the means to attack continue to exist. In such a kill or be killed combat situation, the physical elimination of an opposing unit or force is definitive. Once destroyed, the opposing unit or force can no longer pose a threat.

Yet, we also pointed to another understanding of destruction. Destruction of capabilities may be a means to an end, or a way of enabling other kinds of effects to be created. It may force a re-evaluation of a course of action. It may shock. It may wear down resistance. It may lead to other effects or be the agent for other effects both physical and psychological.

2. Physical Attrition

Although on the tactical level of conflict, the destruction of an opponent's force or capabilities may be carried out in a single operation, such destruction on the operational or military strategic level is likely to involve a campaign or series of campaigns.[12] The focus would shift from physically killing the enemy in a tactical engagement to gradually wearing down enemy capabilities in repeated operations.[13] Although the physical result of attrition may be the same as that of destruction (the elimination of all or part of a foe's capability to wage war), the character of the effect is very different because of the longer time that it takes to produce a result. Among other things, this slower, longer time line permits the foe to assess what is going on and perhaps to adapt to the challenge and deal with it, thus extending the timeline of the interaction.

This longer timeline also provides more opportunity for psychological factors to operate and means that any psychological impact is likely to revolve about weariness or a calculation of the futility of further action rather than a sudden collapse. Like destruction, physical attrition of an opponent's forces and means of waging war can be an agent for generating other psychological kinds of effects.

The role of physical attrition in the three Middle East crises is most apparent in the 1973 war. Instead of a 4-year long grinding down of an opponent's capacity to wage war as in the World Wars, in the 1973 war, it only took 1 week for the belligerents to exhaust nearly their entire supply of ammunition, tanks, aircraft, and missiles, and to then turn to the United States and the Soviet Union to compensate for the shortfall. President Sadat, in particular, appears to have realized that Israel, even with American arms, could not support a long war because of its manpower limitations, and used this to push Israel into negotiations, a different form of behavior modification.[14]

3. Chaos

Where destruction and physical attrition very obviously fall under the heading of a physical effect, chaos is both physical and psychological in nature. Chaos works from the premise that rendering a foe unable to react coherently or to control the forces he has available, or throwing those forces into disarray, is tantamount to destroying capabilities. Such confusion created in the minds of decisionmakers conveys that they are unable to command or fight their forces effectively. This idea is reflected in the concept of entropy-based warfare. The greater the degree of confusion and disorganization that can be induced into an enemy's decisionmaking process, the less able the foe will be to use the capabilities he has effectively and efficiently. This was clearly demonstrated in the Trafalgar example.

In this respect, the effect of chaos embodies some elements of both physical and psychological effects. Psychological factors (disorientation, confusion, fear) yield a physical result, the inability to use otherwise applicable forces and capabilities, however the cause of this effect is inherently rooted in behavior, the inability of commanders and subordinates to handle the pace and scope of operations required to deal with the challenge.

The drawback here is that, unlike the effects of destruction and attrition, such induced chaos is not a permanent state. Thus, the effect is not definitive and the capabilities can be brought to bear again if ever and whenever the foe is able restore order.

4. Foreclosure

A recurring facet of all three of the Middle East crisis reactions at all levels was the idea of somehow curtailing an opponent's options or foreclosing potential courses of action. Such foreclosure, indeed, is a fundamental tenet of positional or maneuver warfare. It can derive from the destruction of the capabilities that might be needed to pursue a certain course of action, or from their being rendered somehow inapplicable. But as numerous crisis reactions over the past 50 years have pointed out, it may also derive from maneuvering forces so as to put a particular capability at risk and thus invalidate the would-be enemy's risk assumptions underlying a particular course of action.

In the crisis histories that we have reviewed, we can distinguish two different types of foreclosure:

- *Active Foreclosure.* Most of the examples of foreclosure encountered in the discussion focused on what might be termed active foreclosure, the use of military forces to block a course of action that a foe has already initiated. This may take the form of a modern version of positional warfare in which a military force is interposed between the would-be enemy and his objective. This approach was very much evident in all three of the Middle East crises of 1967-1973, but has also been present at all levels of peace enforcement operations in the 1990s most demonstrably in Bosnia and Kosovo. Foreclosure may take the form of a threat of a response so massive or dire as to invalidate all previous risk assessments.

• *Passive Foreclosure*. Another less obvious
aspect of foreclosure is the ongoing balance of
military power that brings stability to a given
area. This passive foreclosure is analogous to
Mahan's concept of a "Fleet-in-Being."[15] The
foreclosure revolves around the fact that a
sufficient array of capabilities exists or can be
brought to bear in a given region to prevent a
destabilizing course of action from being
carried out. Such foreclosure hinges not only
on the relative capabilities of both sides over
time, but also on convincing the challenger that
those capabilities are likely to be used in the
event of aggression. Successful passive
foreclosure is likely to produce one of two kinds
of behavior. Either the would-be challenger will
not apply the resources necessary to creating
the capabilities to pursue the course of action
in the first place, or if the capabilities do exist,
the challenger will risk them on an endeavor
that is doomed to failure.

In the three Middle East crises, the resort to active
foreclosure in each case indicated some failure of
the regime of passive foreclosure in the area. This,
indeed, was one of the historical roles of the U.S.
Sixth Fleet presence in the area. In each of the three
crises, therefore, the immediate reaction of the
guarantor powers was to attempt to restore passive
foreclosure. In 1967, the United States and Great
Britain attempted to break the Egyptian blockade of
the Strait of Tiran and restore the balance in the
Sinai, but failed. In the 1970 crisis, the foreclosure
was restored by Jordan's military success against
the Syrians, Iraqis, and Palestinians, a success that

precluded the United States' having to intervene. In the 1973 crisis, both the United States and the Soviet Union initially attempted to restore order via passive foreclosure, but again failed and soon found themselves at loggerheads with each other pending the creation of some new balance of power.[16]

Like chaos, the effect of foreclosure is not permanent. Foreclosure will remain operative as long as the challenger continues to assess that the risks of pursuing an aggressive course of action outweigh prospective gains. In practical terms, the effect will remain only as long as the imbalance of forces that deterred action persists. If the balance between opposing forces shifts toward the challenger during active foreclosure, as was the case during the Soviet and American reactions to the 1973 war, then the foreclosure effect can diminish, disappear, or be reversed. Over a longer term, the same is true of passive foreclosure. The local balance of power can similarly shift, or over a far shorter time, the willingness of one side to actually use the forces can lapse, provoking a challenger to reassess the risks involved in aggressive conduct.

As the above chains of reasoning intimate, foreclosure is prominently within the domain of the reason and ultimately hinges on the ability to create a situation in which the proverbial "reasonable man" would conclude that a desired course of action simply cannot succeed and adjusts his behavior accordingly.

5. Shock

Where foreclosure is in the domain of the reason, shock is clearly in that of the emotion. Shock centers about a sudden collapse of the foe's belief in his ability to produce an acceptable outcome in a given situation. It may be paralleled by a sense of despair and resignation to a fate that can no longer be avoided. It can be induced by the constant surprise created by an overwhelming tempo of the opponent's operations, or by the unexpected failures of one's own forces and plans. This, indeed, was the case in France when confronted by the German blitzkrieg of 1940.

At the strategic and operational level, the shock effect may be manifest in a semi-catatonic inability to make coherent decisions or in ceding the initiative to the adversary. On the battlefield, it may be seen in the collapse of unit cohesion and the panic of a rout, certainly evident in the Syrian Army's actions on the Golan Heights in the 1967 and 1973 wars.

However, we need to add a caveat. Shock is in the eye of the beholder. Shock and panic are much less likely in an experienced leader or among well-trained and battle-hardened troops than among newly trained conscripts. As noted earlier, in the American Civil War, whereas the battle of Bull Run in 1861 resulted in a panicked rout of Union troops, the Battle of the Wilderness in 1864 resulted in no such reaction, even though the casualties were far greater.[17] Shock, in short, is as much a function of the target's experience, perceptions, and psychological state as it is of the actions taken to induce it.

6. Psychological Attrition

Whereas shock is a sudden collapse of belief, psychological attrition is the product of gradual erosion of the will. The victim of this psychological attrition gradually becomes convinced that nothing he can do will yield a satisfactory outcome to a situation and, at length, the victim agrees to change his behavior in a direction that previously could not have been tolerated. This effect is typified by the reaction of the United States public over the period from 1968 to 1975 during the Vietnam War. The focus in this effect was not on capabilities that might retrieve or alter the underlying situation, but on a mounting belief that those capabilities would ultimately be to no avail. Thus, the course of action was deemed fruitless and ripe for change. This, of course, is the primary effect sought by the physically weaker adversary in an asymmetric conflict.

The kinds of effects outlined above are not mutually exclusive. Any unified overall effect, especially at the military-strategic or geo-strategic levels, is likely to reflect a number of different kinds of effects and the balance of these different kinds of effects will change over time.[14] Moreover, a single action may create different kinds of effects at each level. For example, the destruction of an opposing aircraft may be an effect in its own right at the tactical level. However, it might also be seen as part of an operational level campaign to attrite enemy forces and wear down enemy will to fight. Or it may serve to foreclose options that the enemy might otherwise have attempted using that aircraft. Or the shoot-down might be part of a larger strategic level effort to shock the enemy military and political leadership into reconsidering their behavior. These connections may be accidental and purely serendipitous, but the central notion in effects-based operations is that all these effects and actions can and should be carefully orchestrated to produce a decisive effect on the enemy at one or more levels and in one or more arenas. As this implies, the effects of a particular action will probably not be uniform across all levels and all arenas. The fighter pilot operating at the tactical level is focused on destroying the opposing aircraft. Not only might that be his assigned role, but he may also be forced into that action to save his own life.

At the operational level, the joint commander may have more latitude in this regard and might focus on creating chaos in the enemy decisionmaking process.

At the military-strategic level, the regional Combatant Commander or the Joint Staff might focus on foreclosing certain tactical and operational moves the foe might take.

And, at the geo-strategic level, the national command authorities might look to foreclose certain international actions or to shock the foe into reconsidering his past choices. Yet the action that is directed by each of these levels of decisionmakers in order to create all these diverse effects might be the same: one air-to-air engagement at the tactical level.

We can depict these varying configurations of effects to be sought in a series of vector diagrams. Each of the kinds of effects discussed above can be rendered as one vector (see Figure 41). Then the changing configuration from one level of conflict to the next could be shown by indicating how far along each vector the concern with that kind of effect was at this level or for this unit or command.

Thus, at the tactical level, the configuration of effects sought to create the impact on the opponent might reflect an emphasis on destruction as a reflection of the "kill or be killed" nature of the interaction, but it might also reflect the value of shocking, blocking, or confusing the opponent in such an engagement (see Figure 42).

At the level of the operational commander, this diagram might look very different. Instead of focusing on destruction of an opposing force per se, the commander may be more concerned with foreclosing a particular course of action or with his ability to attrite the opponent physically and psychologically. Yet, he is likely to have a similar interest in shocking and confusing his opponent. This would yield a very different shape from that above (see Figure 43).

At the military-strategic level of the theater or the national military staff, the configuration might be expected to change yet again. Even more than the operational commander, their concern would probably be on the longer term overall effects of an engagement or campaign. Thus, the focus would be on physical and psychological attrition and on foreclosure, both active and passive (see Figure 44). In contrast to the tactical level, the interest of a national level command may be less in destruction

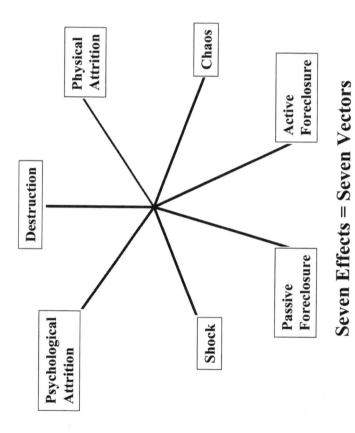

Seven Effects = Seven Vectors

Figure 41. Combining Effects

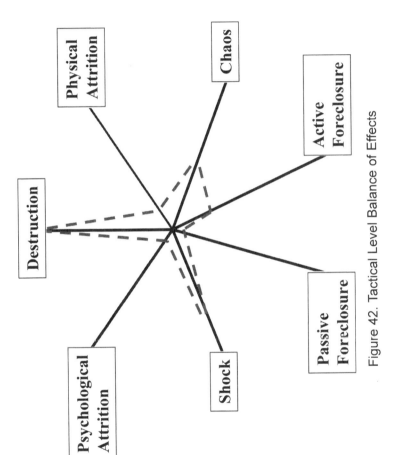

Figure 42. Tactical Level Balance of Effects

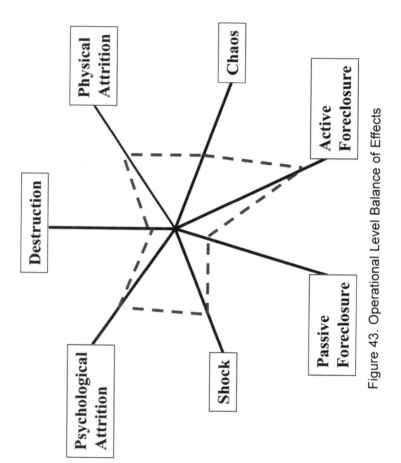

Figure 43. Operational Level Balance of Effects

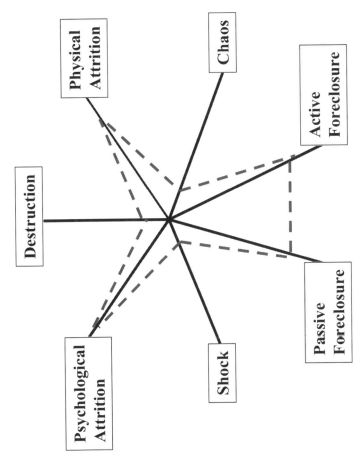

Figure 44. Military-Strategic Level Balance of Effects

than in the avoidance of destruction. Similarly, in an interaction with a power armed with weapons of mass destruction, the interest may not be in inducing shock and chaos but in avoiding those effects.

Finally, at the level of the national command authority, the focus would probably be on still longer-term issues. Thus, psychological attrition would figure prominently in the effects sought, as would the restoration of some form of passive foreclosure (see Figure 45). At the same time, the national commander would probably continue to be concerned with physical attrition and with creating an active foreclosure of unacceptable actions on the part of the foe. As a significant difference, however, the national commander would be looking at each of these effects not from the perspective of just military actions to create these effects, but also the use of political and economic actions to those ends. Thus, active foreclosure, as demonstrated in the three Middle East crises, would combine military action with diplomatic action and domestic political action to achieve the effect sought.

Obviously, each of these effects diagrams will vary with the particular situation and over time. The priorities in the first phase of a crisis are not likely to resemble those of succeeding phases. This evolution through a crisis was demonstrated in each of the three Middle East crises. Typically at the operational level and higher, this evolution went from an emphasis on foreclosure and the astute avoidance of anything that might shock the parties or induce chaos during the initial crisis containment phase, then to active foreclosure with elements of

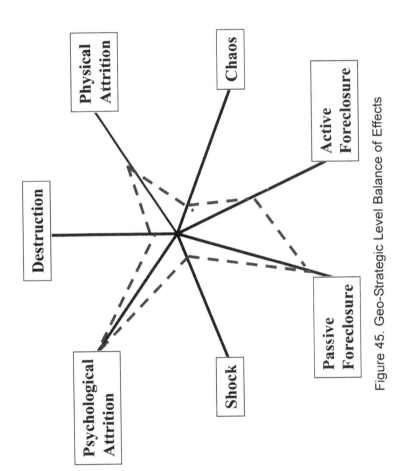

Figure 45. Geo-Strategic Level Balance of Effects

surprise or shock and psychological attrition during the conflict containment stage, and then to passive foreclosure and the avoidance of shock and chaos in the crisis resolution phase.

The Observer

There is an additional aspect to the complexity to be considered here. Not only can a single action create a variety of different effects, but those effects also can vary radically from one observer to the next and from one situation to the next.

While we tend to think of diplomatic and economic actions as efforts to convince, cajole or otherwise induce acceptable behavior and of military actions as efforts to compel or coerce, in actuality, whether the actions in question are seen as positive or negative depends on whether the observer is a friend, foe, or neutral. The same military action seen as a coercive intervention by a would-be aggressor will be seen as reassurance by a local friend who is the object of the intended aggression or by a local neutral who seeks to avoid the regional instability that the aggression might provoke. Thus, a peacekeeping operation would be seen as threatening or coercive by those who stand to gain by disrupting the peace (e.g. the Serbs in Bosnia or Kosovo), and as stabilizing and reassuring by those who wish to maintain the peace (Bosnian and Albanian villagers).[19]

In essence, the action itself is neutral. It acquires its positive or negative dimension as coercion or reassurance in the eyes of the observer and in the context of the situation. From the standpoint of planning and executing effects-based operations, however, this adds to the complexity. Since no action takes place in a vacuum and the observers of any action will be many and varied, we must consider multiple and conflicting cognitive impacts when planning any action.

From Actions to Effects

The above leaves a major question unanswered. How do we orchestrate our actions so as to produce the kinds of effects we seek? By thinking of actions in terms of a set of observable attributes, we have begun to define the nature of the potential military actions we might use and have begun to reduce the variables we must consider to a manageable set. Similarly, by delineating the kinds of effects we might want to create, we have both begun to define the nature of the potential effects and reduced them to a workable set of variables. The real question we must answer, therefore, is how might a certain combination of attributes in our actions lead to a particular kind of effect?

We can instinctively understand that certain kinds of actions are likely to produce certain kinds of effects in a maze of links like that displayed in Figure 46. For example, we could surmise from what we know of attrition-based operations that, in order to produce a certain level of destruction, we would require a particular focus for our efforts, particular kinds of forces, on a particular scale with these operations being sustained at some rate for some specific duration. We might also deduce that the geographic

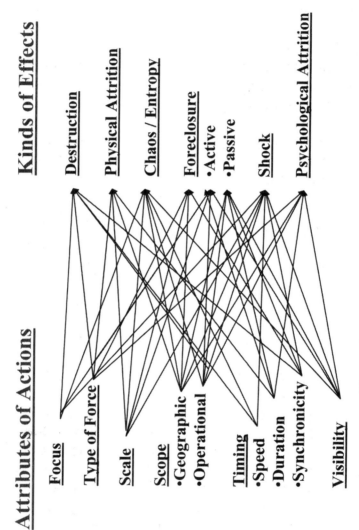

Figure 46. From Actions to Effects

and operational scope of the operation in question, or its synchronicity and visibility might be less relevant to achieving our objective. In other words, we would assess that the destruction meted out will vary as we concentrate our efforts (focus), use more powerful forces (type of force) in greater numbers (scale) at a faster rate (speed) over a longer period of time (duration). However imprecise it may be, the existence of a working link between kinds of actions and the kinds and levels of physical effects is hardly any surprise. And, it suggests that the same kinds of links are at the root of producing psychological or cognitive effects.

Although the cognitive process by which actions become perceptions, understanding, and a sense of the situation and then in turn result in the choice of certain courses of action may be too complex to identify or to permit us to track a cause and effect chain with any reliability, we can arrive at an intuitive sense of the relationship between actions and effects in the same manner as we understand the links in an attrition-based model without necessarily computing them. We can understand, for example, that chaos on the battlefield has something to do not only with the level of destruction inflicted but also of how that destruction was inflicted, factors such as speed and synchronicity or the ability to focus on critical vulnerabilities. In our 1805 Trafalgar example, the French commander knew he was going to be defeated before the first shot was fired. The insurmountable problem he faced was not so much the destructive power of Nelson's fleet, which was inferior to his own. It was the fact that

Nelson's commanders could synchronize their actions independently and thereby sustain a speed of operations that allowed the British fleet to focus its power at will so as to defeat a superior opponent in detail.

The foreclosure effect, in essence the use of military forces to ensure either that the opponent cannot fight as he had intended or that he does not fight at all, is slightly different in character. Yet, we can still discern the links between the nature of the actions and the foreclosure effect. In the three Middle East crises of 1967-1973, the resort to destruction or physical attrition was not a viable option for either the Soviet Union or the United States. Thus, success hinged on how forces were used to create psychological or cognitive effects.

Here we can see the attributes at work.

- The focus or specific nature of the action that the other side would observe was of critical importance either as a negative reinforcement, e.g. undertaking routine port visits to demonstrate a refusal to become involved, or as a positive reinforcement, e.g. conducting potentially threatening exercises to demonstrate a willingness to become involved.

- The type of force used also became a key variable. For example, the Soviets replaced intelligence-collection ship tattletales with missile-firing combatants to underline a tactical challenge that would have made any American strike on Soviet units very costly and thus foreclose it.

- The scale or numbers of forces involved and especially the repeated reinforcement of the opposing Mediterranean fleets similarly became a dominant way in which each side endeavored to foreclose certain courses of action to the other.

- The scope of military operations both geographic and operational also became a central part of the attempts to shape opponent behavior, and that of clients and allies. Forces were alternately held back from the crisis area to show a desire to avoid confrontation, or rushed toward it to block an impending opposition move.

- The role of the speed of actions and reactions by both sides and the need for synchronicity was most evident in the attempts to coordinate specific military maneuvers with diplomatic actions, a coordination requirement that sometimes necessitated visible military action of a particular kind within an hour or less.

In each of these crises, thus, the attributes of the military actions undertaken were consciously manipulated so as to produce active foreclosure of a particular course of action to the opponent or, conversely, to encourage a particular course of action, with the specific course of action to be foreclosed varying over time.

The case for shock is more straightforward. We can readily understand that a combination of numbers, particular types of forces focused on particular objectives, and speed and synchronicity produced the success of the German blitzkrieg in May 1940 and the subsequent collapse of French military and political will. In short, it was the nature of the German actions and not just the destruction they inflicted that collapsed any French hope for finding a way out of the dilemma posed, and thus produced shock.

Finally, there is the case of psychological attrition, arguably the root cause of the American defeat in Vietnam. Actions calculated to induce psychological attrition would clearly seem to revolve about some aspect of duration, the ability to sustain some finite level of operations over a protracted period of time, as in Vietnam. Yet, at the same time, in the context of asymmetric terrorist operations, we can also see factors such as geographic scope entering the equation. The attack on the World Trade Center, for example, derived its impact from the fact that it was an attack upon a major symbol in the American heartland.

As the above indicates, by varying the nature of our actions, we can vary the kinds of effects we are likely to create. This link between actions and effects both reflects and is consistent with our earlier observations on the cognitive process even though it makes no attempt to trace a specific action through all of the steps in that process. In essence, we accept a certain level of ambiguity and uncertainty (or ignorance) and plan and execute our actions within the constraints imposed by bounding the factors involved, actions on the one hand and effects on the other.

Unity of Effect and Synchronization

There is an additional complication here. The effects we create can be positive (driving observers toward the behavior we want), negative (drive them away from that behavior), or neutral, (having no impact on behavior). Observers will view our actions in their aggregate and not as isolated events. Since they have no way of knowing for certain what misunderstandings may have arisen in our execution of actions, they cannot afford not to treat them as a whole, considered, intentional response on our part.[20] Indeed, this process of aggregation is a central part of sensemaking.

Our objective in executing effects-based operations is somehow to create a unity of effect that focuses all actions and thereby masses their effects toward a particular behavioral objective. However, to do this we need to address yet another aspect of the complexity of effects-based operations: how do we orchestrate our actions so as to, at a minimum, deconflict them or, ideally, to achieve the synergy we need? The problem once again centers on what observers see and how they interpret what they see.

Logically, the scope of an observer's aggregation of the effects of our actions will grow geometrically from one level of conflict to the next and with it the scope of the actions we must coordinate to achieve unity of effect. Therefore, where the tactical commander might coordinate the actions of a squadron or company, the Joint Task Force Commander must coordinate the actions of multiple forces over a wider geographic scope and in several warfare environments. The Joint Staff must similarly coordinate military actions on a global basis including those of strategic deterrent forces whose activities might send a particularly strong message one way or the other. However, the greatest challenge lies at the geo-strategic level. The national leadership must coordinate all the diverse elements of national power so as to create a single overall effect at the geo-strategic level of operations in which each action by each element, military, political and economic, reinforces the actions of the other elements in driving observers toward a desired behavior.

We can think of this as outlined in Figure 47. The effects we create may be either positive or negative, causing or preventing some behavior. If we fail to coordinate our actions, then we risk presenting the observer with conflicted actions whose effects would tend to cancel each other out and provide no impetus to shape the desired behavior. If we deconflict the actions so that they do not cancel each other out, then the effects can become additive, but if we can somehow choose the right actions and synchronize them, then we can achieve a synergy in which the effect of one action builds upon the other to multiply the impact. Conversely, if we choose the all the wrong actions and deconflict them, then the negative impact would become additive, and if we do all the wrong things at all the wrong times, that impact too can become synergistic in a negative direction.

Our problem, then, is not only to choose the right actions to drive behavior in the direction we want at

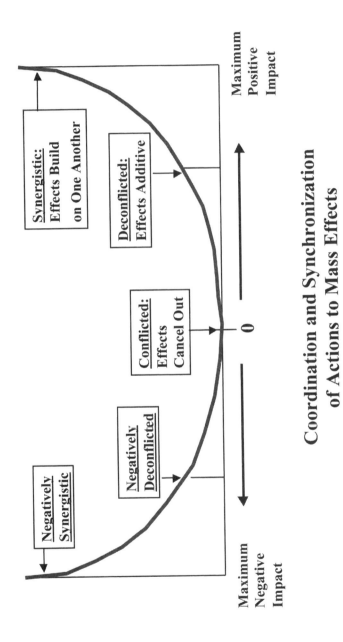

Coordination and Synchronization of Actions to Mass Effects

Figure 47. Unity of Effect

each level and in each arena, but also to avoid those actions that might drive behavior in the wrong direction or that might leave the observer confused and uncertain. Our opportunity is to use the power of networking to coordinate and synchronize all actions to build synergistically upon each other.

There is an additional complication here. Actions will likely be taken in multiple arenas simultaneously and involve a changing weight of military, political-diplomatic, and economic actions in creating a unified national effect. As shown in Figure 48, the relative balance of the national effort changes as the interaction moves from peace, to crisis, to confrontation, to war.[21] Generally, political, diplomatic, and economic actions tend to predominate in the early phases of a crisis, but as the crisis worsens, there is an increasing reliance on military action and a diminishing reliance on economic action at least in part due to the time such actions require to have an impact either as an inducement or a means of coercion. And, in the periods of highest tension, as noted during the successive Middle East crises, there is a tendency to rely on rapid political interchange backed up by whatever military actions can be brought to bear and seen by the right observers.

This tradeoff underlines that we must synchronize not only military actions, but also all of the actions of all the different forms of national power that might be observed. Each of these forms will have its own timeline[22] much as different forms of military power have different combat power generation cycles (see Figure 49). Thus, when senior decisionmakers

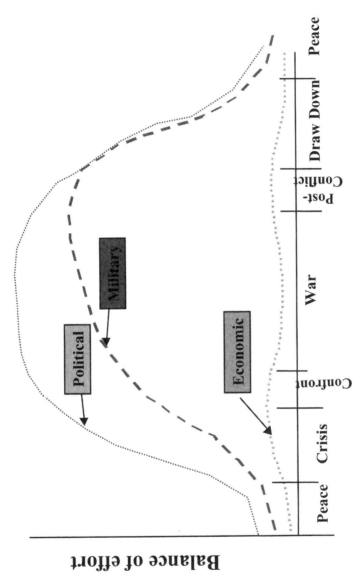

Figure 48. Relative Weight of Effort

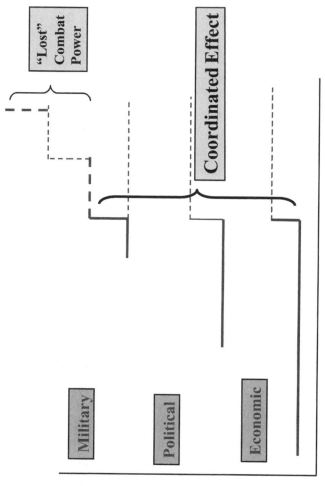

Figure 49. Different Actions, Different Timelines

attempt to coordinate political, diplomatic, economic, and military actions to achieve a unity of effect, they are subject to the same problem that we observed in the efforts of military commanders to coordinate different kinds of military forces, and to the same losses in efficiency as commanders pursuing a planned synchronization.[23] This leaves the national leadership in the same position as the military operational commander who must coordinate the actions of his forces so as to optimize their physical effect upon the enemy. A nation-state's leadership or its equivalent in a non-state organization must adjust the actions of all players in each arena, political, military, and economic, in order to put together a coherent overall effect that drives observer behavior in the desired direction.

Synchronization: The "Fedora Curve"

All of the above bespeaks a need for synchronization in effects-based operations that appears to contradict the aspiration of network-centric operations to be "self-synchronized." What then Is the role of self-synchronization in an effects-based operation? If we look more closely at the crises surveyed, it becomes apparent that the requirement for synchronization is not a constant. Rather, it varies across the duration of a crisis or war (see Figure 50). The requirement for tight synchronization of actions and effects will likely be least in routine peacetime interactions, but will begin to rise sharply in times of crisis as the national or organizational leadership attempts to coordinate and synchronize actions to achieve a synergy of

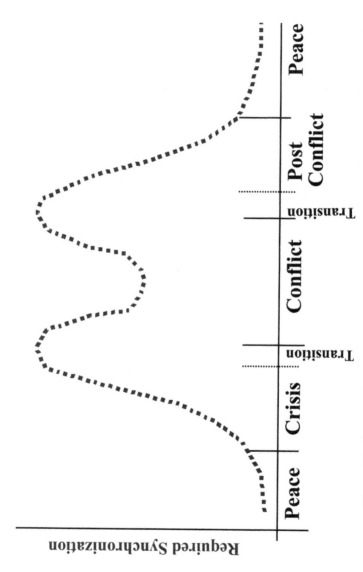

Figure 50. Coordination Requirements: Planned vs. Self-Synchronization

effects. That need for tight control will peak during a period of intense confrontation immediately before hostilities when the risks attached to any individual action being misperceived are at their greatest.[24] However, the requirement lessens as hostilities commence and any attempt to assert close centralized control of a fast-paced tactical or even operational level combat situation would mean ceding the initiative to the enemy. Then, as the combat transitions into an end-state solution, the requirement for control returns as the national and military leadership attempts to reduce the risk of any action undoing the solution being discussed. Finally, once a solution is reached, the requirement for control remains high during the initial stages of a build-down of force levels before gradually returning to a peacetime self-synchronization, giving the curve the shape of a fedora hat.

Bounding Complexity

The picture of effects-based operations that emerges from these examples is above all one of complex coordination requirements. The core challenge in planning and executing effects-based operations is to ensure that all of the actions taken across this diverse spectrum reinforce the effect we are trying to create and to avoid a situation in which those actions negate each other and either confuse friends, foes, and neutrals as to our intentions, or worse still, create an effect that is the opposite of what we seek. It seems obvious that, by thinking in terms not of an infinite variety of possible actions but in terms of the particular combination of attributes of an action that can be observed or felt and thus affect perceptions and behavior, we can bound one aspect of the effects-based planning problem. It also should be evident that, by thinking in terms of the kinds of effects we wish to create rather than in terms of a highly specific outcome for which we cannot trace any semblance of a cause and effect chain, we can bound another aspect of the complexity to the point that we can conduct rational effects-based planning.

Yet, in the last section of this chapter, we have suggested something more: that this planning and bounding of complexity is not to be done just once and then executed. Rather, the planning process must be dynamic and respond to the give and take of an evolving situation. The effects sought and the actions required, as well as the degree of coordination needed to carry out the multi-faceted aspects of a national action, will change over the course of a crisis or conflict.

---

[1]This variety was great enough that, as the history of the crises amply illustrates, the national level decisionmakers were normally unaware of all the actions being taken at the tactical level and the local commanders were almost invariably unaware of the exact role they were to play in the larger, national level scheme of things.

[2]In the sense of creating specific physical effects, it is also what was taking place in the wars reviewed.

[3]Aristotle. *Nichomacian Ethics.*

[4]The United States did have Wheelus Air Force Base in Libya during the 1967 crisis, but was largely unable to use it due to the situation that such use would have placed the Kingdom of Libya with its Arab neighbors, particularly Egypt. Similarly, although the Soviets had large numbers of advisors in Egypt prior to the 1973 crisis, they were ordered out of Egypt a few months before the Egyptian attack on Israel.

[5]Kissinger, *White*, p. 631.

[6]In fact, though manageable, the withdrawal of access can pose problems for resupply as the United States found out in 1973 while trying to refuel two carriers operating east of Suez in the face of an Arab oil embargo.
Zumwalt, p. 455.

[7]In a somewhat different guise, they are also applicable to other nonmilitary actions that a government may take. The effect of a diplomatic note, for example, derives not only from what language was used in the note but also from how that note was presented, to whom, by whom, when, and with what degree of publicity. If we were further to combine a military operation with the presentation of the diplomatic note, then the variables to be controlled or manipulated would include all those attached to the note and all those attached to the military action.

[8]Czerwinski,Thomas. *Coping with the Bounds, Speculations on Non-linearity in Military Affairs*. Washington, DC; National Defense University Press. 1999. p. 9.

[9]This concept was the centerpiece of the decisionmaker school of international relations theory. It was hypothesized that if we can know the decisionmaker and the influences upon him or her well enough, we can begin to predict the decision that will be made. To that end, social-psychological laboratory studies in the late 1960's and early 1970's sought to profile subjects, insert them into a controlled problem set, and analyze the results. However, a criticism of the approach was that the results, even with a relatively homogeneous subject population, were not conclusive and even less credible when postulated for very different cultures and backgrounds.
Singer, J. David, ed. *Human Behavior and International Politics, Contributions from the Social-Psychological Sciences*. Chicago; Rand McNally. 1965. pp.153ff.

[10]Lieber. *Theory and World Politics*. Cambridge; Winthrop. 1972. pp. 18ff.

[11]Beyerchen, Alan D. "Clausewitz, Nonlinearity and the Unpredictability of War" *International Security*. Winter, 1992. p. 60.

[12]Although there remains the possibility of discovering some "golden node" that would bring about the collapse of an entire system or war effort and, thus, for a single destruction operation to win the war rather than merely the engagement, it is questionable whether such a node would exist and still more questionable whether we would be wise to rely upon creating such a far-reaching effect.

[13]Carried to its logical extreme, the total physical elimination

of the adversary, as in Rome's destruction of Carthage, might so totally remove a threat as to make the question of creating psychological effects on the foe entirely moot.

[14]Sadat, pp. 215ff.

[15]Mahan, Alfred. *Mahan on Naval Warfare: Selected Writings on Rear Admiral Alfred T. Mahan.* Boston: Little Brown. 1918. p. 243.

[16]Laqueur, W. *The Road to War: The Origin and Aftermath of the Arab-Israeli Conflict 1967-8.* London: Penguin. 1968. p. 109.

[17]Steere, Edward. *The Wilderness Campaign.* Harrisburg: Stackpole Company. 1960. p. 457.

Johnson. *North to Antietam.* p. 494.

[18]The collapse of France in 1940, for example, involved a complex variety of effects acting together. The destruction of French and British forces in the field and the attrition of the French Air Force accompanied by the chaotic inability of the French General Staff to salvage the military situation produced shock at all levels of the French Government. This in turn built upon a certain level of defeatism and war weariness that lingered from the First World War to produce France's defeat. In this process, the German Army and the blitzkrieg served as the agents of this complicated series of effects and the subsequent change in French behavior.

Shirer. pp. 805ff.

[19]On a different level, this positive/negative perception of the same action is true of strategic nuclear deterrence as well. A reinforcement of the nuclear deterrent that might be judged threatening by an opponent might be seen as reassuring to an ally whom that reinforcement might protect.

[20]The 1962 Cuban Missile Crisis presents a good example of both dimensions of this problem. On the one hand, the U.S. military often failed to understand that their actions were being used by President Kennedy as a means of signaling American intent and that, under such circumstances, normal military precautions such as raising the DEFCON level might either confuse the Soviets or create an effect contradictory to what the NCA sought. On the other hand, the stark discrepancies between the communications from General Secretary Khrushchev and the later official Soviet position both confused and alarmed the American NCA, quite the opposite of what Khrushchev intended.

Kennedy. *Thirteen Days.* p. 98ff.

[21]Observed in newspaper analyses during four crises, the 1967, 1971, and 1973 Middle East crises and the Cuban Missile Crisis of 1962.

Smith, Edward A. Jr. *Naval Confrontation, The Inter-superpower Use of Naval Suasion in Times of Crisis.* Unpublished dissertation, The American University. 1979.

[22]Military, diplomatic, political, and economic actions are physical in nature and can move only so fast. Arranging for a call on the head of a foreign government or for a meeting of the United Nations Security Council takes time and proceeds according to a schedule over which the United States and/or its coalition partners may have little or no control. Economic actions, for example, might require approval from Congress or actions by industry and financial centers at home and abroad.

[23]The physical actions necessary for the State Department to make a public announcement can be condensed into hours or even minutes, while moving a military force into a position where it can sustain and lend credence to the announcement may take days. One reason for the repeated resort to the use of forward naval forces for signaling was that they were already forward and being monitored and thus, could reinforce rapid-fire diplomatic actions within minutes.

[24]As that demonstrated in the confrontation stages of the 1962, 1967, 1971, and 1973 crises, the balancing of military and political-diplomatic actions can become so tightly controlled and dynamic that the action-reaction cycles are reduced to less than an hour.

CHAPTER 7

From Dealing with Complexity to Exploiting It

If effects-based operations are to be anything more than an interesting theory, we must figure out a process by which we can reliably translate the multifaceted actions we have been describing into the kinds of effects that we need to shape the behavior of friends, foes, and neutrals. In brief, we must be able to plan and execute real-world effects-based operations that apply this theory.

Orchestrating our actions so as to have the greatest probability of producing a desired effect is a task that is easier said than done. The sets of variables described in the preceding chapter, even when bounded by defining the elements of military actions or by delineating the kinds of effects, remain complex. And, there are at least two additional levels of complexity in the problem that we still have to address before we can hope to undertake the planning and execution of effects-based operations.

One aspect of this additional complexity has already been intimated. The orchestration we need to undertake involves not only choosing the right combinations of actions to influence observers' behavior in the desired direction, but also identifying and avoiding those actions that might drive the behavior in the wrong direction. In essence, if we fail to orchestrate our efforts correctly, the variables we seek to manipulate can become a cacophony of signals in which the different aspects of our actions will tend either to cancel each other out, or to so confuse observers as to have no impact at all. Even worse, the actions may produce effects and behavior that are quite the opposite of what we intended. In planning effects-based operations, therefore, we must be able not only to focus our actions but also to deconflict them across four levels of command and three or more arenas of effects-based operations. What is more, we must be able to deconflict our actions not only with respect to a single observer, but also with respect to the multiple and very different perspectives suggested by the "friends, foes, and, neutrals" in our definition of effects-based operations.

Influencing this behavior means dealing with the perceptions of human beings, each of whose reactions will be different and none of whose reactions will be either linear or entirely predictable. Yet, to plan effects-based operations, we must somehow anticipate how each complex adaptive system observing our action, whether an individual or an organization, might adapt and respond to the stimulus it presents. On the surface, this task sounds like a contradiction in terms. How do we predict the reactions of a complex adaptive system whose reactions are, by definition, not entirely predictable? And, how do we make the same action appear differently to different observers? Are we setting an impossible standard for effects-based operations?

The task of coordinating all of these elements so as to create a unity of effect certainly seems daunting. However, we can take some solace from two facts.

First, a failure to address these levels of complexity does not remove them. Indeed, we can logically surmise that, in the absence of any effort on our part to orchestrate our efforts, the likelihood of cacophony of actions and effects will be even greater.

And second, the fact that the examples used throughout this work are drawn from history should send a message. Successful coordination of effects is neither impossible nor new. We have done all of this before. Indeed, the great military and political leaders in history have been "great" at least in part because they have been able to put these pieces together in their heads. The question for us is rather how the new technological revolutions and network-centric concepts let us do these tasks better, more quickly, and more precisely.

Dealing with the Additional Levels of Complexity: Elements of the Problem

The first step in dealing with these new dimensions of complexity is to fit together the pieces of the effects-based puzzle that we have explored so far. In our discussion of a general evolving concept of effects-based operations, there are three major pieces of the puzzle that stand out.

- First, in looking at the cognitive cycle, we began to describe the human dimension of the decisionmaking process. We traced how human beings and human organizations perceive actions, make sense of them, and then use this deep understanding of an emerging situation to respond. This cognitive process described not only the variables inherent in our own decisionmaking process, but in the context of an effects-based action-reaction cycle, provided an insight as to the variables involved in shaping the behavior of others. While such an insight may not remove the complexity from human reactions, it does provide us with a logical base for further bounding the complexity involved.

- Second, using the insights gained from the cognitive process, we began to define the dimensions that actions and effects might take on in the human mind. As illustrated in Figure 51, the attributes of actions described which elements of our actions were likely to alter perceptions, affect decisions, and produce the kinds of effects that shape an observer's

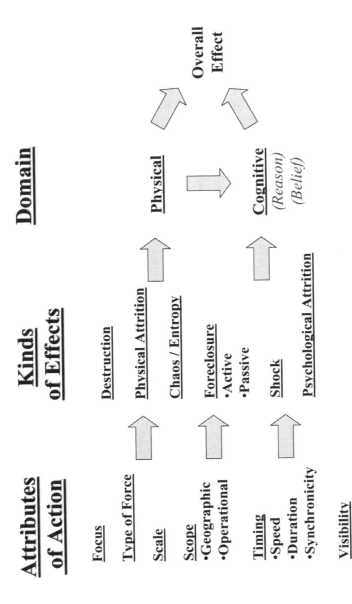

Figure 51. Creation of Overall Effect

decisions and behavior in a certain direction. By defining actions and effects in terms of two sets of variables rather than leaving them as an infinite variety of possible actions and effects, we bound the problem and also create a menu of the options available to us in orchestrating the effects needed to achieve a unified overall effect. We even used a series of Middle East crises to illustrate historically how we have used these options and varied the nature of military actions to create specific effects. This relationship between actions and effects provides the core element for planning and executing effects-based operations

• Third, we also began to define the action-reaction cycle mechanics of an effects-based operation. The effects-based rule set that we derived from the Middle East crises and several wartime examples laid out a rough idea of how the action-reaction cycles actually work in real-world effects-based operations. The rule set also began to define the decisionmaking and organizational structure used in such operations. Although this functional description was primarily drawn from decisionmaking on the American side of the conflict, the crisis interactions make it clear that the model could also be roughly extrapolated to the structures and reactions of any "state" actor.[1] Thus, the rules set mechanics provide a framework within which the planning and execution of at least state-to-state effects-based operations can be considered.

These insights into the cognitive process and into the system mechanics are particularly relevant to the process of planning and executing effects-based operations so as to achieve the nonlinear impacts we seek.

Much of the problem that we confront in the planning and execution of effects-based operations derives from a need to predict the responses of the individual or organization that we intend to stimulate. If we are to plan deliberately and logically, we must be able to anticipate how an initial or direct effect created by our actions will propagate additional effects. This step is critical because our hope of creating nonlinear impacts grows at least in part from the expectation that our actions will set off a chain reaction or cascade of indirect effects whose scale and scope may dwarf the initial effect we create. Planning an effects-based operation then revolves about the challenge of setting off a controlled chain reaction rather than an uncontrolled reaction whose consequences we cannot imagine.

In order to plan effects-based operations, therefore, we must address two questions. First, how does this chain reaction or cascade of effects occur? And second, how might such a cascade of effects operate in the context of the effects-based mechanics outlined in the rule sets that we introduced in Chapter 5?

Exploiting Complexity:
The Logic of Effects Cascades

In the discussion of effects throughout this book, we have drawn a distinction between physical effects and psychological or cognitive effects. We defined physical effects broadly as the physical impact of an action upon others and illustrated that such an impact that might not involve destruction or, indeed, any violent use of military force at all. At Midway, the initial physical effect was simply the act of a Japanese reconnaissance pilot observing an object, the carrier *Yorktown*, and reporting that object. In Information Age warfare, a similar initial physical effect might be the entry of a computer virus into a system network or the discovery of an effort to hack into a network.

However, we need to take this logic a bit further. As we saw in the Midway example, the direct physical effect can indeed provoke a chain of subsequent impacts. In the cyberwar example, similarly, we almost instinctively accept that the initial, direct physical effect will not be the end of the impact. We expect that this initial or direct effect will create additional indirect effects of some sort. And we expect that some combination of these effects will eventually bring changes in behavior, just as the *Yorktown* sighting report caused VADM Nagumo to change his intended course of action and to rearm his planes for a fleet action.[2] Putting this in the terms of our rule sets, we expect that the effects created by our action will not remain isolated but will spread to other dimensions.[3]

Two additional distinctions are needed here:

First, the actions we are considering are, by definition, physical in nature. The alternating of physical actions and reactions was reflected in the action-reaction cycles in the rules sets we examined. Similarly, the cognitive process we described dealt with those actions that could be observed or perceived in some way, and it even defined actions in terms of physical objects and events.

- We saw that, although such a physical event could be the destruction of forces and capabilities, it could equally be a maneuver such as the movement of military forces as illustrated in the Middle East crises. Moreover, as the history of the Middle East crises clearly demonstrates, the event could also be economic, political, or diplomatic in nature. Like military actions, the economic actions such as trade sanctions, the political maneuvers, the press announcements, and the exchanges of diplomatic messages all rely on some form of physical action intended to be observed and perceived. Logically, if we are to create a unified overall effect, these actions need to be coordinated with all other actions that might be seen by the same observers.

- We also saw that a physical action, such as the sighting of the *Yorktown* in the Midway example, might simply be an object that is placed (intentionally or unintentionally) in the right place at the right time to be seen by the right observer. Again, a physical presence was required to create the effect.

Notice that in each of these cases, both the objects and events involve real physical entities and thus, are actions in the physical domain.

Second, we have already drawn a distinction between a direct physical effect (the immediate physical impact of an action) and an indirect effect (one of a series of follow-on or derivative impacts that result from the direct effect). These indirect effects may also be physical in nature, but as in the *Yorktown* sighting in the Battle of Midway, they may also be psychological and cognitive effects that grow from the action and its initial physical impact.

These distinctions are at the core of our concept of effects-based operations and of nodal targeting. We use physical actions to create a stimulus, a direct physical effect that sets in motion a chain reaction or cascade of additional indirect effects. We also hope that, if the stimulus is properly planned, this chain of effects will sooner or later cross from the physical to the psychological or cognitive domain so that the resulting psychological and cognitive effects will in some way affect the behavior of observers.

Normandy, 1944

Clearly, the idea of creating a cascade of effects is not new. The World War II bombing campaign in support of the June 1944 Allied landings in Normandy is a good example of a deliberately planned cascade of physical effects.

Normandy: Physical Effects

The direct physical effect sought by the planners of the Allied air campaign, the so-called "Transportation Plan," was the destruction of the French rolling stock and the rail yards, bridges, and junctions leading toward the Normandy beachheads.[4] In Churchill's words, the bombing was to create "a railroad desert" around Normandy.[5] However, the objective of the Allied planners of the air campaign was not limited to the direct physical effect of destroying the rail system. Their real objectives were two indirect or derivative physical effects: to incapacitate the railway system in northern France so that rail movement became difficult or impossible; and to thereby prevent the movement of German panzer divisions into the Normandy area in the critical hours and days after the D-Day landings.[6]

Had the planners of the air campaign approached the problem by simply looking at the initial direct physical effects of the bombing (from the standpoint of pure attrition[7]) and disregarded the indirect or derivative effects, they might have adopted a general, almost random approach to the bombing. They might have chosen to attrite the capability of the entire French rail system, much as von Falkenhayn had attempted to bleed the French Army white at Verdun in 1916. However, it would have certainly been clear to the Allied air planners that, even if such an attrition campaign were confined to a given region or to the given categories of rail facilities, it still would have been too costly, too slow, and given some level of enemy capability to repair the damage,[8] might even have been doomed to failure from the start.

Instead, to all intents and purposes, the strike planners worked backwards from their ultimate objective. They started with the second cascade indirect effect they hoped to create: blocking German movements toward the invasion beaches. Then, they identified the reduction of the performance of the French rail system as the first cascade indirect physical effect they needed in order to bring that about. Finally, they used their knowledge of the rail system and how it functioned to identify the 93 rail yards, bridges, and junctions that would be most significant in creating this indirect effect.[9] In short, they focused their direct effect (the bombings) so as to achieve two levels of indirect physical effects. This was a nodal targeting approach that focused upon the cascade of indirect physical effects that they thought would likely flow from the direct physical effect they inflicted.

Notice that in both the attrition and effects-based approaches, the generic initial direct physical effect of the bombing campaign (the destruction of rail facilities) would have remained the same. However, by adopting an effects-based targeting approach, the planners refined and focused the bombing campaign by looking at the successive cascades of indirect physical effects that might be produced by a given set of targets. In the planners' calculations, the impact of the bombing on the throughput capacity of the French rail system was the first cascade indirect physical effect.[10] The inability of the German troops, especially the armored divisions, to reach the Normandy battlefield was the second cascade indirect physical effect, and the ultimate objective of the campaign.[11]

Cascades of Psychological Effects

In the psychological and cognitive effects, the physical effect of an action takes on a human dimension. Again this is not new. The impact of physical actions upon the will or decisionmaking is repeated time and again throughout military history. Classically, if the disruption of a military operation is particularly sudden or severe, or if there are no good alternatives, then the psychological impact of the physical destruction may be to shock the opponent. It may also induce an incapacitating despair either immediately or as a result of repeated stimuli over some period of time. Physical destruction can cascade into psychological effects, which in turn can cascade into a series of further effects far beyond the immediate tactical impact of the targets destroyed.

Normandy: Psychological Effects

Although the two cascades of indirect physical effects outlined earlier were consciously sought by Allied air planners, further cascades from these physical effects into a series of indirect psychological effects do not appear to have been an immediate part of the air planning. Yet, clearly there were such psychological effects. The inability to move the forces needed to mount a counter-attack might have been expected to undermine German morale and discourage German commanders[12] even as it encouraged the boldness of the French Résistance. It is even possible to speculate about a series of cascading indirect psychological effects stretching from the German inability to mass forces for a successful counterattack in June 1944 to the participation of senior German commanders in the July 1944 plot to kill Hitler.

We can also observe in the Normandy air campaign an attempt to prevent one particular psychological effect. The Allied forces hoped to hide the site of the invasion from the Germans and avoid revealing their strategy through the targets they chose. There was ample reason for concern. Most of the potential German reinforcements were located in the region of the Pas de Calais where the German High Command was convinced that the actual invasion would take place. Thus, the Allied air campaign planners had to keep the Germans convinced that the invasion would in fact take place in the area of the Pas de Calais so that the German forces in that area would not be committed to the Normandy battle. They dealt with this problem by enlarging the scope of the bombing campaign to include the rail system leading into the Pas de Calais as well as into Normandy, and by ensuring that the scale of the bombing in that area was even greater than in Normandy.[13]

Since behavior is the real focus of our effects-based operations, the cascade from direct or indirect physical effects to indirect psychological effects, which is only slightly evident in the Normandy example, needs further examination. In fact, the process of translating physical actions into psychological effects is another way of looking at the stimulus and response interactions at the root of our concept of effects-based operations. The physical effects are stimuli that the observer must take into account in his decisionmaking process.

In the example, the direction of the bombing either toward Normandy alone or toward the Pas de Calais alone would have been a stimulus applied to the German decisionmaking process. The response would have been a confirmation of the Germans' existing mental model that the invasion was to come at the Pas de Calais, or an impetus to consider a new mental model based on an Allied invasion through Normandy. The care exercised by the Allies to divide the bombing, to orchestrate the nature of the physical actions undertaken, deprived the Germans of that stimulus. And in its absence, they were left with their existing Pas de Calais model intact, a model that continued to dominate the thinking at both the German Western and Headquarters Commands even after the Normandy invasion was well underway.

The Normandy example does point to two important differences between the cascades of physical effects and those of psychological and cognitive effects. These differences were at the center of the air campaign planning.

- First, psychological effects did need not to be observed in the same sense as those of a cascade of physical effects.[14] In the Normandy example, it was not necessary for the German Command in the West to receive reports of the level of bomb damage to the railway system, or to measure the level of performance of the railway system after the bombing in order to reach the conclusion that their mental model of an invasion at the Pas de Calais was wrong. It was only necessary for the German commanders to know that a focused, large scale bombing campaign was in progress and where.

Although physical effects can set off a cascade of psychological effects and a continuing cascade of physical effects can certainly contribute to it, the cascade of psychological effects itself may be largely independent of the physical cascade or, indeed, in the case of panic, it may be independent of any physical reality at all. This is important for how we calculate the nonlinear impact of our actions because it indicates that psychological effects can propagate far more quickly than an equivalent cascade of physical effects.

The example that comes to mind here is the shock and panic that set in among the French senior military and political leadership as the German blitzkrieg rolled across northern France in May 1940. Although the panic was set in motion by a cascade of physical effects stemming from the success of German military forces, the cascade of psychological effects soon attained a life of its own. The spreading panic then debilitated French efforts to deal with the physical effects of the blitzkrieg or, in fact, to continue the war from France's vast overseas empire.[15]

- Second, as the extent of the coordination required for successful effects-based operations underlined, the scope of the effects possible in the psychological domain is far greater than that possible in the physical domain. In the Normandy example, the cascade of physical effects from the direct effect of physical damage to rail yards to the indirect effects of degraded rail system performance and the inability of the Germans to move armored divisions into the beachhead area was relatively narrow and closely interconnected.

The cascade of psychological effects need not be so bounded. The impact extends to anyone who can observe the action or even the follow-on psychological effects of the action with the latter potentially spreading at a geometric rate. That impact, further, is not limited to those observers directly involved in the action-reaction cycle but includes the passive observers.[16] [17] The only criterion for the cascade of psychological effects is that some portion of the effect has to be observable in some fashion.

A Cascade Model: Applying the Logic to Military Operations

We can use the Normandy air campaign model and the earlier examples of noncombat interactions seen in the Middle East crises to construct a model of how these "effects cascades" work.

Cascades of Physical Effects

The starting point, as illustrated in Figure 52, is a physical action, an object or event of some kind. In the manner outlined in the cognitive cycle, the object or event is perceived by observers. The direct effect produced may be the destruction of capabilities, as in the case of the Normandy bombing campaign, or it may be simply observing and reporting a maneuver, as in the cases both of the Battle of Midway and all three of the 1967-1973 Middle East crises.

However, what we really hope is that the initial direct effect will not be the end of this stimulus and response interaction. We hope that the impact of the direct effect will be such that it will provoke other physical effects, that the direct effect will cascade into at least one more indirect effect (see Figure 53). In the Normandy example, the first cascade, indirect physical effect of the bombings would have been the impact on the performance of the French railway system and specifically the reduction of its throughput capacity.

We might further hope, as did the Allied air planners, that this first cascade, indirect physical effect would produce an additional second cascade consisting of additional indirect physical effects (see Figure 54). In the context of the Normandy air campaign, the first cascade (reduction of the French railway system performance) would have been meaningless unless it produced the second cascade impact on the German ability to move reinforcements into the area of the intended

Figure 52. Effects Cascades: Physical Action to Direct
Physical Effect

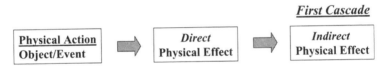

Figure 53. Effects Cascades: First Cascade of Indirect Effects

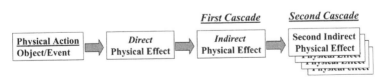

Figure 54. Effects Cascades: Second Cascade of Indirect
Physical Effects

invasion. Moreover, the second cascade impact on the performance of German military forces might also have produced an indeterminate number of additional cascades of indirect physical effects in the manner of the "for want of a nail...the kingdom was lost" nursery rhyme.

These successive cascades of indirect physical effects are the context for the application of an effects-based approach to attrition-based warfare, and are the focus of effects-based targeting and nodal targeting. In such targeting, we choose highly specific direct physical effects exactly for their potential to set off a chain reaction so that we can multiply the impact of our actions on the forces and capabilities of our opponent.

Cascades of Psychological and Cognitive Effects

However, as our discussions of actions and of stimulus and response make clear, the indirect effects are not limited to a chain reaction of indirect physical effects. The cascades of effects can also jump from physical to psychological effects. This is indeed the phenomenon we considered in the context of the cognitive process (see Figure 55). In the Midway example, the direct physical effect (the *Yorktown* sighting) created an immediate impact on VADM Nagumo's cognitive decisionmaking process, an indirect psychological effect. The same is true of the maneuvers and reinforcements of Soviet and American fleets during the three Middle East crises. In a negative sense, this jump from a physical effect, the bombing, to a cognitive effect, a German

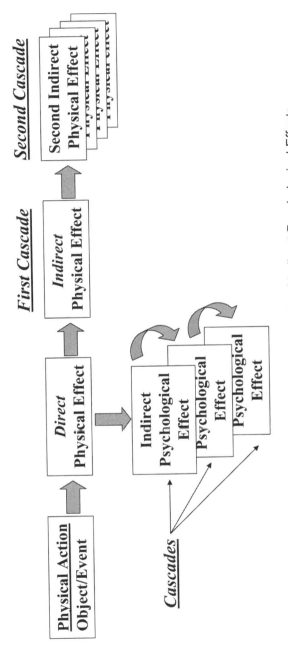

Figure 55. Effects Cascades: Cascade of Indirect Psychological Effects

conclusion that the Allied invasion would come in Normandy rather than the Pas de Calais, was exactly what the Allied planners of 1944 feared would happen and were at pains to avoid.

Like the chain of indirect physical effects, the impact of the indirect psychological or cognitive effect is not necessarily limited to this first cascade. Instead, we hope that it will produce successive cascades of other psychological and cognitive effects, that the direct physical effect and the first cascade indirect psychological or cognitive effect will set off a further chain reaction of additional cascades of psychological and cognitive effects. The spread of panic in France both in the government and the civilian population in the face the German blitzkrieg of 1940 is a case in point.

However, notice as well something else that is perhaps even more significant. As illustrated in Figure 56, each of the physical effects in the diagram (both the initial direct physical effect and all the subsequent indirect physical effects) can set off indirect psychological and cognitive effects. These in turn can themselves likewise set off cascades of psychological and cognitive effects.

Again, we can see this in the Normandy campaign. The overall psychological and cognitive effect of the bombing campaign can be traced to three distinctly different sets of physical effects. In part it arose from the direct physical effect of the bombing, in part from the indirect physical effect of the collapse of the French railway system, and in part from the indirect physical effect of the German

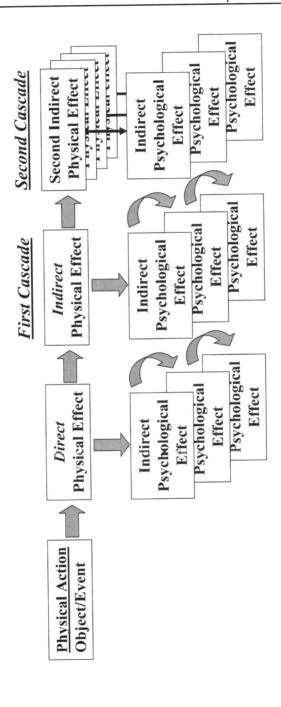

Figure 56. Effects Cascades: Derivative Cascades of Indirect Psychological Effects

inability to move reinforcements to Normandy when the invasion began. The overall effect is to multiply the impact of the initial action and the resulting direct effect geometrically. This phenomenon is a key aspect of the nonlinear impact we seek in effects-based operations.

However, there is another aspect of this model that we need to note. The cognitive audience would have been at least slightly different for each of the direct and indirect physical effects cited above. Thus, the direct effect of the bombing might perhaps have posed a more pressing dilemma for those charged with railway repair. The indirect effect of the collapse of the railway system might have had more of an impact on the thinking and decisions of the German railway administrators and the German High Command in the West. The inability of the armored divisions to move into Normandy might have had more of an impact on the thinking of the German Headquarters Staff.

What this suggests is that, like each of the direct and indirect physical effects, each of these indirect psychological effects can also produce other indirect psychological and cognitive effects. And what is still more, the path of this cascade is likely to vary from one incident to the next and from one observer to the next. While the diagrams assume for the sake of illustration that the initial direct effect will, in fact, provoke a chain reaction, the implication is clear. The cascade of effects set in motion by our original action can extend to an expanding set of indirect effects both physical and psychological.

Planning an Effects Cascade

The difficulty in orchestrating our actions exists not so much in simply setting off cascading effects as it does in determining where these cascades of physical and psychological effects might actually lead. This is no small challenge. If we bear in mind that the wars and crises as well as peacetime activities like exercises and port visits are interactions between complex adaptive systems (e.g. states, militaries, or other human organizations), and if we consider that these interactions occur at multiple levels (e.g. units, military forces, and entire states), then it becomes clear that the ultimate extent of the effects cascade or chain reaction could potentially be breathtaking in both its scope and complexity. Setting such a cascade in motion and predicting even roughly where it will lead is both the promise and the challenge of effects-based operations. To address that challenge, however, we must understand something more of the complexity involved.

An example frequently used to describe complexity is that of a butterfly flapping its wings in Beijing and thereby producing a hurricane in the distant Atlantic Ocean. The idea portrayed in the analogy is that, in complex systems, very minute changes in one area can provoke enormous changes in another, apparently unrelated area. The problem is that we cannot trace or explain the cause and effect chain by which the butterfly produces the hurricane nor figure out how to duplicate it. In a complex system, the cause and effect chain from the butterfly flapping its wings to the creation of the hurricane is simply too complex to either fully understand or predict.

In the effects cascades, we too must deal with sets of complex systems and what we seek to exploit in effects-based operations is exactly the possibility of engineering the right set of relatively small actions to create a set of disproportionate effects. If those disproportionate effects are to shape behavior in the direction we want, however, we must figure out first how to trace the path of an action to a certain effect, and then how to plan the right actions to set the chain in motion.

Of Dominoes and Ping-Pong Balls

At first blush, this sounds impossible. However, the facts argue otherwise. The many historical examples considered thus far demonstrate that we can in fact cope with this kind of complexity. But the examples do more than simply indicate that this is possible. They show us how to deal with this complexity.

The model of the effects cascades and the Normandy example points to a dichotomy between chains of physical effects on the one hand and those of psychological and cognitive effects on the other. Both of these cascades are complex, but in the Normandy and Middle East crisis examples, we can identify two distinctly different sorts of complexity at work.

Falling Dominoes

The chain reactions of physical effects operate in a fashion analogous to falling dominoes. These domino chains may be relatively simple or, as challenges to Guinness World Records exemplify, they may be very complex in nature with many additional chains branching off and they may be of very substantial length and scope. Despite this complexity and even though we may not know where the chains end, we can nevertheless trace the flow of physical effects along the chain rather readily. More than that, we can predict a cause and effect relationship between any two adjacent dominoes or even along entire stretches of the domino chains with some degree of certainty.

Like the chains of physical effects, the fall of dominoes takes a predictable duration of time to occur. One domino must physically strike and push over the next for the chain reaction to continue. The longer the chain, the longer time it will take to complete the entire reaction. Similarly, in the Normandy air campaign, the bombing had to produce one effect (the reduction in the capacity of the French railroads) before the next effect (the prevention of panzer movements toward Normandy) could occur.

Ping-Pong Balls

The relative predictability of the above physical chain reaction contrasts sharply with the chain of psychological and cognitive effects. That chain reaction is both more complex and more instantaneous than that represented by the dominoes. The psychological chain, instead, is more analogous to a demonstration in which Ping-Pong balls are placed on spring loaded mousetraps across the entire floor of a room, and are then set off by tossing a single ball into the room. Even though the cause of the subsequent chain reaction is obvious, we cannot predict with any certainty the exact course that chain reaction will take, the exact sequence in which the reactions will occur, or which of the original balls if any might remain untouched at the end of the reaction. As this suggests, we also cannot predict the amount of time that the reaction will take. We simply know that it will spread very rapidly, and indeed geometrically, until there are either no more mousetraps left un-sprung or until there are no more balls in the air and thus no further ability to set off new reactions.

The situation is similar with the cascades of psychological and cognitive effects. An initial stimulus provokes a series of responses that in turn are the stimuli for still more responses. This pattern was very evident in the interaction of political, military, and economic actions and reactions during the three Middle East crises. Where we could predict cause and effect relationships along a domino chain of physical effects, we could not entirely predict the parallel chain of psychological and cognitive effects.

How do we deal with these two different kinds of complexity so as to plan effects-based operations?

Chain Reactions of Physical Effects

The relationship between a physical action and a direct physical effect and from one physical effect to the next as exemplified in the fall of dominoes is relatively straightforward and understandable (at least for a limited number of causes and effects). The problem here is that, while we may be able to understand and predict this limited and largely linear relationship over a limited number of links in the chain, we cannot predict all of the potential cascades that might take place. By extension, we cannot know the ultimate impact or all of the ways in which the direct effect we propose might potentially affect a particular situation.

"Pruning"

In the case of the Normandy air campaign, as in most nodal targeting, we solve this problem at least in part by bounding the complexity involved in some way. Typically, planners follow two approaches to this end. They ignore the course of a cascade beyond some certain point, which is usually the ultimate objective they set for themselves, or they may elect to ignore some entire chains of effects that their actions might set in motion.

In the Normandy example, the Allied air planners looked closely only at the first two cascades of indirect physical effects: first, the railroad throughput capacity degradation; and second, the ability of German panzer divisions to move to the front. They deliberately ignored several entire additional chains of indirect physical effects that might have resulted from their initial direct effect.

For one, however accurate Allied pilots might try to be, the bombing of rail junctures and rail yards in densely populated areas would have inevitably created significant collateral damage and large numbers of French civilian casualties, which in fact happened. Given the stakes involved in a successful invasion, however, the Allies at least partially ignored the importance of that possible cascade of physical effects. It was subordinated to the pressing military need to reduce the performance of the rail system and thereby keep the German armor away from the invasion beaches.[18] Similarly, while rendering the rail system incapable of operation would have had the indirect effect of preventing the German armored divisions from moving toward Normandy, it would also prevent the movement of food and goods to support the local French civilian population.

In the context of a war for survival, the Allied planners deliberately chose to ignore a series of possible effects that might otherwise have put an end to any hope of meeting their primary objective of defeating Nazi Germany.

We can recognize here that the approach taken by the planners was to bound the complexity of the problem by "pruning" the tree of potential effects chains to some limited number for consideration (see Figure 57).

In planning effects-based operations, we can do likewise. We can set a limit to how far we are willing to pursue a particular chain of cascading effects. We can also identify which chains of effects we want to consider, and which we can prudently set aside. Where we do this "pruning" is a function of the risk calculus we apply. In the Normandy case, it was the result of decisions made by Roosevelt and Churchill as to which political, military, and economic risks they were prepared to accept and where.

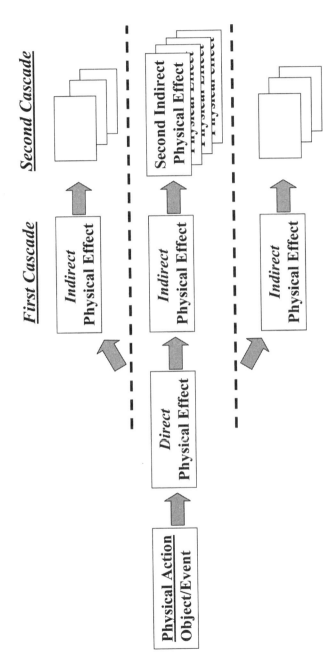

Figure 57. Effects Cascades: Bounding Complexity by Pruning

These risks, as the Normandy example makes plain, will be a function of a particular situation. In general, the less dire the circumstances to which we must respond, the less will be the differences in the risks and consequences of each chain and the more difficult it will be to ignore some chains. The more dire the circumstances, as in the case of a war for survival, the easier it will be to prune the chains and accept the risks.

Psychological Effects Chains

In the Normandy example, as in the chains of dominoes, there was a predictable relationship from one physical effect to the next. The number of bridges and rail yard junctions destroyed had a direct, predictable, and quantifiable relationship to the performance of the railroad system.[19] In turn, the railroad performance had a direct and understandable relationship to the Germans' ability to move armored divisions to the invasion area. Similarly, among those pruned chains of physical effects to be ignored was the effect of the decrease in railroad performance upon the ability to provide food to the local French population.

This relative predictability is not the case in the chains of psychological and cognitive effects. Instead, the degree of complexity involved in the psychological chains is multiplied by two factors evident in the Ping-Pong ball chain reaction. First, because there is no need to wait for one set of physical effects to engender a physical outcome before giving rise to a succeeding effect, the speed at which the cascade can propagate is far greater.

In essence, the speed of the reaction is the speed of communications because it is by the communications that the reaction spreads. Second, because there are no physical limits to the chain, the ultimate scale and scope of the psychological-cognitive cascade can be global.

As in the example of the butterfly and the hurricane, the relationship between the links in the chain of psychological and cognitive effects is usually indirect and nonlinear. They are not predictable in the sense of the relationship between railway performance and German mobility, nor are they easily quantified. We cannot predict the ultimate outcome of the psychological cascade (for example, a cause and effect linkage between the effectiveness of the bombing campaign in Normandy and the plot to kill Hitler in East Prussia). We may not even be able to predict an initial set of outcomes reliably. Thus, we will not be sure of the form the cascades may take or the speed and extent of the chain of psychological and cognitive effects we set in motion.[20]

If we were to assume the kind of seemingly random spread that is implied by the complexities involved in the psychological cascades, then the number of possible outcomes that might accrue from an action becomes nearly infinite. The core question for planning and executing psychological and cognitive effects, therefore, becomes that of somehow bounding the scope of this complexity to a workable size. Here again, the problem we face is not new. We have dealt with similar complex chains in the past. Accordingly, the history of what has succeeded or failed in past wars and crises provides an insight to bound the complexity. As in the three Middle East crises examined earlier, it is apparent that the decisionmakers at all levels reacted as they did and chose the courses of action that they did exactly because they could predict roughly what parts of the cognitive chains would be. It is also evident that, in these crisis interactions, commanders and decisionmakers at all levels did not assume a complex and perfectly random spread of psychological effects.

If we study the history of the Middle East crises, it becomes apparent that the decisionmakers at all levels did two things. First, they again pruned the number of chains and cascades of psychological and cognitive effects that they would consider, bounding the complexity involved. Second, they assumed that there would be a structured flow to the cognitive effects that they created.[21]

Part of the complexity of the cascade of psychological and cognitive effects arises from the fact that any action taken can be observed by virtually anyone, and that these actions shape the behavior of "friends, foes, and neutrals" (see Figure 58). Since each observer, whether a human being or organization, will perceive a single action in light of a particular idiosyncratic mental model, background, and agenda, a single action will tend to produce a large number of very different chains of psychological and cognitive effects for each observer. A single action or set of actions, therefore, will tend to produce different behavior in a friendly observer from that in an enemy observer.

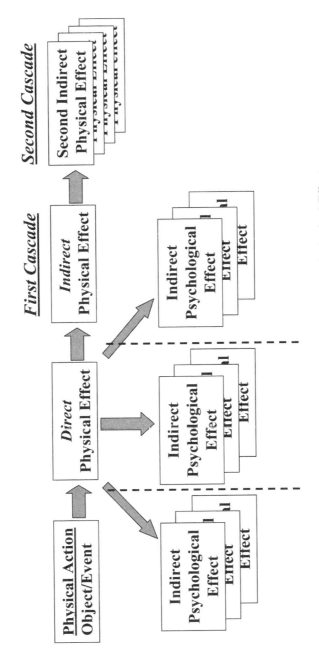

Figure 58. Effects Cascades: Pruning Psychological Effects

If we look to the examples presented by the 1967-1973 Middle East crises, it is evident that decisionmakers pruned this complexity by deliberately limiting the number of potential psychological chains to certain players or groups of players in some order of priority. While this is to some degree analogous to the decision to ignore many of the psychological repercussions of the 1944 Normandy bombings, there is an important difference. In the Normandy case, the pruning was nonreactive. It largely took place in the planning process that preceded the strike operations and does not appear to have been significantly revised.[22] In all three of the Middle East crises, by contrast, we can trace distinct changes to the pruning as the crisis evolved.

In the early stages of the Middle East crises, both Soviet and American decisionmakers tended to look at the effects of their actions in terms of multiple chains of cognitive effects. At a minimum, they considered the potential responses of their superpower opponent, the reactions of their respective NATO or Warsaw Pact Allies, those of their local client states, and those of the neutrals in the area (four principal chains, each of which might have ancillary chains for each country comprising the category). However, in the most dangerous moments of the Soviet-American confrontations, the cognitive focus of the decisionmakers focused on the single chain of cognitive effects that was most consequential: the potential reactions of the other superpower.[23]

In essence, the decisionmakers pruned the decision tree as they went. They were aware that additional chains of psychological and cognitive effects would inevitably be created by their actions, but when pressed by events, they subordinated these considerations to their most dangerous concern, the reactions of the opposing superpower.

Structured Flow of Effects

Although this pruning may reduce the number of chains of psychological and cognitive effects to be considered at any one time, it still leaves us with the problem of trying to anticipate the flow of effects along those chains that remain. Given a large number of potential observers and decisionmakers in the remaining chain, we are still left with the potential for a nearly infinite number of possible variations in where and how fast a cognitive effect will spread and the impact it will have on behavior. How then might we bound this complexity to the point that we could plan operations based on a rational assessment of the changes in behavior that would result from a particular set of actions?

If we reexamine the three Middle East crises, it is clear that the decisionmakers at each level of the interaction accompanied the process of pruning psychological and cognitive effects with another form of complexity bounding. They assumed that the flow of psychological and cognitive effects *would not be random* and, thus, infinitely varied. They assumed that the observers of their actions were rational decisionmakers who were operating in the context of a rational decisionmaking structure.[24]

Notice that this does not mean that they were "mirror-imaging" or assuming that the other decisionmakers would react as they would. Rather, they assumed that the other decisionmakers would perceive and react logically within the rationality of their own national and institutional cultures. They further assumed that organizations (governments, military units, and bureaucracies) would do likewise. Then, into this logical framework of the rational decisionmaker, they inserted what they knew of the particular foe or ally and the particular decisionmaking structure they faced. This is to say, the decisionmakers attempted to bound the chaotic complexity of a purely random spread of psychological effects by assuming that any effects created would flow in a rational, structured manner.

We can represent this rational, structured flow in terms of an ordered "nesting" of effects (see Figure 59). In the nest, we assume that actions observed at the tactical level would create a cognitive effect that would be propagated from the tactical level all the way to the national command authority. That is, we assume that psychological and cognitive effects would flow in some logical pattern.

While this nesting was used to explain the interrelationship of effects and actions on our own side, it was also a major feature of the military operations of both superpowers and their client states during all three of the Middle East crises. More to the point, the model of a nested, logical flow of effects was employed by decisionmakers at the national or geo-strategic level to direct military actions. Thus, the movement of the U.S. Sixth Fleet

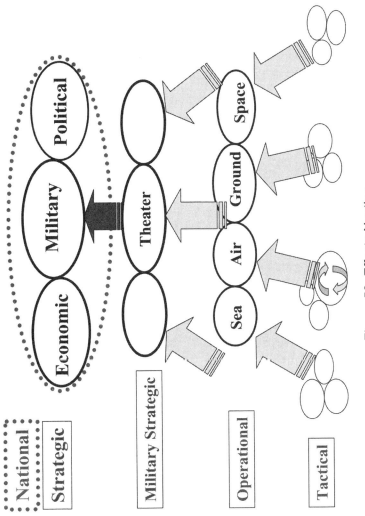

Figure 59. Effects Nesting

toward the coast of Syria in the 1967 crisis, the dispatch of a carrier transport aircraft to Israel during the 1970 crisis, and the movements and reinforcement of the Sixth Fleet during the 1973 crisis were all executed specifically because they would be observed and reported and because the cognitive effect would be rapidly propagated along a rational and predictable path.

In each case, the assumption of a logical flow went a step further. The decisionmakers from the operational level upwards assumed that specific tactical military actions would create cognitive effects that not only would rise through a military chain of command, but also that these military effects would cross over into at least the political arena. They also assumed that the cognitive effects growing from these military actions would combine with the psychological and cognitive effects wrought by diplomatic, political, and economic actions so as to create a single overall effect that would then shape the observers' behavior in the desired direction (see Figure 60).

There is, of course, a down side to this. For both the military and political decisionmakers, the assumption of a structured flow also meant accepting two things: (1) the effects of any military action undertaken would not and could not be limited to the military outcome of a specific individual engagement; and (2) the effects of any military action might extend to anyone who could observe that action.

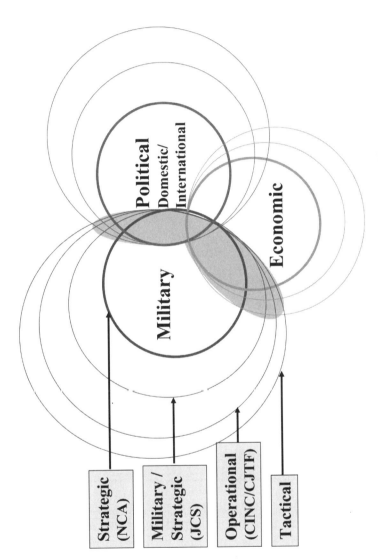

Figure 60. Effects Nesting: Multiple Overlapping Nests

Coalition Operations: Ours and Theirs

Implicit in these nesting assumptions is yet another level of complication. The interactions represented by the nest are not likely to be those of just one state or just one organization trying to coordinate its actions so as to deal with the reactions of another single state or even with those of a single organization.[25][26][27] The likelihood of multi-nation or multi-organizational interactions has two significant impacts. It multiplies the complications of coordinating a unified effect, and in the case of an opposing coalition, it provides an additional complexity to exploit.

Conducting Coalition Operations

Over the past half-century, many of the crises and conflicts in which we have found ourselves engaged involved either alliances such as the North Atlantic Alliance, or coalitions.[28] This fact suggests that, far from being able to prune complexity by largely ignoring or diminishing the reactions of our partners, we will instead be confronted by a pressing need to factor these chains of psychological and cognitive effects into the complexity of our effects nest. This challenge is threefold.

- First, we need to recognize that, in the strictest sense of an alliance or coalition, there is no single unified objective and therefore, no single unified effect that can be created. Rather, any alliance or coalition will represent a collection of national or organizational objectives that may more or less coincide, but that will never be entirely the same. The national interests of each state (or non-state) actor will always be different in some respect. In an alliance, the coincidence of national interests and objectives and thus, a general agreement on the effects to be sought may be long-term and habitual. In a coalition, any such accord may be very temporary. Deciding on the overall effect or outcome to be achieved by the coalition is therefore likely to involve some considerable degree of negotiation and compromise.[29] In other words, multi-state or multi-actor effects-based operations are likely to have a strong political aspect to them. This means that coordinating the actions and desired effects of a coalition and responding to the actions of a foe are likely to be cumbersome. This process will be still more cumbersome where there is no history of cooperation and no established modality of resolving conflicting national objectives.

- Second, whereas in a one-on-one, state-on-state interaction an adversary would tend to regard all of the actions of an individual government as interrelated parts of a coordinated effort, in alliance or coalition operations, the contrary is likely to be true. The adversary or adversaries will be looking for exploitable discord in the coalition and will search out any indication of such discord in the actions of individual coalition members. Thus, however unified the coalition effort, any misstep or conflict of actions failure at any level of the operation will tend to be treated as an opportunity to split the coalition and will have a disproportionately negative impact on the overall effect the coalition may be trying to create.

- Third, as we have seen, effects are cumulative over time and create a history of previous actions that either can be built upon or that must be overcome. However, in the case of an alliance or a coalition, this history is additive across the membership. The previous actions of each individual member contribute to a history of the coalition as a whole. If a coalition member has a history of weak governments and desultory participation in joint efforts, or of military forces with little capacity for the kinds of operations required, then these factors will diminish the effect that can be achieved. Similarly, if the members have a colonial history in a given area, this will be part of the mental models and experiences of the observers that the coalition must either overcome or build upon.

Coalition Effects Nests

If we return to the diagram of an effects nest, and if we assume the same basic rule sets that applied to the original nest, we can postulate a coalition nest along the lines depicted in Figure 61.

In this diagram, all of the problems associated with trying to coordinate actions and plan effects over the four levels of military operations and over three or more arenas are multiplied by the number of active members in the alliance or coalition. Each

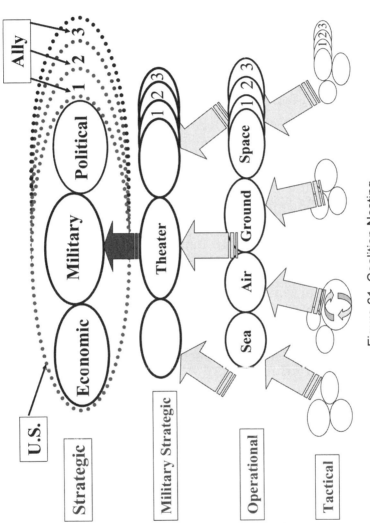

Figure 61. Coalition Nesting

actor will have operational commanders trying to coordinate the actions of various tactical units. Each will also have a military staff trying to coordinate a broader military effort. Each will have a national leadership trying to balance political, economic, and military actions so as to accomplish a national objective. Thus, the complexity represented by the nest is multiplied by the number of active participants in the coalition operation.

We also need to look at this coalition nesting structure from the standpoint of how it deals with the stimulus and response of effects-based operations. Each of the partners, for example, might have air, sea, and/or ground forces in the field and thus, the possibility of tactical level interactions with the adversary. Hence, the number of potential physical and psychological chains that could be created would also be multiplied by the number of participants. While the physical effects of each such interaction might remain confined to the local area of the engagement, this cannot be said of the cognitive effects.[30] These latter effects are likely to spread not only through the coalition partner's own nest, but also through those of other members.

To make matters worse, this spread is not likely to be simply from one national command authority to the next, but will also be from one member to the next at each level of command. Thus, a tactical level action might spread to other nations' forces in adjacent areas, from one commander to his peers in other forces, and from one national military staff to the next. This suggests a geometrically expanding opportunity for confusion and misinformation that would only be mitigated by a common understanding of the ground truth situation awareness. This suggests that the ability to control coalition confusion will only be as good as the awareness of the weakest link.

Still worse, each interaction will have the potential for providing an uncoordinated, contradictory, or nullifying stimulus to the opponent. Each may equally be the recipient of a stimulus that will resound through the coalition. As indicated in our discussion of the cascade of psychological effects, these effects will spread at the speed of communications. In each case, the speed of those communications and the extent of the spread will tend to vary with the nature of the effect. The more serious the implications of an action, the farther and more rapid the spread is likely to be.

As difficult as all of the above sounds, it does underline two things. First, the better the situation awareness and understanding of intent are across the coalition, the more likely it is that the participants will be able to deconflict their actions so as to achieve a unity of effect. Second, the more experience nations and forces have in operating together, the more likely they are to be able to deal with the complexities of coalition operations.

Exploiting the Hostile Coalition

Although most of our threat scenarios deal with situations in which the United States and coalition partners confront a single nation-state opponent, we may not be confronted with a single entity, but rather with some group of actors. Although such an opposing coalition may be of states in the sense of a classic symmetric conflict, it also may be of tribes, ethnic dissidents, and/or terrorist organizations in an asymmetric conflict.

If we look more closely at the wars and crises of the last half-century, we often have had to deal with some form of coalition ranged against us, even if multi-state military operations against American forces were not the norm. Each of the three Middle East crises surveyed can be described as a confrontation between two loose coalitions (the Soviet Union and its local clients versus the United States and its local clients), even though the armed conflict in each case was confined to the local clients. Similarly, in the Cuban Missile Crisis, we can see not only a confrontation between the Soviet Union and the United States, but also actions by coalition partners on both sides such as Cuba and the Organization of American States. We can further see in the Afghan War another loose coalition between the Taliban Government of Afghanistan and an international terrorist organization, al-Qaida. With al-Qaida, we can even trace a loose coalition of radical Islamist groups to pursue operations around the world with the whole coalition sponsored both by states and a series of nongovernmental organizations.

If we look more closely still, we can see that in most governments or organizations, power is shared in some form of internal coalition. These internal coalitions may be formalized in the context of a parliamentary government, or it may reflect precarious and potentially very tenuous balancing of political factions, social, and ethnic groups, as in the case of the Milosoevic government in Yugoslavia during the NATO peacekeeping operation in Kosovo. In many respects, these internal arrangements also function as a classic interstate coalition.

The salient point here is that the complexities of coalition operations work both ways. However difficult it is for us to coordinate a coalition operation, it is equally hard for the opposing coalition, whether it is of nations, organizations, or groups. Herein lies an opportunity. If we look closely at the historical examples of coalitions and the problems they encountered, two things become obvious. First, the same problems that confront us in coordinating coalition effects-based operations also afflict the adversary. Second, the same kinds of rules and some version of coalition nesting continue to apply.

In each coalition, we can see that an action creates a physical effect that somehow crosses into the cognitive domain as an indirect effect. That indirect psychological effect then stands to propagate through the successive levels of some form of control structure (intrastate, state or otherwise), that probably has discernible tactical, operational, and strategic levels. It may also propagate into other arenas, for example to the political arm or financing of a terrorist organization.[31] Where this structure operates with other groups in a coalition, the psychological effects will propagate to other coalition members. The same complexities that confront us are likely to plague the opposition as well and they may be similarly exploited.

We do not need to mirror an arrangement of states as coalition partners in order to conduct such anti-coalition effects-based operations. On the contrary, the ability to exploit the complexities involved is likely to be most pronounced in those coalitions farthest from the standard models of states-versus-states or of an internal parliamentary arrangement. Five aspects of this coalition complexity are of primary concern.

- Any accord on a course of action within a coalition is likely to be time-sensitive. The interests of nations, organizations, and factions change over time and tend to do so especially rapidly as they attempt to adapt to a challenge. The looser the coalition and the more heterogeneous the membership, the more fleeting the accord is likely to be. In most cases, the partners in an asymmetric conflict coalition will not have had a long history of operations together. In many cases, they will not have anything more than a negative general agreement. They may agree only on the need to strike at America and the West, but not on any specific long-term plan. As a result, each will tend to react separately to stimuli and coordination of efforts is likely to be difficult.

- Also, an ad hoc coalition of entities with no history of working together is likely to be subject to the same problems that we experience in managing our own coalitions and may be considerably more susceptible to fracture. Partners often bring a history of distrust and suspicion to the coalition, which compounds the tendency to look at each misaction as evidence of ill intent or an attempt to pursue individual interests at the expense of the group.

- As in our own coalition nesting model, stimuli applied to the nest at any level will tend to produce a chain reaction of psychological effects that propagates throughout the nest. The right stimulus applied to one part of the coalition therefore has the potential to alter the behavior of the entire coalition.[32]

- The opposing coalition will also have some rational decisionmaking structure through which the stimuli and the psychological effects will flow. The closer an actor resembles a state, the more stable the structure is likely to be. The less like a state the member is, the less stable the decisionmaking structure is likely to be. And, when a coalition mixes state and non-state actors, the tensions between the various decisionmaking structures and the ways in which they react to stimuli are likely to be pronounced.

- Finally, the speed of communications at which the flow of stimuli and effects occur will vary between members depending on the level of shared awareness within the coalition, and the organization and sophistication of the individual coalition partners. This can also provide seeds of discord.

Each of the above suggests a difference between two opposing coalitions that is analogous to the edge of chaos we discussed in Chapter 2. Like the better trained and equipped unit, the coalition with the superior organization, communications, shared awareness, and stability wrought by a history of collaboration will have a distinct advantage. Each also represents a potential opportunity to exploit adversaries' vulnerabilities by planning and executing effects-based operations to create and exacerbate the differences that are part of any coalition.

Complexity and Planning

The message of this chapter is that complexity is inherently a part of effects-based operations and is indeed what gives them their nonlinear impact, whether from cascading physical or psychological effects. What we have sketched here are both ways of bounding the complexity involved in planning and executing an effects-based operation and ways of exploiting the parallel complexities faced by our opponents. As this underlines, the better able we are to deal with the complexity (in our thinking, in our internal and coalition organization, and in our support to decisionmaking at all levels), the less likely an opponent will be to use it successfully against us and the more likely it is that we will be to exploit the complexity to our own advantage.

---

[1]The fact that these descriptions are historical rather than theoretical is significant here because it demonstrates that the complexities described above, however daunting they may be, have routinely been handled in military and diplomatic interactions for centuries. The challenge is deriving

the lessons from these interactions that will better enable us to understand what was going on and to apply the emerging capabilities of network-centric operations to them.

[2]It is worth noting again that at Midway, neither the action (the *Yorktown*'s presence) nor the observation and reporting was intentional on the part of the Americans, and that the subsequent cascade of effects was neither planned nor understood by the Americans at the time.

[3]Even though we routinely accept this idea of a chain of effects, we should also note that this expectation of a succession of derivative effects differs somewhat from the expectations involved in a pure attrition model. One difference is obvious. In both of the cases shown above, no physical damage was inflicted in the initial physical effect nor could the outcome of the entire chain be described in terms of a level of destruction, whereas in a pure attrition model, success would be defined in terms of what was destroyed. However, another, perhaps greater difference is that in straight-line physical attrition such as that at Verdun in 1916, the destruction itself would have been the objective of the operation and the question of any other effects would have been largely ignored. In an attrition model, there are only direct physical effects. Yet, the fact of the matter is that examples of straight-line attrition such as Verdun are relatively rare. In most military combat operations, we *do* seek to create chains of physical effects in order to multiply the impact of our actions. Also, we *do* seek in some way to break the opponent's will and move from simply creating a physical effect to creating a still more far-reaching psychological effect.

[4]Pogue, Forrest. *The Supreme Command.* Washington, DC; Department of the Army. 1954. pp. 124ff.

[5]Churchill. *Closing the Ring.* p. 528.

[6]Pogue. p. 127.

[7]Taken in the context of pure Lanchestrian attrition, the destruction of the rail facilities had a logic all of its own. The bombing of rail targets as a category served to eliminate some portion of the French railroad transportation network in the expectation that, when a large enough portion of that network was destroyed, the system would be unable to function and thus produce the desired effects. If we were to follow the logic of pure attrition-based warfare, we might expect that strikes on rail yards would cumulatively achieve the requisite level of destruction for the system to collapse.

[8]In fact, the Germans showed a remarkable ability to repair the damages to the rail system as a result of Allied air strikes, often opening junctions within 48 hours of their destruction.

Similarly, although Allied bombings destroyed some 1,700 locomotives and 25,000 rail cars in the weeks before D-Day, this amounted to only a small percentage of the total available rolling stock. SHAEF Weekly Intelligence Summary. No. 11, 3 June 1944.

[8]Churchill. *Closing the Ring.* p. 528.

[9]That capacity had been reduced to 69 percent of the January 1944 level by mid-May 1944, and to just 38 percent of that level by D-Day.

Ambrose, Stephen. *D-Day June 6, 1944.* New York; Touchstone. 1994. p. 97.

[10]Tedder, Sir Arthur. *With Prejudice.* London; Cassell. 1966. pp. 524ff.

[11]It is clear from the comments of German generals interviewed after the war that the Allied success in this regard was very discouraging as it was "ruinous to their counteroffensive plans."

Pogue, p. 132.

[12]Tedder, p. 524.

[13]The direct physical effect that sets off a cascade of indirect psychological effects may be "felt" in terms of destruction inflicted and options foreclosed, or it may be in terms of a maneuver observed, an announcement made, a diplomatic note delivered, or a bank deposit frozen, to name just a few examples.

[14]Churchill's description of this despair and inability to act coherently is vivid.

Churchill. *Their Finest Hour.* pp. 322ff.

[15]Again the example of the reactions to the blitzkrieg of 1940 is relevant. In that case, the sense of panic in the French military and political leadership that occurred as a result of the swift German offensive brought the British Prime Minister Churchill to refuse any further commitment of Royal Air Force assets to what he perceived to be a lost cause. Similarly, the imminent French collapse brought another passive observer, Mussolini, to conclude that he could safely launch an offensive of his own against France. This spread of psychological effects rapidly became pervasive and set off a chain of effects of its own in multiple directions.

Churchill. *The Gathering Storm.* pp. 132ff.

[16]These possibilities were in fact the subject of much debate by both the Allied military and political leadership, despite the agreement of the Free French to the bombing campaign. The matter was deemed of such importance that the final choice to ignore the collateral damage and casualties physical effects paths fell to Roosevelt and Churchill.

Churchill. *Closing the Ring.* pp.528-531.

[17]Eisenhower, Dwight D. *The Eisenhower Diaries.* New York; Norton. 1981. pp. 114-115.

[18]This was done after consulting with the Free French leadership, which endorsed the plan despite the collateral damage entailed.

Pogue, p. 128.

[19]This was certainly reflected in the SHAEF intelligence reporting that, by D-Day 1944, the French rail system was at 38 percent of its pre-bombing capacity.

SHAEF Weekly Intelligence Report No. 11, 3 June 1944.

[20]Although the information revolution has increased both the speed and the scope of communications dramatically, neither the speed nor the scope is uniform across all opponents or all observers. This phenomenon was very evident in the spread of information during the operations in Afghanistan during 2001-2. This "communication quotient" thus becomes yet another variable to be considered in plotting the potential spread of psychological and cognitive effects.

[21]In fact, in the Cuban Missile Crisis of 1962, it was the speed of the cognitive effects that made the signaling between the two superpowers possible at critical moments of the crises.

[22]Obviously, the results of the air strikes were closely monitored so as to ensure that the 93 targets on the list were in fact destroyed and to trace any efforts to repair the damage that might necessitate a second strike. However, there was no significant change to the German posture as a result of the bombings and thus no further change in the chains of physical effects at the core of the air campaign plan.

[23]This was most apparent at the geo-strategic level in the interactions between the two national command authorities, but it is also apparent at the level of the operational commanders. Thus, in each crisis, the Commander of the United States Sixth Fleet started the interaction with multiple directions of concern and narrowed his focus to the actions of his Soviet opponent as the crisis turned into a major military confrontation. Not surprisingly, a similar shift in the tactical focus of both sides followed.

[24]These bounding assumptions reflected the prior knowledge and mental models of the decisionmakers involved. Yet, as shown in the Middle East crises, the models and knowledge are not so esoteric as to make them inapplicable to the situation. On the contrary, the assumptions of rational decisionmakers operating in a rational decisionmaking context were shared by all the participants in the crises (not only the Soviets and Americans, but equally by the Arabs and

Israelis and major allies of the two superpowers). They recognized that, at a minimum, the effect of the action would be cumulative over time and contribute to the history of actions upon which an observer's future decisions would be based and, thus, shape his future behavior.

[25]In approaching the problem of multi-actor effects-based operations, we will assume that since the rule sets examined earlier describe effects-based operations in general rather than any peculiarly American approach, those rules will continue to operate and impose similar kinds of coordination problems. As in the case of an individual actor, therefore, we will assume that all of the actions of any player that can be observed will be observed by the other actors. And, in the case of coalition partners, we will likewise assume that the effect created by each action will combine with the effects wrought by all other actions, and have either a positive or a negative impact on the overall effect created by the coalition as a whole.

[26]This was in fact the case in the creation of the "Transportation Plan" aerial bombing campaign in Normandy, which had to take into account not only the different desires of the British and American governments but also the competing demands of the U.S. Army Air Corps and Royal Air Force (which saw the operations as detracting from the strategic bombing campaign against Germany), and the Supreme Commander (who saw the "Transportation Plan" as so essential to the success of the invasion that he threatened to resign his command over the issue).

Eisenhower. p. 114.

[27]Tedder, pp. 524ff.

[28]Churchill. *Closing the Ring.* pp. 528-9.

[29]Coalitions can be defined as ad hoc alignments of states or groups which arise to deal with a particular threat or problem and which disperse when the problem is resolved.

[30]In most cases, this latter situation will mean that each partner would be operating under a set of national rules of engagement or instructions while attempting to coordinate as well as possible with the other partners.

[31]In these engagements, the passive players would include not only national forces in adjacent patrol stations, but also all coalition forces in the area. If the interaction were to result in hostilities, then all coalition units might become active participants and with them, their respective nations. At a minimum, such an uncontrolled interaction would most certainly become a stimulus confronting both the military and civilian leadership at all levels. This is to say that, in a coalition operation, the effect of an action by the opponent

could be not only to expand abruptly the scope of the interaction to other warfare areas, but to do so across the breadth of the coalition.

[32]It should be noted, however, that in a loose coalition of the type described, actions are not likely to be as coordinated as those demonstrated by the United States or the Soviet Union in the three Middle East crises. Thus, the expectation of an almost instantaneous relay and impact of military actions that characterized those crises needs to be tempered by a realistic assessment of what the opposing nest will look like and just how fast its speed of communications is likely to be.

CHAPTER 8

Dynamic Effects-Based Operations: The Challenge of Effects Assessment and Feedback

If we accept the maxim that no plan survives first contact with the enemy, then it stands to reason that it is not enough for a commander to orchestrate the opening engagement of an effects-based operation. No matter how good this preplanning may be and no matter what the scale of any initial strike, no single military action by itself is likely to create the overall outcome sought. What is far more likely, indeed almost inevitable, is that the initial operation will be followed by a succession of additional action-reaction cycles in which each side adapts to the challenges of the other. It is a reality of war that, in these successive cycles, the enemy will not intentionally cooperate with the commander's plans and will seldom fight in the manner expected. Elementary prudence dictates that commanders at all levels assume the reverse. They must plan for an intelligent adversary who will be determined to defeat their efforts by whatever means possible.

Stating the above in terms of complexity theory reinforces this interactive, give-and-take view of battle. In this context, war is seen as a clash between complex adaptive systems, be they states, non-states, armies, guerrillas, or terrorists. In these clashes, each side will attempt to preserve itself as a system and must adapt to and deal with any challenge presented. Furthermore, given the complex nature of the human organizations involved in these clashes, we should expect that these adaptations would take forms that we will never be able to predict entirely.[1]

In the history we have reviewed, we can also see that both these realities of war and the challenges associated with them are not in fact restricted to war. Rather, the realities and challenges are in one way or another true of all interactions between complex adaptive human organizations whether in peace, crisis, or war. Opposing sides maneuver to protect their interests and adapt to the challenges presented in new and innovative ways. This is true even when the challenges are denominated in primarily political or economic terms, rather than military terms. In short, the give-and-take is characteristic of the interactions of all complex adaptive systems and not just of a war between two nation-states.[2]

Accordingly, if our concept is to have any value, we must be able to adapt our effects-based operations to evolving situations in peace, crisis, and war at all four levels of conflict, and across the political-diplomatic, economic, and military arenas. That is, we must be able to conduct dynamic effects-based operations that account for the ebb and flow of a battle, a crisis, and of all the interactions we may have with both the state and non-state actors that populate our national security environment.

However, there is a hitch. If commanders at any level are to adapt effects-based operations to a changing battlefield or crisis situation, and if they are to be proactive rather than reactive, then they will need some form of continual feedback on the effects of their actions. Such effects assessment would also need to address the changes in behavior that an enemy might be trying to force upon us and the direction that any succession of effects-based action-reaction cycles might be taking. It must also tell the commander how his actions affect the behavior of others who observe his actions. Without the right kind of feedback, commanders will neither be able to respond intelligently to enemy actions nor optimize their own actions in the manner foreseen by Network Centric Warfare theory.[3]

This requirement for feedback raises two more questions: First, how do we measure the success of effects-based operations from one interaction to the next so as to determine how best to adapt and respond? And second, how do we do so with a timeliness commensurate with the speed of command that we seek to exploit in network-centric operations? The challenge posed by these questions is even more formidable because it implies that we must somehow measure the behavior of complex adaptive organizations, a behavior that by definition we can never entirely and precisely know or predict.

The abundance of historical examples of effects-based operations makes a salient point here. For the past 50 years and more, successful commanders at all levels have been coping with the same problem. They have done so by mixing intuition and ad hoc metrics, and they have managed to use uncertain and often ambiguous feedback to make decisions. They did so not because the metrics and feedback were what they earnestly desired, but because they had no choice. They had to make decisions at critical moments and therefore had to use whatever information and metrics were available at the time. This suggests that if we study how past commanders at all levels approached the challenge, what they needed to know, and how they obtained and used it, then we might also be able to understand how to apply the capabilities of the Information Age to the task.

The Normandy Air Campaign, 1944

One good example of this coping is the 1944 Normandy air campaign used in the preceding chapter to describe the cascade of effects. We can continue this example to trace the requirements for multiple different kinds of measures of effectiveness, how each contributed to the feedback needed to support the operation, and how different kinds of measurements were balanced to that end. We can also use this example to see how planners and commanders dealt with the ambiguities and uncertainties that were an inherent part of the planning and execution of the campaign.

As we have seen, the Normandy air campaign was focused on a particular end-state or overall military-strategic effect: the isolation of the intended Allied landing areas from a riposte by German armored divisions in the regions of the Pas de Calais and south of the Loire River.[4] Because the successful execution of the air campaign was seen as a prerequisite to the success of the invasion itself, its execution involved decisionmaking at all levels from the tactical through the national leaderships of Britain and the United States. This multi-level involvement of commanders makes the Normandy example particularly useful because it offers us an opportunity to see what the requirements for feedback were at each level and how these requirements were accommodated with a mixture of three different metrics applied to an array of observable actions.

- Bomb Damage Assessment

The first and most obvious measurement of effects used in the air campaign was the assessment of the physical damage to the rail yards, junctions, and bridges along the principal routes leading to the Normandy battlefields. In the context of the effects-based desired end-state, this essentially attrition-based metric assumed a new dimension. The bomb damage assessment was not just a running tally of the amount of destruction in the manner of a body count. Instead, it was an index of whether or not an action had been completed as planned and whether or not it had had the immediate or direct effect that the air campaign planners intended.[5] In the Normandy example, this meant that the planners needed to determine whether the 93 facilities designated as critical nodes in the French railway system[6] were no longer functional or whether they required a restrike so as to ensure that the desired direct effect on the railway system was achieved.

Despite this effects-based context, the process was relatively straightforward, quantifiable, and little changed from the traditional attrition-based application. Post-strike photography was examined to gauge the damage to targets and the results were provided to commanders. The speed of this process varied only with the collection, execution, processing and reading of the photography, variables that could largely be controlled by the tactical and operational commands involved in the operation. This reporting was supplemented by intelligence from the French Résistance, which was more detailed but was delayed to a degree that became unacceptable in the latter days of the campaign as D-Day approached.

• Railway System Performance

For the Allied commanders and operational level air campaign planners involved in the operation, however, the key measure of effects was not simply the destruction of particular rail facilities. Their principal interest was in the cascades of indirect physical effects that they hoped would grow from that destruction. Thus, they sought feedback from two very different measures of effect: the ability of the rail system as a whole to perform; and the ability of additional German armored divisions to be brought forward quickly enough to affect the Allied landings in Normandy.[7] This demanded an assessment not of damage, but of system performance.

This assessment was obligatorily multi-level. It entailed measuring the throughput capacity of the rail lines both before and after the destruction of the critical nodes. It also involved observing and measuring the ability of the rail system to adapt to the destruction inflicted by repairing the damage and/or by finding work-arounds. Finally, it also required the continual observation of the movements of the German armored divisions that were to be prevented from approaching the invasion beaches, both to gauge the threat to Allied operations and to take advantage of any opportunities for Allied air strikes that may have been created by bottling up the divisions along the routes into Normandy.[8]

Such multi-level assessment was more difficult, complex, and time-consuming than simple bomb damage assessment. Measuring the throughput capacity of a rail system meant assembling a database to establish a norm from which changes could be calculated and then observing the movements along the rail lines over time after the rail nodes had been attacked and destroyed. It also meant observing what bypasses were being created[9] and then determining what throughput capacity each work-around would support. It also meant observing how quickly and completely repairs were being accomplished and thus, how the diminished throughput capacity was changing over time. A similar challenge was encountered in tracking the efforts of German military forces to reach Normandy by other means.

Notice that in the case of these performance metrics, real-time feedback was not an option. The information required was both too complex for a simple read-out and it changed continually over time. This delay, however, was quite acceptable in a campaign lasting many weeks and the intelligence reporting of the French Résistance, even though late, became a more critical part of the feedback.

• German and French Behavior

For the air campaign planners, the Allied commanders at SHAEF, and the national leaderships of Britain and the United States, perhaps the most pressing concern was the indirect psychological effects, which almost caused Prime Minister Churchill to turn down the entire project. In the case of the air campaign planners and the SHAEF staff, the concern over these indirect psychological effects appeared in a reverse context. Their most pressing fear was that the focus of the air campaign should not disclose the location of the invasion and thus induce the Germans to reinforce the Normandy area with forces then being held in the area of the Pas de Calais. To avoid this eventuality, the Allies deliberately sought to create a psychological effect (to maintain German confusion) even as they executed an extensive bombing campaign to deny the key German forces access to the invasion area.

Yet, in spite of the importance of this indirect psychological effect to the Allies, they could not directly measure the degree of confusion that had been left in the German cognitive process after the bombings.[10] Rather, Allied intelligence had to rely on indirect evidence such as the continued presence of the German armored divisions in the Pas de Calais area.

Beyond this immediate concern, the Allies' assessment of the cascading effects of the air campaign in the psychological domain was fuzzy at best. There was no real expectation by the Allied leadership that the bombing campaign would cause the German Army to surrender, though there was a continuing hope that the campaign and invasion would shorten the war and aid in an overall German collapse.[11]

Here again reliable information was sparse. Information on the reactions of the German command might have been available from signals intelligence, notably in the Ultra code-breaker intercepts, but each of these sources would have been delayed, subject to chance availability, and subject to varying interpretations by different analysts. Similarly, the impact of the operation upon the national German leadership might have been loosely discernible in subtle changes in propaganda and public announcements, but again with substantial delays and only a tenuous tie to any particular Allied action.

However, the concern of the Allies' national level leaderships was also very much focused on a different set of indirect psychological effects. These centered on the amount of collateral damage and casualties that might be caused by bombing critical rail facilities in heavily populated areas of France. They feared that a cascade of indirect psychological effects might grow from the bombing campaign to the point that an angry or hostile French citizenry would meet the invasion. Although the Free French government of General de Gaulle dismissed this likelihood and advocated the bombing campaign as a necessary step in the country's liberation, Prime Minister Churchill was most apprehensive as to the psychological effect wrought by the bombing. It ultimately required a threat of resignation by General Eisenhower and a subsequent intervention from President Roosevelt to launch and sustain the air campaign.

The quantity and quality of the feedback into the leadership's cognitive processes at the military-strategic and geo-strategic level was minimal or contradictory. The Free French government might offer reassurance, but its input might be considered to be at least partially self-serving. The controlled media in German-occupied France and in what was left of Vichy France might similarly be expected to condemn the bombing as well as to magnify the suffering of the local people for propaganda purposes. Thus, the feedback available to major decisionmakers was sparse and potentially unreliable. Yet, decisions were required and the decisionmakers in question made them on the basis of what they knew both from prior knowledge and what little feedback they did have.

Lessons Learned

In the Normandy example, we can see the above metrics addressing three distinctly different kinds of feedback requirements: the measurement of physical damage (direct effect), the measurement of performance (indirect physical effects), and a looser set of diverse intelligence information (indirect psychological effects).

1. Direct Effects Assessment

As we noted, the Normandy air campaign planners had to assess the level and nature of destruction wrought by their bombs to see whether the action had the immediate, direct effect that they had intended. Even though the purpose of the feedback was different, the effects assessment of the action closely resembled the classic, attrition-based bomb damage assessment.

This applicability of an attrition-based metric should not be surprising since the actions undertaken were air strikes and the kind of direct effect sought was the destruction of a set of ground targets. The bomb damage assessment remained a valid measurement because the physical action was the same as in a straight attrition conflict, even though the ends for which the assessment was to be used differed fundamentally. This contributes to the development of effects-based metrics because such assessments of physical damage are something we know how to do and which we can quantify relatively promptly.

However, as we look beyond this wartime example of destructive direct effects, we are faced with a question: What metric would we use if the direct effect we sought did not or could not involve such measurable destruction? How would we measure the direct effect of an action in peacetime or in crisis response operations, or the impact of an action upon coalition partners, friends, and neutrals? Notice that in all of these situations, the requirement for feedback on the direct effects of our actions remains essentially the same as in the Normandy example. Was the stimulus applied, for better or worse? Was the action seen or felt by the intended observer and other observers in such a way as to enter their cognitive processes? This extension of the direct effects assessment feedback requirement to noncombat situations means that we can no longer think solely in terms of bomb damage assessment as a metric for direct effects. Instead, we must expand the effects assessment process to include metrics that may be significantly different from assessment of physical damage to forces and capabilities. This expanded requirement leaves us looking for new indices not only of actions observed, but also how other observers perceived the action.

A better example is that of the closing days of the 1967 Middle East crisis and the dispatch of the United States Sixth Fleet toward the coast of Syria to signal American opposition to the Soviet threat to send troops into Damascus. The American military action, in conjunction with national level diplomatic actions, sought to foreclose an unacceptably dangerous Soviet behavior. However, in order to become a factor in the Soviet national decisionmaking process, the military action had to be seen, understood, and reported by local Soviet observers. In this example, President Johnson counted upon the fact that the Soviet intelligence collection ships monitoring the Sixth Fleet would observe the American action and that they would immediately report the American action up their chain of command to Moscow. In this case, the measure of a successful direct effect might have been found in the actions of the Soviet tattletales when their American prey came about and headed in the opposite direction at high speed.

The above suggests that the indices of direct effects can take two dimensions: physical effects that we can monitor and possibly quantify, and behavior that we can monitor but must be put into some context (e.g. the difference from established norms) before it can be useful as feedback.

2. Performance Assessment

This latter idea is central to performance assessment. In the Normandy example, air planners carefully monitored activity on the French railway system to determine whether the cascade of indirect physical effects that they had hoped to create was in fact occurring. They had to monitor the physical performance of the system over a period of time both before and after their action, and then use the resulting, changing delta between the baseline and post-strike performance. In this manner, they were able to determine that by the end of May 1944, despite a concerted German-directed repair effort, the rail activity in northern France had been reduced to just 38 percent of its pre-war total.[12] Although such system physical performance assessment cannot provide any immediate feedback, the process of measuring such performance is again something with which we are familiar and is largely quantifiable.

What is significant to note here is what was required before a delta could be determined and measured as system performance. To obtain any meaningful data on the performance of the targeted system,[13] we must first have a relatively good picture of what the system is, how its component parts relate to one another, how the system has performed in the past, and some idea of how it might react to the stimulus provided by the direct effect. In the Normandy case, this meant that the air planners had to thoroughly research the railway system of northern France before they could begin work. This implies that the assessment and feedback process must address not only what the evolving performance of this system may be in a given area, but also the likely causal relationship between the actions taken and that changing performance.

In several respects, the above underscores how the critical element in performance assessment is less the collection of new data on the system than it is the availability of a data or knowledge base from which to calculate change. That knowledge base, as illustrated above, must include how the system works and how it has functioned in the past.

Although this is no minor challenge, it is also familiar territory. We have done all of this not only against the French railway system in the case of the Normandy air campaign but equally against the electrical grid in Iraq during the Desert Storm operations. In most instances, we can identify and monitor a specific set of indices to follow the impact upon the physical systems in question, and we may even be able to predict some of the ramifications of the system's degradation. The problem is that the larger and more complicated the system is, the more difficult it is to estimate all of the possible ramifications of our actions against it. For example, we might be able to predict the impact of the destruction of a transformer on a power grid, but it would be considerably more difficulty to predict all of the potential impacts that might result from the loss of electric power through a country.[14]

If we think in terms of the falling domino model examined in the preceding chapter, we would be limited to looking at just a short stretch of the cause and effect chain reaction. The larger and more complex the chains to be monitored are, the smaller the proportion of the entire chain we are likely to have to judge the totality of the effects we are creating. Thus, the feedback we could supply would be less accurate and more ambiguous.

We also need to recognize that for larger systems (e.g. a national or regional economy), it is more likely that the effects we create will not remain confined to the physical domain, but will cross over into the psychological domain. Indeed, as we saw in the models of chains of effects, each successive falling domino can set off its own series of indirect psychological effects.

How would this performance assessment apply to effects-based operations in peace and crisis? Obviously in such cases, we might not be monitoring the performance of physical systems following a bombing campaign, but we might be seeking indices of changed performance in the sense of system behavior. A good example here is the 1962 Cuban Missile Crisis. During that crisis, a critical moment was the feedback to White House decisionmakers first that Soviet cargo ships en route to Cuba had stopped, and then that a large number of these ships were turning back. The performance of the commercial shipping system of the Soviet Union provided a key indicator of a change in Soviet policy.

Notice that the same kinds of issues and constraints apply here as in the monitoring of the rail system performance in the Normandy example. The performance of the shipping had to be monitored over time in order to determine a set of norms from which a delta might be monitored. In the Cuba case, this meant that the United States had to understand how Soviet commercial shipping operated, what kinds and quantities of shipping would normally have been en route to Cuba,[15] and then what all of the ships en route to Cuba at the time of the crisis were doing on a minute by minute basis. However, in the Cuban case, there was also a difference. Unlike Normandy rail traffic, the ships en route to Cuba could be monitored on a minute by minute basis and, using the Navy's reporting network, that data could be rapidly collated, assessed, and reported to the decisionmakers in a timely enough manner to be of significant use. In the Cuban instance, this timeliness became even more critical in the hours following the initial halt of the ships when some of the ships continued on their way, possibly with submarine escort. The final halt of these ships signaled the beginning of the end of the confrontation.

However, notice that for this timeliness to be achieved, the surveillance system had to set up the entire context for the critical piece of information. It had to know the system well enough to establish an overall norm of routine merchant shipping performance and a sliding norm of what the shipping was doing in the steady state of crisis operations. Given this context, all that needed to be done was to look for one critical datum: divergence from the sliding norm. That datum could then be reported with little further assessment in much the same fashion as the last datum needed to complete a sensor to shooter link.[16]

In the above examples, we can distinguish two types of performance assessment. There is performance reckoning of how the system performs after the target has been destroyed, and there is a behavioral performance metric manifest in the ongoing actions of such systems as commercial shipping, telecommunications, military operations, and diplomacy. We can distinguish between two different kinds of performance metrics. In the Normandy example, the reporting on performance was an *aggregate* indicator, the measurement of a level of throughput capacity of the rail system in a particular area. In the Cuban example, the key feedback was a *point* indicator, the detection and measurement of an event that differed from the established norm (the continued transit toward Cuba of Soviet merchant ships). Both aggregate indicators and point indicators demand a significant database on the system in question to determine a norm, and both demand continued monitoring. In the latter case, the availability of a large, networked surveillance system permitted immediate detection of a change in system performance and timely feedback to decisionmakers.

3. Psychological Effects Assessment

Effects-based operations may be about shaping behavior and creating psychological effects, but how do we assess these psychological effects? Performance assessment can be used to assess behavioral changes. It focuses on the changes in system behavior, which might be monitored as indicators of an ongoing, adapting decisionmaking process. What other indicators of psychological effects might be relevant?

In the Normandy example, we can see this search for indicators at two distinct levels:

- For the Allied campaign planners concerned that their railway bombings might indicate the intended location of the invasion to the German commanders, there was clearly a set of physical indicators of the German Western Command's cognitive process. These indicators reflected the various actions involved in preparing and moving the armored divisions. These were essentially point indicators of divergence from normal operations in the Pas de Calais and could be closely monitored. If detected, they would have provided critical feedback to Allied decisionmaking at all levels.

- By contrast, the cascade of indirect psychological effects that so worried Churchill (a hostile French reaction to the bombing campaign) did not have a reliably measurable index. Instead, the senior commanders and national leaders involved had to fall back on an almost intuitive assessment of the situation. For Eisenhower, this intuition was based on a military perspective that told him that, in the absence of the bombings, the invasion would fail and thus, that the risks of a hostile French public reaction had to be borne. For Churchill and Roosevelt, the intuition was based on a lifetime in politics, an occupation that was built around assessment of public reactions to events. These mental models of public opinion, plus assessments of actual French reactions and military assessments of the risks of invading without blocking the German armored divisions, would have provided the basis for their decisions.

Any feedback inserted into the decision processes of each of these commanders has to have been uncertain and ambiguous, no matter how well analyzed. Ultimately, the decision reached by each commander would have represented both a conscious and unconscious consideration of a wide variety and large number of variables that the leaders themselves would have been hard pressed to explain.

This latter predicament is not new. Successful leaders and commanders at higher levels have always been forced to reach decisions on the basis of metrics that are uncertain. Napoleon, for example, used to claim that his job as a general consisted of setting up the battle to be fought and then watching for the right moment to throw in the reserves so as to break the enemy's will and drive him from the battlefield. Therefore, his primary role during the battle was to gauge when the enemy psychology was such that the addition of a relatively small amount of additional force would turn the tide of battle. In Napoleon's case, as in that of the Allies, determining the right moment was a subjective decision that combined years of experience with whatever was visible on the battlefield. But Napoleon's task was much simpler than that which the World War II leaders faced. After all, Napoleon's decisions were an assessment of a purely military reaction within a relatively confined area that he could himself observe.

In essence, what Napoleon, Eisenhower, de Gaulle, Churchill, and Roosevelt were providing was a particular expertise. That expertise enabled them to integrate an extensive set of variables and to deal with the ambiguities and uncertainties by filling in the blanks from their own knowledge base. Their expertise was supplemented by feedback from other experts, as well as whatever indicators of behavior were gathered by the intelligence and surveillance effort, but it remained highly idiosyncratic.

Our challenge in conducting dynamic effects-based operations is to provide ongoing feedback not only on the immediate tactical and operational level interactions, but also on how those interactions affect a series of larger systems at a national level. In these wider assessments, not only is the link between actions and effects still more tenuous, but any reactions we observe are likely to be long delayed and subject to varying interpretations.[17]

Metrics

The above discussions point to an interesting dichotomy between traditional, attrition-based measures of effectiveness and what might be termed human-based metrics, the measurement of the reactions and behavior of human beings and human organizations. We can see in the Normandy example that commanders' decisions were not based solely on attrition-based metrics, nor were they based solely on the often-vague human-based metrics. The common element in the decisionmaking process was the tendency of commanders to combine attrition-based information with human-based metrics and largely subjective judgments drawn from available estimative intelligence.[18] These "mixed metrics" were then used to assess how well they were succeeding.

However, the mix of attrition-based and human-based metrics was not uniform across the spectrum of commanders. Instead, the relative value of the metrics varied according to the level of command. At the tactical level, the assessment of the level of damage inflicted on the adversary might by itself be a sufficient indicator of success, but at higher levels, such damage assessment is only one of many criteria, which tend to expand as the level of command increases. In fact, as commanders' objectives become increasingly denominated in terms of enemy behavior, the role of attrition-based measurement of damage in decisions decreases.

This dichotomy bears further examination. Why and how are attrition-based metrics useful, and when are imprecise and ambiguous human-based metrics the only alternative? In the latter case, what might we do to choose the right human-based metrics and to make them less ambiguous and contradictory?

Attrition-Based Measures

The presumption at the root of attrition-based metrics is that the destruction of the means of waging war will ultimately result in victory. But what constitutes a victory or success?

At a kill-or-be-killed tactical level, the destruction of the opponent is a clear and usually conclusive victory. If we were to describe victory in a war as the destruction of all of an opponent's forces and capabilities, then the results of each of these tactical victories would be additive. That is, each kill would further diminish the overall enemy capabilities and provide quantifiable progress toward victory. Following this logic at military-strategic and geo-strategic levels, measuring the level of destruction inflicted on a day-to-day basis would provide an accurate picture of our progress toward an overall victory.

Yet, as we have seen in Chapter 2's discussion of the Third Punic War, there are very few such total wars in which victory does equate to the total physical destruction of the enemy. Thus, a purely attrition-based index would not be adequate for the strategic or military-strategic level and would probably be insufficient for operational level decisions as well. The infamously misleading body counts during the Vietnam War are a case in point. Moreover, as we saw in the discussion of the great attrition wars of the past century, there are few operational level engagements that resulted in the total destruction of an enemy's forces and personnel. Instead, even in wars of attrition, the paradigm has been to reduce the adversary's forces and capabilities to the point where his will to wage war collapsed.

In spite of these limitations, we cannot dismiss the attrition-based metrics entirely. We can recognize from our earlier discussion of different kinds of effects that destruction does matter, even in effects-based operations. What we need to understand is how and under what circumstances the attrition-based metrics apply in feedback to commanders. Then, armed with that understanding, we can address their limitations in an effects-based role and begin to overcome them.

To understand the role of attrition-based metrics in feedback to commanders, we must first understand how commanders actually use those measurements. In fact, if we look closely at the role of attrition-based feedback in the decisions of the commanders involved in our crisis examples, it rapidly becomes evident that the measurements of destruction found a very different use at the tactical level of command than at higher levels of command.

For the tactical level combat commander, the effect to be achieved was usually very specific and straightforward. For example, he may have had to destroy a critical railroad bridge or junction, as in the Normandy example. In such a case, the connection between the desired tactical end-state and the destruction required to achieve it was clear. Moreover, the tactical actions themselves usually constituted an independent cycle of finite duration. When the level of destruction required was achieved, then that particular operation was over. Under these circumstances, the measurement of the level of destruction inflicted could provide a clear index of success or failure for a given engagement.

At the level of the operational commander, the clarity of this connection between destruction and success might be expected to diminish. To the degree that the assigned objective remains clear, specific, and denominated in terms of destruction (for example, an order to destroy all of the bridges in Normandy over which German tanks might pass), then the connection between action and effect remains clear. But when the task begins to take on a human dimension, such as an order to prevent enemy armored divisions from advancing into Normandy, a more general direction befitting a higher level of command, then the connection between actions and effects might become more complex. The commander might elect to destroy either the railways or the tank column itself. However, if he chooses to destroy the railways (as Eisenhower did), the choice would involve a decisionmaking process including assessments of whether the foe might find some other way to Normandy, whether the destruction might immobilize the enemy, or even whether the action might break the foe's will to fight.

Notice that in this operational level example, the measurement of the extent of damage to bridges or even to the entire rail network would tell the operational commander only a part of the information that he needed to determine the success or failure of the operation. Assessment of damage to the bridge would not tell the commander whether or not the enemy advance was permanently halted or what the enemy's intentions were.

At the military-strategic and geo-strategic levels of command, the level of Allied Supreme Headquarters and the national leaderships, the connection between destruction and a desired effect or end-state is even more tenuous. At this level, the destruction rendered by one single military operation or even an entire campaign is but one factor in a complex interaction that spans a far longer period of time, multiple arenas, and other military operations around the world. At this level, the measurement of damage inflicted is only a partial index of success in a more complicated picture where success is defined in political or diplomatic, not military, terms.[19]

It should also be noted that, over the 50-year history of American military crisis responses, attrition-based measures of effectiveness provided no index at all of success in the vast majority of operations simply because the operations did not involve destruction. More significantly, this is true of all of the Soviet-American military confrontations, including the three Middle East crises cited, because any violent use of military force would have been the antithesis of success in each of these confrontations.

Nor did attrition-based metrics reflect the impact of military actions upon allies, partners, and neutrals, a persistent and very significant consideration for the upper levels of command during coalition combat operations such as the Kosovo crisis. Attrition-based measures alone were unable to provide meaningful feedback for the nonviolent uses of military power (which constitute the vast majority of military operations) or for gauging effects upon anyone but the enemy.

These limitations are noteworthy because they suggest that for all of their apparent exactitude, the traditional attrition-based measures ultimately become unproductive when applied to the measurement of effects. At any but a kill-or-be-killed tactical level or total attrition war, the attrition-based yardstick still leaves us trying to determine how the action of destroying forces and capabilities translates into a particular behavior, such as the collapse or erosion of the enemy's will to fight.[20]

Human-Based Metrics for Operations in the Cognitive Domain

This inability of attrition-based measurement to describe the human dimension of combat and war is not new.[21][22] It is well recognized, for example, that a level of damage sufficient to cause the will of one unit to collapse and retreat will not necessarily have the same impact on a similarly armed adjacent unit. The differential between units may be one of esprit, as in the case of the performance of German Waffen SS units during World War II, or it may be of experience, as in the case of the Union Army of the Potomac in 1861 versus in 1864. It may be the result of a myriad of human factors that are equally difficult to quantify.

Attempts have been made to measure these human variables (e.g. unit cohesion, fatigue, training, etc.) and to assign values to them so as to predict what level of damage or losses might produce a collapse, most notably by the Soviets.[23] However, in each case, analysts have found themselves trying to quantify intangibles to the point that the validity of each set of numbers quickly came to depend upon human judgments either on the part of the subjects or that of the analysts, or both.[24][25]

Although the above military operations research efforts have tended to focus on the tactical and operational levels of war, there is also a rich history of United States Air Force efforts to assess the links between non-nuclear strategic bombing campaigns and the collapse of national will, or the will of the national leadership. These efforts date back to Guilio Douhet's original air power work and are reflected in the U.S. Army Air Corps bombing studies done in the years before World War II, as well as in the bombing campaigns during the war. In their current guise, these linkages are most evident in the work of Colonel John Worden and especially in his theory of attacking concentric circles of national power to break the will of the leadership, a targeting approach taken during Desert Storm.[26] [27] Most recently, this connection between attrition and strategic effects has taken an additional step in Brigadier General David Deptula's concept of simultaneous strike against large numbers of these targets so as to induce shock.[28]

However, in each of these cases, the same problem resurfaces. How do we detect and measure the relationship between the bombing campaign and the will of an opponent or of the opponent's leadership?

In the case of Desert Storm, and the more recent cases of Serbia and Kosovo, this problem was reflected in the often tenuous connection between regime behavior and target destruction. To make matters worse, in the Kosovo operation, attacks on targets that might possibly have yielded the desired effects on Serbian decisionmaking were foreclosed because the same action might produce undesired effects in the internal politics of the coalition members or on diplomatic efforts to isolate Milosevic from external support. Indeed, the lack of adequate human-based metrics in Kosovo posed a double problem. Not only could we not measure the progress of our effects-based operations with respect to the enemy, but because we could not do so, it became still more difficult to justify the political risks that our coalition partners were being asked to take in order to achieve coalition objectives.

How might we approach this problem?

Indicators

In the Normandy example, each of the three kinds of effects assessments outlined depended on indirect measures of effect. We measured observable phenomena of some sort (damage, performance, or behavior), and then used that measurement as an indicator of the impact of our actions on a cognitive process, the true nature of which depended on a series of factors that we could not observe directly. Thus, in the D-Day example, the damage to railways and facilities could be monitored and quantified, but the damage was only an indication of the desired effect that the planners sought to create: blocking rail movement toward the invasion beaches. Similarly, although the movement of forces over the rail lines could be monitored, given the possibility of rapid repairs, the use of alternative rail routes, road transport around ruined railways, and so on, the effect was neither certain nor exactly quantifiable despite the evident cause and effect relationship.

We can extend this observation to human-based metrics in general. Whether we are assessing the immediate, direct effects of our actions or the cascade of indirect effects through the physical and cognitive domains, what we will really be looking for is a series of observable indicators from which to gauge a particular effect. For the most part, these indicators will not be nearly as straightforward as the bomb damage to the French railway system. Instead, there always will be an element of uncertainty and the value of the measurements will depend heavily on how well we choose and aggregate the indicators and on the context in which we consider them. A single indicator may not suffice to assess an effect or to define a change in behavior, but the combination of all the indicators available may provide a reliable guide.

In this respect, the process of assessing effects begins to resemble the approach to indications and warning intelligence developed during the Cold War.[29] The indications and warning methodology called for the development of extensive lists of indicators of the postulated actions a prospective enemy might take in order to prepare for a surprise attack upon the United States and its NATO allies. These indicators were then made intelligence collection priorities and were regularly observed and reported. Since any observations of potential actions were expected to be incomplete given deliberate concealment by the attacker, those that could be observed were weighted for their significance and for the place they occupied in the likely sequence of preparing an attack. These weighted indicators were aggregated and put into an algorithm to yield an overall, evaluated probability of attack.[30] However, this indications-and-warning model poses another question.

What indicators should we be looking for?

The Cognitive Cycle

What indicators can we observe and how would we do so?

Perhaps the most fundamental criterion for any indicator is that it be in some way observable. That which cannot be observed, cannot be measured, and therefore, cannot provide meaningful feedback. But what are we supposed to observe in human-based metrics and how are we supposed to observe it?

Our stated objective in effects-based operations is "shaping behavior of friends, foes, and neutrals." Since this shaping is something that occurs in the minds of decisionmakers at all levels, it stands to reason that any phenomenon that emerges from this process might provide a human-based index of how well we are shaping behavior. If we follow this logic and consider its implications in the context of the action-reaction cycles examined in the rule sets, it equally stands to reason that the metric we seek is some evidence of a behavioral change that occurs because of an action that we have taken. Combining the two criteria of observability and relevance to the cognitive process, we should be seeking a set of potentially observable phenomena that reflect what is going on in the cognitive process that we outlined in Chapter 4.

We can delimit the large set of potentially observable phenomena somewhat if we further consider that the cognitive process is built around how each side perceives and reacts to the stimuli of the action-reaction cycles that make up an interaction. This would suggest that the phenomena we seek to measure as a human-based metric revolves about what is observed by both sides and how.

Here the earlier discussion of the attributes of actions becomes relevant again. Essentially, we turn the attributes around. We are now the observers of another actor's actions. What is it that we see?

Clearly, what was done as a reaction is key. We can easily see a series of relevant questions building off this reaction. For example, is the reaction symmetric or asymmetric? Does the reaction involve an escalation of force? Or was there no observed reaction? And if so, did that represent a decision not to react, a decision to postpone any reaction, an inability to react, or simply our own inability to detect the reaction? All these questions address essential elements of the feedback commanders might require.

Equally important, especially for operational commanders, is how the reaction we are observing was executed. Which military capabilities, if any, were brought to bear? On what scale? Over what geographic scope? In which warfare areas? Did the reaction represent a lateral escalation of the battle or confrontation? Did the reaction represent an attempt to exploit our vulnerabilities, and if so, which ones? Did the reaction expose the opponent's vulnerabilities, and if so, which ones? How fast was any military reaction? How long was it sustained? How long could it have been sustained? How well were individual military actions coordinated or synchronized? What were we able to see and what aspects of the operation might we have been unable to detect? Finally, when we put all of these facets of the reaction together, what do they tell us about how our last action was perceived and what we should do next?

Again, we can understand that the answers to these questions would be elements of the feedback essential to commanders. But where do we get the questions we need to ask? What observables do we look for? In fact, we can see that all of these questions simply reverse the variables we considered when trying to look at how the qualities of our actions might shape the perceptions of some other observer.[31] Now, the same variables are what we must look for in the reactions of another actor to act as indications of behavioral changes. However, knowing the "what" and "how" of another actor's reaction still leaves an important question to be answered: what might we be able to see?

In approaching an inherently complex interaction like those involved in the conduct of effects-based operations, it is necessary to accept from the beginning that we cannot know everything that we might want to know and that we cannot know anything precisely. What we must deal with are those elements of the action-reaction cognitive cycle that can be seen and to some degree measured. This is to say that our feedback must ultimately be based on a relatively limited set of potential observables.

What We Cannot "Observe"

The process of answering the question "What is observable?" is perhaps best begun by noting what is *not* likely to be observable. To begin with, we recognized and accepted in Chapter 4 that we could not really "get inside the enemy's head," much less measure what was going on in that head. We also accepted that there was a large degree of uncertainty in assessing that cognitive process, both in the data acquired and in the predictions made from it. In discussing the cognitive cycle (see Figure 62), we have repeatedly taken note of its complexity and of the almost infinite number of variables associated with the actual decisionmaking process in the cognitive domain. And, we noted the difficulty of obtaining insights into that process, especially in any way that would be timely enough to provide meaningful feedback to commanders. In essence, we concluded that we could not observe the internal workings of the cognitive domain itself.

By extension, this indicates that we will not be able to know exactly how an observer will perceive a given stimulus, or exactly what mental model he will apply, or how he will transform his perceptions into an understanding so as to make sense of the emerging situation. Nor will we know exactly how the multiple observers of our stimuli within a given organization will interact with each other to influence the understanding of the situation.[32] [33] Similarly, we will not know exactly what options observers will consider, nor all of the factors that might figure in planning a reaction to our stimulus.

Given this inability to directly and reliably monitor the decisionmaking process itself,[34] we are largely limited to examining those reflections of the cognitive domain decisionmaking process that occur in the information and physical domains, the aspects of the emerging behavior itself. This means that we must examine two parts of the cognitive cycle that occur in those domains. What aspects of the opponent's reaction will be observable, and how do we best observe it to support our own decisionmaking?

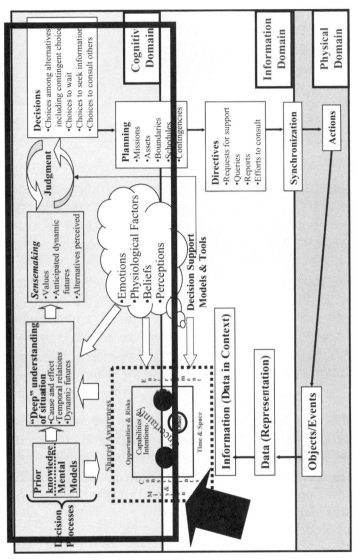

Figure 62. The Cognitive Cycle

What is Observable?

Under our definition of effects-based operations, the focus of our attention is on actions, and the goal of those actions is the shaping of behavior. We also considered those actions to be part of a series of action-reaction cycles as the stimuli and responses in an ongoing interaction between humans and human organizations. Finally in this same context, we postulated that any effects we might create would vary with what an observer could see of our actions or stimuli.

What matters in the action-reaction, stimulus and response cycles is not what action was actually taken, but what its observable dimensions are. In Chapter 4, we pointed to six such dimensions: what is done, with what, on what scale, in what geographical and/or operational scope, with what timing, and with what visibility. However, now the tables are turned. Whereas our earlier concern was with determining how our actions would be observed and understood by a friend or opponent, we now must look to the same dimensions in the reactions of others as indicators of their decisions and behavior.

In the cognitive cycle diagram (see Figure 63), the aspects of the other actors' reactions that are potentially observable fall into two categories: evidence of transmitting guidance for a course of action; and the physical acts that the course of action involves.

If we follow the diagram, therefore, we may be able to observe another actor's attempts to execute a course of action, for example, the orders and

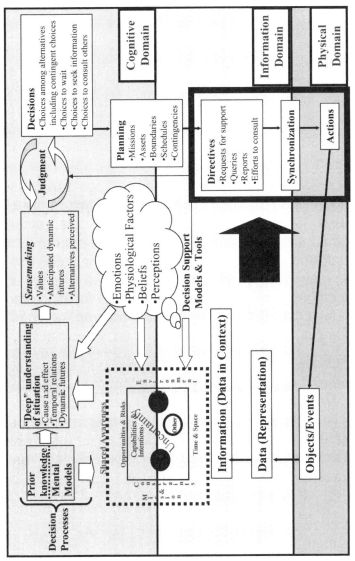

Figure 63. What is Observable?

instructions sent and the dialogues between commands on how to carry them out. These observations need not be precise to be useful. A successful observation does not demand that we break an enemy's codes so as to read all the messages involved. It may be sufficient to know that activity has intensified or that certain national and military entities are communicating with each other. That may be as simple as monitoring the media for announcements or for news on the movements of major decisionmakers.

We might also monitor the efforts of the commanders to coordinate or synchronize their actions. As the location of the diagram's "synchronization" block on the borderline between the information and physical domains suggests, this task may involve monitoring both the command interactions and the physical movements of forces and decisionmakers subsequent to the application of a stimulus.

Finally, we probably will be able to observe at least some part of the physical actions that may make up the emerging behavior itself. These observables may include events such as an announcement or diplomatic note or the movement of military forces, which are the results of the decisions and planning.

Notice here the word *some*. The actions of any actor are likely to include both those that he wants us to see (so as to shape our behavior) and those actions that he would rather we did not see, which he therefore will attempt to conceal. What we see either of the actions we are intended to see or of those that the other actor would prefer to keep hidden is a function of how good our surveillance and intelligence systems are. Notice that in all of the above, we are applying a form of behavioral performance assessment and that the feedback we obtain may be either an aggregate indicator of performance trends, or it may be a point indicator of a sharp divergence from a system norm or some sliding norm.

It should also be underlined that in each of the above cases, the directives, the synchronization, and the actions to be observed are not restricted just to military efforts. If we remember our rule set for effects-based operations, any military reaction by a state actor will almost invariably involve decisions in at least the political and diplomatic arena and very possibly in the economic arena as well. Similarly, political, diplomatic, and perhaps economic moves are likely to parallel those in the military arena.

This does not necessarily mean that there will be intense interaction between, for example, military and diplomatic actors at each level, though such interactions are by no means excluded. It suggests, rather, that any course of action will have multiple parts and that these parts must be coordinated and synchronized in some way. Thus, the steps taken to implement a course of action in one arena may be an indication of a similar and related set of directives and actions in another arena. Therefore, if we look beyond the immediate set of military observables to other arenas, we may be able to find indications that are substantially easier to see and track.

To some degree, the same construct applies to non-state actors. The actions of guerrillas or terrorists, asymmetric military reactions, cannot be isolated from a wider context. The liberation movement or terrorist organization operates as a human organization. It is held together by a commonly held interest in advancing some cause, and therefore must look not only to its own internal cohesion, but also to the external audience whose behavior it is trying to shape. It is going to require assets of some sort to sustain its operations, whether these are the fruits of illegal operations (e.g. robbery and drug sales) or of external contributors, it will have some form of economic arena as well. As the pursuit of the al-Qaida network since September 11th has demonstrated, these financial arenas offer a way of measuring effects that parallel and give at least some indication of effects taking place among the network of al-Qaida/Taliban fighters.

In both of the above cases, we can see the operation of the cognitive cycle and a series of elements of that cycle that may be monitored and measured to provide feedback to commanders on the effects-based operations we are conducting. However, this leads to the second part of the problem, the question of *how* we observe.

How Do We See the Observables?

Creating an Effects-Based Situational Awareness

In Chapter 3, we looked at visibility as a critical aspect of any action, and we concluded that all of the other qualities of an action were meaningless as stimuli unless they could be seen or observed in some way. In Chapter 4, we noted that the observer was a prisoner of his sensors and that what he could see was a function of the surveillance system he created.

The same is equally true of ourselves. The aspects of an enemy's cognitive process that we can or cannot see will be a function of the capabilities of the collectors we have in our surveillance and intelligence system, how we deploy them, and how we task them. To the extent that another actor's physically observable actions lie outside the scope of what the system can see, those observables will play no role in fashioning our effects-based feedback.[35]

To understand how we observe the indicators or how human-based metrics enter into the feedback process, we need to dissect the left portion of the cognitive diagram in the same fashion as we did to the right (see Figure 64).

The left corner of the diagram shows the process by which a physical action of some sort is detected, reported, assessed, and becomes part of our shared situational awareness, the entry point for our own cognitive and decisionmaking process.

In this process, the physical indicators of what is happening in the other actors' cognitive process must first be detected. This detection data then must be collated and aggregated with other data and information, and then integrated into the shared situational awareness.

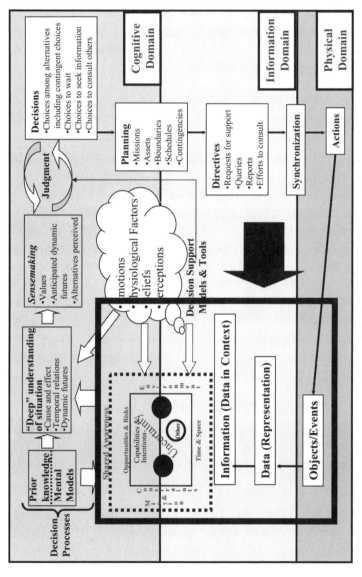

Figure 64. How Do We Observe?

We understand this process well from the standpoint of combat operations. Indeed, most of our experimentation with network-centric operations has focused on creating such shared situational awareness on at least a tactical combat level. The issue here is different. What we seek to create is a shared effects-based situational awareness. The shared situational awareness to support effects-based operations, however, rests on not only the sensor data required for combat operations, but also a broad range of imprecise and ambiguous inputs associated with human behavior that must somehow must be collected and integrated into a comprehensive picture.

Creating such an effects-based situational awareness means that our intelligence collection and surveillance systems must detect, process, and provide data that may be very different from those inherent to tactical combat situational awareness. The first problem here is the sheer breadth of the observable data and information that might be relevant to an effects-based picture. Relevant observables might include most if not all of the tactical data that comprised the common operational picture, but they will also include a wide array of other data and information, much of it from human sources and therefore often ambiguous or subjective. These *human information* inputs will draw not only from traditional intelligence sources, but also from unevaluated reporting from world media, which might possibly be disinformation or propaganda. Moreover, the data will need to include inputs from other government agencies and departments, nongovernmental and international organizations, as well as allies and coalition partners. The wider the net that we cast, the greater the number of observables that is likely to be seen. The better the quality of the net, the more likely we are to see not only what another actor may want us to see, but also what he may not want us to see, and the better our feedback to the commander is likely to be.

However, this is not the end of the problem. The quality of the feedback in any surveillance system is also a function of what we do with the data we collect. The process and challenges of collating tactical data into a common relevant operational picture are relatively clear, however difficult they may be. But that challenge is relatively small compared to what is involved in collating the vast and diverse set of data needed to support effects-based operations. Thus, where the emphasis in a tactical level, network-centric awareness tends to be on sensors and links, effects-based awareness is likely to emphasize how data is processed, collated, and assessed, and the way in which available human expertise is used and integrated.

Obviously, there are two risks involved with dealing with very large numbers of inputs. One is the danger of losing what could be an essential piece of information amid a cacophony of other inputs. The other is that of providing so many inputs to the commander that he becomes overwhelmed with data to the point that the quantity of the effects-based feedback actually hampers the command's decision process. We can hope that advances in information technology will alleviate the problem with better ways of processing information on observables or with decision aids to sort through and at least partially digest the large quantities of information. But there is an additional problem. Since the picture that constitutes a shared effects-based situational awareness is so complex, and since it is not necessarily easy to visualize, the question of how it is presented to commanders will be critical.

Decision Aids

All of the efforts we put into detecting and assessing indicators will be for naught if they cannot be integrated into the thinking of commanders at every level. Yet, the result of an effects-based assessment process may be very different from a conventional military "plot" and the demands placed upon a commander's prior knowledge, understanding, and ability to make sense of a fluid and highly varied situation are likely to be extreme. It is natural, therefore, that many of the opportunities to bring network-centric operations and new information technology to bear focus on what have been dubbed "decision aids," implements to help commanders at all levels deal with the complex variables of an effects-based operation. In the final analysis, there are two parts of the effects-based process that are so complex as to require some assistance.

The first is the dynamic planning and execution of an effects-based operation. In this instance, the decision aids might be developed to draw upon and combine data, knowledge, and expertise in order to provide an assessment both of the situation and of the most likely effects to be generated by different courses of action. This might further extend into highlighting the most likely observable indicators of the success or failure of an effect as the basis for a surveillance and collection plan.

The second type of decision aid might revolve about the feedback process. One key capability would be integrating data so as to establish performance norms on physical or behavioral systems either over history or on a sliding basis within a crisis, war, or other operation. Another element might be to detect and compare relationships between different kinds of data and information so as to collate it and aid assessment. However, perhaps the most significant role may lie in an ability to perform a function similar to that of the collection and evaluation algorithms in the intelligence indications and warning system. This function would not only nominate indicators but give them weights and then assemble the varied collection of pieces into a coherent, probabilistic understanding of the direction or nature of an observer's behavior.

Knowledge and Uncertainty

There are two threads that run through our entire discussion of effects-based operations and the requirements for supporting them. The first is the need not for just information, but for knowledge and understanding. The second is the degree to which uncertainty will be a part of everything we do in an effects-based operation.

Over the course of the preceding chapters, we have considered "knowledge" in three different guises. In discussing network-centric operations, we were primarily concerned with the kind of knowledge that grew from the aggregated data and information of where an enemy was, where he was going, and what he was doing into a primarily tactical and operational level shared situational awareness. However, with effects-based situational awareness, we have seen this definition of knowledge take on two additional dimensions:

- One form of knowledge is exemplified by the database, or more properly a *knowledge base,* which can encompass a pool of very diverse information covering a large number of multi-level, complex adaptive systems. These systems may be physical such as the electrical grid, psychological such as a government or polity, or a hybrid of both, of which Wall Street would be an example.

- The other form of knowledge, present both as an input to situational awareness and on the part of the decisionmakers themselves, is a subjective or intuitive understanding of a situation, actor, or system. This knowledge, reflected as prior knowledge or even understanding in the cognitive cycle, is the basis for either the expert or the decisionmaker perceiving, evaluating, assessing, and making sense of an emerging situation.

When we say that in order to execute successful effects-based operations, we must know the opponent, the "knowing" implied is multi-dimensional. The knowledge we require and the feedback that the commander requires will be some combination of the three dimensions outlined above. For effects-based operations, it is no longer enough to know where the adversary is and where he is going. A tactical or operational picture composed only of such elements is of only limited utility when it comes to dealing with the impressions and cognitive processes of the opponent, and is of even less utility in dealing with friends and neutrals. Rather, what we need is the insight into how a system or an individual will react to stimuli.

The challenge here is more than that of assembling an adequate battlespace awareness, or of developing a picture of what the dimensions of a physical system are and how it functions. However difficult these tasks may be, we have a good idea of how to organize and amass such knowledge and make it available to commanders. The real challenge lies in dealing with the human dimension of war and conflict, and at the core of that challenge lies the necessity of dealing with the complexity inherent in human beings and human organizations. This implies that for all of the knowledge and expertise we might assemble, we will still be faced with some level of uncertainty.

Again, if we examine how commanders have treated this inherent complexity, we can see a process of pruning occurring. One element of this pruning revolves around acknowledging the inevitability of uncertainty and the determination of an acceptable level of ignorance. In our earlier discussion of orchestrating effects, we saw that the requirement for knowing the enemy was not an absolute. We did not need to know enemies, friends, or neutrals so well as to be able to predict their every move, just well enough to delimit a reasonable set of likely reactions from which to plan. We saw that we could derive this level of knowledge by stating the problem we intended to present in neutral enough terms to approximate how others would see it, and by having sufficient insight into decisionmaking processes to understand the pressures on decisionmakers. This model for accepting and dealing with uncertainty applies equally to the task of assessing effects and to the task of estimating what cascade of effects our action is likely to produce.

It should be noted that neither the model nor its results are going to be exact, quantifiable, or certain. Not only will our knowledge of the observers always be inexact and incomplete, but also the measurements we take will be indirect and subject to error. However, our goal is not to eliminate error. That cannot be done. Our goal is to refine the information we do have, and to collate and assess it to provide the best feedback available in a given circumstance.

Dynamic Effects

We stated in the beginning of this chapter that the problem we confront in effects-based operations is dealing with complex adaptive systems called human beings, whether as individuals or as amassed in armies, states, or terrorist gangs. The challenges we have outlined here can help us to parse that problem in a rational way, and the technologies and thinking of Network Centric Warfare can bring new means to bear on solving aspects of the challenges involved. Yet at the core, we will still face a problem and set of cause and effect relationships that can never be entirely defined.

Despite this uncertainty and the challenges involved, the fact remains that we have done all of this before and we will have to do it again. This is the reality of war and peace. What we seek is not a perfect answer. There is none. Rather, we seek a way of using the growing means at our disposal to help commanders and decisionmakers conduct the effects-based operations they have always done in a more dynamic, more precise, and more informed way.

---

[1]Miller. pp. 851ff.

[2]Miller. pp. 853-4.

[3]In Navy Global Wargame 2000, for example, this effects-based feedback was denominated in terms of bomb damage assessment rather than behavioral effects. The result was that, despite their best efforts to plan and fight an effects-based war, the game commanders soon reverted to a traditional attrition conflict. They had no choice. They had little feedback to support doing anything else.
Author's notes as a participant in Navy Global Wargame 2000 effects assessment cell.

[4]Tedder. p. 525.

[5]Note that from the perspective of the tactical level commanders executing the bombing campaign, such "effects-based" bomb damage assessment is almost indistinguishable from the traditional, attrition-based version. For them, the question was simply whether or not they had hit the right target and inflicted the damage ordered. For the planners, the question was not only whether the right target had been struck, but also whether the level of damage was sufficient to achieve the larger effect sought in the campaign plan.

[6]Churchill. *Closing the Ring.* p. 528.

[7]Not only were there additional German armored divisions in the vicinity of the Pas de Calais (temporarily held in place by a successful Allied deception plan), but there were also other armored forces south of the Loire River bridges.

Tedder. p. 525.

[8]Similarly, if the divisions had been moved into the Normandy area before the rail campaign was completed, the planners would have been forced to reconsider whether the strategic bombing assets involved would have been more effective against rail targets or against German petroleum supplies.

Ibid.

[9]This was especially true in view of the unexpectedly good German ability to repair the damage to the rail junctions demonstrated in the weeks before the invasion.

SHAEF Weekly Intelligence Summary. June 3, 1944.

[10]The Allies had Ultra and thus access to some sensitive German communications, however, these intercepts did not indicate a change in the German assessment. But as with any intercept, there is always a question as to whether the opponent has determined that the code has been broken and used messages in that code as disinformation. Similarly, one can also speculate that had an Allied spy been operating in the higher levels of the German Command and had that spy been able to report quickly and reliably, the feedback might have been available. However, such speculation would ignore both how rare such successful high-level emplacement of an intelligence agent is and how brief the source's survival would likely be if any sort of rapid and repeated communications were attempted.

[11]There was, however, a very real concern with the impact on Allied morale and willingness to continue the struggle if the invasion failed.

[12]*SHAEF Weekly Intelligence Summary.* June 3, 1944.

[13]The word *system* is used in a general context that encompasses everything from the railroad system attacked in the Normandy air campaign to a political, economic, or social system. In the sense of an effects-based cascade, it connotes an arrangement of entities bearing enough relationship to one another as to transmit physical and/or psychological effects in some manner to the limits of that relationship, with those limits in turn defining the limits of the system.

[14]The widely reported impact of the loss of electricity upon water purification for the city of Baghdad or on life support for premature infants in Kuwait are cases in point.

[15]This same indicator had a different role at the onset of the crisis because it informed American decisionmakers of the

fact that an unusually high number of ships were en route to Cuba and that these included ships with history as arms carriers. Both of these inputs likewise depended on a knowledge base constructed over some period before the crisis ever began.
Allison, Graham T. *Essence of Decision, Explaining the Cuban Missile Crisis.* Boston; Little Brown. 1971. pp. 128-9.

[16]To make a sensor-to-shooter link work, we have to have already answered all the other questions that might be raised except for the targeting information. We need to know what kind of target we are looking for and that the criteria for the rules of engagement have been satisfied before the sensor-to-shooter link can be used. The same kind of situation applies to using these behavioral indicators in a timely way. We need to have the situation so well defined that all levels know the kinds of indicators we are looking for, so that all that is needed is the actual detection of a particular physical action.

[17]To the above challenges, we must add another. The feedback loop we seek to create must provide information that is appropriate to the level of the commander or decisionmaker receiving it. For tactical level commanders confronted with immediate kill-or-be-killed decisions, feedback on the performance of distant enemy units or on the psychological state of the enemy command are likely to be not only irrelevant but dysfunctional. They need a near real time damage assessment. Is the unit opposing us out of action, or can it still kill us? By contrast, operational level commanders need to know much more. In the Normandy example, Allied commanders needed to know both that the targets had been attacked successfully and what, if any, German forces might still enter their battlespace. To carry the analogy further, at the military-strategic level, the Supreme Commander needed to know how the German counter-offensive was forming so as to better allocate limited mobile resources, and perhaps how the German commanders were reacting to the air campaign as a whole. Finally, at the geo-strategic level, the concern of Roosevelt and Churchill would have been less with the military specifics than with the broader questions of the impact of a failure upon the war effort and the opportunities that might be presented by a quick German collapse. Thus, each level would have required a different level of detail and a different timeliness of feedback to undertake different levels and kinds of effects.

[18]The term *estimative intelligence* is used here to define a distinction between the reporting of aggregated positional information and analyzed intelligence that attempts to deduce

enemy thinking and intentions. A classic example of this estimative intelligence was the role of Admiral Nimitiz's intelligence chief Commander Edwin Layton in the days before the Battle of Midway. Layton, who spoke Japanese, had studied in Japan, and knew Nimitz' opponent (Admiral Yamamoto) personally, was able to assess Japanese intentions accurately despite a paucity of information. He was therefore able to provide the continual feedback that Nimitz required before and during the battle.

Layton, RADM Edwin T. USN. *I Was There.* New York. 1962.

[19]This is the measures of effectiveness quandary that strategic bombing efforts encounter. The air campaign planners can quantify the destruction of a carefully conceived list of targets and they can observe the final behavior of the national leadership that was the object of the bombing, but they cannot trace the exact link from the target destruction to the behavioral outcome observed. The linkage between the two is simply too complex to track, even in historical investigations conducted after the fact with full access to documents and personnel.

[20]Indeed, this should hardly be surprising in as much as destruction and physical attrition are two of the kinds of effects that may derive from an effects-based operation.

[21]This nonlinear human dimension of war was what in fact distinguished Clausewitz's writings from the rational, linear Newtonian conception of war as a function of numbers, capabilities and tactics.

Watts, Barry D. *Clausewitzian Friction and Future War.* Washington, DC; INSS. 1996. pp. 19ff.

[22]Schmitt, John F. "Command and (Out of) Control: The Military Implications of Complexity Theory." *Complexity, Global Politics, and National Security.* David S. Alberts and Thomas J. Czerwinski eds.Washington, DC; NDU/INSS. 1997. pp. 229-238.

[23]The Soviet strategists assigned values to units depending not only on how they were armed but also on factors such as training and nationality. These were then factors in complex formulas to calculate the level of destruction required in order to cause the unit to collapse or the level of numerical superiority Soviet forces would require for a successful offensive.

Sarikin, V.Ye. *The Basic Principles of the Operational Art and Tactics.* Washington; GPO. 1972. pp. 214-223 and 258-260.

[24]Moreover and somewhat strangely, the human factor measurements that were explored in tandem with attrition-based measures tended to be confined to combat operations.

Very little work seems to have been done in applying these or similar human-centric measurements to gauging operations short of combat, especially noncombat operations above the tactical level.

[25]Warden, John A. III. "The Enemy as a System." *Airpower Journal.* Spring 1995. pp. 40-55.

[26]Fadok, David S. *John Boyd and John Warden: Airpower's Quest for Strategic Paralysis.* Air University, Air University Press. 1995.

[27]Deptula, BG David A. USAF. "Firing for Effects," *Air Force Magazine.* April 2001, pp.46ff.

[28]*Effects-based Operations, Change in the Nature of Warfare.* Arlington, VA; Aerospace Education Foundation. 2001.

[29]Much of this process grew from the epochal work of Prof. Roberta Wohlstetter examining the "surprise" at Pearl Harbor. Wohlstetter concluded that all of the indications needed to realize that a Japanese attack was forthcoming were available to the Americans but that, for various reasons, they treated each indication separately as being inconclusive. The failure in American intelligence thus stemmed from a failure to aggregate individual indications into a clear warning.

[30]It can be argued that a simpler form of this process was what intelligence analysts and air planners undertook to determine the effect of their air operations upon German movements toward the Normandy battlefield.

[31]Notice that we have been very careful to use neutral terms such as *observer* and *actor* rather than *foe* or *opponent*. The reason is that in an effects-based operation, the reactions that concern us are not only those of the opponent or potential opponent. They are equally those of our allies and coalition partners, and of those actors who remain neutral. All of these actors will have behavior that we will seek to shape either by reinforcing their support for our efforts against another party, or winning support in this or future efforts

[32]Robert F. Kennedy's account of the decisionmaking in the Kennedy White House during the Cuban Missile Crisis is a fascinating picture of just such group dynamics and underlines the nonobservable influences that may be expected to affect outcomes.
Kennedy. *Thirteen Days.* New York; Norton. 1969.

[33]Graham Allison's *Essence of Decision* dissects in detail the decisionmaking process and both the group and the organizational dynamics involved.
Allison, Graham T. *Essence of Decision, Explaining the Cuban Missile Crisis.* Boston; Little Brown. 1971.

[34]This does not mean that we cannot have an expert intuitive

insight into the processes that are likely to take place in the cognitive domain, as exemplified by Napoleon, Churchill, and Roosevelt. It means rather that we will have few indicators of the actual cognitive process that might be taking place in reaction to our stimuli.

[35]This basic problem was demonstrated in the weeks after the September 11th attacks and throughout the Afghanistan campaign. The intelligence collection system was not oriented to collect the information needed to provide adequate effects-based feedback to commanders. Moreover, while sensors could be readily sighted to provide some coverage of physical movements of al-Qaida and Taliban forces, the lack of human intelligence sources and of linguists able to read the information that became available was not an easily fixed problem. In essence, the way in which the intelligence and surveillance system had been set up and funded created a filter that cut off some of the physical reflections of Taliban and al-Qaida decisions that might otherwise have been observable.

Economist. April 14, 2002.

CHAPTER 9

Effects Beyond Combat: Deterrence and Reassurance

Thus far we have been examining our concept of effects-based operations in the context of combat or crisis response operations. This focus on combat, whether actual or potential, is proper since the only military force that has any value is one that can fight and win. Yet, if the mark of a truly successful military force is the ability to prevent such combat in the first place, then clearly no study of network-centric and effects-based operations can be complete without also examining this peacetime dimension as well. This is especially true because the peacetime tasks of war prevention and crisis/conflict containment constitute the vast majority of what military forces actually do. In short, we need to begin to think not only in terms of effects-based combat operations, but also in terms of effects-based deterrence, reassurance, forward defense, presence, and containment.

In assessing the role of effects-based operations in this peacetime dimension, we need to recognize that the task is twofold. We need to prevent wars, contain crises and conflicts, and deal with threats to our citizens and interests. But deterrence of would-be aggressors is only part of the answer and cannot produce an enduring peace by itself. Rather, the task has a two-faced quality to it. We must not only deter challengers, but must reassure allies and neutrals, often at the same time and with the same actions. Accordingly, any assessment of the role of network-centric and effects-based operations in peacetime must address how they help us both deter and reassure.

The central question here is how might effects-based operations and network-centric operations help us to deter would-be opponents and to reassure allies and neutrals? However, to address that question properly, we must also deal with two additional and more pressing questions. How might this effects-based deterrence and reassurance function in the post-September 11th global threat environment in which we find ourselves? And how might we use it to create a stable regional deterrence/reassurance regime?

Niche Competitors and the Post-September 11th Security Environment

In the opening chapter of this book, we discussed challenges from peer or near-peer competitors with symmetric means and will, and challenges from smaller states or non-states that have limited means, but believe themselves to have superior will and endurance. We noted that the strategic nuclear deterrence regime of the Cold War has given way to a new, more complex requirement: deterring not only the symmetric, peer competitor, but also the asymmetric competitor whose objective is not to avoid conflict, but to create it, and who has little at risk in attacking our homeland.

The problem posed by the emergence of a symmetric peer competitor of course remains, but since September 11th, the more immediate challenge has been that of asymmetric competitors such as terrorists and their state-sponsors, a challenge for which we have no tried and true deterrence/reassurance regime. This kind of threat demands an approach to homeland defense and strategic deterrence that is heavily dependent on conventional rather than nuclear deterrence, that is focused on prevention rather than retaliation, and one in which peace maintenance and forward defense are critical.

How then would our concept of effects-based operations better enable us to deal with this challenge?

To answer this question, we can start by looking at these asymmetric adversaries as "niche" challengers, would-be foes who seek to identify and exploit a political, temporal, geographic, and/or military niche where American and Allied power either cannot be brought to bear or is too weak, slow, or dysfunctional to meet a challenge, but in which challengers can realize their own political, ideological, economic, or military objectives. A successful niche challenge depends not only on the choice or creation of a situation that conforms to these constraints, but also upon an ability to limit the interaction with the larger power to the niche of choice. A successful niche strategy, therefore, might be expected to hinge on damage infliction vice military victory and on psychological vice physical attrition.[1]

Because niche competitors generally have little at risk themselves, they can afford to continually probe suspected vulnerabilities and to attack whenever and wherever they believe that they have found a likely niche. Moreover, because their strategy is based on damage infliction and psychological attrition, they can use the element of surprise to attack in one niche, inflict the required damage, and then move on to exploiting other potential niches as soon as the original probe is met or foreclosed. In the case of al-Qaida, for example, the niche exploited on September 11, 2001 was presented by the gaps between internal and external security in the United States and between the United States and other states in an era of mass movements of people. This loss of surprise and closure of the niche was evident even on September 11th itself as passengers, alerted by cell phone calls as to what *hijacking* now meant, struggled to retake one plane before it could be used as a missile against an additional target. As this implies in niche competition, as security gaps or other niches are plugged in one area, we should expect the direction and nature of the probes to shift continually as the competitor seeks to surprise us by exploiting new vulnerabilities.

Logically, to deter such attacks, we would need to demonstrate that we had both the will and the means to negate the political, temporal, geographic and military niches that the competitor might seek to exploit. Or we might demonstrate a willingness and ability to escalate any confrontation beyond the challenger's niche of choice. In essence, this was the tack taken by the United States and its allies in the destruction of the Taliban regime in Afghanistan. Also, to reassure friends and neutrals, we have to demonstrate that we had the means and will to block or respond to any niche challenge while maintaining a local order conducive to peaceful change.

Notice that there are two elements to this deterrence and reassurance: will and means. The *will* component has been the principal thrust of our concept of effects-based combat operations and the reason for our focus on operations in the cognitive domain. This focus on the cognitive domain is even more pronounced in deterrence and reassurance. Indeed, the *means* component of deterrence and reassurance comes to be defined in terms of its impact on the cognitive domain as the physical capabilities that can be used to shape will. In the context of a niche strategy, the primary military actions would center on the demonstration of the range of options at our disposal to meet a probe, to negate a perceived niche or vulnerability, or otherwise deal with a challenger.

In a sense, we have already laid the groundwork for such a peacetime application of military power in our concept of effects-based operations. Because we defined effects-based operations in terms of actions rather than weapons on targets, we opened the way to considering nonkinetic, peacetime uses of military force in everything from maneuver to presence. Similarly, by defining *effects* in terms of the impacts of our actions on the behavior of "friends, foes, and neutrals," we moved beyond focusing solely on a hostile opponent and into the multi-sided interactions typical of a deterrence/reassurance regime.   Furthermore, by looking at military effects not as independent phenomena, but as components of a unified national effect that encompasses all of the elements of national power, we created the basis for examining the wider interplay of political, diplomatic, economic, and military power across the peace-crisis-war spectrum. Finally, by considering effects-based operations as "operations in the cognitive domain," we began to view actions and effects from the complex perspective of an observer trying to make sense of an emerging situation and attempting to decide on a course of action.

In examining the kinds of effects that we might create, we also began to define the deterrence side of our mission. We looked at the question of *foreclosure*, the use of military forces to block an adversary's likely course of action either by demonstrating an ability to prevent success or by raising the risks of such a course of action until they become unacceptable. We noted that foreclosure can take two forms. *Passive foreclosure* is where the scope and scale of our capability dissuades aggressors from challenging the regime. *Active foreclosure* is where the response to any challenge is so immediate and overwhelming that challengers must reassess their risk calculus and desist in mid-action.

We now need to take this effort two steps further. First, we need to look specifically at the role of effects-based operations in deterrence and reassurance.[2] Then, we need to examine how the concept of effects-based operations itself might serve as a framework for defining a new security regime and for determining the capabilities that forward presence and crisis response forces would need to be successful in preventing as well as fighting wars.

Deterrence and Reassurance as Effects-Based Operations

On the surface, an effects-based approach to deterrence and reassurance seems eminently reasonable. After all, both deterrence and reassurance are inherently matters of human behavior, and shaping the behavior of human beings and human organizations is what effects-based operations are all about. More specifically, deterrence and reassurance both involve using some combination of military, political, diplomatic, and economic actions to influence what goes on in the decisionmaking processes of both individual observers and groups of observers.[3] This is to say that the military side of deterrence and reassurance inherently entails operations in the cognitive domain.

The above suggests that a good starting point for understanding the role of effects-based operations in deterrence and reassurance is the cognitive cycle (see Figure 65). If we extend the logic of the cognitive process diagramed in Chapter 4 into peacetime operations, we can postulate that the military, political, diplomatic, and/or economic actions we take to deter or reassure are in some respect physical actions that occur in the physical domain. These actions are then somehow monitored and reported through the information domain to observers so as to become part of the observers' situation awareness, an awareness that varies with quantity and quality of the reporting or of the surveillance system. However, the key to understanding how we deter and reassure lies less in understanding how actions are detected and reported than in understanding how situation awareness impacts the cognitive domain (how observers understand the actions and react to the stimuli provided).

In the cognitive domain, observers (consciously or unconsciously) will compare the actions observed in the situation to a set of mental models and prior knowledge that is based both on a history of what they perceive has happened in similar situations and on personal experience that they perceive to be relevant. The observers will then apply these models to determining one or more probable cause and effect chains, to assessing temporal relationships between events, and to forecasting how the situation is most likely to evolve (dynamic futures). These assessments together constitute a deep understanding of the situation observed. This

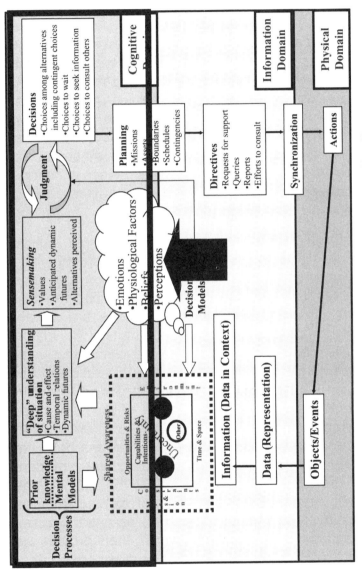

Figure 65. Deterrence, Reassurance, and the Cognitive Process

deep understanding combined with the observers' own value system, the observers' national, ethnic, religious, organizational, and generational culture, and with an assessment of how they might shape the perceived futures contribute to how the observers make sense of what they see. The sense the observers make of the situation in turn influences their assessment of what options might be open to them to respond or shape the situation to conform to their needs or desires, and the decisions or choices they make as to which course of action to pursue. The resulting choices constitute the observer's behavior, the outcome we are trying to shape or influence.

Although we looked at each of these steps previously from the perspective of combat and conflict situations in which these cognitive processes were part of rapid-fire action-reaction decisionmaking, the same processes are in fact basic to deterrence and reassurance. As in the conflict-centered cognitive cycle, deterrence and reassurance will probably involve a succession of action-reaction decisionmaking cycles on the part of both sides over some period of time. In these interactions, we would strive to identify and orchestrate our actions so as to drive the behavior of the targeted observers in a particular direction. On the other side, those observing our actions would assess them and attempt to calculate the risks involved in pursuing various potential courses of action. Their reactions would then provide us with feedback and possibly the stimulus for another action-reaction cycle. This interchange is two-sided, with other actors attempting to shape our behavior even as we try to shape theirs, so that these two-sided interactions occur simultaneously with multiple actors. The creation of a stable deterrence/reassurance regime may involve prolonged successions of these action-reaction cycles over a period of years and even decades.

In the case of deterrence and reassurance, as in the case of the conflict-centered cognitive process, there are only two points in this entire cognitive cycle at which we can hope to influence observers' behavior. One is in the immediate actions we take to create a certain combination of effects that will drive the chain of deep understanding, sensemaking, judgment, and decisions to some acceptable short-term behavior. The other is the accumulated history of all the actions that we have taken that constitute the prior knowledge yardstick of the observers and which therefore shapes the mental models by which those observers will measure any current action. This history may either support the current action, such as a history of good relations and cooperation might support coalition formation, or it may prove a hurdle to be overcome, such as a history of distrust might need to be overcome before a coalition can be formed.

Context

Notice that, in the above description of operations in the cognitive domain, no action or effect occurs in a vacuum. Deterrence and reassurance are in the eye of the beholder and the beholder always will have some mental baggage. Stated differently, the deterring or reassuring effect we create with our actions arises from those actions being put into some context by the observer. In the diagram of the cognitive process, this context is embodied in prior knowledge and mental models, in the various aspects of a deep understanding of the situation, and in the cultural and other factors that support sensemaking, including physiological factors. Since these factors will never be exactly the same for any two human observers or for any two human organizations, the cognitive context for any action can vary radically. Indeed, the shift from one observer to the next may be so radical as to make the same action carry completely opposite meanings for the different observers.

How then do we bound this infinity of potential perceptions and reactions so as to be able to make a rational choice of actions to deter and/or reassure?

Two basic facets of this varying context are most significant: the context provided by the observer's own intentions and plans, and the context that we ourselves provide by our actions, past and present. To some degree, we have already been talking about the context provided by the observer's plans and intentions when we broke the down observers into the three categories of friends, foes, and neutrals. Implicit in this categorization is the idea that the plans and intentions of observers are going to be different and those differences are going to shape how an action is perceived. Is the observer the would-be aggressor or the likely victim? To a would-be aggressor, the movement of a great power military force into the region and, thus, into the context of an invasion the aggressor may be planning probably would appear threatening. In that case, the impact of such a movement might be to disrupt those plans so badly as to foreclose any possibility of success or to change the risk calculus enough to keep that aggressor from a course of action leading to hostilities. By contrast, to the state that was to be the aggressor's target, the move would likely be seen as reassuring and affect its calculation of the costs and risks of resisting aggression or of cooperating, for example, by granting access to air bases.

The context will also be provided by history[4] and the individual observer's own experience. While a substantial proportion of this historical preconditioning (including national history, religion, ideology, organizational or political affiliation) cannot be controlled or changed by our actions, it is where our actions contribute to shaping the prior knowledge and mental models of the observers and thereby create the context for our future actions to be observed. To be successful in deterrence and reassurance, we need to construct a history of previous actions against which our future actions can be assessed by the intended observers.

Forward American military operations including military exercises with local friends must be understood in this role of creating context or preconditioning, as a means of shaping the context within which all of our future actions will be considered. For the friend, the exercises reassure by demonstrating the will and capability to act when necessary. For the challenger, the exercises demonstrate the combined capabilities of the outside power and the local partner against which the challenger must weigh the risks and probabilities of success. This latter contextualization occurs not only on the part of the state with which the exercise is conducted, but also on the part of any other local entity that observes it. For each observer, the interaction becomes a part of the history by which they will measure future interactions.

This is fine as far as it goes, but is still too general. We need to carry the logic another step and answer the same question that we posed in examining the cognitive process in combat and crisis operations. What kinds of actions might actually shape this context? In terms of the cognitive cycle, we must understand what aspects of our capabilities and/or actions would be seen by observers and then how the resulting perception might shape their risk versus gain calculations.

Observe What?

What do the observers see that would shape their behavior and either deter or reassure them either over the short term or over the longer term? Our discussion of actions and effects in Chapter 6 proposed that observers' perceptions and subsequent behavior are shaped not just by what we do, but also by how we do it. We described this "what" and "how" in terms of six attributes that defined the observable character of any action. Since the actions we undertake are the only means at our disposal to shape observer perceptions, the six attributes become the variables at our disposal to create the perceptions and effects we desire and the aspects of our actions that we need to manipulate to create a unified effect. Actions taken to deter or reassure are no different. The attributes of an action (focus, type of force, scale, scope, timing and visibility) provide the basis for a risk-gain security calculus by local observers. They are what would drive a would-be aggressor to ask the hard questions, the answers to which would define his ability to succeed and risks in a particular course of action. The attributes define the military niche within which a challenger must operate, determine his likelihood of success, and anticipate potential consequences.[5] To the extent that any aggressor concludes that a particular geographic, temporal, or warfare niche is not viable, we are likely to deter disruptive courses of action and reassure local allies and neutrals.

We break the six attributes down in terms of this deterrence/reassurance risk calculus along the following lines.

1. Focus

The focus is the nature of the physical actions that can be undertaken to deter or reassure either immediately or over time.[6] It is the prospect of what is being done or might be done to deter and reassure, rather than how it is or might be done. The "what" determines the character of the problem a would-be aggressor might face or the ways in which concrete support or reassurance might be provided to a friend. From the standpoint of the observer, it is the "what can be done to me?" (opponent) or "what can be done for me? (friend). It equates to the nature of a potential foreclosure.

In practical terms, it brings a challenger's planners, including those of a terrorist cell, to ask questions as to how a particular course of action might be thwarted and what the consequences of the probe or a conflict might be. For purposes of reassurance, the focus helps drive the friend or neutral's assessment as to whether an intervention might in fact provide the support needed to deal with an emerging situation. For example, a purely naval capability offshore might be judged irrelevant to an urban guerrilla threat and therefore fail to reassure, but the combination of such offshore support with a marine force that could be inserted from the sea would probably be judged as relevant and therefore would tend to reassure.

The "what" also begins to define the nature of any military niche that a challenger might seek to exploit. Logically, if a military force that is meant to deter the challenger actually has no capability for certain kinds of warfare, those gaps are likely to be seen as warfare niches to be exploited and will shape the challenger's niche strategy in that direction. For example, an inability to put "boots on the ground" might evoke a probe that focuses on ground operations, but which minimizes exposure to long-range precision strikes, such as in urban guerrilla operations. Similarly, an inability to deal with sea mines might invite an anti-access or area denial strategy that focused heavily on mining offshore waters.

For local friends and neutrals, the same inability to cover a perceived military niche would leave those friends and neutrals to fill the niches themselves, or to conclude that they cannot oppose the enemy and that some accommodation with the challenger must be found. In either event, the result would be a failure to reassure, one that would be felt not just when an active threat was encountered, but rather as soon as the inability became obvious.

2. Forces

The nature of the forces themselves (standoff or close in, ground, sea, or air) is distinct from the warfare capabilities they represent and defines a different element of the would-be foe's problem.[7] Instead of a "what can be done to me or for me?" it forces a consideration of how the action might be undertaken and how plausible a threat or promise of support might actually be. To the degree that the deterring or reassuring forces rely on close-in forces or "boots on the ground," a challenger might see an opportunity to inflict or to threaten to inflict sufficient damage and casualties to counter-deter and plan accordingly. Conversely, if the deterrent force were to rely on standoff precision weapons, the challenger might calculate that there was a greater likelihood of a reaction. Notice in both these cases that the nature of the forces deployed can be observed by both the would-be foe and would-be allies, each of whom may be expected to make their own deductions.

We must also take into account that our capabilities are by no means restricted to military means. Economic and political pressures may likewise be applied, as in the forced British withdrawal from the Strait of Tiran in 1967,[8] and these pressures may work better than any military equivalent. Conversely, if the only pressures that can be generated are nonmilitary, the military option is likely to be seen as a niche to be exploited.

3. Scale

The scale of the action that is possible (passive foreclosure) or that is being undertaken (active foreclosure) establishes the quantitative size of the problem the would-be aggressor must deal with and indirectly affects the range of options available to deter or reassure. When broken down according to the types of military capabilities involved, it will also convey the specific kind of threat with which the would-be aggressor must deal.

In passive foreclosure, if the would-be aggressor concludes that he cannot deal with the numbers and types of forces ranged against him, his reaction very likely will be either to dismiss that course of action or perhaps to seek another more promising niche to achieve his aims.

For active foreclosure, the idea is slightly different. The fact that the active foreclosure is needed implies that passive foreclosure has failed. Thus, increasing the scale of the force to be applied well beyond the would-be aggressor's expectations is one way of forcing him to reevaluate his probability of success.

4. Scope

The scope equates to the geographic and operational range of action that the would-be aggressor may have to face, and in this capacity, scope becomes a prime consideration in the challenger's planning.

The geographic scope or area over which a counter-action can be credibly presented determines the spatial dimension of the threat the challenger must be prepared to counter and the likelihood of a lateral escalation beyond his chosen niche. At a minimum, it should convey that there would be no sanctuary and, thus, no prospect of a successful anti-access or area denial strategy. Better still, it should convey a sense of risk to the would-be challenger. That may be an unstated threat to retaliate in other geographic areas, but it also may be to pose a direct military problem. For example, if a deterring force's military actions can cover a wide geographic area, the challenger's own forces may become too diluted to defend against it, or if the challenger elects to concentrate defenses about some critical point, the rest of the country or organization will be subject to unimpeded attack.

The operational scope defines a different dimension of the deterrent: the extent of the warfare niche that a challenger might hope to exploit. There are two facets to this exploitation. Limitations in a deterrent force's operational scope might reveal a niche that a would-be aggressor would try to exploit in an anti-access campaign. But at the same time, the deterrent force's strengths in various areas would both define areas that could not be challenged and areas in which the challenger himself might be vulnerable - a reverse niche.

5. Timing

The timing variable for actions was broken into the three elements of speed, duration, and synchronicity. All three shape a challenger's risk/success calculus and the reassurance provided to friends and neutrals.

The speed of a deterrent force response to the stimulus or aggression sets the time element of the niche, the time limits within which the challenger's plan must be successful. Obviously, a challenger is likely to deem it far easier to achieve success in an operation that can be mounted unimpeded over a period of months or even years as compared with an operation that must be carried out within a much shorter span of time of hours or days. The faster the deterring force can move, the fewer the opportunities likely to be presented and the more precarious the niche to be exploited will be. The question of timing implies a series of more specific questions. What capabilities are likely to be available to thwart the aggression at what time? In what numbers would they be available at what time? Together, the answers to these questions would define the would-be aggressor's timing calculus.

The duration sets the standard for how long the challenger might have to endure either a foreclosure of some action or some form of retaliation. If the threatened military actions were limited to a one time, nonrepeatable strike for example, it would invite the challenger to consider "riding out" the action and then resuming the probe, or simply accepting the attack as a one-time cost of doing business and moving on to the next probe. By contrast, if the military actions could be continued for months or years, it would force the risk calculus to consider the impact on future operations, the ability to sustain damage, psychological attrition strategy, and even the challenger's ability to sustain a lengthy confrontation.

Finally, the ability of a deterrent force to time and coordinate its actions so as to optimize their impact forces a worst-case and potentially discouraging risk calculus on the challenger. How might the challenger's vulnerabilities be exploited? How might the consequences of his actions accelerate out of control?

6. Visibility

Everything that we have considered in the guise of tools to reassure friends and to shape a would-be aggressor's risk/success calculus is dependent upon the friend or aggressor seeing and understanding the capabilities in question. The deterrent will only be valuable to the extent that it has been demonstrated to observers, and to the extent that this demonstration is periodically reinforced both by repetition and by continuing adaptation to changing circumstances. As this suggests, whereas an overwhelming surprise response to aggression may help deter further aggression, the fact that the action was a *surprise* would indicate that the capabilities of the deterring force were not sufficiently evident to the aggressor to prevent the aggression in the first place. However, it can also be argued that the capacity to surprise is itself a deterrent because it complicates the risk calculus and leaves a would-be challenger to imagine a worst-case response. This suggests a balance between the two that might itself be manipulated for maximum effect, contingent upon our ability to control the visibility of our actions.

As we noted in the case of effects-based combat operations, the deterrence we seek to create is not a function of any one of these variables by itself, but rather of how we combine them to shape an observer's decisionmaking process. Strengths in one area can balance relative weaknesses in other areas, or can complement and enhance the value of other capabilities. A small force that can be applied immediately can complement a larger force that takes more time to mobilize, creating a more complex problem for the aggressor to handle. Similarly, while the above is written primarily from the standpoint of military forces, the logic extends to political, diplomatic, and economic elements of national power whose actions might be used as part of an overall deterrent. These alternative elements of national power multiply the variety of options by which we might deter enemies or reassure friends and neutrals.

Rules of the Game

What we have done so far is to outline in rough terms how the deterrence-reassurance process takes place in the context of operations in the cognitive domain. We can take this yet another step to examine how deterrence and reassurance might figure in the effects-based rule sets that we presented in Chapter 5. The rules of the game that we deduced from the series of wars and crisis responses were (1) that actions create effects, (2) that effects are cumulative, (3) that action-reaction cycles will have both active and passive participants, (4) that the cycles will occur simultaneously in multiple dimensions, (5) that all actions and effects at all levels and in each arena are interrelated, and (6) that the effects produced are both physical and psychological in nature.

- *Actions create effects.* Any conventional deterrence-reassurance regime ultimately must rest on local observers' perceptions of our actions, past and present and, by extension, their expectation of future actions. The key words in shaping the local security calculus are *actions* and *perceptions*. Having a potential capability to thwart is not by itself sufficient to deter or reassure. We must also demonstrate that capability and our willingness to use it in such a way as to be readily observed by all concerned.[9] We must do this on a regular basis if we are to translate a past history of action into a current and continuing expectation by local observers that future action will be undertaken whenever and wherever needed.

- *Effects are cumulative.* Just as the threats from a niche competitor are likely to be continual, so too must the deterrence-reassurance regime be a continuing process. Effects are cumulative over time. There is no sharp dividing line between peace and war, but rather a continuous chain of observed interactions that stretches from routine peacetime presence to combat operations. Logically, effects-based operations cannot begin with combat or even target planning if they are to succeed in deterring, and especially not if they are to succeed in reassuring. We accept that continued peacetime exercise is critical to wartime success. It is no different with creating a local conventional deterrence-reassurance regime. The peacetime actions are the means by which we condition observers as to what to expect in the face of a threat. The history of peacetime actions, in short, is the experience base upon which crisis and wartime perceptions are built. If we were to wait for a crisis or war before beginning to act and shape perceptions, we would likely discover either that it was too late to achieve the effect we required, or that we had to overcome local perception of inaction or inability before our actions could have any impact on the observers.

- *Any action-reaction cycle will have both active and passive participants.* Actions meant to deter or reassure may be focused on a limited circle of observers, but in fact will inevitably have an effect on anyone who can observe them, and potentially could include an entire regional and global audience and thereby alter the security environment well beyond the original targets. In so doing, each action contributes to the cumulative history and experience base, and in some degree contributes to shaping the perceptions and behavior of all observers across that security environment. We may elect to prune these cascading psychological effects and confine our concerns to the targeted friends or challengers, but we will still need to take the impact of our actions on passive participants into account in future interactions with those actors.

- *Interactions occur simultaneously in multiple dimensions.* The military components of deterrence and reassurance do not exist in a vacuum. All actions, whether tactical, operational, military-strategic, or geo-strategic, and whether political-diplomatic, economic, or military, are interrelated and will be seen by local observers as a single coordinated national effort, regardless of whether we intended them as such. If we are to make deterrence and reassurance work, we too must see our actions as an aggregate. For example, even an action as routine as a port visit by a Navy ship is likely to be seen against a background of our national political, security, and economic policy. Further complicating the situation, the local observers will also see the visit against the backdrop of their own local and national politics, or in the case of terrorists for example, in the context of their organization's internal politics.

- *All actions and effects are interrelated.* Given the multi-faceted character of our own actions, the diversity of the influences on observers, and the relatively small proportion of influences that we can control, it becomes even more incumbent upon us to coordinate our deterrence/reassurance efforts to ensure a unity of effect in those measures. At a minimum, we will need to deconflict our own actions so that they do not leave conflicting impressions or confuse the observers, or still worse, unwittingly build a negative synergy that conveys an effect that is the opposite of what we intended. Optimally, in achieving a unity of effect, we will build a positive synergy that reinforces our effort.

- *Effects have physical and psychological dimensions.* Like the cascades of physical and psychological effects created by military actions in crisis and war, our actions to deter and reassure should be expected to set off cascading effects that will have both physical and psychological dimensions. These cascades are likely to be more nuanced than those of combat operations. Just as in combat operations, determining the success of our efforts and our ability to adapt and innovate will hinge on the feedback that can be provided to decisionmakers and commands. Yet, because of the extended and often times subtle character of this complex cascade, this deterrence/reassurance feedback is likely to be even more heavily psychological, political-diplomatic, and subjective than those of combat operations.

Although these concepts bring us closer to effects-based deterrence and effects-based reassurance, we are still left with a fundamental problem. If deterrence and reassurance are to work, then by definition, they cannot be simply a reactive operation.[10] They must be a configuration of forces, capabilities, and actions that can establish a stable state or regime by presence and continued action. We need to create not so much effects-based deterrence operations as an effects-based deterrent at the center of a new strategic deterrence regime. This is the underlying challenge posed by the collapse of the Cold War strategic deterrence regime on September 11, 2001.

Crafting an Effects-Based Deterrent

What kind of effects-based deterrent force might provide the forward deterrence we need to defend our homeland against an expanding asymmetric threat? In fact, we have now described several components of such a deterrent. We have said that it entails both deterrence and reassurance missions and that it must look equally at friend, foe, and neutral. We have described a set of variables including actions, locations, timing, and visibility. We looked at these variables in terms of their ability to define and limit the niches within which competitors might operate. Lastly, we have applied the effects-based rule set to deterrence and reassurance. We now must put these together.

The rule sets tell us two more things.

- First, they indicate that a stable deterrence regime is a cumulative effect to be built gradually over a period of years. The decisions made and the courses of action pursued that result in deterrence arise from an aggregation of economic, political, cultural, and military perceptions that may take years to evolve. These perceptions are both rational and emotional in nature. In part, they may reflect reasoned assessments of physical capabilities such as the economic and military power of contenders, and of patterns of behavior by those actors that might indicate how these physical capabilities might or might not translate into action. In part, they reflect human elements such as national pride, trust, and personal friendships. This is to say that we must orchestrate not only the responses to crises and threats, but also our peacetime actions and that by doing so, we can gradually shape the history, perceptions, and the context within which local observers will see our future actions. It is within this peace, crisis, and war context that deterrence and its components of presence and crisis response operate, and within this context that we must consider the role of effects-based operations.

- Second, as the above suggests, where strategic nuclear deterrence might be considered to be global in dimension, all conventional deterrence, like politics, is local. The deterrence we are concerned about exists in the minds of regional decisionmakers and local publics. It is about the balance of power and capabilities within a given geographic area. That geographic area may be restricted to a region within the borders of a single country in the case an ethnic "liberation front." It may be restricted to immediate neighbors in the case of smaller powers. Or it may encompass an entire region in the case of large powers.[11] What goes on beyond the bounds of this area is generally of interest only to the degree that it affects the local situation or that capabilities from outside the area that might be brought to bear upon this local balance of power.[12]

Thus, any local deterrence regime will have a "wrong end of the telescope" character about it. Observers are not likely to focus on the totality of events taking place either in the region or in the world, nor will they consider the totality of American power that may be brought to bear. Their perceptions will be shaped by what they can see. Dissidents, for example, will tend to create a security calculus that focuses within their country, or at most across borders to fellow ethnic and religious groups. States will tend to focus their calculations on their neighbors, or at most, those potential coalitions of neighboring states that might affect them.[13]

In this local calculus, the possibility of action by a nonregional power constitutes something akin to a strategic problem. Such an external military challenge could be an order of magnitude greater than any local force and thus, could be the decisive component of the local calculus. But it is also likely to be a factor that may or may not be credible in a given circumstance. Also, like the strategic nuclear challenge, this potential for external intervention may require strategies and capabilities that may be sharply different from those the same local actor might use against local adversaries.[14]

Threefold Military Deterrent

In shaping the local security calculus that is at the heart of stable deterrence, our challenge is to create a local constellation of capabilities that would force a challenger to ask the series of hard questions about the risks and chances of success that we have discussed above. Our effects-based rule set makes clear that military capabilities are only one part of this constellation, even though they are the focus of this book and of the deterrent we have been considering in this chapter. Moreover, as our initial concern with friends and neutrals implies, a deterrent cannot be defined in a vacuum, independently of the situation or solely in terms of American forces and capabilities. Rather, the military component of any deterrent will be marked by a balance of three factors: (1) what local powers can do for themselves, (2) what American or other allied capabilities are routinely present, and (3) what American or other allied forces can be brought to the scene (and how fast and for how long). The three military forces (local, forward deployed, and forward deployable) play complementary roles in the shaping behavior and should be thought of as interlocking parts of the same deterrent.

As one would expect in any interaction between complex actors, these capabilities are not simply additive, but instead resemble a three-dimensional continuum. The greater the capabilities of the local allies and the greater their will, the less reinforcement will be required from nonregional powers in order to maintain the same level of local deterrence and reassurance. The same is true of the internal security apparatus that might have to deal with threats from non-state organizations, including terrorist attacks. Similarly, the greater the immediately available capabilities of the forward deployed nonregional forces, the less dependent the deterrent will be on either the forces of local allies or those deploying from distant bases. Finally, the greater the forces that can be deployed and the more rapid their deployment, the less reliant the deterrent or reassurance will be on either local or forward deployed forces. There is no cookie cutter, one-size-fits-all forward presence force or crisis reaction force. The force needed will vary from one region to the next and one situation to the next. We can, for example, readily extrapolate the above to the situation of an international security force in a peacekeeping operation. In that case, the degree of support required to reassure would depend on what local security capabilities remained, the threat to local order, the capabilities of the peacekeepers, and how rapidly they could be reinforced if necessary.

In this deterrence equation, the local forces are the independent variable. That is, the amount of outside intervention that will be required to maintain a given level of deterrence and stability will depend on the level of local capabilities, and not the reverse. The United States, for example, might encourage local allies to take a greater part in their own defense, but in the final analysis, it cannot control what they actually do or the proficiency that they will bring to the task. When all is said and done, the United States and other outside powers have the choice of making up any deficiencies with their own forces or accepting the instability and risks of conflagration that may result from a failure to do so.

...and in Combat

Finally, there is another aspect of deterrence and reassurance that we must not ignore. Deterrence is far from being a peacetime-only mission that disappears when combat begins. It is a fundamental facet of military operations in combat as well. This concern with deterrence during combat was apparent in one way during the Cold War when any open combat at all between the superpowers had the potential for escalating into a global thermonuclear war. However, the same problem presents itself in any combat situation at any level.

The question of reassurance is equally present in wartime and other combat operations. We very seldom fight alone and almost never engage in combat operations without some degree of support from friends and allies. Such support rests on an ability to reassure allies, an ability that is every bit as continual a task as deterring the vertical escalation of a conflict.

These questions of deterrence and reassurance are a fundamental aspect of achieving an acceptable end-state in any crisis or conflict, and of determining how to contain the conflict and prevent lateral as well as vertical escalation. This may involve simultaneously deterring the adversary from lateral escalation while reassuring and encouraging friends and neutrals to resist. Or, particularly in the last stages of a crisis or conflict, it may involve reassuring an adversary to make an end-state work.

Here the variables and rule sets apply. Especially in the latter case, every aspect of how we act will come under scrutiny as an indicator of whether the solution proposed is in fact an end-state rather than a maneuver for advantage. Political, diplomatic, and military actions will be inseparable parts of what will be regarded as a unified national or coalition action, however inchoate it may be.

Effects-Based Deterrence

If the above sounds commonsensical, it is. We have done all of this before and usually on an intuitive ad hoc basis. However, in this case, by applying the framework of effects-based operations concepts and theory that we have been exploring in this book, we also lay the foundation for applying the advantages of the network-centric revolution to this old problem. It is the mounting urgency of the deterrence problem in the wake of the September 11th attacks and particularly the potential for the terrorist attacks taking on a nuclear, chemical, or biological dimension that make the combination of network-centric and effects-based operations so essential.

[1]Thus, the niche challenger might be expected to avoid actions that so enrage the larger power as to negate the challenger's perceived advantage in will. This judgment, of course, would not pertain where the challenger is trying to provoke just such a conflict or where the challenger perceives that his actions are simply carrying out a divine mandate in the face of which questions of human will might be presumed irrelevant.

[2]For purposes of this work, we will confine the consideration of *reassurance* to the military domain and to the primary military function of providing security, either in the sense of supporting a general deterrence-reassurance regime or that of specific actions to support it. We will not attempt to assess the nonmilitary components of reassurance or the use of military forces in purely humanitarian operations (as opposed to humanitarian operations requiring an a priori establishment of security), even though these too can be factors in reassurance.

[3]We established earlier that all who could see an action would in some way be affected by it. However, such a broad definition of the set of observers would be so unwieldy as to be impossibly complex. In Chapter 7, however, we postulated that this set could be pruned to limit it to the particular sub-set of all these observers who are the targets of our actions.

[4]This history may be purely tactical or operational in nature and basically factual. However, it also may be a perceived history shaped by culture, propaganda, self-deceit, and a variety of other factors both personal and organizational. This latter perceived history, therefore, will vary from one observer to the next.

[5]The niche will probably not be limited to military capabilities alone. It will almost inevitably include political, economic, and military actions.

[6]As discussed, this can be either over time, in the case of passive foreclosure, or in response to a specific incident, in the case of active foreclosure.

[7]Here again, the power that is applicable may not be military. However, the unavailability of a military component to deterrence would itself shape the would-be aggressor's perceptions of what was or was not possible and produce a different calculation as to risks.

[8]Wilson, Harold. *A Personal Record.* Boston; Little Brown. 1971. pp. 397-9.

[9]This means planning such demonstrations from the standpoint of what observers are likely to see and configuring them so that the intended observers cannot miss seeing the capabilities we are trying to demonstrate.

[10]Our problem is complicated by the fact that we tend to regard the military role here in terms of operations, such as the evacuation of American nationals threatened by local unrest or as crisis responses to block aggression. Yet, as we pointed out earlier, these are responses to deal with the symptoms of an incipient failure of local deterrence/reassurance and not a description of the underlying deterrence regime needed to ensure the stability that would prevent such challenges or make them far less likely.

[11]It is worth noting that even in the midst of the Cold War, the conventional confrontations between the superpowers tended to be on a region by region basis and seldom gave rise to a lateral escalation, even though both the Soviets and Americans had the capability to do so.

[12]There is a rich anecdotal history of this phenomenon epitomized by the "campanilism" or disinterest in anything that could not be seen from the campanile (bell tower) of the local church, something that was the bane of Italian nationalists in the nineteenth century. From the perspective of a local decisionmaker, this horizon corresponds to the limit of his span of control or to that portion of the world upon which he feels able to have any impact.

[13]Terrorists such as al-Qaida will tend to focus on a particular region, such as the expanse of the mythic Islamic caliphate. However, within that wide region, there will be a tendency to focus on individual local campaigns such as Afghanistan, the Philippines, Somalia, or even a country-by-country campaign against the Western nations. Each locale represents an individual geographic niche to be exploited, and like other more conventional threats, will have to be deterred one niche at a time.

[14]For example, the would-be aggressor might resort to a damage infliction effects-based strategy in dealing with the extra-regional power while continuing to use an attrition-based approach to dealing with local peers.

CHAPTER 10

Putting the Pieces Together: An Operational Example

We have now used a series of examples drawn from wars and crisis response operations to outline a definition and a rule set for effects-based operations, including the cascade of physical and psychological effects. We have also used a model of the cognitive process to examine the nature of actions and effects, and have looked at the attributes of both in the context of the same examples as well. However, most of these historical examples have focused on the military-strategic and geo-strategic levels of the interactions. Yet, the cutting edge of effects-based operations lies at the operational level of warfare and crisis reactions. We must now draw all of these elements together so that they become something more than an abstract collection of observations and apply them to real-world planning at the level of the operational commander.

We can do this by treating all of the elements we have discussed in the context of a single example that demonstrates how an operational commander has applied the ideas we have been examining and has coped with the complexities of the effects-based thinking and processes we have outlined, preferably one that involves both kinetic and nonkinetic uses of military forces. Then we can trace the planning and execution of an effects-based operation from the tactical level upwards, noting how actions were chosen and executed, and observing the effects manifest in the reactions and behavior of an opponent.

Attain Document: Operations in the Vicinity of Libya, 1986

One example of what might now be termed *effects-based operations* occurred off the coast of Libya during the first months of 1986.[1] These operations are of particular interest in the aftermath of the September 11th attacks in that, like the 1970 Jordanian Crisis, they responded to a series of terrorist attacks on Americans conducted with the aid of a state sponsor.

Background to the Crisis

The Attain Document series of predominantly naval operations off Libya came in response to an upsurge in anti-American terrorism in 1985 at the hands of first Hizballah and later the Abu Nidal organization. The Hizballah, with the support of Syria and Iran, had begun an anti-American terrorist campaign in response to the Israeli occupation of areas of Lebanon. Hizballah operations in Lebanon ranged from the bombing of the U.S. Marine barracks in Beirut in 1983 and of a U.S. Embassy annex in 1984, to the seizure of U.S. hostages. However, the operations expanded in June 1985 with the hijacking of an American aircraft carrying American tourists. That aircraft was seized in Greece, then flown to Beirut where a U.S. Navy diver was "executed." Subsequent U.S. pressures on Syria and Israel brought about the release of the passengers, but the question of halting "the spread of international terrorism" had become a major concern of the U.S. national leadership.[2]

In the following months, it became increasingly clear that Libya was expanding its support for Middle Eastern terrorism and was "talking to Iran and Syria about a joint terrorist war" against the United States.[3] In October 1985, 6 days after an Israeli air strike against Palestinian Headquarters in Tunisia, Libyan-supported terrorists seized an Italian liner, the *Achille Lauro*, and murdered a wheelchair-bound American passenger.[4] Then, more Libyan supported terrorists attacked groups of largely American tourists in the airports of Rome and Vienna on December 27, killing 20 people including 5 Americans, an action praised by Libyan leader Colonel Muammar al Qadhafi as "a noble act."[5]

In response, the U.S. leadership decided that America needed "to express in a concrete way [their] displeasure with his terrorism" and began to draw up contingency plans and to reinforce the U.S. Sixth Fleet. One element of these contingency plans was a naval operation off the coast of Libya. Attain Document, also known as Operations in the Vicinity of Libya (OVL), took place in a series of three phases: Attain Document I in January 1986, followed by Attain Document II in February, and Attain Document III in March. Attain Document III involved Libyan attempts to shoot down American aircraft over the Gulf of Sidra with surface-to-air missiles and attempts to attack U.S. warships with anti-ship missiles. The American response included attacks on the missile sites and the sinking of the missile patrol boats moving toward Sixth Fleet units. Attain Document III was followed in April by yet another Libyan supported terrorist operation, the bombing of a Berlin discotheque frequented by American soldiers, and then by Operation El Dorado Canyon, a series of strikes by Air Force and Navy aircraft into Libya.

Attain Document: The Operational Problem

In apparent reaction to American outrage, the visible reinforcement of the U.S. Sixth Fleet,[6] and the rising prospect of American military action, al-Qadhafi responded on January 24, 1986 by declaring a denial area in international waters of the Gulf of Sidra off the Libyan coast, which he demarcated with a heavily propagandized "line of death" (see Figure 66). Two days later, the United States Battle Force Sixth Fleet began Attain Document I, the first of three "Freedom of Navigation" (FON) operations off the denied area of the Gulf.

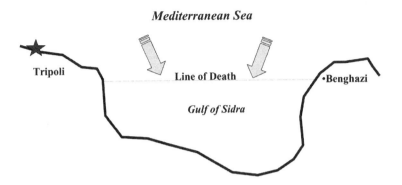

Figure 66. Libyan Crisis (1986)

The objectives of the Battle Force in the Attain Document series of operations were twofold. On one level, in keeping with the national objectives, it needed to convey a message to al-Qadhafi that he could not fend off the consequences of his support for terrorism and that the United States could and would act forcibly if further provoked. On another more concrete level, it needed to undertake a longstanding presence mission by challenging the Libyan restrictions on freedom of the sea embodied in the "line of death." The latter became the operational level framework for the former.

It was recognized from the start that the true national-level objective of the Battle Force's operations, a change in Libyan behavior, was more political than military in nature. If the Battle Force were able to operate visibly and repeatedly in the declared denial area and the Libyans were unable or unwilling to respond, it would send two messages. To al-Qadhafi, it would signify that he could not evade a forcible

United States reaction to his sponsorship of anti-American terrorism. To other regional powers, it would send a message both that there would be a forceful American reaction to state-sponsored terrorism and that neither al-Qadhafi nor any other state sponsor could forestall it.[7] In short, the demonstration of military power inherent in the Freedom of Navigation operations was intended to be sufficient to achieve the desired political outcome.

In the event that the Libyans decided either to continue terrorist operations or to launch a large-scale attack on the Navy ships and aircraft in the Gulf of Sidra, national-level contingency planning called for the execution of a "contingency strike package" code named Prairie Fire.[8] However, with the blessing of the Sixth Fleet commander, then-Vice Admiral Frank B. Kelso, the commander of the Battle Force, then-Rear Admiral David E. Jeremiah, also began planning potential Battle Force responses to a more limited exchange with Libyan forces, a set of contingencies not directly covered by the Prairie Fire strike planning.

This Battle Force planning process proceeded with the instruction that the news of any Libyan action and any U.S. reaction must be reported in the same issue of the Washington Post (within 24 hours). This caveat, which the Battle Force staff irreverently dubbed "the Washington Post factor," reflected a keen insight into the nature of the problem. The timing and proportionality of any American response to a limited Libyan action were more important than which targets were struck. That is, the key to success in any interaction lay not in what destruction was inflicted, but in understanding and anticipating how any American action would be perceived by the Libyans, by U.S. Allies, by others in the region, and by the U.S. public at home.

This perspective, with its requirement for reacting within 24 hours or less, signaled a different approach to operational level planning. Strikes against a pre-planned list of targets in Libya were certainly possible given a political decision to do so. Indeed, this was embodied in the Prairie Fire contingency strike plan. But, a Prairie Fire-type pre-planned target list was unlikely to have anything to do with the nature of a specific Libyan action against the Battle Force and would therefore likely fail the proportionality test in any case but that of a large-scale attack on American forces. On the other hand, if the Battle Force were to wait until the Libyans took action before developing a response and asking for approval, the process would result in delays that would likely make it impossible to meet the timing criterion.

The solution was to define a limited number of al-Qadhafi's most likely hostile actions toward the Battle Force, and then to plan a specific and proportional reaction that could be swiftly executed with the forces at hand for each postulated Libyan action. This set of paired actions and proposed reactions was then briefed all the way up the chain of command through the White House. Its approval brought not only standing permission to conduct the proposed responses, but also the allocation of the requisite rules of engagement to the Commander of the Sixth Fleet. As a result, in the March 24-25, 1986 engagements during Attain Document III in which the Libyans fired a surface-to-air missile at a Navy aircraft and then sent missile patrol boats against U.S. surface forces, the U.S. response was not only proportional but timely. It also required no further direction from the National Command Authority.[9]

Attain Document as an Effects-Based Operation

Even in the brief description of Attain Document given above, the effects-based nature of the operation and of its planning is already evident. This effect-based core becomes still more evident as we examine the operation to see how our proposed definitions of effects-based operations, actions, and effects are reflected, how the action-reaction, stimulus and response, cognitive cycles worked, how cascades of effects were sought, and what kinds of feedback were required and available.

Definitions and Rule Sets

What is perhaps most apparent in this brief description of Attain Document is how well it conforms to our proposed definition of effects-based operations as "coordinated sets of actions directed at shaping the behavior of friends, foes, and neutrals in peace, crisis, and war." As we delve into the operations, we will see this in three ways:

- First, the series of three Attain Document operations clearly comprised "coordinated sets of actions" over a 3-month period. However, this coordination was not limited to the

American national leadership and the operational level commanders; rather, it involved a complex coordination of operations at each level of interaction and across all the arenas of national power.

- Second, from the beginning, it was apparent that the "actions" commanders considered were far more than air or missile strikes. Instead, from the initial reinforcement of the Sixth Fleet onwards, the actions or stimuli chosen more often took noncombat forms and each action was calculated to shape local behavior in some way.

- Third, at the national level in particular, it is also clear that the behavior to be shaped extended far beyond that of Colonel al-Qadhafi and the Libyans. The actions were equally tailored for a temporarily passive regional audience that included Syria, Iran, Israel, Egypt, the Palestinians, and America's NATO allies.

We can see this definition being played out in a series of action-reaction, stimulus and response cycles at the tactical, operational, military-strategic and geo-strategic levels of the crisis interaction. Indeed, as we trace these cycles at each of these levels and in each of the arenas of national power, we can begin to see our set of six effects-based rules reflected as well.[10]

Levels and Nature of Interactions

As we look at the Attain Document I, II, and III Operations, we can distinguish action-reaction cycles taking place on four different levels of the military command structures of both Libyans and Americans. For the Americans, the tactical level was represented by the actions and reactions of the U.S. air and naval units operating in and around the Gulf of Sidra.[11] The operational level was to be seen in the actions and reactions of the United States Sixth Fleet and Battle Force Sixth Fleet Commanders, and the military-strategic level in the activities of both the European Theater Commander and the Joint Staff in the Pentagon. Finally, the geo-strategic level was manifest in the actions and concerns of the Reagan White House.

It can also be surmised that the actions and reactions of the Libyan side roughly paralleled this breakdown. At the tactical level, the Libyans also had air and naval units operating in the area of the Gulf of Sidra, as well as air defense and ground forces located along the coast. They had naval and air defense commanders at the operational level who, like their Sixth Fleet and Battle Force counterparts, were trying to make sense of a developing situation and to direct the actions and reactions of their forces. And, they too had a national military staff under al-Qadhafi, who in this case seems to have functioned both as the military leader and the national command authority.

The action-reaction cognitive cycles of both the Americans and the Libyans could be observed on all of these levels during the crisis. Actions were taken and effects created on four different levels of a tactical, operational, military-strategic, and geo-strategic nest. In turn, the actual Libyan reactions were felt and the potential Libyan reactions had to be considered on each of these levels. Since the impacts of both the actions and the reactions were not and could not be limited to any one level, both the planning of effects and the execution of the required actions and of reactions to any Libyan reaction had to reach across all levels of the nest. Especially on the American side, we can trace a cognitive cycle in which actions were perceived and evaluated, choices were made, and physical reactions were directed at each level. We can also see the operation of the rule set mechanics at each level. In fact, what we are describing is something akin to a multi-faceted nest of interactions and decisionmaking. Indeed, this construct provides a useful way of tracing the effects-based operation through the successive levels and arenas we must consider.

Nest: Tactical Level

At the tactical level of the nest, the most frequent interactions between Americans and Libyans came in the form two-versus-two, air-to-air engagements. These occurred in both Attain Document I and Attain Document II and are illustrated by the arrows in Figure 67.[12] These air-to-air interactions typically involved two sets of active players, one pair of U.S. Navy aircraft and one pair of Libyan Air Force aircraft. The object of the resulting aerial ballet was not to destroy the opposing aircraft (something that the U.S. operational commander at least deliberately avoided).[13] It was rather to maneuver the aircraft so as to preclude or foreclose an unacceptable tactical

| Sea | Air | Ground | Space |

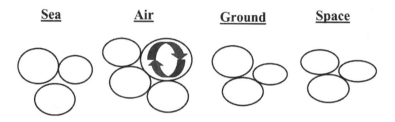

Figure 67. Nesting: Tactical Level

action, such as the Libyans approaching the American fleet, and the Americans approaching Libyan territorial seas, respectively.

For the pilots involved, these objectives reduced to the kind of straightforward cognitive cycle envisioned in the original tactical OODA loop, but with one important difference. The objective in these 1986 engagements was not to destroy the opposing aircraft, it was rather to foreclose certain kinds of behavior on their part. The added difficulty was that in each of the Attain Document I and II engagements, there was a relatively strong possibility that the other side might initiate hostilities, either intentionally or by accident. Thus, each pilot had to monitor the actions of his opponent closely for any clue that might indicate some hostile intent. Rules of engagement obviously were critical guidelines in making this judgment. However, the speed of the air-to-air interaction meant that the pilots were called upon to make a succession of instantaneous, life-or-death decisions and to act upon them with scant time for further guidance.

Because a judgment as to intent hinged on a great deal more than sensor data, the pilots' observations of the opposing aircraft had to focus not only on what those aircraft did, but also on how they did it, for instance, how "aggressively" the aircraft were maneuvered. This meant that pilots had to balance those adversary actions they were currently observing against those that they had seen in the past and against their own mental models of the actions an opposing pilot might take as a prelude to opening fire. This pilot-centered cognitive cycle was continuous throughout the engagement, and for most experienced pilots, was almost subconscious and intuitive. This was what the American pilots had been trained to do.

As the above suggests too, the effects of these air-to-air engagements were cumulative over time and especially across the air operations of the Attain Document series. To start with, both the Libyan and American pilots were familiar with the recent history of Libyan-American air interactions in the same region. That history included the shoot-down of Libyan aircraft by U.S. Navy aircraft just 5 years earlier, a factor that would have shaped the mental models of both sides before the first Attain Document intercept ever took place. To this initial mental model were added the effects from the growing number of Attain Document intercepts. In these latter engagements, the Libyans were constantly out-matched by the better-trained American side, a situation reflected in the growing confidence of the American pilots and very likely by a growing discouragement among the Libyan pilots.

In this tactical engagement, however, the action-reaction cycle was not limited to the two sets of aircraft actively engaged in the aerial duel. Rather, the air interaction took place as part of a larger tactical level context that involved other players who remained passive observers throughout the engagement.

The most immediately concerned of these passive players were the other aircraft in the combat air patrol stations adjacent to the scene of the interaction and the Libyan fighters on alert around the Gulf of Sidra (see Figure 68). The passive role of these assets would have ended when any aircraft undertook a hostile action,[14] abruptly changing the mental model of an engagement that was not intended to take offensive action. Any such action would have instantly broadened the scope of the engagement to include these passive pilots and aircraft as active participants. Thus, these pilots and their commanders closely monitored the ongoing air-to-air action-reaction cycle for any clue that it might be breaking away from the bounds of expected behavior.

Also immediately concerned were the ships operating in the area. During Attain Document I and II, U.S. surface warships were also manning combat stations throughout the area of the Gulf of Sidra north of the "line of death," and Libyan missile patrol boats were located at bases on either side of the Gulf. The ships on both sides would also have been

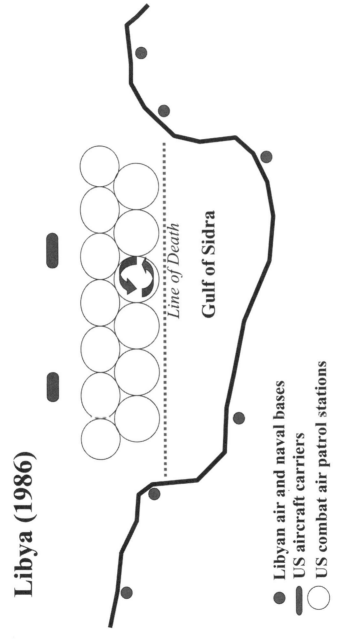

Figure 68. Attain Document I and II (Libya 1986)

deployed as search and rescue platforms or might also have become parties to the combat. This in fact did happen during the subsequent Attain Document III Operation.

Finally, we might speculate that, had our initial two-versus-two air engagement gone sour, the web of concerned parties reacting would have included Libyan ground and air defense forces along the periphery of the Gulf of Sidra. Similarly on the American side, the surveillance platforms that were monitoring the Gulf and Libyan actions would likewise have dramatically altered the scope and direction of their collection activity.

As the above makes plain, even at the tactical level of conflict, we can see all of the elements of the rule sets and the cognitive cycle at work. And, we can also see a tactical level assessment of intent that depends upon a great deal more than location, heading, and speed. The breadth of these expended requirements for information becomes even more apparent as we move to the operational level of the interaction.

Nest: Operational Level

Together, all of these elements of tactical level interaction comprised the larger and constantly changing operational level action-reaction cycle (see Figure 69). The problem of the operational commander was considerably more complex. His core challenge was to orchestrate the actions and reactions of the diverse array of forces under his command so as to create a single, unified military

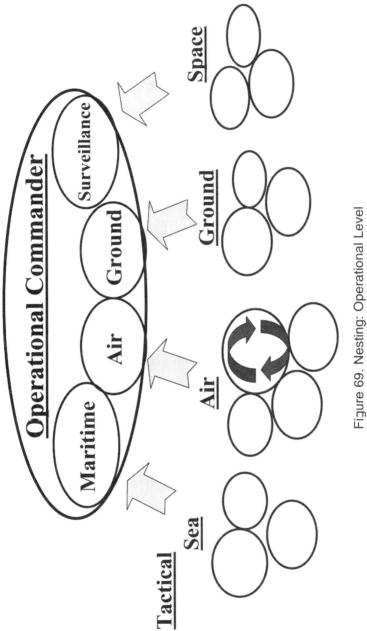

Figure 69. Nesting: Operational Level

effect at the operational level that would reinforce the overall effect sought by his superiors. That challenge had several different elements to it. First, the commander had to configure the actions of his forces so that they would be observed and understood by the adversary in a way calculated to produce the desired overall effect. Second, he had to anticipate roughly how his forces' actions would be seen and how the adversary might then react. Third, he had to monitor the adversary's actions and reactions well enough to assess roughly his own success and adapt to changes imposed by the adversary's actions. Finally, he had to ensure that all of the operational level actions and induced effects in fact conformed to the overall national and military-strategic effect sought.

In orchestrating the actions at the operational level, the air-to-air engagement constituted of what was obviously the most visible and active measure by which the respective operational commanders might hope to shape their opponent's perceptions and behavior. But, it was hardly the only one, nor was it necessarily the most potent. The real impact at the operational level and higher probably derived more from the full scope of the actions taken by the force as a whole over time. This larger dimension of the operational level interaction was reflected in the operational commanders' preparations for the engagement of their assigned forces. Admiral Jeremiah, the U.S. Battle Force Commander, very carefully calculated where the combat air patrol stations would be located and how they would be filled. That calculation was made as part of an overall plan that positioned ships and submarines throughout the area. In each case, the decisions were made not only with an eye to Battle Force defense, but also as to how the actions of each might be observed by the Libyans, if at all.[15]

Command Intent

As the above begins to indicate, the Battle Force or operational commander's challenge in creating and orchestrating effects was far more complex than that of the tactical commanders', who tended to be either direct, active participants in an engagement themselves or were in immediate control of the forces involved. For the operational commander, the scope of the forces to be directed would have made such a degree of control a difficult proposition at best. The greater the number of tactical engagements that occurred at one time, the more difficult the problem became. Yet this span of control problem was only partially a question of communications. The driving question was actually one of knowledge and understanding. Who could best know what was going on and when?

This consideration was most apparent in the high-speed air-to-air engagements. The Battle Force Commander in the Sidra Operations could and did monitor closely what transpired in these engagements, but in many ways he remained a prisoner of what the sensors and communications of the information domain could deliver to him. He recognized not only that there would be situations in which he could not react fast enough to control the tactical action, but also that his appreciation of what was going on would always be inferior to that of the pilots actually engaged.

This predicament might be attributed to some delay in sensor data reaching him, however brief that delay might be. In part, it might be attributed in a fundamental difference in data presentation. The pilot's eyeball picture of what was going on was naturally superior to the commander's form of visual display. Yet where new information technologies might address these problems, there remained two more decisive factors: the intensity and immediacy of the observer's involvement and the need to inject this human-derived information into the decision process.

A pilot focused on what might be a life-or-death interaction not only was in a better position to act and react more quickly, but also probably had a better deep understanding of what was going on than an operational commander confronted with multiple other demands. Even in a straight line combat air intercept in which an aircraft simply sought to detect and destroy an opposing aircraft, this consideration would have argued strongly in favor of a decentralized command structure that delegated a great degree of freedom of action to the pilot.

In air-to-air engagements (such as those in the Attain Document I and II Operations) that call for frequent, rapid cognitive judgments by pilots as to their opponents' behavior, the ability to act quickly and decisively depended on the input of information from a human source, the pilot-observer. Given these factors, there clearly was no alternative but for the operational commander to delegate authority and trust to the judgment of the on-scene actor.[16]

To prepare tactical commanders to self-synchronize in such situations required more than rules of engagement drills. Thus, the Battle Force Commander took great pains to ensure that tactical level participants not only knew the governing rules of engagement, but that they also had a clear understanding of command intent, the role he expected them to play and why. To this end, Admiral Jeremiah called a series of commander's conferences in the days leading up to Attain Document I so as to draw all the tactical commanders into the planning process by soliciting their views on how each unit might be most effectively used. This participation enabled tactical commanders to contextualize their actions at any given moment and to act both quickly and with a minimum of further guidance as a tactical situation unfolded.[17]

We can assume that some similar effort to coordinate actions also took place on the Libyan side. However, in the Libyan case, neither the training of the pilots nor an air doctrine that revolved about "controlled intercepts" permitted a similar freedom of action for tactical commanders or the resulting degree of flexibility and adaptability.

To support the tactical efforts and to monitor Libyan movements, the Battle Force Commander had also meticulously positioned his organic surveillance assets[18] and tasked available national collection assets so as to ensure the optimum feedback on Libyan actions and reactions in the crisis area. Of these two surveillance elements, the more important for the operational commander were the organic assets including Air Force and Navy land-based reconnaissance assets, carrier-based airborne early warning platforms, ships, and netted electronic warfare assets. These assets had a threefold advantage over national assets. Not only could they report faster, but they could also be tasked and respond to tasking faster, and perhaps most significantly, they could be queried in a dialog between collector and operator.

The surveillance commanders were also drawn into the planning process and participated in the commander's conferences. Like the tactical commanders, they needed to have a sense of the plan to be executed, of the anticipated Libyan actions, and of their role in the commander's plan. Given this understanding, they too functioned in a rather self-synchronous manner, focusing on those rapidly unfolding events that warranted the most attention, undertaking initiative reporting, and filtering a volume of reporting that might otherwise have overwhelmed the operational and tactical commanders. In actuality, by introducing at least the Battle Force surveillance commanders into the planning process,[19] the operational commander had enabled them to combine information and cognitive domain functions on a single platform.

Operational Level Contingency Planning

At the heart of the planning effort and the commander's conferences was an effort to anticipate Libyan actions and reactions and to think through a series of likely contingencies. In this respect, the conferences were a forum for reviewing more detailed planning already conducted by the Battle Force Commander and his staff. This planning involved not only the effort to craft the maneuver actions of the Battle Force to shape Libyan perceptions and behavior in a certain way, but also an effort to flesh out potential responses to likely contingencies. These contingency scenarios focused on the most likely ways in which Libya might deliberately begin hostilities, rather than on an accidental misstep by a Libyan pilot along the lines of the 1981 shoot down. To that end, Admiral Jeremiah directed his staff to produce a list of the five most likely ways in which al-Qadhafi might take hostile action and then to propose a way of responding to each.

In undertaking this planning effort, as we have previously noted, the Battle Force Commander sought to address the questions of timing and proportionality of response in a way that the military-strategic and geo-strategic levels of command did not and perhaps could not. That is, he was using his cognitive grasp of the local situation in much the same way his tactical commanders were expected to exercise their judgment in the field. In practice, this meant that whereas directives from the Joint Staff focused on how the Battle Force ought to respond to a large scale Libyan attack on U.S. forces, the operational commander focused on a series of lesser contingencies that could more readily be fine-tuned. The planning effort gave him an opportunity to look closely at the variables in any response. What kinds of force might be used in what numbers? How widespread should the response be? How fast should it be and over how long a time? In each case, the effort was not to predict what the Libyans would do, but to delimit a range of what they might do.

The planning effort likewise provided a nucleus for coordinating the effects sought by the Battle Group Commander with those sought by higher levels of command. The five contingencies examined by the Battle Force Commander and the proposed actions for each were briefed to successive levels of command. Each higher level could then not only come to understand what was being proposed, but could also factor that understanding into its own actions.

Obviously, there would have been no need for this up-the-chain coordination if the higher levels of command had simply dictated top-down exactly what the operational commander was to do.[20] But, in rapidly evolving effects-based operations such as Attain Document, this centralization and synchronized planning also had two drawbacks.

First, it was in many ways a holdover from an attrition-based approach to warfare in which the operating forces were simply expected to bomb some number of very specific targets calculated to have some specific derivative physical effects. In such an evolution, the local operational commander's insight might be valuable, but it probably was not essential. However, in an effects-based operation that focused on shaping or changing an opponent's behavior, the forward commander's deep understanding of the situation and the opponent became critical.

Second, by centralizing direction, higher-level commanders would largely sacrifice the cognitive insight that the local operational commander could contribute. The value of that insight, moreover, grew with time as the local commander's understanding of the situation and the opponent grew. In this case, the Attain Document I and II Operations in January and February 1986 provided a training ground for the more dangerous Attain Document III Operation in March.

Again at the level of the operational commander, we can see all of the elements of the rule sets, cognitive cycle, and action variables at work. The Battle Force Commander's efforts to position his forces reflects a concern both with what his opponent would perceive and how to manipulate his actions to create the right effect. The efforts to draw both tactical and surveillance commanders into the planning process points to a recognition of the nature of the cognitive processes involved in his actions, as does the creation of a set of contingency plans. However, the latter likewise suggests the need to look further up the chain to how all of this activity by the operational level commander fits into the problem of the military-strategic level.

Nest: Military-Strategic Level

The tasks of the European Theater Commander and the Joint Staff in Washington on the one side and of the Libyan military staff on the other side represented a still wider and still more complex dimension of the military problem (see Figure 70). Theirs was the task of managing the overall military response so as to produce a coordinated set of military actions whose direct and indirect, physical and psychological effects might achieve the ends set by the national political leadership at the national level. This task was fourfold:

- First, they had to identify and task the elements of national military power that were most applicable to the area and situation at hand.

- Second, they had to forecast roughly the actions and reactions of the opponent so as to anticipate additional calls on national military resources that might be forthcoming, and then include these in national-level contingency planning.

- Third, they needed to undertake what might be termed *military diplomacy* to coordinate the military actions of the operational commanders with any allied actions and to ensure that all military actions would be perceived in the right way by other military actors, neutrals, friends, coalition partners, and allies.

- Finally, they were responsible for coordinating these military actions with parallel political and diplomatic actions so as to create a unified overall national level effect.

All of these elements were intertwined in the actions of the U.S. Joint Staff and the U.S. European Theater Command. For these American military planners, the central challenge was determining how

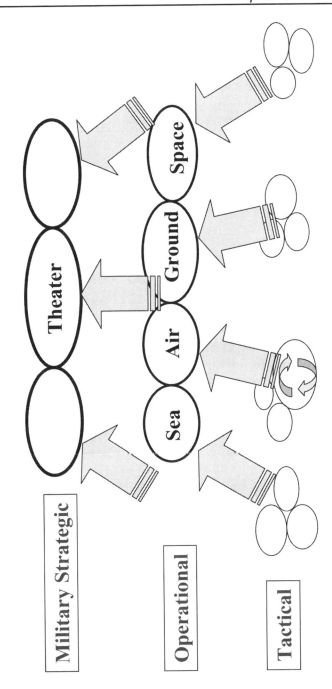

Figure 70. Nesting: Military-Strategic Level

to use United States military power to support national efforts to compel a change in al-Qadhafi's defiant sponsorship of anti-American terrorism. The military component of this response was a substantial Freedom of Navigation operation in the Gulf of Sidra, an action calculated to raise the military pressure on al-Qadhafi and induce a change in his behavior.[21]

From the military-strategic perspective, the FON operations had a number of advantages to them.

- First, the action could be conducted without initiating hostilities that might derail diplomatic and economic efforts that had been directed by the White House.

- Second, because the action relied on naval forces operating in international waters, its scale, scope, and activity could be varied at will, and could be sustained virtually indefinitely.[22]

- Third, as would be apparent to the Libyans, the units conducting the operations were quite capable of striking with force if the United States were provoked either by further acts of terrorism or by Libyan military action in the Gulf.

In keeping with the latter, the Joint Staff and Theater Commander began preparing contingency plans for Prairie Fire strikes, while the operational commander on-scene prepared plans for proportional responses to more limited Libyan action against the Battle Force. To support military action, the European Theater initially had one carrier battle group in the Mediterranean Sea headed by the smallest and oldest carrier in service, the U.S.S. *Coral Sea*. This group was moved into the area north of the Gulf of Sidra in early January as the crisis flared. To increase the scale and scope of the action possible, the Theater Commander also asked for a covert return to the Mediterranean of the *Saratoga* carrier battle group, then in the Pacific Theater in the Indian Ocean. And, in conjunction with the U.S. State Department, it began negotiations with Egypt for the *Saratoga* group's safe passage through the Suez Canal.[23] Finally, in preparation for the March Attain Document III Operation, the Theater received a third battle group centered around the carrier U.S.S. *America*.[24] The Battle Force for Attain Document III then consisted of 26 warships, including 3 aircraft carriers and 250 aircraft.[25]

To coordinate this effort, the Joint and Theater Commands had several different levels of control embodied both in rules of engagement to guide the operational commanders and in direct approval of contingency plans. The latter consisted both of the Battle Force Commander's proposed options for dealing with a set of limited Libyan actions duly reviewed without change at successive levels of command, and of the staff's own contingency plans for dealing with a large scale Libyan attack on the force.[26]

This review of the Battle Force Commander's options by the military-strategic and national levels of command had another impact. When hostilities began in Attain Document III, there were no surprises and no further intervention required. The standardized list of rules of engagement (ROE) recognized the need for on-scene commanders to deal with the exigencies of a fast moving battle and permitted the senior military and civilian leadership to give them a delimited freedom of action to deal with them by granting particular ROEs. In Attain Document, some of these were allotted to the Battle Force Commander or to unit commanders and some were reserved to the Sixth Fleet Commander, then-Vice Admiral Kelso. In Attain Document III, Kelso was also granted the freedom to decide that a Libyan attack against one unit was to be considered an attack on all and to react accordingly.[27]

From the Libyan military perspective, the problem would have been dealing with the military consequences of two political actions: the Libyan support of Abu Nidal in his campaign of anti-American terrorism; and more immediately, al-Qadhafi's declaration of a "line of death," which, based on previous history, the Americans were sure to challenge. To deal with any American action, the Libyan command had a relatively modern arsenal of aircraft, surface-to-air missiles, and missile patrol boats,[28] but were probably under no delusion as to their ability to defeat a still better-armed and considerably better-trained American force in open combat. Both the reach of these Libyan forces and the lack of any long-range surveillance capability precluded a direct military attack on American bases or upon American forces too far out at sea.[29] As a result, the options exercised by the Libyan command revolved about the Americans coming to challenge Libya in territorial seas. The military goal in this was most likely not to defeat U.S. forces outright, but to aggressively meet the intruders and, if hostilities were to erupt, to inflict damage on American forces in a "heroic" defense of the homeland. In the latter, the behavior to be shaped was probably less that of the United States than a local and regional public. That is, to be successful in their military actions and the resulting effects, the Libyan command did not have to win so much as it had to avoid losing badly.

Nest: Geo-Strategic Level

Finally, this entire military picture was but one facet of the overall national problem that had to be considered at the level of the President and the national leadership. In the case of the Libyan Operations, that national problem was of coordinating the military operations with both a domestic and international political dimension that included dealing with the media, briefing Congress, consulting with local allies and neutrals, and activities in international arenas.[30] The White House's challenge in this effects-based endeavor was especially great as it involved coordinating very diverse and often seemingly unconnected actions in three arenas so as to create a coordinated, unified effect.

Some of the White House's first actions reflect this perspective. In a press conference on January 7, 1986, the President announced "an executive order bringing Americans and American business home from Libya and canceling relations."[31] The effect of the action was to put economic and political pressure on Libya while moving quietly to reinforce military forces in the theater. The decision to order American citizens out of Libya likewise prepared a geo-strategic battlespace by removing the possibility of al-Qadhafi's seizing American hostages to thwart a U.S. military action in the area.[32]

The challenge faced by the Administration was further complicated by the fact that the effects sought created overlaps from one arena to the next (see Figure 71). The White House staff would have been left to explain the nature of a tactical action in the event that the interaction resulted in a shootdown on either side. The State Department, already charged with explaining the U.S. position and the reasons for the operation to the international community, would have been left to field similar inquiries from overseas allies.

From the standpoint of the White House, the Freedom of Navigation context of the Attain Document operations served multiple purposes in these dimensions, and not all of them related to shaping Libyan behavior. If forcible military action became necessary, then the Libyan closure of international waters provided a clear violation of international law as a justification. That in turn would make it difficult for local fellow travelers to support the Libyan position in a face-off. Also, Attain Document was a confrontation between military forces in an international environment in which there were few civilians likely to be harmed inadvertently if hostilities did erupt.[33]

These factors enabled the White House and the Joint Staff to give the local operational commander a bit more discretion in handling the Libyan actions than was evidenced in the planning for a Prairie Fire contingency strike package or the El Dorado

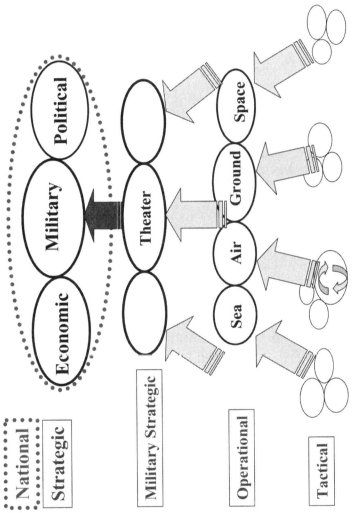

Figure 71. Different Actions, Different Timelines

Canyon Operation. The tighter leash in the latter cases was dictated by White House concern over the possibility of civilian casualties and the effect that such casualties might have on American support. These concerns were not minor and, in the preparation for the El Dorado Canyon strikes, were voiced by close allies, notably British Prime Minister Margaret Thatcher.

The White House's concern over the likelihood of al-Qadhafi taking American hostages is instructive in a different sense. The departure of the Americans became a prerequisite to any significant American military action, such as that undertaken in April in the El Dorado Canyon strikes.[34] This meant that however prepared military forces may have been to respond in early January 1986, there were consequences that the White House needed to consider that proceeded along an entirely different timeline, as depicted in Figure 72. Moreover, the same timing concerns would have been a determining factor for any diplomatic action that needed to be accomplished before power could be applied. This was a major factor in the El Dorado Canyon where permission was sought from Britain and France for an over-flight of Air Force F/B-111 aircraft en route to Libyan targets.

However necessary this planned synchronization may have been, and in this case it clearly was needed, it also posed problems. From the start of the Libyan operations, it was obvious to the Battle Force Commander that the likely interactions with the Libyans would be too rapid and dynamic to be tightly controlled by the Joint Staff or the White House. If

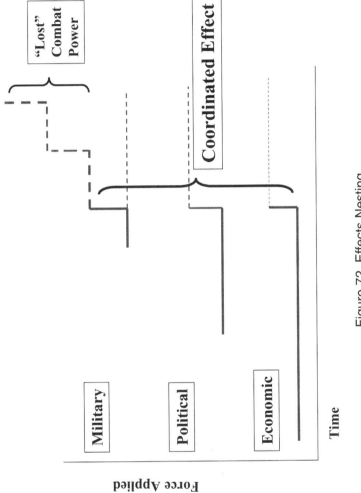

Figure 72. Effects Nesting

the planning of responses to immediate Libyan actions were centralized, they could no longer be as timely as they needed to be to succeed. It was accepted at all levels that some of the rules of engagement[35] for independent action would need to be delegated to local commanders.[36] However, such routine grants of ROE were normally confined to questions of self-defense, and the Cold War-era process of approving operations plans and granting ROEs for larger operations could be lengthy and cumbersome.

All told, the time delay that would be involved in the process of approving action would likely have left the Battle Force unable to meet the time line indicated by the "Washington Post factor" and thus, to achieve the political-military effect sought. Admiral Jeremiah's innovative solution to the problem was to look beyond the essentially negative ROE process and to propose instead a series of options to deal with a set of the most probable Libyan actions. The approval of these options by successive levels of command through the White House then provided not only the ROE required, but also a common understanding of the national level commander's intent that could be translated into local commanders' intent and what might be called a common effects-based operational picture.

Actions and Effects

Throughout the more detailed breakdown of Attain Document above, we can see the multidimensional nature of both actions and effects at work. This multidimensional nature was clearly more than the difference between the kinetic impact of weapons on targets and the nonkinetic impact of force movements upon an observer. Rather, in the choices made by decisionmakers at all levels, we can see the various attributes of both actions and effects as factors in the decisions.

Actions

In one respect, the decisionmakers' active use of the multifaceted character of actions should not be surprising. The interactions in the Attain Document series focused on how American actions would be observed both by the Libyans and by local friends and neutrals. Therefore, we would expect to see commanders pay a great deal of attention to what those observers would see and thus, to not only *what* U.S. forces did, but *how*. Their concern with the what and how becomes even more apparent as we break the two terms into the component attributes we derived from looking at similar crises in the Middle East.

Focus

The "what" of the American operations, a Freedom of Navigation operation in force, set the framework not only for what was to be accomplished militarily, but also for how the action would be explained politically and diplomatically. At the military-strategic and geo-strategic level, this focus offered a way of "taking the moral high ground" and forcing the Libyans either to accept the lesson offered by the maneuvers or to become the aggressor. Moreover, by conducting the operations at sea, the effects of any Libyan propaganda that sought to exploit the civilian casualties of any combat that might ensue were very limited. At the operational level, this focus enabled the commander to play to one of the greatest strengths of the battle group (its defense in depth) and to force the Libyans to come out to challenge the United States in the face of that strength. Finally, at the tactical level, it narrowed the range of likely Libyan actions to the point that they could be roughly anticipated.

Forces

The heavy reliance on sea-based forces during the Attain Document operations took advantage both of the power of the Battle Force and of the international status of the high seas. The power of the force meant that it could take on Libyan forces largely unaided, but the real key was the fact that it could legitimately operate immediately off the Libyan coast. The international status of the seas also meant that, in contrast to the difficulties experienced in getting F-111s from European bases to the target area during the later El Dorado Canyon operations, no over-flight permission was required for the Battle Force's air operations. Further, once at sea, the Battle Force could be sustained off the Libyan coast without resort to land bases. This relative independence removed any Libyan potential to bring political or economic pressure to bear on a U.S. ally to curtail the American action, yet posed a potent threat that could not be ignored, but that could be applied at will in response to any untoward Libyan action.

Scale

The question of scale was probably most apparent in the reinforcement of the Sixth Fleet both before and during Attain Document. This was one of the first concerns of the White House and of the Theater Command when the operation was first outlined on January 7, 1986. It was clearly seen by President Reagan as one element of teaching al-Qadhafi that he could not support anti-American terrorists without risking an overwhelming retribution.[37] From the perspective of the Battle Force Commander, the reinforcements served not only to help cow a Libyan opposition, but also in a more practical way by increasing the number of days that the force could sustain heavy, round-the-clock air operations (virtually indefinitely with three carriers). Finally, the impact of the scale at the tactical level likely grew from the realization of Libyan pilots that any American aircraft they engaged in one patrol area were surrounded by other American aircraft in adjacent patrol areas that could swiftly be brought into the fray.

Scope

The combat air patrols in Attain Document covered an offshore international sea area that stretched along about two-thirds of the Libyan coastline. From the White House perspective, this span and the obvious ability to extend it further, lent further credence to an implied American threat to respond forcefully to any further Libyan-backed terrorism at a time and place of our choosing. From the operational and tactical perspective, the span of the

Battle Force operations coupled with its defense presented the Libyan military with a challenge that they knew they could not handle and in which Libyan forces stood to be overwhelmed, no matter where they tried to attack.

Similarly, the operational scope of the American forces applied did not offer the Libyans any obvious exploitable niche. The Americans were clearly superior in the air, at sea, and under the sea even though the Libyans had some capability in each of these areas. From the perspective of the White House and the Theater Command, this meant that they could probably count on the Libyans knowing that they would not be able to win any engagement, and that American forces would likely win it handily. From the perspective of the operational commander, this breadth of capabilities translated into a list of options for Battle Force responses to possible Libyan actions, and thus into a flexibility to adapt to the exigencies of a rapidly changing crisis interaction.

Timing

The speed of action and reaction was reflected in two very different ways. At the operational level, there was the Battle Force Commander's concern that any Libyan action against the force be met promptly and proportionately, the "Washington Post factor." At the national level, however, the concern was not only with responding to any Libyan provocation, but also to ensuring that the timing of American actions in various arenas be coordinated. Thus, while the response to any Libyan attack needed to be immediate, the White House also preferred to postpone any such encounter until after American citizens had been evacuated from Libya, and economic and diplomatic efforts had been given a chance to work.[38]

The 3-month duration of the Battle Force operation certainly conveyed the notion that the U.S. threat was not going to go away, but could be sustained as long as necessary. It also enabled the White House to complement the ongoing and time-consuming American economic and diplomatic efforts with a visible military option that could be exercised if diplomacy and economics failed.

As this latter point implies, the ability of the Battle Force to conduct sustained operations also enabled its actions and postures to be synchronized with U.S. activities in other arenas with very different timelines so as to optimize the impact on the Libyans. A different form of this synchronization was reflected at the operational and tactical level, both in the rapid intercepts of Libyan aircraft challenging the Force during Attain Document I and II and in the response to the Libyan missile firings in Attain Document III. In the latter case, this synchronization involved one group of aircraft exciting the enemy missile batteries to activate their radars so that other aircraft could fire anti-radiation missiles to destroy them.

Visibility

From the perspective of the White House, the whole purpose of Attain Document was that the operations be observed by the Libyans and affect their behavior, specifically the support for anti-American terrorists. Once the Saratoga battle group returned to the Mediterranean Sea, therefore, no secret was made of the fact that the FON operation was being conducted in precisely the area to be denied by the "line of death." Indeed, the intention to operate in the area was published as notices to airmen and mariners for each operation in the series. For the Battle Force Commander, visibility was a mixed problem. Combat air patrol stations were established with the full recognition that they could be seen by Libyan air defense radars that would then report the scale and scope of American activity. It was also assumed that the Libyan Intelligence would be aware of the numbers of surface ships in the American force. However, any Libyan reconnaissance aircraft that approached the surface ships to observe them at close range might equally have posed a threat as a suicide bomber intent on causing major damage to a carrier and a major blow for Libyan propaganda. Therefore, a balance had to be struck between what was shown and what was made less visible.

Effects

In the Attain Document series of operations, the United States set out to produce a strategic-level psychological objective, the alteration of Libyan behavior with regard to terrorism. To do that, it first relied on a mix of psychological effects. We can clearly distinguish an element of passive foreclosure in the effort to convince the Libyans that any further support to terrorism would bring an

American military response that the Libyan military would be unable to handle or mitigate. We can also distinguish an element of active foreclosure in the handling of the Libyan air probes during Attain Document I and II. Each time the Battle Force was challenged, the challenger was out-maneuvered and driven off, with each such event reinforcing in the Libyans a mental model that they would lose in any such confrontation and thus also reinforcing passive foreclosure. We can perhaps read psychological attrition into the Libyan Air Force's failure to engage during the actual penetration of the line of death in Attain Document III, as well as in the ultimate outcome of the operations: the cessation of Libyan support to terrorists.

The shock and chaos psychological effects in this case, however, appear to have resulted more from the physical effects the United States inflicted first in the engagements of March 24-5, 1986, and in the El Dorado Canyon strikes less than a month later. Even though the Libyans obviously anticipated that there was a good probability of an American reaction if they fired a missile at a U.S. aircraft, there was considerable confusion and perhaps shock on the Libyan side after the Battle Force's strikes began. Indeed, this was most evident in the almost haphazard reactions of Libyan missile boats in the Gulf of Sidra. However, the greater shock appears to have resulted from the El Dorado Canyon strikes, particularly as some of the bombs fell close to al-Qadhafi's own residence.

Cascades and Feedback

The primary cascade of concern to decisionmakers in Attain Document was that a series of physical actions and the psychological effects would produce a change in Libya's behavior.

Direct Effects

The direct physical effects were visibly of two types, damage and maneuvers.

The physical damage inflicted in Attain Document III and in El Dorado Canyon differed somewhat as to the direct effect intended and the type of damage assessment required as direct feedback. In Attain Document III, the targets were operational level military targets struck in a limited response to Libyan hostile actions and held little prospect of including civilian casualties. In the El Dorado Canyon, they were strategic level targets chosen at the White House and Joint Staff level to produce an immediate impact on the Libyan leadership's decisionmaking. In both cases, the bomb damage assessment was immediate and sufficient to ascertain that the direct effect had indeed been achieved. However, in the case of El Dorado Canyon, which bore a far greater potential for civilian casualties and thus for creating a cascade of negative psychological effects, the strategic level damage assessment emphasized the targets that might have been unintentionally struck and what civilian casualties might have been involved.

Maneuvers offered a considerable range of possibilities, particularly to the degree that they could be exercised in a terrain-free international environment. This freedom gave Battle Force maneuvers three axes along which actions could be varied for greatest impact.

- First, the size and composition of the force might be changed to emphasize the scale and scope of the threat to be implied or supported. This was clearly evident in the reinforcement of the fleet and, in El Dorado Canyon, by the addition of Air Force bombers.

- Second, the activities of the force could be varied to increase or decrease the level of the implied or actual threat. To be sure, in the succession of Attain Document operations, periods of intense operations off Libya alternated with port visits and more routine fleet operations. However, within the operations themselves there was a gradual ratcheting up of pressure as more patrol stations were manned.

- Third, the forces might be moved toward or away from the area of the crisis. In this case, air combat patrol stations were moved ever closer to the "line of death," and then in Attain Document III, the patrol stations were established well south of the line in full view of the Libyans.

The drawback with maneuvers was detecting and measuring the direct effect upon observers. The Battle Force could and did monitor both the incidence and timing of Libyan air probes and the immediate behavior of Libyan forces on a day-to-day, engagement-to-engagement basis. The air probes provided an indication that the Battle Force presence, rough numbers, and levels of activity were being reported up the Libyan chain of command. Likewise, the performance of the Libyan aircraft involved in the engagements provided some index of the effect of the interactions at the tactical level. Each of these factors was reported up the Battle Force's own chain of command.

Indirect Effects

The key element in the entire Attain Document and El Dorado Canyon operations was the cascade of indirect effects that the United States was attempting to create and those that it was trying to avoid creating.

In its targeting effort, the primary American concern was not with potential cascades of physical effects. Indeed, the indirect physical effects sought from Attain Document were very limited. The radars on Libyan surface-to-air missile batteries were destroyed to produce one obvious cascade, to incapacitate any Libyan efforts to acquire and fire upon American aircraft in the Gulf of Sidra, and this could be readily tracked in the performance of the Libyan air defense system subsequent to the attack. Since the strikes were to be a proportionate response to Libyan hostile actions, they represented no real effort to set in motion a chain of physical effects that might destroy or incapacitate significant proportions of Libyan military and/or economic systems. Such cascades would have been more in keeping with the large-scale response envisioned in the Prairie Fire contingency operations, which were not executed. It is worth noting that, in the later El Dorado Canyon planning, targets that might have yielded a cascade of economic effects were deliberately excluded in part because of two cascades of negative indirect psychological effects that could have resulted, one in the Libyan population and one among those of America's European allies who were heavily invested in Libya.[39]

The real focus of Attain Document was rather on the cascade of indirect psychological effects that might be set in motion. This was the case both in the initial Battle Force operations in the Gulf of Sidra and in the air strikes in response to the Libyan attack on the American forces in the Gulf. And, it was equally the case in the El Dorado Canyon response to the terrorist bombing in Berlin. These cascades could be identified at all levels.

The simplest indirect psychological effect sought was at the tactical and operational levels. There it was hoped that the drubbing given to the Libyan Air Force in Attain Documents I and II would forestall any Libyan attempt at a large-scale air raid against the Battle Force during the Attain Document III operations in the "zone of death."[40] By succeeding in this effort, the Battle Force in essence reduced the scope of probable Libyan actions and lessened the risks of both tactical and operational surprise.

The Battle Force Commander's problem in this regard was simpler than that at the military-strategic and White House levels. The question was not only one of creating the right cascade of indirect psychological effects to change Libyan behavior, but equally sending a message to other state sponsors of terrorism, especially to Syria and the Iranian hard-liners who had been supporting the Hizballah attacks of the preceding 3 years. Further complicating the problem at this level was the need to avoid creating undesired cascades of negative psychological effects among area neutrals, regional friends, and European allies. These multiple and complex concerns were probably somewhat assuaged by the measured nature of the Battle Force responses proposed to deal with a limited Libyan action. However, in the case of the larger responses of Prairie Fire and El Dorado Canyon, they mandated a closer monitoring of the planning and execution simply because the potential for unwanted indirect psychological effects was much greater.

The feedback required to support the assessment of indirect effects was considerably more complicated than the measurement of bomb damage assessment.

At the operational level, the Battle Force could and did monitor the behavior of Libyan pilots and the Libyan Air Defense System during the numerous interactions of Attain Document I and II. However, jumping from that feedback to assessing whether or not the Libyan Air Force would launch a mass attack on the Battle Force during Attain Document III required something more. It demanded that the impressions of Libyan pilot performance be combined with the prior knowledge of the commander and planners and the mental models built on experience and an understanding of the situation and how it appeared to be evolving. Even then, as the continued possibility of an air attack indicated, there could be no certainty.

Similarly, for feedback, the White House closely monitored any changes in Libyan government behavior following the initiation of Attain Document I, but had little to indicate any direct link between those U.S. military actions and overall Libyan conduct. Further, it remained very much a question up until the time that Attain Document III was initiated whether the combined political and economic measures might also be shaping that conduct. This is to say that, with the resources of the entire U.S. intelligence community involved, there was still insufficient feedback to produce certainty.

This continued to be true in the wake of the Attain Document III strikes against the Libyan Air Defense System and Navy. Despite vocal Libyan outrage, there was no firm indication whether al-Qadhafi's behavior would change or whether he would simply choose a new niche within which to respond. When terrorists linked to Libya bombed the Berlin disco 2 weeks later, it was obvious that the pressures still had not succeeded in producing the desired behavior, even though they had produced some change in that behavior.

Finally, it should be noted that, even in the aftermath of the El Dorado Canyon bombing, the feedback as to a change in Libyan conduct was not conclusive. The public stance became still more circumspect, but the terrorist operation against the Pan American flight over Lockerbie, Scotland indicated that al-Qadhafi had not ended his search for other niches to exploit.

Putting It Together

The picture of effects-based operations that emerges from the Attain Document example is above all one of complex coordination requirements from one level to the next, across multiple arenas, and over time. The core challenge in planning and executing these effects-based operations, especially from the level of the White House and Joint Staff/Theater Commander level, was to ensure that all the actions taken across this diverse spectrum reinforced the overall effect sought. This meant that planners at all levels needed to deconflict those actions that might negate each other or might confuse friends, foes, and neutrals as to American intentions, and they had to somehow avoid creating a cascade of psychological effects that was the opposite of what was sought.[41]

Amid this complexity, however, we can once again see the rule set and definitions borne out. Decisionmakers clearly thought in terms of actions rather than simply of targets, and they clearly considered those actions to have dimensions that included both the *what* and *how* of the military operations. Indeed, the care given to the targeting in contingency operations underlines the degree to which even the targets themselves were defined in such action terms, rather in the simpler terms of physical attrition. In the actions of the decisionmakers, we can see the basic rules at work: the effects created are both physical and psychological in nature, cumulative and interrelated, across four different levels of command and three arenas.

Perhaps we can see how these factors figured in the planning and execution of an effects-based operation by operational commanders, in this case, Vice Admiral Kelso, the Commander of the U.S. Sixth Fleet, and Rear Admiral Jeremiah, the Commander of the Battle Force Sixth Fleet. In no way did these commanders have all of the feedback that they needed and in no way were they able to eliminate the uncertainties of a complex operational problem. Rather, they improvised and innovated, and then made do with what was available.

---

[1]Since the author was assigned to the Battle Force Sixth Fleet staff as the relieving Assistant Chief of Staff for Intelligence and actively participated in the planning and execution of the Attain Document series, the 1986 Libyan Operations offer the advantage of permitting a firsthand account of the operation from the level of the operational commander.
See also: Stanik, Joseph T. "Swift and Effective Retribution." *The United States Sixth Fleet and the Confrontation with Qaddafi*. Washington, DC; Naval Historical Center. 1996.
[2]Reagan, Ronald. *An American Life*. Norwalk, Connecticut. 1990. pp. 489-499.
[3]Reagan, p. 496.
[4]The hijackers turned themselves in to Egyptian authorities, but when they were being flown out of Egypt, they were intercepted by U.S. Navy aircraft and forced down in Italy where the men were taken into custody. Ironically, the U.S. aircraft that intercepted the hijackers came from the same carrier that was later to serve as the Battle Force flagship for the Attain Document Operations.
[5]Reagan, p. 511.
[6]The USS *Saratoga* carrier battle group, which had been

operating in the Indian Ocean, had been pulled back to the Mediterranean Sea to reinforce the *Coral Sea* carrier battle group and had transited the Suez Canal a few days earlier.

[7]President Reagan's comment here was, "If Mr. Qaddafi decides not to push another terrorist act, okay, we've been successful with our implied threat. If on the other hand he takes this for weakness and does loose another one, we will have targets in mind and instantly respond with a hell of a punch."

Reagan, p. 515.

[8]In 1986, the most obvious targets would have been terrorist bases in Libya, but the physical destruction of a terrorist camp promised to be little more than a relatively minor setback. The camps, if indeed they were still in use, could be replaced. Thus, the major impact on future operations would depend largely on whether the terrorists themselves were killed during the attack, a feat of timing and intelligence prediction that was unlikely. In addition, even if the terrorists were killed, it would be only a matter of time before more candidates were recruited and the process began anew.

Accordingly, the real goal of any operation was not destruction of terrorist capabilities as such, but a change of Libyan behavior that would deny terrorists any bases or support at all. To this end, any strike package had to hold at risk something that mattered to Libya, rather than to the terrorists. Questions of what targets and what scale of destruction would be needed to this end became central issues of the targeting debate that endured through the Prairie Fire contingency strike planning during the first 3 months of 1986. These debates concluded with the El Dorado Canyon strikes by Air Force and Navy aircraft in April 1986.

[9]In actuality, the only NCA intervention in executing the approved option was a query from the White House shortly after the missile firing to ascertain that the Battle Force Commander and Commander Sixth Fleet still intended to execute the agreed course of action, and a request that the White House be notified as soon as this was done.

[10]As outlined in Chapter 5, these are:

Actions create effects.

Effects are cumulative.

Any interaction will affect both active and passive observers.

Effects can occur nearly simultaneously in multiple dimensions.

All effects at each level and in each arena are interrelated.

Effects are both physical and psychological in nature.

[11]Although the bulk of the U.S. forces involved in the Attain

Document series were the U.S. Navy units assigned to the Battle Force U.S. Sixth Fleet, U.S. Air Force reconnaissance aircraft provided much needed support.

[12]Such tactical level interactions took time and might involve a succession of maneuvers and counter-maneuvers by the aircraft involved and, thus, a succession of tactical OODA loop type interactions each of which might be considered an action-reaction cycle. However, for our purposes here, the entire intercept and subsequent maneuvers will be taken as one tactical action-reaction cycle

[13]A shootdown of a Libyan aircraft might have resulted in the cessation of the Attain Document Operation before the desired effect on Libyan behavior had been achieved.

[14]This could have been an aircraft that opened fire, or it could have been either a Libyan aircraft that made a dash toward the fleet or an American aircraft that made a dash for the Libyan coast.

[15]It was surmised, for example, that the Libyan radars would be able to detect the aircraft manning most of the combat air patrol stations, but that they would be unable to detect the movements of the ships north of the "line of death" and that they similarly would not be able to detect the movements of any submarines.

[16]Although the Battle Force Commander could and occasionally did intervene in a given ongoing interaction, such intervention was almost invariably to contribute a situational awareness that was beyond the perspective of the aerial dogfight, rather than to direct the engagement.

[17]This process was repeated shortly before Attain Document III in March 1986 when another carrier battle group with USS *America* joined the Attain Document force bringing the total force to three groups.

[18]That is, those surveillance platforms that were part of the Battle Force or could be launched from it, and those platforms that may have operated from shore bases but were under the direct control of the Battle Force Commander.

[19]The land-based surveillance assets did not participate in these commanders' conferences. That fault in the process was remedied in the operations of 1987 when both Air Force and Navy land-based surveillance commanders were brought out to the Battle Force flagship for extended discussions before the start of the operation.

[20]This was largely the case in the Prairie Fire contingency planning that was to go into effect in the event of a large-scale Libyan attack on the Battle Force. For various reasons that will be discussed later, this was also the case in the El Dorado

Canyon operations that occurred in April 1986.

[21]Stanik, p. 16.

[22]That is to say, Libya could not stop the action by making threats to those Mediterranean nations whose bases might be used to support it as it might have been able to do in the case of any sustained American land-based strike operation.

[23]Although warship transits of the Suez Canal are guaranteed by treaty, given the circumstances and obvious destination of the battle group, Egypt had to take extraordinary security measures along the banks of the canal in order to ensure safe passage.

[24]In fact, the *America* group was on its routine deployment cycle and the concentration in force was achieved by holding the *Saratoga* group that had been scheduled to leave for home on station in the Mediterranean for several weeks beyond its normal departure date.

[25]Sobel. *Israel.* p. 106.

[26]These consisted of detailed lists of targets that were updated throughout the course of the first two Attain Document Operations. Under standard U.S. Navy practice, the missions to destroy the targets were then planned by the air crews that would fly the actual mission.

[27]To ensure that the exercise of these ROE proceeded smoothly and that both the Fleet and Battle Force Commanders were proceeding from the same understanding of the developing situation, VADM Kelso transferred his flag to the Saratoga for the critical first stage of the Attain Document III Operation and sat next to RADM Jeremiah in Saratoga's Flag Plot. In this situation, the actual grant of the ROE to the Battle Force Commander consisted of a glance toward the Fleet Commander and an affirmative nod. The two had an identical appreciation of the situation and what was required to the point that no further conversation was needed.

[28]Excluded here are the ground forces that would have been inapplicable short of an American invasion. The Libyans also had old Foxtrot-class Soviet submarines that could potentially have been deployed against the Battle Force, but the ability of these to get underway much less to submerge was questionable.

[29]Terrorist attacks, of course, remained a possibility, but as the subsequent attack on an American frequented disco in Berlin and upon a Pan American airliner over Scotland indicate, even the terrorism option was of only limited use against a relatively hard military target such as a protected base and of even less use against defended ships at sea.

[30]Reagan, pp. 515ff.

[31]Reagan, p. 515.

[32]The White House estimated that there were some 1,000 American citizens, mostly oil workers, in Libya as of the beginning of 1986 and feared that they would become hostages just as soon as any military operation began to unfold. It became essential to get them out of Libya before any offensive operation could be undertaken.
Reagan, pp. 511 and 515.

[33]In fact, there were airline routes through the area that had to be continuously monitored as to ensure that no danger was posed. Additionally, warning of American live-fire operations area in the Gulf of Sidra was published in notices to airmen and mariners to further reduce civilian traffic.

[34]Reagan, p. 518.

[35]These codified and numbered rules of engagement define what actions a commander may or may not take under given sets of circumstances. Some of these ROE are routinely delegated to local commanders, while others, especially permission to conduct offensive operations of any sort, are tightly controlled by national authorities. At their core, the ROE constitute political rather military guidance and consequently vary from one country to the next. In the case of the combined ROE used for NATO operations, a decision to grant particular ROEs can involve lengthy political negotiations before a consensus can be reached.

[36]In the Libya operations, some ROEs would have been delegated to the Battle Force Commander and others to his immediate superior, the Commander of the Sixth Fleet. However still others, would have been retained by the National Command Authority, i.e. the President and the Secretary of Defense.

[37]Reagan, p. 515.

[38]Stanik, p. 15.

[39]Stanik, p. 33.

[40]The possibility of such an attack was indeed addressed as one of the likely Libyan responses to a crossing of the "line of death." It had been planned as a contingency and had been one of the action-reaction options that were proposed to higher command. However, at least in part due to the belief that the air actions in Attain Document I and II would discourage such an attempt, that contingency was placed lower on the list. This proved to be a good decision and the actions taken by the Libyans were in fact numbers one and two on the contingency list: surface-to-air missile firings; and attacks by anti-ship missile patrol boats.

[41]The 1962 Cuban Missile Crisis presents a good example of

both dimensions of this problem. On the one hand, the U.S. military often failed to understand that their actions were being used by President Kennedy as a means of signaling American intent. Under such circumstances, normal military precautions such as raising the DEFCON level might either confuse the Soviets or create an effect contradictory to what the NCA sought. On the other hand, the stark discrepancies between the communications from General Secretary Khrushchev and the later official Soviet position both confused and alarmed the American NCA, quite the opposite of what Khrushchev intended.

Kennedy, Robert F. *Thirteen Days.* p. 98ff.

CHAPTER 11

Network-Centric Contributions to Effects-Based Operations: Options, Agility, Coordination, and Knowledge Mobilization

In the introduction to this book, we recounted Admiral Boorda's lament that "it sure would be nice if we had some clear idea what it was we were trying to do" with the new technologies and capabilities of the Information Age before we buy them. In response, we proposed that there were three different levels of potential improvement in military effectiveness to be derived from new technologies. The most basic level of improvement accrued from

501

simply applying the new technologies to existing military doctrine, organization, and concepts, much as Britain and France had done with tanks, aircraft, and radios during the years before World War II. A second, greater level was to be attained by applying the technologies to *new* doctrine, organization, and warfare concepts conceived to exploit the new technologies, as the Germans had done in creating the blitzkrieg and as we are hoping to do with the introduction of network-centric operations. Finally, we postulated that a third and still greater increase could come from applying our newfound network-centric military level of improvement to effects-based operations that were focused on the human behavioral dimension of conflict. In essence, we treated network-centric operations as a means to an end, a tool for better implementation of the longstanding ideas of effects-based operations. Even more than this, we also pointed to effects-based operations as the conceptual gateway to applying the new network-centric capabilities to military operations short of combat in everything from deterrence to crisis response, exactly the areas of concern in building a post-September 11th security regime.

The concept of effects-based operations that we have outlined in this book is based on two ideas:

- First, as the name *effects-based* implies, effects-based operations are about ends rather than means. They focus upon the outcomes that might be obtained by military actions in concert with other elements of national power and upon choosing the most expeditious and efficient way of obtaining these outcomes at any level. The conduct of effects-based operations, therefore, demands that we reason backwards from the outcome we desire to the set of actions that might produce that result.

Since these outcomes are dynamic and can vary throughout the course of an interaction, the planning and execution of effects-based operations must be a dynamic, interactive process in which we constantly assess how each new action moves us toward the desired overall objective of the operation at each level. In this effects-based context, more efficient destruction means very little unless it somehow contributes to achieving the desired outcome. Indeed, as a number of the examples in preceding chapters attest, "kinetic solutions" of any kind may be the exact antithesis of the outcome we seek.

- Second, the focus of effects-based operations is on human behavior and specifically on the use of military operations to shape that behavior. To this end, effects-based operations constitute a human-centric, stimulus and response approach to military operations. Such an approach strikes at the heart of the battlefield problem. After all, it is this will of an opponent to fight and his ability to do so coherently and effectively that is the true determinant of victory. Moreover, since the human dimension is the most nonlinear aspect of any battle, effects-based operations potentially offer the greatest impact per unit of force applied and thus, the greatest operational efficiency.

This human-centered, stimulus and response approach is especially important in dealing with the problems of the post-September 11th security environment because it provides a framework for applying military power short of combat to deter attacks or to contain conflict. It also forces us to consider military actions in the context of the overall national power being applied, and as they affect allies, neutrals, and foes.

Neither of these ideas is new. The concepts are as much a part of Clausewitz's writings 200 years ago as they are of Sun Tzu's more than 2,500 years ago.[1] Their practical application can be seen as easily in Caesar's commentaries on the Gallic wars as it can be in the examples cited in this book. Thus, the real issue in moving from network-centric operations to effects-based operations is how we might best use the concepts and technologies of a network-centric transformation to carry out a classic effects-based approach to military operations in a new and better way.

As this implies, the process of applying network-centric innovations to effects-based operations is not one that hangs on the creation of some future technology or decision aid about which we can now only dream. The examples we have used amply underline the fact that U.S. military forces have been conducting effects-based crisis response operations focused on influencing the behavior of observers for a half-century and more. They are doing so now in Afghanistan and elsewhere even as this book is being written. And, as is all too apparent in the wake of September 11th, they will be called upon to do so again and again in the future.

Our challenge, therefore, is to apply the network-centric capabilities of today to the effects-based operations of today; and to optimize the emerging network-centric thinking and capabilities for the effects-based operations of the future. However, the starting point for meeting this challenge lies in a better definition of what network-centric operations bring to effects-based operations.

In laying out a basic concept of effects-based operations, we have made frequent references to network-centric thinking and capabilities as an enabler. We now need to draw some more specific connections and to ask two pointed questions. Just what do Network Centric Warfare and network-centric operations (with all of the thinking and capabilities they imply) bring to effects-based operations? And equally important, what more do we need to build into our network-centric thinking and capabilities if we are to apply our concept of effects-based operations to the post-September 11th security environment?

If we accept that some network-centric concepts have already been adapted in ad hoc ways to real-world operations, then we should be able to identify the critical functional elements involved in network-centric effects-based operations, understand better how the network-centric capabilities contribute, and identify where they must do more.

Operations Off Libya, 1987

One particularly useful example in this regard is the little known, low-key sequel to the 1986 Attain Document I, II, and III and El Dorado Canyon Operations that we examined in the previous chapter. Just as in the original Attain Document series, these new FON operations took place in the international waters of the Gulf of Sidra off the Libyan coast, but in this case, the operations occurred over a year later in September and October of 1987.[2] This 1987 sequel is valuable as an example because it involved the same battle group with the same carrier, same air wing, and same staff that had planned and executed the original Attain Document series of operations and that had participated in the El Dorado Canyon contingency planning.[3] Thus, this example contains important constants, but from the network-centric perspective, also has two important differences. First, the introduction of a digital display (the Joint On-line Tactical System or JOTS) linked and integrated force data, data from organic sensors, and data from theater and national sources. Second, the Attain Document/El Dorado Canyon "lessons learned" were applied to the preparation and execution of a new operation with similar forces under similar conditions.

Like Attain Document III, the 1987 Freedom of Navigation operation involved a three-battle group[4] Battle Force of the U.S. Sixth Fleet directed to conduct operations in the Gulf of Sidra (see Figure 73). In the 1987 operation, the objective was similar, to reinforce the lessons and mental models created

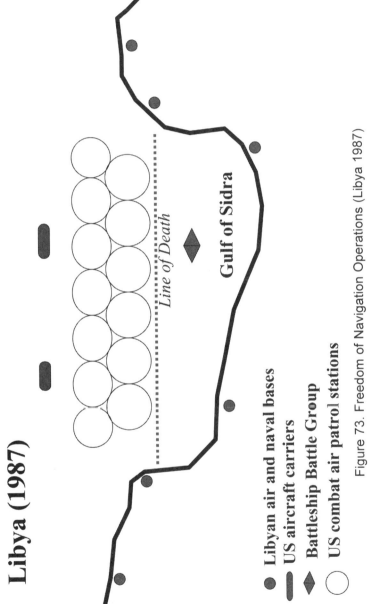

Figure 73. Freedom of Navigation Operations (Libya 1987)

by the 1986 Attain Document and El Dorado Canyon Operations. This is to say that, without the urgency wrought by the Libyan-sponsored terrorist bombings in 1985 and 1986, the effect to be achieved by the Battle Force in the 1987 action was roughly the same as it had been in Attain Document.

The new operations involved large-scale air operations in the Gulf, as had the Attain Document series, and a Surface Action Group penetration of Colonel al-Qadhafi's vaunted "line of death." Unlike Attain Document, however, this Surface Action Group was in fact a Battleship Battle Group under the Commander of the U.S. Sixth Fleet, which conducted extended operations in the area south of the line.

The effects-based planning for the new operations also proceeded in much the same fashion that it had for the original Attain Document series. Again, the objective was to shape future Libyan behavior by reinforcing not only the international character of the waters of the Gulf of Sidra, but also the fact that the United States remained ready and able to strike again in response to any further Libyan-sponsored terrorist activity. Again, the Battle Force planning effort assessed the most likely potential Libyan actions in response to specific aspects of the operations and then drew up a series of "if-then" contingency plans for likely Libyan actions and reactions.

As in the 1987 operations, combat air patrols were set up in areas north of the "line of death" and then were progressively moved southward until they were well into the "denied" area, although still outside Libyan territorial airspace and waters. Unlike the Attain Document Operations, however, these air operations were not challenged by the Libyan Air Force nor were anti-aircraft missiles fired at U.S. aircraft participating in the operation. Finally, unlike Attain Document III, the operations were conducted without incident. No missiles were fired at U.S. aircraft and no missile patrol boats attempted to intercept surface units in the Gulf of Sidra.

1987: Movement Toward Network-Centric Operations

While the attempt to create shared situational awareness using the Joint On-Line Tactical System by no means approached the awareness foreseen for future network-centric operations, it did reflect a direct application of network-centric solutions to the tactical and operational level problems presented by Attain Document. These solutions took the forms of the JOTS itself and the tactics, techniques, and procedures developed for using the information provided.

In the 1987 operations, JOTS provided a medium for linking together the sensors that were organic to the Battle Force, as well as displaying positions and movement of military forces and neutrals, similar to the outline in the Chapter 4 diagram of the cognitive cycle (see Figure 74). This Battle Force JOTS picture covered not only the immediate area of the operation, but much of the central Mediterranean Sea and more importantly, the air corridors

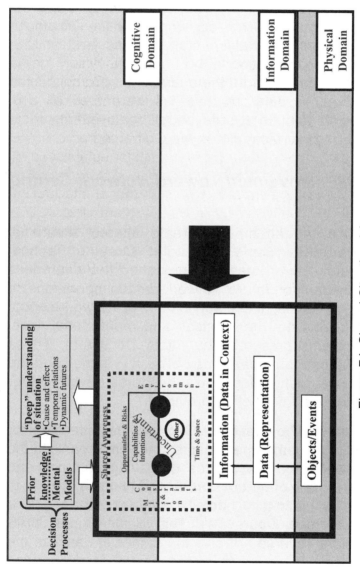

Figure 74. Shared Situational Awareness

traversing the operations area. The JOTS also provided a medium for inserting positional data from both Air Force and Navy theater reconnaissance assets. Furthermore, as in the Attain Document operations, the Battle Force drew upon the nodal intelligence network of the Navy's Ocean Surveillance Information System (OSIS). This intelligence data could be fed into the JOTS and then displayed not only in the flagship's Flag Plot, but also in similar displays on all units in the Battle Force.[5] Finally, networks were further established to link the Battle Force intelligence plot to national overhead sensors and area operational intelligence analysts.[6] Some of this data was entered into JOTS. The result was a JOTS-centered shared situational awareness that, although imperfect by current and future standards, did extend across the Battle Force and provide the basis for developing a shared understanding of the emerging operational situation and for coordinated operations by the component commands.

However, this linkage of hardware and information flows was only a relatively small part of the problem. The Battle Force Commander, then-Rear Admiral J.M. Boorda, was also deeply concerned with how the new situational awareness would be used by the force. His concern was focused on the organization of command responsibilities and the fashioning of the tactics, techniques, and procedures best suited to exploiting the new information flow.

Command Responsibilities

Under the Combined Warfare Commander (CWC) concept used by the Navy in both Libyan operations, the Battle Force Commander decentralized the command structure into a series of subordinate warfare commanders, each of whom was responsible for a given warfare problem (e.g. air warfare, surface warfare). The introduction of JOTS meant that the Battle Force/Joint Task Force Commander and each of the warfare commanders could work from the same picture, a shared situational awareness that gave all parties the confidence to adopt a modest form of self-synchronization. In this context, Boorda used the situational awareness provided by JOTS to operate in something approaching a command by negation mode. Within the constraints of command intent and the rules of engagement, warfare commanders could take the initiative in acting but with any action subject to being countermanded by the Battle Force Commander if necessary.[7] While the Commander could readily revert to direct control whenever an issue of particular concern arose, the system left him free to concentrate his attention on the most pressing aspects of the overall situation while the warfare commanders handled the less pressing cases.

To support this decentralization, Admiral Boorda was careful to build a common understanding of command intent. In this case, not only did he discuss his plans and assumptions in detail with each of the unit commanders, but he also took the care to conduct reciprocal "familiarization" visits with the crews of both Navy and Air Force theater reconnaissance assets. The crews of these assets would therefore understand his plans and intent in the operations, and he, his staff, and the warfare commanders could understand the capabilities and constraints under which the reconnaissance assets themselves were operating.

To this end as well, Admiral Boorda also conducted a series of ROE exercises that posed scenario questions to be answered by an officer in each unit in the battle force, with the solutions personally reviewed by the Admiral himself. Although the exercises provided critical training for all concerned, they also provided Admiral Boorda with an index of just how well the command intent was understood and what he could expect from his subordinates when the operation off Libya actually began.

Organization, Tactics, Techniques, and Procedures

Admiral Boorda was also deeply concerned with how the organization, tactics, techniques, and procedures would operate using the new capability.[8] Every effort was made to move beyond the installation of new technology, to probe the way in which information was displayed and used, and to consider the human factors involved by comparing performance with the performance from the previous Attain Document operations.

The admiral mandated a series of exercises/ experiments that looked closely at the information flow within the ships of the *Saratoga* Battle Group to ensure that gains made in awareness capabilities external to the ship were not negated by an inability to move the information internally. In this series of "Intelligence Exercises," the Cruiser-Destroyer Group Eight/Battle Force intelligence staff tested 10 different ships over a 6-month period. In each case, in the context of an accelerating-pace scenario, some 90 to 100 simulated timed inputs of information were provided to seven different sensor and information nodes onboard the ship. The subsequent arrival of that piece of information in the hands of the Tactical Action Officer (TAO)[9] was noted and similarly timed. Ships could then be assessed as to the time delays involved in getting information to the TAO (if it did reach the TAO).[10] The results passed to the commanding officers and Admiral Boorda highlighted shortfalls in training and procedures for handling information and, in one case, uncovered the fact that a circuit for transmitting key information had never been connected when the ship was built.

Further, with Boorda's encouragement, his entire Flag Plot command center on the U.S.S. *Saratoga* was made into a sensitive intelligence space so as to ensure that the Flag TAO and all watch personnel would have continuous access to all available intelligence and sensitive information. To this end, the Battle Force watch staff was also extended to include a dedicated intelligence watch as part of each of the regular rotating watch sections so as to ensure that needed information passed freely.[11]

Results

In the end, the 1987 operations were not stressed to the degree that the Battle Force experienced in the 1986 operations. There was no combat with the Libyans, and Libyan behavior was marked by a sharp reduction in normal military activity. Nor was there the degree of national level interest that had accompanied the 1986 operations. Nevertheless, it was clear to those who had participated in both operations that the creation of a "network-centric architecture" and the revisions in procedures, doctrine, and organization had better equipped the 1987 Battle Force to handle any evolving situation in the effects-based FON operations. Indeed, the closer the Battle Force moved toward even a rudimentary form of network-centric operations, the better able it was to serve as a precise tool in effects-based operations.

1987: What More Was Needed?

The increased shared situational awareness and common understanding of command intent that had been developed across the Battle Force was imperfect and left considerable room for improvement, but it worked sufficiently well to deal with the tactical requirements of the 1987 operations. In fact, we can see in the architecture of the system and the procedures for its use an embryonic version of the capabilities we are seeking in network-centric operations. We can likewise see elements of self-synchronization and speed of command in the Battle Force actions during the operations. Moreover, the Battle Force's tactical picture could be monitored at higher levels of command and incorporated in their decisionmaking.

What more was needed? The underlying problem was that the system, for all of the efforts to improve it, remained configured to support linear attrition-based combat operations rather than effects-based operations requiring some form of "deep understanding" of a complex interaction in the cognitive domain. The situational awareness to which the JOTS and other information improvements had been applied was largely concentrated in the tactical arena. It focused on giving commanders a better and more comprehensive picture of the whereabouts and movements of their own forces, of Libyan forces, and of white traffic such as commercial craft and neutral military forces. All of this was very much necessary and a definite improvement over the grease pencils and display boards that had preceded JOTS, but it created an understanding that was largely at the tactical level of operations. Despite the improvements, what the system did not provide in 1987 was a way of assessing the larger, nontactical aspects of Libyan behavior and reporting on the impact of the Battle Force's actions were having on al-Qadhafi and the Libyan leadership at any given moment.

As Battle Force Commander, Admiral Boorda understood the effects-based dimension of the operation and had focused his thinking and planning on the behavioral objectives involved.[12] However, to support this thinking and planning, he and his staff needed something more than sensor-derived tactical information provided by JOTS. They needed a base of prior knowledge[13] and a deep understanding of what was going on in the Libyan decisionmaking process,[14] and that meant a different set of metrics, information flow, and knowledge/databases upon which the existing information infrastructure[15] was focused.

In the 1987 operations, as in those of 1986, the flow of information to support the effects-based aspects of the operation was largely ad hoc. Every bit of information available to the Battle Force that might have provided an indication of Libyan behavior (including wire service and radio reporting) was tapped and used,[16] as was the formal intelligence reporting provided by the national intelligence community and the Navy's Ocean Surveillance Information System.[17]

However, the OSIS system also offered the possibility of creating an ad hoc, on call, back channel, "old boy" network, *community of expertise* that permitted free and informal access to experts at multiple levels.[18] In essence, this informal community of expertise was composed of one vertical community and four lateral communities. The vertical element in the overall network revolved about a network of senior naval intelligence officers at each level. These officers were colleagues in a relatively small intelligence corps, each of whom commanded a section of the intelligence analysis capability, and each of whom had experience in battle group operations and in theater/national intelligence (see Figure 75). These participants included the Battle Force/JTF and Fleet Assistant

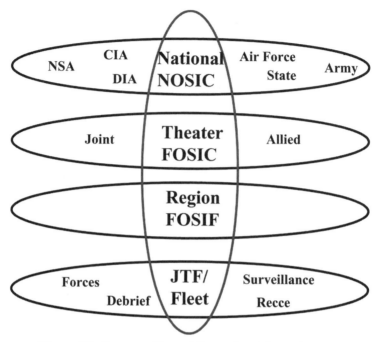

Figure 75. Communities of Expertise: Libya (1986-7)

Chiefs of Staff for Intelligence, the commander of the Fleet Ocean Surveillance Facility (FOSIF) supporting Navy Mediterranean operations, the Commander of the Fleet Ocean Surveillance Information Center (FOSIC) supporting the theater commander, and the Navy Ocean Surveillance Information Center (NOSIC). Each combined two very different experience bases, fleet operations and intelligence community operations, which enabled them to serve as interfaces that had a deep understanding of the limitations and needs of both sides. Each of these players also had a lateral network of experts who could be tapped for their thinking. At the FOSIF level, this network included all the analysts who were minutely following military activity in the Mediterranean Basin each day and who often had years of experience. At the FOSIC level, the informal lateral network extended into the joint theater intelligence structure and to Allied intelligence services. At the national level, the informal network extended directly to analysts in multiple intelligence agencies.

The vertical network operated on a pull-push basis. On the pull side, informal queries could be made directly to any level of the network, or a general but equally informal request for information might be addressed to one element that then would pulse the remainder of the network to obtain the necessary information.[19] On the push side, not only could the formal intelligence reporting be tailored to the specific needs outlined over the network, but also the experience base at each level permitted the identification and forwarding of any information not requested but deemed to be relevant.[20]

The lateral networks operated as ad hoc communities of expertise with analysts in an eclectic mix of fields and from a variety of agencies contacted to deal with a particular question or issue. The interplay among the analysts was often further enhanced by the fact that there had been frequent or even routine (but informal) analyst-to-analyst exchanges on subjects of interest in a manner that unconsciously mimicked academic communities.[21] The communities of expertise so created were evanescent. They came together to deal with a specific question and disappeared when the question was answered or transmuted into a different community of experts when different requirements for knowledge/expertise arose.

The underlying problem with this system lay not so much in the flexible organization of the network, which in fact permitted a largely unsanctioned flow of information and intelligence around the regimented structure of the intelligence community. Rather, the problem was both that the work-around had been necessary in the first place and that the information/knowledge focused on the adversary's behavior was not readily available through the formal reporting process. The latter problem was itself twofold. The data and information to support military operations in the cognitive domain was either not collected or not available in the military intelligence databases, and there was no ready way to contact outside experts to obtain additional inputs. The limitations were less those of technology than of organization, techniques, and procedures at levels above that of the Battle Force.

At the root of these limitations is the need for a new paradigm for shared situational awareness defined in effects-based terms.

Effects-Based Shared Situational Awareness

The lack of relevant effects-based feedback in the 1987 Libyan operation (despite the efforts to otherwise improve the situational awareness of the Battle Force) underscores a key point. The shared situational awareness required for effects-based operations is not the same as that required for the combat operations. Naturally, if forces are to be able to meet the minimum criterion for effects-based operations, that they be able to fight and win, they unquestionably will need this combat-focused shared situational awareness. But, that is not enough for effects-based operations. Those operations require a different focus and one that is in many ways considerably wider than the tactical and operational military picture. They require what we might term an *effects-based, shared situational awareness.*

Providing this effects-based situational awareness poses two major challenges for network-centric capabilities over and above those reflected in the creation of a tactical level situational awareness.

- First, in effects-based operations we must deal with human beings and their responses to the stimuli presented by our actions. That means that our awareness must somehow integrate large numbers of imprecise, often subjective data and information containing complex variables into a picture that includes all of the elements of the tactical and operational picture. Historically, this has been the function of experts, the community that both the 1986 and 1987 operations sought to tap informally.

- Second, because many of the inputs needed to fashion an effects-based awareness are imprecise, subjective, and meaningless without a context, we must also create and maintain a knowledge base to provide that context. As outlined in the Chapter 4 discussion of the cognitive cycle, this context knowledge appears in two forms. First is the knowledge required to predict how our actions will be perceived by the opponent and others, a context that includes the relationship between our own actions and those of other elements of national power. Second is the knowledge required to detect and assess feedback on the effects created by our actions and on how others are trying to shape our own behavior (see Figure 76).

Both of these elements were reflected in the Libyan operations of 1986 and 1987. However, we need to emphasize here that this requirement for effects-based awareness is not something restricted to Joint Task Force Commanders and above. It is also very much present at the tactical level. This was certainly evident in the judgments required of the pilots of the intercepting aircraft during the Attain Document Operations and of the pilots monitoring civilian airliners in 1987. But, it is also the case in a far wider range of tactical operations well beyond the Navy or airborne intercepts. For example, there are few operations as effects-based and knowledge-centric as a soldier on a peacekeeping patrol in Bosnia or Kosovo, or as the Special Forces fighting the Taliban in Afghanistan in 2001. The same problems of culture and language, of creating and using communities of expertise, and of tapping resources beyond a formal intelligence chain of command will apply to asymmetric warfare and peacekeeping operations elsewhere in the world.

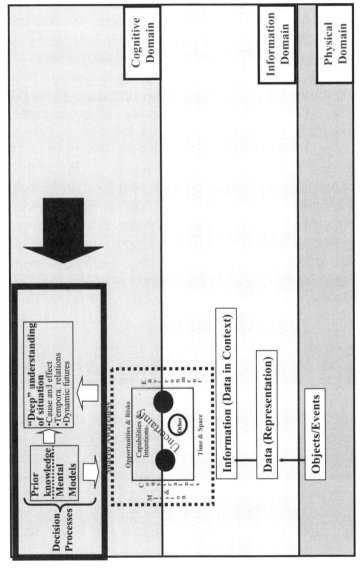

Figure 76. "Context" in the Cognitive Domain

Knowledge and Understanding

At the heart of the delineation between tactical/operational and effects-based situational awareness are the natures and relative roles of knowledge and understanding in that awareness. In order to operate successfully in the cognitive domain, we must understand the enemy, the friend, or the neutral. Such understanding requires more than data and information as to his location, direction of movement, and even current intentions. It requires that we know something of how the observer perceives and thinks,[22] and it requires that this knowledge of the observer has somehow been internalized by commanders as deep understanding. The knowledge required to support our effects-based actions falls into three categories: knowledge of the enemy (or observers); knowledge of ourselves; and knowledge of the situation.

Knowledge of the Enemy

The most obvious requirement is knowledge of the enemy. Clearly, if we want to orchestrate a set of actions to produce a particular kind of effect, we must have some notion of how the enemy is going to see that action, but this "seeing" has a double meaning. On the one hand, we must know the enemy surveillance and data collection capabilities well enough to determine what he is likely to observe of our action and what he will not. We must also know something of how he will perceive the stimulus he observes, what sense he is likely to make of it, and how he then might translate it into a response.

One aspect of this knowledge, the parameters and limitations of the physical domain, is relatively straightforward. For example, we can calculate what an air search radar will see because we can determine the detection radius using basic physics and geometry, and we routinely include this kind of data in our tactical level situational awareness. However, the problem can become considerably more subjective if we look at the information domain and all the other ways in which our actions might be communicated to targeted decisionmakers. For example, how is an action likely to be reported on CNN or in local media and which decisionmakers are likely to monitor these media? The variables here are numerous and not at all straightforward. We can speculate as to whether some decision aid based on extensive modeling and simulation might be developed, but the simpler answer is that we can rely on an expert with the necessary knowledge to frame the variables and provide an opinion as to what will be reported and how. This kind of knowledge and expertise mobilization was what was reflected in the ad hoc "old boy network" that arose in 1986 and 1987.

The cognitive domain question of how observers will perceive the reports of our action and how they will react to it is still more subjective. It implies that we must get into the mind of the opponent to see the action as he sees it. This is no small task and means that we again will have to rely on expert judgment on the part of a knowledgeable regional analyst and on the part of the local operational commander with expertise on the military dimension of his battlefield. This interface between regional and operational expertise was exemplified in Admiral Boorda's use of the back channel "old boy" intelligence network to support his decisionmaking during the 1987 Libyan operation.

Knowledge of Self

The Sun Tzu maxim that "if you know the enemy and know yourself, you need not fear the result of a hundred battles" carries a special twist in effects-based operations and in effects-based shared situational awareness. If the effect we create is the product not just of our action, but of all actions that our country is taking at all levels, then to coordinate our actions we must know not only what those other actions are, but also how the whole fits together.

Such knowledge of self is reflected in command intent, but the breadth of command intent in tactical combat battlespace awareness is not the same as that required for effects-based operations. What is needed is a multi-level understanding of command intent from the national level downward that is tailored to the missions of the units at each level. Moreover, in dynamic effects-based operations, this command intent is never final. Like the actions and plans of the commands involved, it must be continually updated to reflect ongoing multi-level and interagency[23] (and in coalition operations, intergovernmental) interactions.

Knowledge of the Situation

The knowledge of the situation commences with the commanders' appreciation of the battlespace situation and of what is or will likely be unfolding in that battlespace. However, in the effects-based operation, there is a larger context to this appreciation, an understanding of the cascades of physical and psychological effects that might intentionally or unintentionally be precipitated by a given action. Since these cascades are not restricted to the targeted opponent, the required knowledge extends equally to how actions might affect other actors in the region. It is this knowledge of the situation that gives the commander the means of pruning the complexity of a nearly infinite range of potential responses so as to assess the options or actions best suited to the effect to be created. This process was in fact at the heart of the "what if" planning that the Battle Force Commanders and staffs undertook in both the 1986 and 1987 operations.

How do we assess cascades? Assessing these potential spin-offs requires the availability of experts. However, as the division into physical and psychological cascades implies, the expertise required will similarly be divided into those with knowledge of physical systems and those with regional knowledge to assess the cascades of psychological effects within an opposing military, leadership, or public.

Feedback

The effects-based situational awareness created for the Libyan operations was perhaps weakest in its ability to provide timely feedback to commanders on the impact of their actions and those of other elements of national power on the Libyans' cognitive processes. Clearly, if we are to deal with a dynamic battlefield or crisis engagement or are to make speed of command relevant to effects-based operations, the situational awareness that we create must also support a rapid assessment of the effects we create. Specifically, commanders will need to assess three aspects of the effects they create: (1) whether the direct effects of their actions were observed or felt as intended; (2) what cascade of physical effects were produced; and (3) what cascade of psychological effects was produced. The feedback to support this assessment was of three types: damage assessment; performance assessment; and behavioral change. The first two lie essentially in the physical domain and are subject to current metrics. The latter lies in the cognitive domain and is subject to all of that domain's ambiguities. Logically, the situational awareness we need must support these very different kinds of assessment and then integrate the feedback to answer a commander's questions.

Damage Assessment

The simplest problem is that of damage assessment, which already falls under the conventional tactical level network-centric understanding of shared situational awareness. However, because what we are measuring here is whether or not the desired direct effect was created, damage assessment feedback is only relevant where such damage was in fact the direct effect sought. When the direct effect sought is not discernable damage to forces and capabilities but changes in behavior, what is measured must shift from damage assessment to some form of performance measurement.

Thus, during Attain Document III, the Battle Force Commander had access to photography of the bomb damage to Libyan missile sites and radars as well as photography of sinking Libyan missile patrol boats. These provided an index of direct physical effects, but they did not address the more fundamental question of Libyan perceptions or of any shift in Libyan behavior that might have resulted, which was the objective of the operations

Performance Assessment

Performance assessment, whether for direct or indirect effects, consists of the performance of physical systems (usually before and after a direct effect), and the observable behavior of forces or actors. Here again, context is key. We can neither task the collection of data on performance and behavior nor use changes in performance as an indication of effect unless first we know which kinds of performance will in fact reflect the information we need for the assessment. Similarly, we cannot detect a change in performance unless we already have a knowledge base including data as to the observed norms for a system's or an actor's performance. To make a performance assessment, therefore, our situational awareness must include a sufficient knowledge base both to identify candidate measures and to assess a delta and its probable meaning.

Behavioral Change

The object of effects-based operations is to shape behavior, but how does a decisionmaker know he has succeeded or when? Detecting and assessing changes in behavior is perhaps the greatest effects-based challenge. To some degree, we can observe changes in behavior by observing and assessing performance, but where the behavior is the result of complex influences in a decisionmaking process, this may not be conclusive. We noted earlier the model of indications and warning intelligence in which large numbers of observations were assembled and weighted in an algorithm to provide an assessment of behavior. Assessment of the complex multi-faceted changes in behavior resulting from effects-based actions would likely be amenable to the same approach. However, that too has major implications for how we provide worthwhile situational awareness in effects-based operations because it mandates that these capabilities be networked to support the commander on a continuing basis. Specifically, those providing the assessment must be able to identify which indicators to use and then how to weight them in an algorithm to produce the desired rolling assessment.

Options, Agility, Coordination, and Knowledge Mobilization

This brings us back to our starting questions. What do network-centric operations bring to effects-based operations? And what might they bring in the future? The discussions of the two Libyan operations and of the concepts outlined in preceding chapters suggest that network-centric operations have the potential to make four major contributions to the conduct of successful effects-based operations. These can be succinctly summarized in terms of options, agility, coordination, and knowledge mobilization.

Options

The first contribution of network-centric operations seems intuitively obvious. Network-centric military forces[24] can simply do a wider variety of tasks and do them better. They present more options to decisionmakers. We have already noted how network-centric capabilities can enable us to target critical enemy vulnerabilities, to overwhelm an enemy, or to get "inside the enemy's OODA loop." We have pointed to how shared situational awareness, collaboration, understanding of command intent, and self-synchronization can multiply the power of combat forces in pace, scale, and scope far beyond non-network-centric forces and thereby give them a distinct advantage in battle. This is what the Battle Force was striving to do In 1987 with its adaptation of JOTS, the use of CWC, and the development of new techniques and procedures to optimize the information and awareness that was becoming available.

The metrics for evaluating these capabilities can be defined in attrition-based terms, a quantifiable ability to inflict more damage on an opponent's forces and infrastructure, and to do so more quickly. However, from the perspective of effects-based operations and our post-September 11th security environment, the critical measure is not how much damage we can inflict or how quickly we can do it, but rather the utility of these network-centric capabilities in "shaping the behavior of friends, foes, and neutrals." This effects-based utility hinges on the variety and applicability of the military capabilities denominated in terms of options. The role of these options (maneuver, presence, or strike) was evident in the two Libyan operations, as well as in the succession of crisis response examples outlined in the preceding chapters.

The network multiplies the range of options inherent in military forces because it enables us to bring disparate and geographically separated military capabilities to bear on a problem, not simply for destruction, but to precisely configure our actions to create the right effect on the right observer. As we saw in preceding chapters, these actions have multiple dimensions. It is not only what we do but also how we do it, the force employed, the scale of the action, the geographic and operational scope of the action, its timing, and its visibility that must be made to fit the requirements of the situation. Under these conditions, the ability to knit together ad hoc "coordinated sets of actions" from the often-disparate capabilities or forces available becomes the critical network-centric contribution in both peace and war.

We can also extend this thinking into the problems of deterring an asymmetric niche competitor in the current security environment. The better we can demonstrate our network-centric ability to link our capabilities into an effective and innovative response, the fewer exploitable niches we will present to a foe and the better the deterrent value of our forces will be. Similarly, the more options military forces can present, the more likely that military actions can be coordinated with political, diplomatic, and economic actions to create a unity of effect in which diverse actions not only are deconflicted, but also build synergistically upon each other to multiply effects.

In brief, the greater the range of actions that a military force can undertake, the more options it presents to decisionmakers to tailor the right action at the right place at the right time to create a desired effect. If we were to express this notion in terms familiar to the acquisition process, the *Pk* (probability of kill) of attrition-based metrics would be replaced by a *Po* metric in which the "o" is the number of "options" that a given force or capability will present in a given situation.

Agility

The ability to network forces and capabilities expands the range of military options available, but it also does something more. Implicit in the ability to do more and different tasks better and to operate at a pace, scale, and scope of operations far greater than an opponent is an ability to focus those operations on the right task at the right time as often as required to win. In providing more military options, network-centric thinking and capabilities can also give us agility, the innovative ability to develop options that adapt to changing circumstances, the flexibility and robustness to tap additional or different capabilities, and the responsiveness to change and act quickly enough to seize fleeting windows of opportunity. It is worth noting that, in the Libyan operations, the Battle Force did not content itself with planning for a single "what if" contingency. Instead, it planned for a series of most likely "what ifs" and depended on the agility of the forces involved to shift to one or another response to emerging Libyan behavior as required.

Such agility is critical to successful effects-based operations because such operations are dynamic interactions between complex adaptive systems in which all of the possible outcomes can never be known and there will often be a succession of evolving action-reaction cycles[25] producing different repercussions among a range of observers. Under these conditions, we cannot expect to pre-plan all of our actions for the course of an interaction, however good our planning process may be. Rather, we must be prepared to adapt our actions to evolving circumstances and the actions of the friends, foes, and neutrals of most concern. This requirement for adapting and agility exists at each level of conflict (tactical, operational, military–strategic, and geo-strategic) and across the political, diplomatic, and economic arenas.

This must be taken a step further. If we are to deal with an intelligent opponent exploiting a quickly changing situation, it may not be enough simply to have a preplanned list of options for which our forces are prepared. We certainly have no guarantee that we would have chosen the correct "what ifs," and our opponent would have every reason to thwart our efforts in any case. Our problem is rather to create an agility that is so great that we can generate ad hoc options from the capabilities at hand and fuse them into the proverbial right action at the right place at the right time. The shared situational awareness, common understanding of command intent, and collaboration that are integral to network-centric operations provide the basic infrastructure to do this.

Coordination

The third contribution may be slightly less obvious than the preceding two, but is still more important. We somehow have to coordinate all of the actions involved in creating an effect. The need for such coordination is obvious at the tactical and operational levels. A failure to coordinate would at a minimum produce an ineffectual overall impact on the enemy, and at worst might result in fratricide and self-defeat. That fear has been one of the principal drivers behind the concern with a common operating picture and with developing shared situational awareness and a common understanding of command intent. Yet, this degree of coordination, however necessary, is clearly not sufficient for creating the kind of unity of effect that is essential for successful effects-based operations. To achieve a unity of effect in which individual efforts do not cancel each other out, but instead multiply synergistically, demands a coordination that stretches across all military forces, warfare areas, Services, and entire coalitions. It will demand that such coordination equally extend across the political, diplomatic, and economic arenas as well as the military in a degree of coordination that we have seldom managed before and that was only peripherally evident in the Libyan operations for all of their ultimate success.

Achieving this unity of effect will not be easy. In looking at the planning and execution of effects-based operations, we identified three different areas of complexity with which we were obliged to deal. To create an impact in the cognitive domain, we have to orchestrate all of the variables of a complex set of actions so as to have the best possible chance of creating the effect we desire. We equally have to assess where the cascades of physical and psychological effects would lead, and to identify and balance the risks involved. Finally, we have to somehow monitor the changes in an observer's behavior by aggregating many diverse indicators. These three levels of complexity are an inescapable part of operating in the cognitive domain, but exploiting them also offers the nonlinear impacts we desire from effects-based operations.

Network-centric capabilities can give us the tools not only to deal with this complexity, but also to exploit it to our advantage. Note that the issue here is not an inability to conduct effects-based operations in the absence of network-centric capabilities. Indeed, it is the ability to master these complexities on an intuitive basis that is the mark of great commanders and statesmen. What network-centric capabilities bring is rather a new ability to deal with the problems of complexity inherent in effects-based operations on a routine basis. This ability may take the form of decision-aids for commanders, or of planning tools. It may take the form of bringing diverse communities of expertise to bear on a problem. It may equally be the ability to database, identify, collate, aggregate, and assess the indicators of changed behavior.

Knowledge Mobilization

It is almost axiomatic to say that the more precise we attempt to be either in our actions or in our targeting, the more dependent we become on knowledge as opposed to data and information. In effects-based operations, this dependence is multiplied. We must *know* and then *understand* the friend, foe, or neutral sufficiently well to anticipate reactions and to couch our own actions accordingly, and our knowledge must be sufficiently timely to enable us to adapt to the actual reactions as they occur. This knowledge must include both a sufficient database/historical record to lend context to the actions and reactions encountered and a looser expertise that blends large quantities of often-indefinable information into a coherent whole. To make matters still more challenging, the knowledge we require is based on information that is often ambiguous, subjective, incomplete, or even deliberately deceptive.

In looking at the Libyan operation, we encapsulated this knowledge requirement in situational awareness and understanding of command intent that include the knowledge to plan actions, the knowledge of oneself to coordinate a unity of effect, and a knowledge of the broader situation that enabled a commander to put his actions into the context of a national effort. In short, effects-based operations point to some very different requirements for data, information, and knowledge than the predominantly sensor-based data and information we would normally consider in pursuing network-centric operations.

This is where the use of the term *knowledge mobilization,* as distinct from knowledge or knowledge management, becomes critical. In effects-based operations, we cannot assume that the knowledge required will be available in a clean, machinable, displayable form, or even that any database will contain what we need. Yet, the implication of the word *mobilization* is that knowledge, however imperfect, will probably be available somewhere and that the wider our network is, the greater that probability becomes that we can access it. The task of our network-centric capabilities will be to tap that knowledge and expertise wherever it is and to make it available to the warfighters and decisionmakers who need it. The ad hoc communities of expertise that arose during the Libyan operations provide a paradigm for such mobilization, as do Internet chat rooms. The expert[26] tapped in this mobilization may not be an intelligence analyst, or even a government employee. It may be an ally with special knowledge. It could be the last Navy ship into port that filed a report on a chat room, or it may be an academic who has studied a region or leader. In each case, we mobilize available knowledge by networking warfighters with experts, databases, and centers of experience, our own and those of our friends, civilian and military, government and nongovernment, in a link that will vary from one situation to the next, potentially from one hour to the next. The good news is that with effort, such a virtual network is technologically feasible in very short order. The bad news is that it demands a change in how we think about information, intelligence, and support to commanders and commands at every level.

...and in the Future?

Network-centric capabilities and thinking are clearly still evolving and will need to take the requirements of effects-based operations into account. Initially, this will probably take the form of simply figuring out how to best use the power of the network, as in the creation of communities of expertise. However, over the longer term, new information technologies can clearly help us to deal with the three levels of complexity at the core of operations in the cognitive domain. In fact, the discussions above point to two areas of great promise.

One is the development of decision-aids to handle the multiple levels of complexity, that manage what an observer sees, and demonstrate the cascading effects that a given option may produce. Notice that we are not talking about computer-directed responses, but rather of presenting harried decisionmakers with some way of considering the available options in an orderly way. Indeed, we have already been experimenting with decision-aids that can provide relative probabilities for a given behavior in a given situation.

Another area of promise is in the use of indicators to provide feedback on the effects our actions actually produce. Because of the number of variables and potential indicators of changes in behavior or even in performance, one key to any effective use of indicators will probably revolve around data mining of open source materials on a scale unimaginable with today's technology. However, to use what we have mined, we would also have to set up automated algorithms to spot behavioral and performance changes that constitute definitive indicators and then render the indications in terms of probabilities of a particular behavior taking place.

These Information Age capabilities could clearly play a major role in the future of effects-based operations. The results will never be perfect. After all, effects-based operations will always be about human beings, and humans will never be either entirely predictable or constant. What is clear is that the faster we identify the parameters of what we need, the faster they will be in commanders' hands.

To complete the above, we must also add a note of urgency. The effects-based operations we are discussing are not an academic exercise, but are applicable to the problems of the new security environment in which we are now bemired. Thus, the question is not just what might we do to implement network-centric, effects-based operations tomorrow, but how we might best support the effects-based operations we undertake today with whatever elements of Network Centric Warfare we may have at our disposal.

Conclusion

In a sense, the connection between network-centric and effects-based operations is very straightforward. Network-centric operations are the means to an end: effects-based operations. We have only begun to appreciate the power and promise of network-centric operations. But, like any other capability, that power and promise lie chiefly in how they are applied. Combining network-centric operations with effects-based operations to exploit the human dimension of war, with its potential for nonlinear combat efficiencies, would make enough sense by itself to justify proceeding.

However, with the September 11th attacks and a dramatic shift in the strategic threat to the American homeland, we have a still more pressing imperative. We need a way to apply the power of network-centric operations to dealing with an asymmetric opponent, to contain the unrest that threatens our cities and citizens, and to establishing a stable deterrence regime to replace a now tattered balance of terror. All of these tasks focus on the human dimension of war addressed by effects-based operations, our gateway to bringing network-centric power to bear.

Effects-based operations are

coordinated sets of actions

directed at shaping the behavior

of friends, foes, and neutrals

in peace, crisis, and war.

[1]Griffith, Samuel B. trans. *Sun Tzu, The Art of War.* London, 1963. p. 11.

[2]The author was Assistant Chief of Staff for Intelligence for the Battle Force Sixth Fleet coordinating much of the information and intelligence support during the operation. In his role as Assistant Chief of Staff for Intelligence for Commander, Cruiser-Destroyer Group Eight (the battle group commander designated commander of Battle Force), the author participated in drawing up the "lessons learned" from Attain Document. He also helped prepare the battle group for deployment in the months before the 1987 operations.

[3]The flagship of the Battle Force was the USS *Saratoga* with the same air wing embarked, and with the same Battle Force staff, this time under the command of then Rear Admiral J.M. Boorda, later to become Chief of Naval Operations, the same Admiral Boorda whose lament opened this book.

[4]In this case, the Battle Force was composed of two carrier battle groups and one battleship battle group.

[5]Due to the concerns over the sensitivity of the material on the intelligence system, much of the classified intelligence material was entered into the JOTS via a cumbersome process that required intelligence watch personnel to sight a report, make a determination on its releasability, and send it to the JOTS. This process continued 24 hours a day and, however awkward it may have been, provided a far more rapid turn-around of intelligence to the operating forces than would have been possible with hard copy reports or daily intelligence briefings.

[6]To reduce the bandwidth required, the inputs from the national sensors were readouts that reported only the delta from the information already held by the Battle Force, e.g. changes to the numbers and disposition of aircraft at field X.

[7]The decentralization represented by the CWC concept was not new, but was greatly enhanced by the increased degree of shared situation awareness introduced by JOTS. As a practical matter in both Attain Document and the 1987 Freedom of Navigation Operations, the combination of the concept and the shared awareness permitted the Battle Force/Joint Task Force Commander himself to focus on the fastest breaking and most sensitive interactions where his input would be most critical.

[8]The need for this had been brought to Boorda during one of the pre-deployment "work-up" exercises for the battle group during which the newly installed information capabilities and the makeshift procedures for using them essentially collapsed under the workload of exercise operations. As a result, he

became very insistent on both configuration control within the deploying battle group and on working out and exercising procedures for using the new capabilities.

[9]Under the standard organization for Navy ships, the Tactical Action Officer is the watch officer responsible for "fighting" the ship and for directing any operation in which the ship may be engaged. The TAO watch is located in the ship's "combat," where all information whether from organic or nonorganic sources was to come together.

[10]One impact of these tests was to change the procedures for passing information to the Tactical Action Officer, including that of placing the most junior and least trained personnel in the role of the "phone talkers." Such phone talkers passed information verbally from the nodes to similar talkers in the ship CEC for passage to the TAO. Their lack of experience and training compounded itself, often resulting in comically distorted reporting.

[11]Under prodding from security personnel and with Admiral Boorda's encouragement, the author ran an experiment three times in which the door to the intelligence section of the Flag Plot was to be closed until any piece of information failed to reach the Flag Tactical Action Officer. The longest the door remained closed was 25 minutes.

[12]Admiral Boorda had been the Executive Assistant to the Chief of Naval Operations during the 1986 Attain Document and El Dorado Canyon Operations and, in that capacity, had been privy to the military-strategic and geo-strategic level decisionmaking involved. He carried that perspective into planning the 1987 operation and specifically into defining its objectives in behavioral terms.

[13]This prior knowledge was supplied by the experience of those who had participated in the previous year's operation. Moreover, that experience was largely limited to the tactical and operational interactions with the Libyan military and no attempt had been made subsequent to those operations to brief personnel on the actions undertaken by other levels of the U.S. government or on what was known of Libyan government reactions.

[14]Boorda, who subsequently served as NATO's CINC South during the Bosnia Operation in 1992-3, made a similar comment to the author upon his return. He stated that all he could get from the intelligence staff in Bosnia were reports of where things were, when what he really needed was to talk to someone who understood the area and the people involved.

[15]That is, organization, database, collection, analysis, and dissemination.

[16]This quest for feedback before the Internet included

monitoring wire service reporting for any indication of change in Libyan political or economic behavior.

[17]This formal reporting from the national intelligence community had been organized and tasked for the operation well in advance with the information fed into the Flag intelligence plot and from thence to the TAO and Battle Force Commander.

[18]Boorda recognized the utility of this informal back channel network, encouraged its use, and frequently posed questions arising from his "what if" thinking through it.

[19]During the operations in 1986 and 1987, as the pace of operations and the workload on the JTF and Fleet level operational and intelligence personnel increased, so did their reliance on the information "brokers" in the vertical community. The brokers' ability to identify and "push" critical pieces of information from a mass of data, which might otherwise have overwhelmed the limited resources of the harried operational commander, was crucial.

[20]During any major operation such as those in 1986 and 1987, the quantity of intelligence reporting can overwhelm the interface with the operational commander who has to combine this nonorganic information with the organic information derived from the command's sensors and human sources so as to assess a continuously rapidly changing situational awareness. Given the intensity of this interchange and the tendency of agencies to "push" forward an excess of information, it was necessary to supplement the command's "pull" of taskings and questions with a knowledgeable but less pressed interface that could filter the information so as to avoid inundating and distracting the interface at the operational level.

[21]One example of this was a "writings analysis group" of experts (including the author) on the Soviet military from across the intelligence community and the government who met monthly to assess and discuss new Soviet military writings. This human networking then provided the basis for rapid but informal queries among its members on ad hoc questions posed to any one member.

[22]We need to underline once again that knowing how the observer perceives and thinks is not an absolute. Almost by definition, we will never truly know how the other observer will actually perceive our actions, nor how he will translate these perceptions into behavior. Rather, the knowledge and understanding we access must be sufficient to prune the myriad of possible reactions down to a set of most likely perceptions and resulting behavior from which planning may proceed. This was the approach taken in both the 1986 and 1987 Libyan operations.

[23]The interagency requirement extends to both nongovernmental and international agencies as needed.

[24]It is increasingly clear from the data emerging from both real-world operations and experimentation, both in the United States and abroad, that network-centric operations do bring an increase in the combat efficiency of military forces.

Department of Defense, Network Centric Warfare, pp. 8-1ff.

[25]Even if we were to limit our perspective to wartime and the foe, short of the total destruction of all of that foe's means of waging war in the manner of the Third Punic War, we would still have to face the prospect of further interactions before we could declare victory. This is especially true in the face of a threat from a non-state organization such as al-Qaida in which an action successfully countered in one area is likely to result in a different challenge in anther area.

[26]If we follow Admiral Boorda's logic in "cross-training" theater reconnaissance personnel and their battle force interlocutors, then this pool of experts ought to have enough of an understanding of the military commander's situation to provide relevant input. Conversely, the military commander needs to have enough of an understanding of the region to appreciate what the expert can and cannot tell him.

Bibliography

Abu-Lughod, Ibraham. The *Arab-Israeli Confrontation of June 1967: An Arab Perspective*. Evanston; Northwestern University. 1970.

Alberts, David, John Garstka, and Frederick Stein. *Network Centric Warfare, Developing and Leveraging Information Superiority.* Washington, DC; CCRP. 2000.

Allison, Graham T. *Essence of Decision, Explaining the Cuban Missile Crisis.* Boston; Little Brown. 1971.

Ambrose, Stephen. *D-Day June 6, 1944*. New York; Touchstone. 1994.

Barnett, Roger. *Naval War College Review.* Newport, RI; Naval War College Press. Spring 2002.

Blechman, Barry M. and Stephen S Kaplan. *Force without War.* Washington, DC; Brookings. 1978.

Boyd, Colonel John A. USAF. "A Discourse on Winning and Losing." Air University Lecture. 1987.

Cable, Sir James. *Gunboat Diplomacy, The Sea in Modern Strategy*. New York; St Martin's Press. 1981.

547

Colton, Joel. *Léon Blum, Humanist in Politics.* New York; Knopf. 1966.

"Conventional Deterrence," Comparative Strategy, Fall 2000. "Review Of Empirical Studies of Conventional Deterence," Working Paper, Columbia International Affairs Online (CIAO), Columbia University. July 1999.

Czerwinski, Thomas. *Coping with the Bounds, Speculations on Non-linearity in Military Affairs.* Washington, DC; National Defense University Press. 1999.

Department of Defense. *Network Centric Warfare, Department of Defense Report to Congress,* 27 July 2001. Washington, DC. 2001.

Deptula, BG David A., USAF. "Firing for Effects." *Air Force Magazine.* Arlington, VA; Air Force Association. April 2001.

Douhet, Giulio. *The Command of the Air.* Washington, DC; Office of Air Force History. 1983.

Durant, Will & Ariel. *The Age of Napoleon.* New York; Simon and Schuster. 1975.

Effects-based Operations, Change in the Nature of Warfare. Arlington, VA; Aerospace Education Foundation. 2001.

Eisenhower, Dwight D. *The Eisenhower Diaries.* New York; Norton. 1981.

Fadok, David S. *John Boyd and John Warden: Airpower's Quest for Strategic Paralysis.* Air University, Air University Press. 1995.

Finney, John W. "Backing Reported for Plan to Test Aqaba Blockade." *New York Times.* June 1, 1967. Page 1, Col 8.

Foote, Shelby. *The Civil War: A Narrative.* Time-Life, Vol. 10. Alexandria, VA. 2000.

Friedman, Kenneth I. *The Afternoon of the Rising Sun, The Battle of Leyte Gulf.* Novato, CA; Presidio Press. 2001.

Friedman, Norman, Thomas C. Hone, Mark D Mandeles. *The Introduction of Carrier Aviation into the U.S. Navy and the Royal Navy: Military-Technical revolutions, Organizations, and the Problem of Decision.* Washington, DC; Office of Net Assessment. 1994.

Galvin, John R. *The Minute Men.* Washington DC; Brassey's. 1989.

Gell-Mann, Murray. "The Simple and the Complex." David S. Alberts and Thomas J, Czerwinski. *Complexity, Global Politics, and National Security.* Washington, DC; NDU. 1997.

Goldsworthy, Adrian. *The Punic Wars.* New York; Sterling Publishing Company. 1998.

Grant, U.S. *The Personal Memoirs of U.S. Grant.* Easton; Norwalk. 1989.

Gray, Colin. "Thinking Asymmetrically in Times of Terror." *Parameters.* Spring 2002.

Griffith, Samuel B. trans. *Sun Tzu, The Art of War.* London; University Press. 1963.

Hayes, Carlton J. *A Brief History of the Great War.* New York; MacMillan Company. 1925.

Hourani, Albert. *A History of the Arab Peoples.* Cambridge; Belknap/Harvard Press. 1991.

Howe, Jonathan. *Multicrises: Sea Power and Global Politics in the Missile Age.* Cambridge; MIT Press. 1971.

http://www.fas.org/nuke/guide/russia/agency/mf-med.htm. John Pike. September 16, 2002.

Iklé, Fred C and Albert Wohlstetter, Chairmen. *Discriminate Deterrence, The Report of the Commission in Integrated Long-Term Strategy.* Washington DC. 1988.

Israelyan, Victor. *Inside the Kremlin During the Yom Kippur War.* University Park: PSU Press. 1995.

James, Maj. Glenn, USAF. Chaos Theory, *The Essentials for Military Applications.* Newport Paper 10. Newport, RI; Naval War College. 1997.

Jewell, Angela et al. "USS *Nimitz* and Carrier Airwing Nine Surge Demonstration." Alexandria, VA. Center for Naval Analyses. 1998.

Johnson, Lyndon Baines. *The Vantage Point: Perspectives of the Presidency, 1963-1969.* New York. 1971.

Johnson, Robert and Clarence Clough Buel eds. *North to Antietam: Battles and Leaders of the Civil War.* New York; Castle Books. 1956.

Jowett, J.B. trans. *Plato's Republic.* New York; Modern Library. 1982.

Keegan, John. *The First World War.* New York; Knopf. 2000.

Kennedy, Robert F. *Thirteen Days, A Memoir of the Cuban Missile Crisis.* New York; Norton, W. W. & Company, Inc. 1969.

Khadduri, Majid. *Political Trends in the Arab World.* Baltimore; John Hopkins. 1972.

Kidd, Isaac C. ADM. "View from the Bridge of the Sixth Fleet Flagship." Proceedings, February 1972. Interview with the author. November 10, 1972.

Kissinger, Henry A. *Years of Upheaval.* Boston; Little Brown. 1980.

Kissinger, Henry A. *White House Years.* Boston; Little Brown. 1979.

Laqueur, W. *The Road to War: The Origin and Aftermath of the Arab-Israeli Conflict 1967-8.* London; Penguin. 1968.

Layton, RADM Edwin T. USN. *And I Was There.* New York; Morrow, William, & Co. 1985.

Lincoln, President Abraham. *The Gettysburg Address.* 1863.

Luttwak, Edward. *Strategic Power, Military Capabilities, and Political Utility.* Georgetown; SAGE Publications. 1976.

Mahan, Alfred. *Mahan on Naval Warfare: Selected Writings on Rear Admiral Alfred T. Mahan.* Boston; Little Brown. 1918.

Marcus, G.J. *The Age of Nelson, The Royal Navy 1793-1815.* New York; Viking. 1971.

Marshall, Andrew W. "Opening Remarks." *Navy RMA Roundtable.* SAIC. 1997.

May, Ernest R. *Strange Victory, Hitler's Conquest of France.* New York; Hill and Wang. 2000.

Miller, James Grier. *Living Systems.* Denver; McGraw-Hill Professional. 1995.

Morrow, Walter. "Technology for a Naval Revolution in Military Affairs." *Second Navy RMA Round Table.* 1997.

Muir, Rory. *Britain and the Defeat of Napoleon, 1807-1815.* New Haven: Yale University. 1996.

Murphy, RADM Daniel. "Surface Warfare." *Navy RMA Round Table.* 1997.

Murray, Williamson et al. *An Historical Perspective on Effects-based Operations.* Alexandria, VA; Institute for Defense Analyses, Joint Advanced Warfighting Project. October 2001.

Navy Warfare Development Command. Draft Network Centric Operations: A Capstone Concept for Naval Operations in the Information Age. http://www.nwdc.navy.mil/Concepts/NetCen. asp. 2002.

"Network Centric Warfare: What's the Point?" *United States Naval War College Review.* Newport, RI; Naval War College. Winter 2001.

Nixon, Richard M. *RN, The Memoirs of Richard Nixon.* Norwalk; Simon & Schuster. 1978.

Pogue, Forrest. *The Supreme Command.* Washington, DC; Department of the Army. 1954.

Ready, J. Lee. *World War Two: Nation by Nation.* London; Arms and Armour. 1995.

Reagan, Ronald. *An American Life.* Norwalk, Connecticut. 1990.

"Report of the Workshop on Sensemaking, 6-8 March 2001." Tysons Corner, VA; DODCCRP/Evidence Based Research. 2001.

Rhodes, Edward. "Conventional Deterrence: Review of the Empirical Literature," Second Navy RMA Round Table. Tysons Corner, VA; SAIC. 4 June 1997.

Sadat, Anwar As. *In Search of Identity, An Autobiography*. New York; Harper. 1978.

Sandburg, Carl. *Lincoln, The Prairie Years and the War Years*. Easton; Norwalk. 1984.

Sarikin, V.Ye. *The Basic Principles of the Operational Art and Tactics*. Washington, DC; GPO. 1972.

Schmitt, John F. "Command and (Out of) Control: The Military Implications of Complexity Theory." *Complexity, Global Politics, and National Security*. David S. Alberts and Thomas J. Czerwinski eds. Washington, DC; NDU/INSS. 1997.

SHAEF Weekly Intelligence Summary. June 3, 1944.

Shirer, William L. *The Collapse of the Third Republic, An Inquiry into the Fall of France in 1940*. New York; Simon and Schuster. 1969.

Siegel, Adam. *The Use of Naval Forces in the Post War Era: U.S. Navy and U.S. Marine Corps Crisis Response Activity, 1946-1990*. Alexandria, VA; Center for Naval Analyses. 1991.

Singer, J. David, ed. *Human Behavior and International Politics, Contributions from the Social-Psychological Sciences.* Rand McNally; Chicago. 1965.

Smith, Allen. *The Road to Vichy, The Writings and Journals of Constant Caulry, 1938-1945.* Unpublished thesis, College of William and Mary; Williamsburg, Va. 2002.

Smith, Edward A. Jr. *Naval Confrontation, The Inter-superpower Use of Naval Suasion in Times of Crisis.* Unpublished dissertation, The American University. 1979.

Sobel, Lester A. *Israel and the Arabs: The October 1973 War.* New York; Facts on File, Inc. 1974. pp.90-111.

Stanik, Joseph T. "Swift and Effective Retribution." *The United States Sixth Fleet and the Confrontation with Qaddafi.* Washington, DC; Naval Historical Center. 1996.

Steere, Edward. *The Wilderness Campaign.* Harrisburg; Stackpole Company. 1960. p.457.

Strausz-Hupé, Robert. "The New Protracted Conflict." *Orbis.* Eugene, OR; Oregon University. April 2002.

Tedder, Sir Arthur. *With Prejudice.* London; Cassell. 1966.

U.S. Air Force, Air Staff. *The United States Air Force and U.S. National Security: A Historical Perspective*. Washington, DC; USAF Historical Office. 1991.

Warden, Col. John A. III, USAF. "The Enemy as a System." *Airpower Journal*. Alabama; Maxwell AFB. Spring, 1995.

Waters, Maurice. *The United Nations*. New York; MacMillan Company. 1967.

Watts, Barry. *Clausewitzian Friction and Future War*. Washington, DC; National Defense University. 1996.

Wilson, Harold. *A Personal Record*. Boston; Little Brown. 1971.

Zelikow, Philip D. "Force without War, 1975-1982." *The Journal of Strategic Studies*. London; Frank Cass & Co. March 1984.

About the Author

Edward A. Smith, Jr. is a retired U.S. Navy Captain with 30 years of service. He holds a BA in International Relations from Ohio State and a MA and doctorate in International Relations from The American University (Dissertation: *Naval Confrontation: The Inter-Superpower Use of Naval Suasion in Times of Crisis*).

He saw combat in Vietnam as the Intelligence Officer on the staff of Commander Delta Naval Forces and Senior Advisor Vietnamese Riverine Command, completing almost 200 combat missions in helicopters and OV-10 Broncos. His other assignments included duty in the Navy Field Operational Intelligence Office and in the Defense Intelligence Agency, as Executive Assistant to the Political Advisor to CINCLANT/SACLANT, and as Assistant Naval Attache to Paris. He also served as the Assistant Chief of Staff for Intelligence for Cruiser Destroyer Group Eight/Battle Force Sixth Fleet, a tour that included participation in the intercept of the *Achille Lauro* hijackers and the 1986 and 1987 operations off Libya. He then moved to the staff of the Director of Naval Intelligence and was a primary player in creating the seminal Navy white paper *"...From the Sea."* Subsequently, he set up the Intelligence Directorate in the new Office of Naval Intelligence and served as its first Deputy Director for Intelligence. His final tour in the Navy was on the staff of the Chief of Naval Operations in the CNO

Executive Panel where he directed the Navy's RMA wargames and was the author of the Navy's *Anytime, Anywhere* vision. He retired from the Navy in 1998 and is now Boeing's senior analyst for network-centric and effects-based operations.

Dr. Smith's publications include:

"They Can Buy It, BUT.." *Proceedings.* (Feb 94).

"What '...From the Sea' Didn't Say." *Naval War College Review.* (Winter 94-5).

"Putting it through the right window." *Proceedings.* (June 95).

"The Navy RMA Wargames." *Naval War College Review.* (Autumn 97).

Chapter: "The Process of Defining a New Role for Naval Forces in the post-Cold War World." Turbowitz et al. ed *Strategic Adjustment.* (Columbia University Press, 1999).

"Network Centric Warfare: What's the Point?" *Naval War College Review.* (Winter 2000-1).

He also has contributed a chapter on anti-access/area denial strategies to a forthcoming book, *Globalization and Maritime Power*, to be published by the National Defense University Press.

Catalog of CCRP Publications

(* denotes a title no longer available in print)

Coalition Command and Control*
(Maurer, 1994)

Peace operations differ in significant ways from traditional combat missions. As a result of these unique characteristics, command arrangements become far more complex. The stress on command and control arrangements and systems is further exacerbated by the mission's increased political sensitivity.

The Mesh and the Net
(Libicki, 1994)

Considers the continuous revolution in information technology as it can be applied to warfare in terms of capturing more information (mesh) and how people and their machines can be connected (net).

Command Arrangements for
Peace Operations
(Alberts & Hayes, 1995)

By almost any measure, the U.S. experience shows that traditional C2 concepts, approaches, and doctrine are not particularly well suited for peace operations. This book (1) explores the reasons for this, (2) examines alternative command arrangement approaches, and (3) describes the attributes of effective command arrangements.

Standards: The Rough Road to the Common Byte
(Libicki, 1995)

The inability of computers to "talk" to one another is a major problem, especially for today's high technology military forces. This study by the Center for Advanced Command Concepts and Technology looks at the growing but confusing body of information technology standards. Among other problems, it discovers a persistent divergence between the perspectives of the commercial user and those of the government.

What Is Information Warfare?*
(Libicki, 1995)

Is Information Warfare a nascent, perhaps embryonic art, or simply the newest version of a time-honored feature of warfare? Is it a new form of conflict that owes its existence to the burgeoning global information infrastructure, or an old one whose origin lies in the wetware of the human brain but has been given new life by the Information Age? Is it a unified field or opportunistic assemblage?

Operations Other Than War*
(Alberts & Hayes, 1995)

This report documents the fourth in a series of workshops and roundtables organized by the INSS Center for Advanced Concepts and Technology (ACT). The workshop sought insights into the process of determining what technologies are required for OOTW. The group also examined the complexities of introducing relevant technologies and discussed general and specific OOTW technologies and devices.

CCRP Publications

Dominant Battlespace Knowledge*
(Johnson & Libicki, 1996)

The papers collected here address the most critical aspects of that problem—to wit: If the United States develops the means to acquire dominant battlespace knowledge, how might that affect the way it goes to war, the circumstances under which force can and will be used, the purposes for its employment, and the resulting alterations of the global geomilitary environment?

Interagency and Political-Military Dimensions of Peace Operations: Haiti - A Case Study
(Hayes & Wheatley, 1996)

This report documents the fifth in a series of workshops and roundtables organized by the INSS Center for Advanced Concepts and Technology (ACT). Widely regarded as an operation that "went right," Haiti offered an opportunity to explore interagency relations in an operation close to home that had high visibility and a greater degree of interagency civilian-military coordination and planning than the other operations examined to date.

The Unintended Consequences of the Information Age*
(Alberts, 1996)

The purpose of this analysis is to identify a strategy for introducing and using Information Age technologies that accomplishes two things: first, the identification and avoidance of adverse unintended consequences associated with the introduction and utilization of information technologies; and second, the ability to recognize and capitalize on unexpected opportunities.

Joint Training for Information Managers*
(Maxwell, 1996)

This book proposes new ideas about joint training for information managers over Command, Control, Communications, Computers, and Intelligence (C4I) tactical and strategic levels. It suggests a substantially new way to approach the training of future communicators, grounding its argument in the realities of the fast-moving C4I technology.

Defensive Information Warfare*
(Alberts, 1996)

This overview of defensive information warfare is the result of an effort, undertaken at the request of the Deputy Secretary of Defense, to provide background material to participants in a series of interagency meetings to explore the nature of the problem and to identify areas of potential collaboration.

Command, Control, and the Common Defense
(Allard, 1996)

The author provides an unparalleled basis for assessing where we are and were we must go if we are to solve the joint and combined command and control challenges facing the U.S. military as it transitions into the 21st century.

Shock & Awe:
Achieving Rapid Dominance*
(Ullman & Wade, 1996)

The purpose of this book is to explore alternative concepts for structuring mission capability packages around which future U. S. military forces might be configured.

Information Age Anthology:
Volume I*
(Alberts & Papp, 1997)

In this first volume, we will examine some of the broader issues of the Information Age: what the Information Age is; how it affects commerce, business, and service; what it means for the government and the military; and how it affects international actors and the international system.

Complexity, Global Politics,
and National Security*
(Alberts & Czerwinski, 1997)

The charge given by the President of the National Defense University and RAND leadership was threefold: (1) push the envelope; (2) emphasize the policy and strategic dimensions of national defense with the implications for complexity theory; and (3) get the best talent available in academe.

Target Bosnia: Integrating Information Activities in Peace Operations*
(Siegel, 1998)

This book examines the place of PI and PSYOP in peace operations through the prism of NATO operations in Bosnia-Herzegovina.

Coping with the Bounds
(Czerwinski, 1998)

The theme of this work is that conventional, or linear, analysis alone is not sufficient to cope with today's and tomorrow's problems, just as it was not capable of solving yesterday's. Its aim is to convince us to augment our efforts with nonlinear insights, and its hope is to provide a basic understanding of what that involves.

Information Warfare and International Law*
(Greenberg, Goodman, & Soo Hoo, 1998)

The authors, members of the Project on Information Technology and International Security at Stanford University's Center for International Security and Arms Control, have surfaced and explored some profound issues that will shape the legal context within which information warfare may be waged and national information power exerted in the coming years.

Lessons From Bosnia: The IFOR Experience*
(Wentz, 1998)

This book tells the story of the challenges faced and innovative actions taken by NATO and U.S. personnel to ensure that IFOR and Operation Joint Endeavor were military successes. A coherent C4ISR lessons learned story has been pieced together from firsthand experiences, interviews of key personnel, focused research, and analysis of lessons learned reports provided to the National Defense University team.

Doing Windows: Non-Traditional Military Responses to Complex Emergencies
(Hayes & Sands, 1999)

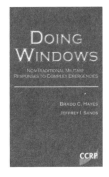

This book provides the final results of a project sponsored by the Joint Warfare Analysis Center. Our primary objective in this project was to examine how military operations can support the long-term objective of achieving civil stability and durable peace in states embroiled in complex emergencies.

Network Centric Warfare
(Alberts, Garstka, & Stein, 1999)

It is hoped that this book will contribute to the preparations for NCW in two ways. First, by articulating the nature of the characteristics of Network Centric Warfare. Second, by suggesting a process for developing mission capability packages designed to transform NCW concepts into operational capabilities.

Behind the Wizard's Curtain
(Krygiel, 1999)

There is still much to do and more to learn and understand about developing and fielding an effective and durable infostructure as a foundation for the 21st century. Without successfully fielding systems of systems, we will not be able to implement emerging concepts in adaptive and agile command and control, nor will we reap the potential benefits of Network Centric Warfare.

Confrontation Analysis: How to Win Operations Other Than War
(Howard, 1999)

A peace operations campaign (or operation other than war) should be seen as a linked sequence of confrontations, in contrast to a traditional, warfighting campaign, which is a linked sequence of battles. The objective in each confrontation is to bring about certain "compliant" behavior on the part of other parties, until in the end the campaign objective is reached. This is a state of sufficient compliance to enable the military to leave the theater.

Information Campaigns for Peace Operations
(Avruch, Narel, & Siegel, 2000)

In its broadest sense, this report asks whether the notion of struggles for control over information identifiable in situations of conflict also has relevance for situations of third-party conflict management—for peace operations.

Information Age Anthology: Volume II*
(Alberts & Papp, 2000)

Is the Information Age bringing with it new challenges and threats, and if so, what are they? What sorts of dangers will these challenges and threats present? From where will they (and do they) come? Is information warfare a reality? This publication, Volume II of the Information Age Anthology, explores these questions and provides preliminary answers to some of them.

Information Age Anthology: Volume III*
(Alberts & Papp, 2001)

In what ways will wars and the military that fight them be different in the Information Age than in earlier ages? What will this mean for the U.S. military? In this third volume of the Information Age Anthology, we turn finally to the task of exploring answers to these simply stated, but vexing questions that provided the impetus for the first two volumes of the Information Age Anthology.

Understanding Information Age Warfare
(Alberts, Garstka, Hayes, & Signori, 2001)

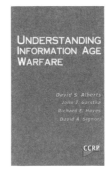

This book presents an alternative to the deterministic and linear strategies of the planning modernization that are now an artifact of the Industrial Age. The approach being advocated here begins with the premise that adaptation to the Information Age centers around the ability of an organization or an individual to utilize information.

Information Age Transformation
(Alberts, 2002)

This book is the first in a new series of CCRP books that will focus on the Information Age transformation of the Department of Defense. Accordingly, it deals with the issues associated with a very large governmental institution, a set of formidable impediments, both internal and external, and the nature of the changes being brought about by Information Age concepts and technologies.

Code of Best Practice for Experimentation
(CCRP, 2002)

Experimentation is the lynch pin in the DoD's strategy for transformation. Without a properly focused, well-balanced, rigorously designed, and expertly conducted program of experimentation, the DoD will not be able to take full advantage of the opportunities that Information Age concepts and technologies offer.

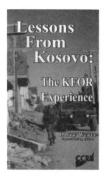

Lessons From Kosovo: The KFOR Experience
(Wentz, 2002)

Kosovo offered another unique opportunity for CCRP to conduct additional coalition C4ISR-focused research in the areas of coalition command and control, civil-military cooperation, information assurance, C4ISR interoperability, and information operations.

NATO Code of Best Practice for C2 Assessment
(2002)

To the extent that they can be achieved, significantly reduced levels of fog and friction offer an opportunity for the military to develop new concepts of operations, new organisational forms, and new approaches to command and control, as well as to the processes that support it. Analysts will be increasingly called upon to work in this new conceptual dimension in order to examine the impact of new information-related capabilities coupled with new ways of organising and operating.

Effects Based Operations
(Smith, 2003)

This third book of the Information Age Transformation Series speaks directly to what we are trying to accomplish on the "fields of battle" and argues for changes in the way we decide what effects we want to achieve and what means we will use to achieve them.

The Big Issue
(Potts, 2003)

This Occasional considers command and combat in the Information Age. It is an issue that takes us into the realms of the unknown. Defence thinkers everywhere are searching forward for the science and alchemy that will deliver operational success.

Power to the Edge: Command...Control... in the Information Age
(Alberts & Hayes, 2003)

Power to the Edge articulates the principles being used to provide the ubiquitous, secure, wideband network that people will trust and use, populate with high quality information, and use to develop shared awareness, collaborate effectively, and synchronize their actions.

Complexity Theory and Network Centric Warfare
(Moffat, 2003)

Professor Moffat articulates the mathematical models and equations that clearly demonstrate the relationship between warfare and the emergent behaviour of complex natural systems, as well as a means to calculate and assess the likely outcomes.

Campaigns of Experimentation: Pathways to Innovation and Transformation
(Alberts & Hayes, 2005)

In this follow-on to the Code of Best Practice for Experimentation, the concept of a campaign of experimentation is explored in detail. Key issues of discussion include planning, execution, achieving synergy, and avoiding common errors and pitfalls.